I0118573

ATTP 3-06.11 (FM 3-06.11)

Combined Arms Operations in Urban Terrain

June 2011

Headquarters, Department of the Army

Published by Books Express Publishing
Books Express Publishing, 2011
ISBN 978-1-78039-977-5

Books Express publications are available from all good retail and online booksellers. For
publishing proposals and direct ordering please contact us at: info@books-express.com

Army Tactics, Techniques, and Procedures
No. 3-06.11 (FM 3-06.11)

Headquarters
Department of the Army
Washington, D.C., 10 June 2011

Combined Arms Operations in Urban Terrain

Contents

Distribution Restriction: Approved for public release; distribution is unlimited.

*This publication supersedes FM 3-06.11, 28 February 2002.

PART TWO   COMPANY AND PLATOON

Figures

Tables

Preface

Army Tactics, Techniques, and Procedures (ATTP) 3-06.11 establishes doctrine for combined arms operations in urban terrain for the brigade combat team (BCT) and battalion/squadron commanders and staffs, company/troop commanders, small-unit leaders, and individual Soldiers.

The continued trend worldwide of urban growth and the shift of populations from rural to urban areas continues to affect Army operations. The urban environment, consisting of complex terrain, dense populations, and integrated infrastructures, is the predominant operational environment in which Army forces currently operate.

Each urban environment is unique and differs because of the combinations presented by the enemy, the urban area itself, the major operation of which it may be part (or the focus), and always changing societal and geopolitical considerations. Enemy forces will take advantage of this complex environment by intermingling with the populace.

ATTP 3-06.11 describes the fundamental principles, tactics, techniques, and procedures (TTP) of urban operations (UO) across full spectrum operations, using the UO operational construct (understand, shape, engage, consolidate, and transition) to outline the discussions. ATTP 3-06.11 is based on current BCT structure and lessons learned from ongoing UO.

ATTP 3-06.11 primarily addresses offensive and defensive operations in an urban environment. Stability operations are briefly discussed in the context of transition considerations. Stability operations are inherently among the people and generally in urban environments. Field manual (FM) 3-07 is the source manual for stability doctrine and addresses BCT considerations for conducting stability UO. FM 3-07.1 is the primary source for BCT and below considerations for interaction and support to host nation (HN) security forces. This material is not repeated in ATTP 3-06.11.

This publication applies to the Active Army, the Army National Guard (ARNG)/Army National Guard of the United States (ARNGUS), and the United States Army Reserve (USAR) unless otherwise stated.

The proponent for this publication is the U.S. Army Training and Doctrine Command (TRADOC). The preparing agency is the U.S. Army Maneuver Center of Excellence (MCoE). You may send comments and recommendations by any means–U.S. mail, e-mail, fax, or telephone–using or following the format of DA Form 2028, *Recommended Changes to Publications and Blank Forms*.

E-mail:	Benn.mcoe.doctrine@conus.army.mil
Phone:	COM 706-545-7114 or DSN 835-7114
Fax:	COM 706-545-8511 or DSN 835-8511
U.S. Mail:	Commander, MCoE
	Directorate of Training and Doctrine (DOTD)
	Doctrine and Collective Training Division
	ATTN: ATZB-TDD
	Fort Benning, GA 31905-5410

Uniforms shown in this manual were drawn without camouflage for clarity of the illustration.

Unless otherwise stated in this publication, masculine nouns and pronouns refer to both men and women.

Introduction

Urban operations are among the most difficult and challenging missions a BCT can undertake. Most UO are planned and controlled at division or corps level but executed by BCTs. The unified action environment of UO enables and enhances the capabilities of the BCT to plan, prepare, and execute offensive, defensive, and stability operations. Urban operations are Infantry-centric combined arms operations that capitalize on the adaptive and innovative leaders at the squad, platoon, and company level. Combined arms is the synchronized and simultaneous application of the elements of combat power to achieve an effect greater than if each element of combat power was used separately or sequentially. The eight elements of combat power are leadership, information, movement and maneuver, intelligence, fires, sustainment, mission command, and protection. Leadership and information are applied through, and multiply the effects of, the other six elements of combat power. These six—movement and maneuver, intelligence, fires, sustainment, mission command, and protection—are collectively described as the warfighting functions. (See FM 3-0 for details.) The BCT is the Army's largest fixed combined arms organization and the primary close combat force. A key component in UO is the inherent ability of the BCT to tailor its force to meet the requirements of the urban environment. This introduction provides an overview of UO considerations that shape the subsequent discussions of operations at BCT and below.

SECTION I – UNDERSTANDING THE URBAN ENVIRONMENT

The special considerations in any UO go well beyond the uniqueness of the urban terrain. JP 3-06 identifies three distinguishing characteristics of the urban environment—physical terrain, population, and infrastructure. FM 3-06 identifies three key overlapping and interdependent components of the urban environment: terrain (natural and man-made), society, and the supporting infrastructure.

The following urban-related terms are critical to understanding this manual. All discuss some aspect of the physical terrain, man-made structures, or the population. To ensure clarity, their definitions follow:

- **Terrain.** Urban terrain is a complex man-made physical terrain superimposed on existing natural terrain. This physical terrain consists of man-made structures of varying types, sizes, materials, and construction arranged sometimes in an orderly manner and sometimes randomly. It may be modern or built around an ancient core; it may contain towering buildings or none over three stories. (See JP 3-06 for details.)

- **Area.** The urban area is a topographical complex where man-made construction or high population density is the dominant feature. (See FM 3-06 for details.)

- **Environment.** The urban environment is the physical urban area as well as the complex and dynamic interaction among its key components—the terrain (natural and man-made), the population, and the supporting infrastructure—as an overlapping and interdependent system of systems. (See FM 3-06 for details.)

- **Population.** The urban population is of significant size and density inhabiting, works in, and uses the man-made and natural terrain. Urban areas are frequently defined according to size, from villages of fewer than 3,000 inhabitants to large cities with populations of over 100,000. Large cities vary greatly in size, ranging in population from 100,000 to over 20,000,000 and in area from several to hundreds of square miles. (See JP 3-06 for details.)

- **Infrastructure.** Urban infrastructure is upon which the area depends that occupies man-made terrain and provides human services and cultural and political structure for the urban area and often beyond, perhaps for the entire nation. An urban area may have a significant influence beyond a city's boundaries. It may influence a region within the nation, the nation itself, or other countries within a geographical region. (See JP 3-06 for details.)

For full spectrum UO, all groupings of man-made structures and densities of population—especially if the population is the hub of political, economic, and cultural activity of the surrounding area—are militarily significant. Any populated place, even those too small to be classified as urban areas (minimum population of 2,500), can affect operations.

The size or density of a population is not the determining factor of whether an area is urban terrain. It is the size or density of the man-made structures that makes an area urban terrain. Therefore, an uninhabited industrial complex; a large, dense homestead; or a well-developed settlement or village may be urban terrain even though they do not fit the definition of an urban area.

TERRAIN

Urban terrain, both natural and man-made, is the foundation upon which the population and infrastructure of the urban area are superimposed. The physical environment includes the geography and man-made structures in the area of operations (AO). A city may consist of a core surrounded by various commercial ribbons, industrial areas, outlying high-rise areas, residential areas, shantytowns, military areas, extensive parklands or other open areas, waterways, and transportation infrastructure. City patterns may consist of a central hub surrounded by satellite areas, or they may be linear, networked, or segmented. They may contain street patterns that are rectangular, radial, concentric, irregular, or a combination of patterns. (See appendix A for details.) They may be closely packed where land space is at a premium or dispersed over several square miles. The infinite ways in which these features may be combined make it necessary to approach each urban area as a unique problem.

The natural terrain features that lay beneath urban cities also influence UO. They dictate where buildings can be constructed and how streets align and, thus, influence schemes of maneuver. In addition, the slopes of roads are included in the overall terrain analysis of a city since they often follow the underlying terrain's natural contours.

Understanding the physical characteristics of urban terrain requires a multidimensional approach. Commanders operating in unrestricted terrain normally address their AO in terms of air and ground. However, operations within the urban environment provide numerous man-made structures and variables not found in unrestricted terrain. Commanders conducting UO must broaden the scope of their thinking. The total size of the surfaces and spaces of an urban area is usually many times that of a similarly size piece of natural terrain because of the complex blend of horizontal, vertical, interior, exterior, and subterranean forms superimposed on the natural landscape. Introduction figure-1 illustrates the types of physical characteristics found in urban terrain. The following terms are provided as they relate to UO.

- **Airspace.** Airspace is the area above the ground usable by aircraft and aerial munitions. In urban areas, airspace is broken up by man-made structures of different heights and densities and the irregularities of natural terrain. This produces an urban canyon effect that can adversely impact operations. Urban canyons often cause higher wind speeds with unpredictable wind direction and turbulence that can cause some munitions to miss their targets (increasing risk for both collateral damage and fratricide) and that significantly increase risks for rotary-wing operations near the surface.
- **Surface Areas.** Surface areas include exterior ground-level areas of streets and roads, parks and fields, and any other exterior space. For purposes of analysis, the ground floor of buildings and the surface of waterways are also part of the surface dimension. These surface areas follow the natural terrain and are broken up by man-made features.
- **Supersurface Areas.** Supersurface areas are the roofs and upper floors of buildings, stadiums, towers, or other structures. These areas also include the internal floors or levels (intrasurface).

- **Subsurface Areas.** Subsurface areas are below ground level that consist of sewer and drainage systems, subway tunnels, utility corridors, or other subterranean spaces. This dimension includes areas both below the ground and below water. These areas can be used for cover and concealment, movement, and engagement, but their use requires intimate knowledge of the area.

Equally important are considerations of exterior and interior space – what is visible from outside buildings or subsurface areas and the significant range of people, infrastructure, and activity that occurs unseen in the interior of those structures. Understanding the full physical nature of an urban area requires a holistic approach, with an appropriate awareness of the lateral, horizontal, vertical, interior, and external nature of the city.

Units should conduct a terrain analysis to relate the terrain's effects on the courses of action (COA) available to both enemy and friendly forces. During the evaluation, it is important to discuss the military aspects of terrain in detail. (See FM 2-01.3 for details.) The four techniques for evaluating the terrain's effect on COAs are—

- Concentric ring.
- Belt.
- Avenue in depth.
- Box.

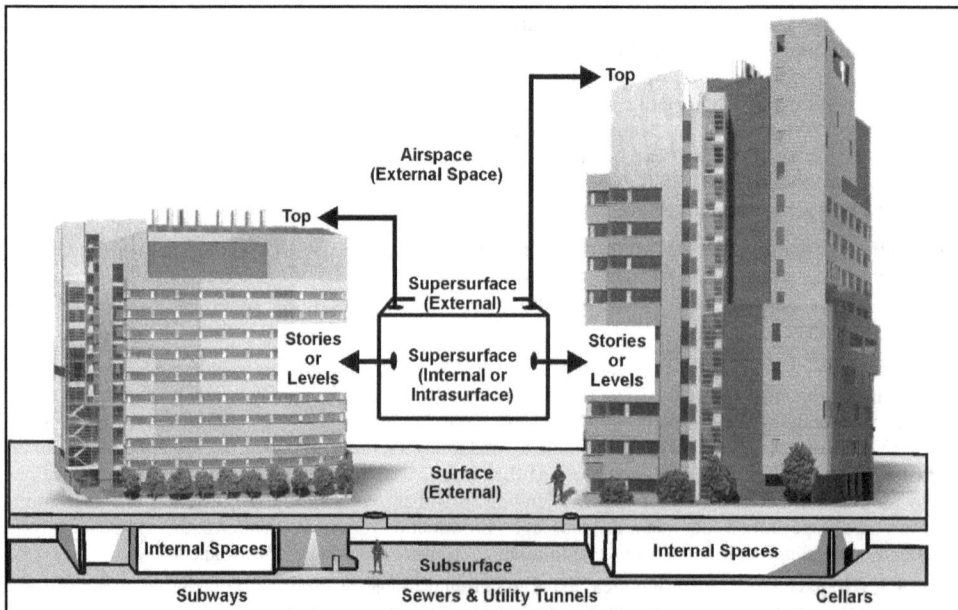

Introduction Figure-1. Multidimensional urban environment

SOCIETY

Urban operations often require forces to operate in close proximity to a high density of civilians. Even evacuated areas can have a large stay-behind population. The population's presence, attitudes, actions, communications with the media, and needs may affect the conduct of the operation. Commanders should take into account the characteristics of a population whose beliefs and interests vary. Analysis and understanding of these factors is critical to successfully inform and influence activities and, thus, the entire operation. To effectively operate among an urban population and maintain its goodwill, it is important to develop a thorough understanding of the population and its culture, to include values, needs, history, religion, customs, and social structure.

The demographics of the HN can complicate BCT operations. The Army is likely to conduct full spectrum UO in countries with existing or emerging cultural, ethnic, or religious conflicts. When these conditions exist, the local population may be sympathetic to enemy causes. Refugees and displaced persons are likely to be present. For these and other reasons, cultural awareness is imperative to mission success.

Accommodating the social norms of a population is potentially the most influential factor in conducting UO. Soldiers function well by acting in accordance with American values but may encounter difficulties when applying American culture, values, and thought processes to the populace or individuals the unit and leadership is trying to understand.

Defining the structure of the social hierarchy is often critical to understanding the population. Identifying those in positions of authority is important as well since they often influence the actions of the population at large. In many societies, influence rather than nominal titles equals power. Many "leaders" are figureheads and the true authority lies elsewhere.

Many governments of developing countries are characterized by nepotism, favor trading, sectarianism, and indifference. Corruption can be pervasive and institutionalized. The power of officials can be based on family and personal connections and not governmental or elected authority. Some areas around the world are not governed by the rule of law as western Armies and cultures understand it. Rather, they rely on tradition. Often, ethnic loyalty, religious affiliation, and tribal membership provide societal cohesion and the sense of proper behavior and ethics in dealing with matters of social conflict, norms, and disagreements, as well as a framework to address those outside their system.

The density of the local populations and the constant interaction between them and U.S. forces greatly increase the importance of social considerations. The fastest way to damage the legitimacy of an operation is to ignore or violate social mores or precepts of a particular population. The urban populace behaves according to their own self-interest and will focus on the different interests at work in the AO–U.S. and multinational forces, hostile forces, and international and nongovernmental organizations.

Another consideration when dealing with the local population is their ability to disrupt full spectrum UO. Regardless of causes or political affiliations, civilian casualties are often the focal point of press coverage to the point of ignoring or demeaning any previous accomplishments. Within the operational continuum, and especially during the conduct of UO, commanders can expect to encounter restrictions on their use of firepower and challenges in their ability to conduct sustainment missions.

Religious beliefs and practices are among the most important yet least understood aspects of the cultures of other peoples. In many parts of the world, religious norms are a matter of life and death. Failure to recognize, respect, and understand the cultural and religious aspects of the population can rapidly lead to an erosion of legitimacy of the U.S. or multinational mission.

Another significant problem is the presence of displaced persons within an urban area. Noncombatants without hostile intent can inadvertently complicate UO. They may be a source of information on enemy forces. However, enemy soldiers, criminal gangs, vigilantes, or paramilitary forces may be hiding within these groups. The enemy knows that it is not easily distinguishable among neutral or disinterested parties. Local combat situations can change rapidly as the seeming neutrals become the enemy within close quarters.

INFRASTRUCTURE

A city's infrastructure is its foundation. Restoration or repair of urban infrastructure is often decisive to mission accomplishment. During full spectrum operations, destroying, controlling, or protecting vital parts of the urban infrastructure may be a necessary shaping operation to isolate an enemy from potential sources of support. An enemy force may rely on the area's water, electricity, and sources of bulk fuel to support his forces. To transport supplies, the enemy may rely on roads, airfields, sea or river lanes, and rail lines. Controlling these critical infrastructure systems may prevent the enemy from resupplying his forces.

The infrastructure of an urban environment consists of the basic resources, support systems, communications, and industries upon which the population depends. The key elements that allow an urban area to function are significant to full spectrum operations. The force that can control and secure the water, telecommunications, energy production and distribution, food production and distribution, and medical facilities controls the urban area. It is important to note that these facilities may not be located within the city's boundaries.

Infrastructure varies from city to city. In developed cities, the infrastructure and service sectors are highly sophisticated and well integrated. In developing cities, even basic infrastructure may be lacking. Many infrastructure systems may exist, and each system has a critical role in the smooth functioning of the urban area.

All systems fit into six broad categories. Commanders should analyze key facilities in each category and determine their role and importance throughout all phases of UO. (See FM 3-06 for details.) The six categories of infrastructure are—

- **Communications and Information.** This is comprised of the facilities and the formal and informal means to transmit information and data.
- **Transportation and Distribution.** Transportation and distribution includes roads, railways, subways, buses, airports, and harbors.
- **Energy.** Energy consists of the industries and facilities that produce; store; and distribute electricity, coal, oil, wood, and natural gas. It also encompasses alternate energy sources, such as nuclear, solar, hydroelectric, and geothermal power.
- **Economics and Commerce.** Economics and commerce encompass business and financial centers; recreational facilities; and outlying industrial, mineral, and agricultural facilities.
- **Administration and Human Services.** Administration and human services covers urban administrative organizations and service functions concerned with an urban area's public governance, health, safety, and welfare.
- **Cultural.** Cultural encompasses many organizations and structures that provide the urban populace with its social identity and reflect its culture, to include religious organizations, places of worship, schools and libraries, museums, archeological sites, and historic monuments.

Each element of infrastructure consists of both a physical and human component. For example, the physical component of the electrical segment of the energy infrastructure consists of power stations; a distribution network; and necessary vehicles, supplies, and equipment. The human component of this same segment consists of the supervisors, engineers, linemen, electricians, and system operators. Commanders should understand and recognize the physical and human components in their assessments.

Perhaps more than any other element of the infrastructure, communications and information link all the other elements. It helps coordinate, organize, and manage urban activities and influence and control the urban population. Urban governments and administrations are generally less prepared than trained Army forces to deal with a loss or degradation of communications and information infrastructure.

The BCT commanders should understand that destroying or disrupting any portion of the urban infrastructure can have an effect (either intentional or unintentional) on the other elements of the infrastructure. They may be able to gain a tactical advantage while minimizing unwanted and unintended effects by relying on the expertise of Army engineer and civil affairs units; local urban engineers, planners, and public works employees; and others with infrastructure-specific expertise. Although exceptions exist, commanders cannot expect the population to remain friendly to U.S. or multinational forces after destroying or significantly damaging the infrastructure of an urban area.

Requirements to protect, restore, or maintain critical infrastructure may divert substantial amounts of resources and manpower needed elsewhere and place additional constraints on subordinate commanders. The potentially large and sprawling nature of many systems makes their protection a challenge. In full spectrum operations, the safeguard or restoration of critical urban infrastructure for military or civilian use may be a decisive point in the overall UO.

THREAT

The changing nature of the threat is described in FM 3-0 through a range of four major categories or challenges—traditional, irregular, catastrophic, and disruptive. (See FM 3-0 for details.) During UO, the BCT should be prepared to face and defeat traditional, irregular, and hybrid threats.

- **Traditional.** Traditional threats compose regular armed forces employing recognized military capabilities with large formations conducting offensive or defensive operations that specifically confront the BCT's combat power and capabilities.

- **Irregular.** Irregular threats are forces composed of armed individuals or groups who are not members of the regular armed forces, police, or other internal security forces. They engage in insurgency, guerrilla activities, and unconventional warfare as principle activities.

- **Hybrid.** Hybrid threats are likely to simultaneously employ dynamic combinations of traditional and irregular forces, including terrorist and criminal elements to achieve their objectives. They will use an ever-changing variety of conventional and unconventional tactics within the urban AO to create multiple dilemmas for BCT forces. Commanders at all levels should organize and equip their forces so they do not rely on a single solution or approach to problem sets. Furthermore, commanders should be prepared to alter plans and operations accordingly when approaches to problems do not work as anticipated. Hybrid threats attempt to avoid confrontation with the BCT's combat power and capabilities and may use the civilian population and infrastructure to shield their capabilities from BCT fires. They are most likely based in and target urban areas to take advantage of the density of civilian population and infrastructure.

Potential enemies (traditional, irregular, and hybrid) in UO share some common characteristics. The broken and compartmented terrain is best suited for small-unit operations. Typical urban fighters are organized in squad-size elements and employ small-unit tactics that can be described as guerrilla tactics, terrorist tactics, or a combination of the two. They normally choose to attack (often using ambushes) on terrain that allows them to inflict casualties and then withdrawal. They attempt to canalize BCT forces and limit their ability to maneuver or mass. Small-arms weapons, sniper rifles, rocket-propelled grenades (RPG), mines, improvised explosive devices (IED), and booby traps are often the preferred weapons.

Enemy forces in conventional major combat operations oppose U.S. forces with a variety of means, including high technology capabilities built into mechanized, motorized, and light Infantry forces. These forces may be equipped with newer generation tanks and Infantry fighting vehicles and have significant numbers of antitank guided missile systems, Man-Portable Air Defense System (MANPADS) weapons, advanced fixed- or rotary-wing aviation assets, missiles, rockets, artillery, mortars, and mines. They may field large numbers of Infantry and robust military and civilian communications systems. In addition, they may possess weapons of mass destruction. Enemy forces in major combat operations may be capable of long-term resistance using conventional formations, such as divisions and corps. They may also conduct sustained unconventional operations and protracted warfare.

The enemy in unconventional small-scale contingency environments employs forces characterized by limited armor. Some are equipped with small numbers of early generation tanks, some with mechanized forces but most forces are predominately Infantry. Guerrillas, terrorists, paramilitary units, special-purpose forces, special police, and local militias are present in the environment. These forces are equipped primarily with antitank guided missile systems, MANPADSs, mortars, machine guns, and explosives. Their forces are expected to have robust communications, using conventional military devices augmented by commercial equipment, such as cell phones. These forces may not be capable of long-term, sustained, high-tempo operations. They can conduct long-term, unconventional terrorist and guerrilla operations.

INSURGENTS OR GUERRILLAS

Insurgents are members of a political party who rebel against established leadership. Guerrillas are a group of irregular, predominantly indigenous personnel organized along military lines to conduct military and paramilitary operations in enemy-held, hostile, or denied territory.

Insurgents and guerrillas are highly motivated and can employ advanced communications; some precision weapons, such as guided mortar rounds and MANPADS missiles; and some ground-based sensors in varying combinations with conventional weapons, mines, and IEDs. They usually conduct psychological and other information warfare against the HN government and population, sometimes using assassinations, kidnappings, and other terrorist techniques. Because of this, the BCT should communicate clearly with the population and operate in support of HN government forces rather than act independently as the main security and combat force. (See FM 3-07 and FM 3-07.1 for details on establishing security and security force assistance.)

Under the conditions of insurgency within the urban environment, the commander should emphasize—

- Developing population status overlays showing potential hostile neighborhoods.
- Developing an understanding of how the insurgent or guerrilla organization operates and its organization.
- Determining primary operating or staging areas.
- Determining mobility corridors and infiltration/exfiltration routes.
- Determining most likely targets.
- Determining where the enemy's logistic facilities are and how they operate.
- Determining the level of popular support (active and passive).
- Determining the recruiting, command and control, reconnaissance and security, logistics (to include money), and operations techniques and methods.
- Locating neutrals and those actively opposing these organizations.
- Using pattern analysis and other tools to establish links between the insurgent or guerilla organization and other organizations (to include family links).
- Determining the underlying social, political, and economic issues.

ENEMY TACTICS

Adaptive urban enemies seek to modify their operations to create false presentations and reduce signatures to influence and disrupt accurate intelligence preparation of the battlefield (IPB). They also attempt to deceive the BCT by showing it exactly what it expects to see. Enemy forces and organizations position decoys and deception minefields in locations where the BCT expects to see them and emplace real mines where the BCT does not anticipate them. This complicates indications and warnings in an attempt to alter the commander's selected COA.

In complex urban terrain, the enemy can close undetected with BCT forces and employ low-signature weapons against command posts (CP), communications nodes, sustainment units, and uncommitted forces. This makes the survivability of these elements and forces at the BCT level more difficult in an urban environment. The need to find, engage, and defeat the enemy must include an understanding that all forces within the BCT must be prepared to fight and secure themselves, their equipment, and their means to move and maneuver. This, combined with commercially available deception measures available to the enemy, raises the level of uncertainty and slows the pace of BCT maneuver, potentially making it more vulnerable.

Urban enemies seek to complicate BCT targeting by "hugging" BCT forces or through shielding their forces among civilian populations or within important cultural landmarks and social or religious structures. Enemy use of high technology systems also makes discerning the signatures of high-payoff systems more difficult, further confounding BCT targeting efforts. Differentiating between valid and invalid targets is time-consuming and impacts reconnaissance and security capabilities through enemy deception and dispersion.

Damage assessments are difficult to determine due to line of sight limitations, urban structures, dispersion, and signature reduction efforts. The enemy also attempts to mask the impact of effects through the same deception and denial techniques used against targeting.

SECTION II – URBAN OPERATIONAL CONSTRUCT

BCT leaders who have an urban area in their AO follow an urban operational construct. It is not sequential nor a planner's tool for phasing an operation. The urban operational construct enables commanders to function as catalysts of the operational process by helping them to understand, visualize, describe, and direct the staff processes and the conduct of operations.

COMPONENTS

The components of the urban operational construct provide a means for conceptualizing the application of combat power and capabilities in the urban environment. Commanders should combine the urban operational construct with the—

- Principles of war.
- Elements of operational art.
- Operations process.
- Considerations for full spectrum operations (including design as outlined in FM 3-0).
- Sustainment characteristics.
- Running estimates.
- Commander's critical information requirements (CCIR).
- Experience of each commander.

The five essential components of the urban operational construct are described below.

UNDERSTAND

Understanding requires the continuous assessment of the current situation and operational progress. Commanders use visualization, staffs use running estimates, and both use the IPB process to assess and understand the urban environment. Commanders and staffs observe and continually learn about the urban environment (terrain, society, and infrastructure) and other mission variables. They use reconnaissance and security forces; information systems; and reports from other headquarters, services, organizations, and agencies. They orient themselves and achieve situational understanding based on a common operational picture and continuously updated CCIR. The commander's ability to rapidly and accurately achieve an understanding of the urban environment contributes to seizing, retaining, and exploiting the initiative during UO.

SHAPE

Reconnaissance, security, and inform and influence activities are essential to successful UO. These shaping operations set the conditions for decisive operations at the tactical level in the urban area. Isolation, decisive action, minimum friendly casualties, and acceptable collateral damage distinguish success when the AO is properly shaped. Failure to adequately shape the urban AO creates unacceptable risk. Urban shaping operations may include actions taken to achieve or prevent isolation, understand the environment, maintain freedom of action, protect the force, and develop cooperative relationships with the urban population. Some shaping operations may take months to successfully shape the AO.

ENGAGE

In UO, the BCT engages by appropriately applying the full range of capabilities against decisive points leading to centers of gravity. Successful engagements take advantage of the BCT's training; leadership; and, within the constraints of the environment, equipment and technology. Engagement can be active or passive and has many components, but it is characterized by maintaining contact with the threat and population to develop the situation. Successful engagements also require the establishment of necessary levels of control and influence over all or portions of the AO until responsibilities can be transferred to other legitimate military or civilian control. Engagements may range from the overwhelming and precise application of combat power in order to defeat an enemy to large-scale humanitarian operations to HN security force assistance characterized by information and influencing activities.

CONSOLIDATE

BCT forces consolidate to protect and strengthen initial gains and ensure retention of the initiative. Consolidation includes actions taken to eliminate or neutralize isolated or bypassed enemy forces (including the processing of prisoners and civilian detainees) to increase security and protect lines of communications. It includes the sustainment operations, rapid repositioning, and reorganization of maneuver forces and reconnaissance and security forces. Consolidation may also include activities in support of the civilian population, such as the relocation of displaced civilians, reestablishment of law and order, humanitarian assistance and relief operations, and restoration of key urban infrastructure.

TRANSITION

When planning UO, commanders ensure that they plan, prepare for, and manage transitions. Transitions are movements from one phase of an operation to another and may involve changes in the type of operation, concept of the operation, mission, situation, task organization, forces, resource allocation, support arrangements, or mission command. Transitions occur in all operations. However, in UO, they occur with greater frequency and intensity, are more complex, and often involve agencies other than U.S. military organizations. All operations often include a transition of responsibility for some aspect of the urban environment to (or back to) a legitimate civilian authority. Unless planned and executed effectively, transitions can reduce the tempo of UO, slow its momentum, and cede the initiative to the enemy.

FUNDAMENTALS OF URBAN OPERATIONS

Urban operations often differ from one operation to the next. However, some fundamentals apply to UO regardless of the mission, geographical location, or level of command. They are particularly relevant to the urban environment that is dominated by man-made structures and a dense noncombatant population. These fundamentals help to ensure every action taken by a commander conducting UO contributes to the desired end state.

MAINTAIN A CLOSE COMBAT CAPABILITY

Close combat is inherent in full spectrum UO. Close combat in any UO is resource intensive, requires properly trained and equipped forces, and has the potential for high casualties. The ability to decisively close with and destroy enemy forces as a combined arms team remains essential.

In stability UO, a lack of respect and fear of Army forces can hinder recovery as much as the ill-advised use of force. All BCT Soldiers should be properly equipped and trained to fight in an urban environment. This allows the BCT to deter aggression, compel compliance, morally and physically dominate an enemy and destroy his means to resist, and terminate or transition UO on the BCT commander's terms.

AVOID THE ATTRITION APPROACH

Previous Army doctrine was inclined towards a systematic linear approach to urban combat. This approach emphasized standoff weapons and firepower. It can result in significant collateral damage, a lengthy operation, and an inconsistency with the political situation and strategic objectives. Enemy forces that defend urban areas want Army forces to adopt this approach because of the likely costs in resources. BCT commanders should only consider this approach to urban combat as an exception and justified by unique circumstances. Instead, commanders should seek to achieve precise, intended effects against multiple decisive points that overwhelm an enemy's ability to react effectively.

CONTROL THE ESSENTIAL

Many modern urban areas are too large to be completely occupied or even effectively controlled without a large force. Therefore, units should focus their efforts on controlling only the factors essential to mission accomplishment.

All principles of war can apply to UO. The principles of mass and economy of force are particularly important in guiding UO and providing mission focus. BCT forces mass combat power only to control requirements essential for mission success. This permits conservation of combat power. It also implies economy of force and associated risk in those areas where BCT forces choose not to exercise control.

MINIMIZE COLLATERAL DAMAGE

Commanders should continually assess the short- and long-term effects of operations and firepower on the population, infrastructure, subsequent missions, and national and strategic objectives. They should also consider what, if any, provisions should be made to amend or address potential collateral damage.

By avoiding unnecessary destruction of infrastructure, minimizing harm to the populace of the urban environment, commanders help sustain legitimacy for their operation. Minimization of collateral damage facilitates the return of the urban area to civilian self-sufficiency.

SEPARATE NONCOMBATANTS FROM COMBATANTS

Promptly separating noncombatants from combatants (psychologically and physically) may make UO more efficient and diminish some of the enemy's potential advantages. This separation may also reduce firepower restrictions, enhance survivability, and strip the enemy of its popular support base. Separation becomes more difficult when the enemy is an unconventional force that blends with the civilian populace.

PRESERVE CRITICAL INFRASTRUCTURE

Commanders should attempt to preserve and protect critical infrastructure during full spectrum UO for the overall health and well-being of the population. BCT forces may have to initiate actions to prevent an enemy or a hostile civilian group from removing or destroying critical infrastructure and assets, to include medical, political, and cultural infrastructure, such as religious and historical places.

RESTORE ESSENTIAL SERVICES

Essential services include power, food, water, sewage, medical care, security, and law enforcement. BCT forces plan and assist HN, international and intergovernmental organizations and agencies to restore essential services that may fail to function before or during an operation. Failure to do so can result in serious health problems for the civilians, which can affect the health of BCT Soldiers and negatively impact overall mission success. Army forces seek to coordinate and assist in transferring responsibility for providing essential services to other agencies, nongovernmental organizations, or the local government as quickly and effectively as possible.

UNDERSTAND THE HUMAN DIMENSION

BCT commanders carefully consider and manage the perceptions, allegiance, and morale of civilians during UO. Sound policies, proper discipline, adequate consideration for local culture, and rapid engagement of urban leaders positively affect the attitudes of the civilian population toward Army forces. The commander's assessment of the environment needs to accurately identify the attitudes of the people toward Army forces. Operational guidance to subordinates—including rules of engagement (ROE), protection, sustainment operations, and fraternization—is based on this assessment. They cannot inadvertently apply Western cultural norms to a non-Western urban population. As the environment of conflict becomes more complex, the human dimension takes on greater importance and may have the greatest potential for affecting the successful outcome of UO.

CREATE A COLLABORATIVE INFORMATION ENVIRONMENT

The complexity of the urban environment, particularly the human dimension, requires rapid information sharing at all levels, to include joint services, multinational partners, and participating governmental and nongovernmental agencies. The analysis of urban information necessary to refine and deepen a commander's understanding of the urban environment and its infrastructure of systems also demands collaboration among the various information sources and consumers.

TRANSITION

Because UO are resource intensive, commanders should plan to end them as quickly as possible. The objective of all UO is to transfer control of the urban area to another agency or return it to legitimate civilian control and responsibility. However, commanders often conduct a relief in place/transfer of authority to another unit. Rapid transition releases Army resources for use elsewhere and improves the civilian morale and disposition toward Army forces. Transition planning should be conducted before the onset of operations and continually adjusted as the situation develops.

SECTION III – URBAN OPERATIONS CONSIDERATIONS

The BCT faces a number of challenges during the planning, preparation, and execution of UO. This section discusses some of the tactical challenges the urban environment presents.

PLAN

The elements of operational art is the conception and construction of the framework that underpins a major operation plan and its subsequent execution. The elements are essential to identifying tasks and objectives that tie tactical missions to achieving the strategic end state. Commanders use elements of operational art appropriate to their UO to help them formulate their guidance. (See FM 3-0 for details.) The elements of operational art are—

- End state and conditions.
- Centers of gravity.
- Direct or indirect approach.
- Decisive points.
- Lines of operations and lines of effort.
- Operational reach.
- Tempo.
- Simultaneity and depth.
- Phasing and transitions.
- Culmination.
- Risk.

Intelligence plays a major role during the planning phase of UO. Initial collection of information and IPB is undertaken to provide intelligence products for the military decision-making process. The basic factors that should be considered in a complex urban environment remain the same regardless of the type of mission BCT forces are conducting. The priority given to individual factors may change based on the type of mission and specific situation. Since urban areas are often closely connected with other urban areas and surrounding rural areas by physical terrain, sociocultural factors, and infrastructure, operations within any given urban area should not be considered and planned in isolation. Events or activities that occur in other urban or rural areas may have a direct impact on events or activities in the urban AOs for which a unit is responsible.

Generate intelligence knowledge is the foundation for performing IPB and mission analysis. It begins before mission receipt and provides the relevant knowledge required regarding the operational environment for the conduct of operations. The primary product of the generate intelligence knowledge task is the initial data files and intelligence survey. (See FM 2-0 for details.) Generate intelligence knowledge includes five tasks. The first four tasks are translated into a database or data files based on the commander's guidance to support the commander's visualization.

- Develop the foundation to define threat characteristics.
- Obtain detailed terrain information and intelligence.
- Obtain detailed weather and weather effects information and intelligence.
- Obtain detailed civil considerations information and intelligence.
- Complete studies.

Intelligence support to operations in this complex environment often requires a higher degree of specificity and fidelity in intelligence products than in operations conducted in other environments. Every city has discrete and discernible patterns of daily activity. Analyzing the civil considerations (areas, structures, capabilities, organizations, people, and events [ASCOPE]) with the components of the urban environment provides a useful structure for BCT intelligence personnel to focus their IPB, and organize the requirements of providing intelligence products to commanders for the conduct of UO planning, execution, and assessment. The civil considerations should not be considered as separate entities but rather as interdependent. Understanding this interrelationship of systems provides focus and allows the commander a greater understanding of the urban area. (See FM 2-01.3 for details on civil considerations.)

ISOLATION

Shaping operations conducted to achieve or prevent isolation are critical in UO. If the attacker fails to isolate the urban area, the defender can reinforce and resupply his forces, prolonging the operation and significantly decreasing the attacker's resources and will to continue. If the defender is isolated, the attacker seizes the initiative and forces the defender to take high-risk actions, such as a breakout or counterattack, to survive.

Mounted forces are optimal for executing isolation operations because they possess the speed, agility, firepower, and protection necessary to successfully shape the urban area for full spectrum operations. Within the BCT, the reconnaissance squadron and military intelligence (MI) company provide essential capabilities to the BCT commander to isolate the urban AO and bring combat power to specific points or activities that disrupt or defeat the enemy outside the AO.

CONTIGUOUS AND NONCONTIGUOUS AREAS OF OPERATIONS

The BCT can conduct contiguous or noncontiguous operations in an AO. In either instance, the BCT commander ensures mutual support and security of key nodes and lines of communications and synchronizes and integrates the warfighting functions to achieve the desired end state.

Contiguous AOs have traditional features, including identifiable, common frontages, and shared boundaries between forces. For the BCT, relatively close distances between subordinate units characterize operations in contiguous environments.

In noncontiguous AOs, some or all subordinate units may operate without common boundaries, connected only by lines of communications and support and an integrated BCT concept of operations and scheme of maneuver. Operations in noncontiguous AOs complicate or hinder integration of warfighting functions because of extended distances between subordinate units. Noncontiguous AOs place a premium on—

- Leader initiative.
- Identification of risk and mitigating considerations or actions.
- Effective inform and influence activities.
- Extended communication requirements.
- Reconnaissance and security missions focused on the enemy and the protected force.
- Decentralized security operations and innovative logistics measures.

JOINT, INTERAGENCY, INTERGOVERNMENTAL, AND MULTINATIONAL COORDINATION

BCTs conducting UO are likely to encounter various organizations, to include—

- Other U.S. governmental agencies.
- International governmental organizations.
- Multinational and neutral national government agencies.
- Multinational and HN forces.
- Local governmental agencies and politicians.
- Nongovernmental organizations.

Even in major combat operations, many organizations operate in the AO as long as possible before combat and as soon as possible after combat. Therefore, coordination with these organizations is essential. Working with these agencies and organizations within the BCT's AO requires the commander and staff to develop effective relationships and procedures to share information and provide mutual support. In many cases, the operative coordinating and integrating process is unity of effort and not unity of command. Effective coordination is challenging, time-consuming, and manpower intensive. The staffs of larger headquarters (divisions or higher) usually have the resources and experience to conduct the coordination.

The density of the urban environment often requires that smaller tactical units coordinate with other agencies and the local civilian leadership (formal and informal) because of their physical presence in the units' AOs. In UO, mission accomplishment requires effective civil-military coordination.

PREPARE

During the preparation phase of UO, intelligence staffs, supported by collection units, further refine their products, collection plans, and reporting procedures. In urban environments, nonlethal targeting may be more prevalent than lethal targeting and should be fully integrated into the process.

When conducting UO, many products may be required. (See FM 2-91.4 for details.) These products may be used individually or combined as the mission requires. Many of the following intelligence products are created in conjunction with multiple staff elements:

- **Population Status.** Population status overlays depict how the population of a designated area is divided based on a single characteristic such as age, religion, working class, ethnicity, or income. This type of overlay is a group of products rather than a single product. The products also highlight lines where single characteristics border each other, as these may be places in which conflict is likely to occur.
- **Urban Terrain.** Urban terrain overlays depict specific aspects of terrain unique to the urban environment. These overlays can depict the details of a single building, a group of buildings, a section of an urban area, or even an entire urban area. This type of overlay can also depict the different terrain zones apparent in an urban area.
- **Building Type.** Building type overlays depict particular types of buildings. Each of the buildings can be numbered or otherwise identified depending on the needs of the commander and his staff. Additionally, entire sections of a city can be marked depending on the construction type prevalent in a particular area.
- **Street Width.** Street width overlays depict street widths in terms of major weapon systems, which can help identify the most advisable formations or routes for an area. Also, depicting buildings that exceed the depression or elevation capabilities of vehicle weapons systems can identify areas of concern and potential enemy ambush positions.
- **Lines of Communication.** Lines of communication overlays identify major lines of communications within and around an urban area, to include roads, airfields, waterways, railroads, radio and television stations (to include the furthest distance the signal can be received), and footpaths.
- **Line of Sight.** Line of sight overlays can help define avenues of approach to an objective. Just as important are reverse line of sight overlays that show the friendly avenues of approach from the enemy standpoint. It includes intervisibility lines that can provide concealment with the line of sight. They can also assist the commander in developing the communication plan.
- **Key Infrastructure.** Key infrastructure overlays depict the locations of key infrastructure in an urban environment. Like population status overlays, this type of overlay is a group of products rather than a single product. These overlays can be produced by using a map, aerial photography, or graphic design that is appropriately marked with a numbering or a color-coded system that indicates the type of asset and its specific attributes.
- **Subterranean.** Subterranean overlays identify the major underground infrastructure that supports the city such as electric, sewer, and subway networks.

EXECUTE

Executing UO requires continuous updating and refining of intelligence priorities and information collection plans as the situation changes in order to provide the necessary intelligence to the commander in a timely manner.

Regardless of the mission, UO are inherently combined arms operations that require the commander to determine the task organization requirements to meet the mission. Typically, the effects of terrain (three-dimensional and compressed operational environment) require commanders to push key combat enablers to the lowest level. As an example, a BCT may have a combat engineer battalion attached to address a mobility requirement identified during planning. The BCT commander can determine that it is more applicable to further task organize engineer companies down to the maneuver battalions to execute the specific breaching or mobility tasks. The modular BCT is well suited to receive augmentation and enablers. The organic reconnaissance squadron, fires battalion, sustainment battalion, and key enablers in the brigade special troops battalion (separate companies in an Stryker brigade combat team [SBCT]) allow the BCT commander to tailor his force to allow for reconnaissance, security, support, breach, assault, and sustainment elements.

Larger open areas, such as stadiums, sports fields, school playgrounds, and parking lots, are often critical areas during UO. They can provide locations for displaced civilians, interrogation centers, holding facilities for enemy prisoners of war (EPW), and detainee holding areas. These areas can also afford suitable aircraft landing zones (LZ) and pickup zones (PZ) and artillery firing locations. Because they are often centrally located, they can provide logistic support areas and aerial resupply possibilities.

Streets often provide primary avenues of approach and the means for rapid advance. However, buildings and other structures often canalize forces moving along them. As such, obstacles on urban surface areas usually have more effect than those in open terrain since bypass often requires entering and transiting buildings or radical changes to selected routes.

The surface of large bodies of water or major rivers bordering urban areas may provide key friendly and enemy avenues of approach or essential lines of communications and, therefore, may be a significant consideration for BCT commanders. As such, amphibious and river-crossing operations may be an integral part of the overall UO.

Mortars are the most responsive indirect fires available to BCT commanders and leaders. Their mission is to provide close and immediate fire support (FS) to the maneuver units. Mortars are well suited for combat in urban areas because of their high rate of fire, steep angle of fall, short minimum range, and the smaller bursting radius of 60-mm and 81-mm mortar ammunition. Commanders ensure that mortar support is integrated into all FS plans.

ASSESS

Urban operations can be extremely fluid. Staffs should constantly reevaluate the tactics of the enemy, affects on the urban population, and capabilities of the BCT's units due to the rapid changes in the situation and the enemy's adaptation. New enemy tactics or potential changes are identified by reconnaissance and security operations, close combat operations, and contact with the enemy. The intelligence officer and staff analysts must quickly provide the commander and operations staff with updates to intelligence estimates and products so that tactics and techniques used by the BCT can be adjusted accordingly.

Intelligence staffs continually evaluate and update intelligence collection plans based on changes in the urban environment, changes in enemy tactics, and assessments of which reconnaissance operations were successful. Continuous IPB updates and constant reevaluation of the relative interests of potential enemies are essential.

SECTION IV – WARFIGHTING FUNCTION CONSIDERATIONS

Understanding the potential effects that the urban environment may have on the integration of warfighting functions permits a commanders to better visualize his operational environment, conduct a more thorough assessment, and determine the most efficient and effective means of shaping the environment and employing BCT forces.

MOVEMENT AND MANEUVER

The urban environment can significantly affect the BCT's ability to move and maneuver. Urban environment considerations include—

- Canalization.
- Compartmentalization.
- Increased civilian vehicle traffic and congestion.
- Increased vulnerability due to explosive devices and the three-dimensional urban terrain characteristics.

An effective combined arms force, task organized with increased dismounted Infantry and Armor and combat engineer units, allow BCT forces to overcome these challenges and maneuver successfully.

Urban operations present unique and complex challenges to aviation assets. (See FM 3-06.1 for details.) The following factors can affect aviation operations in the urban environment:

- Restricted or limited LZs and PZs.
- Increased tower, antenna, and wire hazards.
- Foreign object damage to aircraft from flying debris.
- Increased risk of civilian casualties when operating in areas with high concentrations of civilians.
- Degraded night vision system operations in the vicinity of city lights.
- Degraded communications.
- Irregular and unusually strong air currents, especially when flying low in and around urban canyons.
- Increased risk of collateral damage to property.
- High risk to aircraft from close-range, small-arms, and MANPADS fire.

INTELLIGENCE

Urban environment considerations for the intelligence warfighting function include—

- Degraded reconnaissance and surveillance capability.
- Degraded sensor capabilities.
- Complex and detailed IPB process.
- Increased importance of credible human intelligence, including the contribution of local civilian liaisons, and an established intelligence reach capability.

Soldier surveillance and reconnaissance in the AO can cue commanders and staff to change the employment or organization of maneuver, fires, and sustainment forces. The BCT's response to these effects can result in timely, accurate, and actionable intelligence that permits the effective application of other warfighting functions in the UO.

FIRES

Both the physical and human components of the urban area affect how the BCT uses FS weapon systems. Urban environment considerations include—

- Masking and dead space.
- Collateral damage limitations.

- Acquisition and arming ranges.
- Type and number of indirect fire systems.
- Positioning of artillery in or outside the urban area.
- Mix of munitions.
- Fires.
- Clearance of fires and indirect fires ROE.

SUSTAINMENT

BCT commanders should understand the diverse logistic requirements of conducting UO. They should also understand how the environment (to include the population) can impact sustainment support. These requirements range from minimal to extensive, requiring forces to potentially provide or coordinate all sustainment essentials to a large urban population.

Urban operations are sustainment intensive, demanding large quantities of materiel and support for military forces and noncombatants displaced by operations. Though the infrastructure of an urban environment may be a source of valuable resources (such as supply systems, services, personnel, and facilities), sustainment planners should know the potential enemy and protection requirements that urban populations may present. Urban environment considerations include—

- Criminals, gangs, or riotous mobs may serve to disrupt sustainment operations.
- Urban operations may result in increased ammunition consumption (including terminally guided munitions), higher casualty rates, and transportation difficulties resulting from rubble.
- Units need to accomplish maintenance operations, such as equipment recovery, expeditiously as disabled vehicles may block narrow streets or roadways.
- Sustainment assets are a high-payoff target (HPT) for potential adversaries in UO. Sustainment and support elements within the BCT and attached to the BCT must be able to provide for their own protection and security. When possible, sustainment elements should move with or co-locate with combat units to enhance their security.
- Lines of communications are more difficult to maintain. Access may be limited to a few key routes easily blocked by rubble or man-made roadblocks that Soldiers cannot easily bypass. Sustainment units conducting resupply must be able to plan and execute their mission, including their own security, with organic personnel, vehicles, and equipment.
- Routes may be limited, making sustainment more easily interdicted than in open terrain. Congestion, rubble, debris, and craters may limit wheeled and tracked vehicle movement, requiring alternative modes of transportation.

MISSION COMMAND

The urban environment influences both the commander and his mission command networks and systems. Mission command networks and systems is the coordinated application of personnel, networks, procedures, equipment and facilities, knowledge management, and information management systems essential for the commander to conduct operations. The BCT commander's ability to physically see the AO, his interaction with the human component of the environment, and his intellectual flexibility when confronted with change all impact UO. Mission command networks and systems face difficulties placed on the tactical Internet and system hardware by the urban environment, the increased volume of information, and requirements to support the dynamic decision making necessary to execute successful UO. (See FM 3-0 for details on mission command.)

Although severely challenged, the principle of unity of command remains essential to UO. The number of tasks and the size of the urban AO often require BCT units to operate noncontiguously. Noncontiguous AOs stress the mission command networks and systems and challenge the commander's ability to unify the actions of subordinate battalions, apply the full force of his combat power, and achieve success. Applying this crucial principle in UO requires centralized planning, mission orders, and highly decentralized execution. Mission command permits subordinates to be innovative and operate independently according to clear orders, intent, and ROE.

The four commander's tasks of mission command are—

- Drive the operations process.
- Understand, visualize, describe, direct, lead, and assess operations.
- Develop teams among modular formations and joint, interagency, intergovernmental, and multinational partners.
- Lead inform and influence activities.

The three staff tasks of mission command are—

- Conduct the operations process (plan, prepare, execute, and assess).
- Conduct knowledge management and information management.
- Conduct inform and influence and cyber/electromagnetic activities.

PROTECTION

Survivability in the urban environment is a significant force multiplier. Preserving the force includes enhancing survivability; properly planning and executing air and missile defense; and performing inform and influence, cyber/electromagnetic, and chemical, biological, radiological, nuclear (CBRN) activities. (See FM 3-37 for details.)

Properly positioned BCT forces can take advantage of the increased survivability afforded by the physical terrain. Even a limited engineer effort can significantly enhance the combat power of small forces. In full spectrum UO, properly planned and constructed survivability positions can enable small units to withstand the assaults of large forces, snipers, and indirect fire. Commanders increase survivability by ensuring that all Soldiers have necessary protective equipment and are trained and disciplined in their use.

Properly planned and executed urban air and missile defense prevents enemy air assets from interdicting friendly forces and frees the commander to synchronize movement and maneuver and other warfighting functions.

Enemy rotary-wing aircraft may target key logistics, CPs, communication nodes, and troop concentrations outside the urban area, simultaneously attacking key infrastructure both in and out of the urban area. Some enemies may use unmanned aircraft systems (UAS) to obtain intelligence and target acquisition data on BCT forces.

The intermediate range missile capability of potential enemies is the most likely air threat to an urban area. Urban areas make the most attractive targets because of the sometimes limited accuracy of these systems. By firing missiles at an urban area, an enemy seeks to—

- Inflict casualties and materiel damage on opposing forces.
- Inflict casualties and materiel damage on the urban population.
- Undermine the confidence or trust of the civil population in the ability of U.S., multinational, and HN forces to protect them.

Personnel recovery operations occur within a complex framework of environmental factors that shape their nature and affect their outcomes. Commanders need to understand the operational environment and the impact of political, military, economic, social, information, infrastructure, physical environment, and time (PMESII-PT) to ensure that personnel recovery is incorporated into and supports each mission.

PART ONE

Brigade Combat Team and Battalion

Chapter 1

Urban Operations

The modular BCT is the primary headquarters that receives combat enablers and augmentation to facilitate mission-specific task organization. It employs combined arms teams at the battalion and company to execute UO. The BCT is equipped and manned to defeat all types of enemy forces operating in an urban environment. However, the capabilities organic to the BCT do not include Army aviation, air and missile defense, civil affairs units, explosive ordnance disposal, bridging and assured mobility engineers, specially trained advisors and security transition teams, interpreters, or Army Special Operations Forces (SOF). When required, these capabilities are added through force tailoring and task organization. The BCT does not fight in the urban environment alone. Joint, interagency, and intergovernmental agencies as well as multinational forces are integrated into the close fight. Each brings unique and complimentary capabilities as well as additional coordination and synchronization requirements. Chapter 1 provides information needed to plan and execute missions in an urban environment as an Infantry brigade combat team (IBCT), heavy brigade combat team (HBCT), and SBCT.

SECTION I – ORGANIZATION

1-1. Each BCT has unique characteristics. The modular IBCT, HBCT, and SBCT operate as an integral force in both shaping and decisive operations. Based on the mission variables, each of these BCTs has units and capabilities to isolate the enemy and prevent its reinforcement during UO. This combined with the close combat forces in the BCT to fix and defeat the enemy by maneuver, fires, and close combat makes the BCT the ground force commander's primary means to enforce his will on the enemy. The BCTs operate with their organic Infantry forces in the close fight, augmented and task organized with combat enablers organic to the BCT or attached. These combat enablers provide protection, precise and overwhelming firepower, mobility, situational awareness, and the ability to gain positional advantage over the enemy.

1-2. The BCTs complement each other and can expect to fight together in UO, either pure or task organized with cross attachment of battalions to maximize Infantry close combat capability, protection, lethality, and mobility. The HBCT does not deploy rapidly, although it can draw from pre-positioned supplies. The HBCT offers the best protection and is best employed against enemy mechanized and armored forces. The SBCT cannot deploy as easily as an IBCT but is capable of supporting early-entry operations. The SBCT does not have the protection and all-terrain mobility of an HBCT. However, it does offer the Army a force that is highly mobile with a smaller logistics footprint than HBCTs once deployed. The IBCT has exceptional strategic and operational movement and mobility and is best suited for forced- and early-entry operations. The IBCT does not share the mobility of the SBCT or the protection of the HBCT, but it possesses the core requirement for sustained UO–Infantry. (See FM 3-90.6 for details.)

IBCT CONSIDERATIONS

1-3. The IBCT is the Army's lightest BCT and is organized around dismounted Infantry capable of airborne or air assault operations. The IBCT is best employed when the Army needs to deploy forces rapidly (figure 1-1).

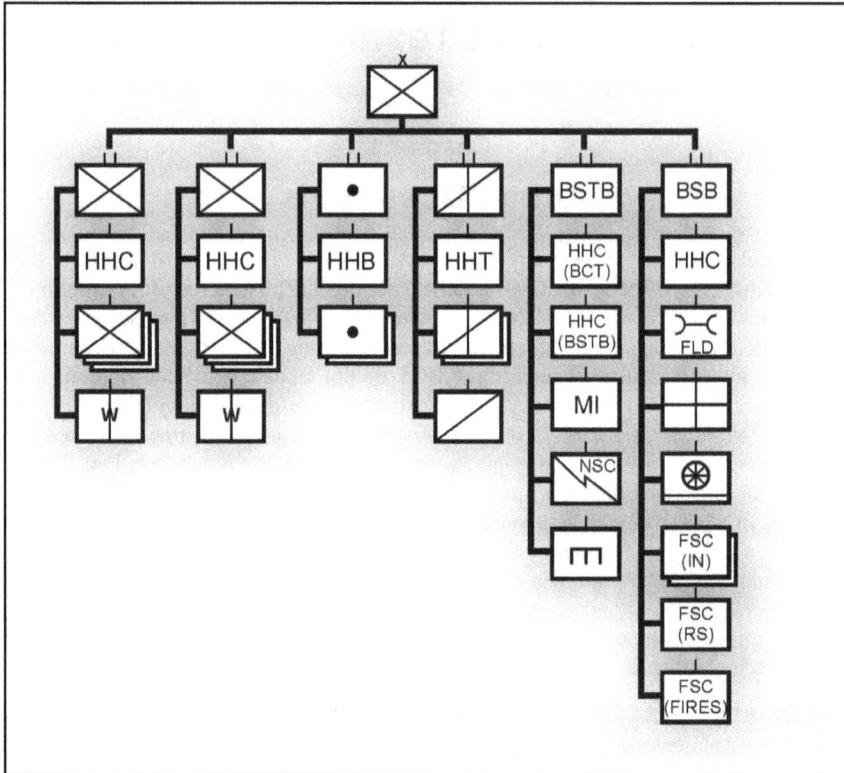

Figure 1-1. Infantry brigade combat team

MISSION

1-4. IBCTs are better suited for full spectrum operations in restrictive and severely restrictive terrain than the other types of BCTs. They are designed to operate best in high-tempo offensive operations against conventional and unconventional forces in rugged terrain. However, they can adapt effectively to a variety of missions, to include urban combat and security missions. The unit's organic elements provide increased flexibility during employment.

CAPABILITIES

1-5. Operational capabilities of IBCTs in UO include—
- Conducting Infantry-intensive dismounted small-unit UO.
- Flexibility and freedom of movement along narrow, rubbled streets.
- Small-unit mobility inside buildings, underground infrastructure, and restrictive interior spaces.
- Conducting operations with SOFs.
- Conducting air assault, air movement, or airborne UO.
- Employing a reconnaissance squadron consisting of both mounted and dismounted personnel.
- Weapons companies and organic mortars to support maneuver and provide supporting fires.

LIMITATIONS

1-6. Operational limitations of IBCTs in UO include—
- Limited firepower, mobility, and armored protection.
- Limited rapid repositioning of forces since maneuver battalions move predominately by foot.
- No armored medical evacuation (MEDEVAC) transport.
- Limited CP positioning options due to minimal protection.
- Limited options for retaining capabilities for a pursuit, exploitation, or reserve force.
- No organic gap crossing capability.
- Limited communication ranges with nonvehicular systems.
- Limited digital systems, which decreases situational awareness.
- Limited transportation assets to facilitate rapid sustainment.

HBCT CONSIDERATIONS

1-7. The HBCT is organized with armored and mechanized units (figure 1-2). It is capable of defeating the military forces of any country when battling force-on-force. It is organized to fight with combined arms at the company team level.

1-8. HBCT units have some characteristics that IBCT and SBCT units do not. The M1A2 and M2A3 vehicles give HBCT units a much greater lethality, protection, and mobility advantage. Also, these units are designed with many organic elements that increase their flexibility during employment.

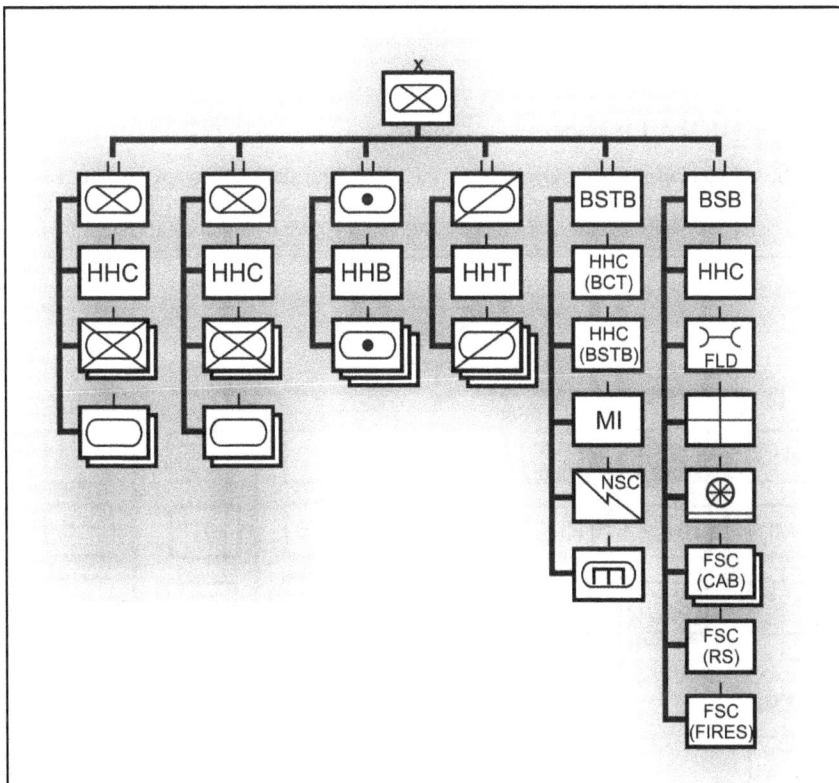

Figure 1-2. Heavy brigade combat team

MISSION

1-9. Primarily, the HBCT is manned and equipped to conduct full spectrum operations, but conditions may develop that require additional capabilities. Its maneuver, mobility, and organic reconnaissance and security units make it invaluable to a division or corps commander in full spectrum UO.

CAPABILITIES

1-10. Operational capabilities of HBCTs in UO include—
- Mobile, protected firepower in organic combined arms teams.
- Armored protection from IEDs.
- Rapid movement and deep penetrations.
- Enhanced optics for reconnaissance and surveillance.
- Psychological impact of tanks and Infantry fighting vehicles (IFV).
- Digital situational awareness down to vehicle level.
- Armored MEDEVAC capabilities.

LIMITATIONS

1-11. Operational limitations of HBCTs in UO include—
- Less dismounted Infantry than other BCTs.
- High usage rate of consumable supplies, particularly Class III, V, and VII.
- Increased vehicle recovery requirement.
- Increased danger to friendly forces, civilian population, and structures due to weapons effects.
- No organic gap crossing capability.

SBCT CONSIDERATIONS

1-12. The SBCT combines the deployability of an IBCT with the mobility of an HBCT. The Stryker vehicle gives the unit a much greater mobility advantage and added protection. The unit is also designed with many organic elements that allow for increased flexibility during employment (figure 1-3).

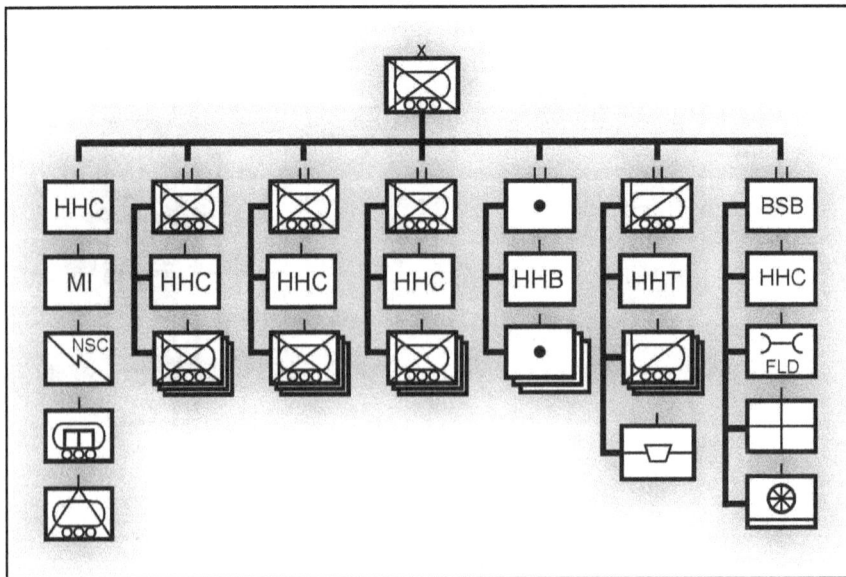

Figure 1-3. Stryker brigade combat team

MISSION

1-13. The SBCT is manned and equipped primarily to conduct full spectrum operations in a small-scale contingency. However, conditions may develop that require added capabilities not residing within the SBCT. Its maneuver, mobility, and organic reconnaissance and security units make it invaluable to a division or corps commander in full spectrum UO. As with any BCT, adjustments to task organization may be required.

CAPABILITIES

1-14. Operational capabilities of SBCTs in UO include—

- Three Infantry battalions for maneuver, which contain organic mobile gun system (MGS) platoons in each Infantry company.
- Rapid maneuvering of forces.
- Digital situational awareness down to vehicle level.
- Organic mortar fires at company level.
- Enhanced optics for reconnaissance and surveillance.
- Sniper teams at company level.

LIMITATIONS

1-15. Operational limitations of SBCTs in UO include—

- High usage rate of consumable supplies, particularly Class III, V, and VII.
- Increased vehicle recovery requirement.
- No organic gap crossing capability.
- Minimal armor protection from direct fire and IEDs.

TASK-ORGANIZATION CONSIDERATIONS

1-16. With their modular organization, BCTs can be rapidly task organized. Task organization is the process of allocating available assets to subordinate commanders and establishing their command and support relationships. (See FM 3-0 for details.) The BCT and battalion commanders designate command and support relationships to weight the decisive operation and support the concept of operations. Task organization also helps subordinate and supporting commanders understand their roles in the operation and support the commander's intent.

1-17. When task organizing his forces, the BCT commander should select the right subordinate force for the mission and balance it with appropriate attachments. The BCT commanders should direct how to organize the small tactical combined arms teams. They should also ensure that battalions and companies have the proper balance of forces from which to form these teams. Successful UO requires small-unit combined arms teams, with Infantry as the base of this force. Commanders decide how to task organize Armor, aviation, engineer, MI, air defense, and mechanized Infantry elements to accomplish the tactical task.

1-18. The BCT may receive units from other BCTs, brigades, or services. Because of the increased need for Infantry and close-in support fires, task organization between brigade or higher level units may be more prevalent in UO. All commanders must understand not only the capabilities and limitations of units within their parent BCT but also the capabilities and limitations of other units. Considerations for the task organization of units from different types of BCTs are the same as the task organization within the BCT. Examples of these task organizations include—

- Infantry battalion assigned to a HBCT.
- Combined arms battalion from a HBCT assigned to an IBCT.
- Stryker battalion assigned to a HBCT.
- Stryker battalion assigned to a combat aviation brigade.
- Combined arms battalion assigned to a Marine Corps Infantry regiment.

SECTION II – MISSION COMMAND

1-19. Mission command develops and integrates those activities enabling a commander to balance the art of command and the science of control. Mission command is the conduct of operations through decentralized execution based on mission orders. Successful mission command demands that subordinate leaders at all echelons exercise disciplined initiative, acting aggressively and independently to accomplish the mission within the commander's intent. (See FM 3-0 for details.)

1-20. In UO, mission command challenges are magnified by the—

- Complexity of the terrain.
- Degradation of communication systems line of sight capability.
- Considerations for positioning CPs in or around the urban area to maximize communication capability while minimizing the enemy threat to the CPs.

1-21. As outlined in the Introduction, the UO construct is understand, shape, engage, consolidate, and transition. Mission command and the integration of the other warfighting functions are integral to achieving and conducting each component of the UO construct.

ROLE OF THE COMMANDER

1-22. The commander is the central figure in mission command, essential to integrating the capabilities of the warfighting functions to accomplish the mission. Mission command invokes the greatest possible freedom of action to subordinates. It enables subordinates to develop the situation, adapt, and act decisively through disciplined initiative in dynamic conditions within the commander's intent. Mission command focuses on empowering subordinate leaders and sharing information to facilitate decentralized execution. (See FM 3-0 for details.)

UNITY OF COMMAND

1-23. Unity of command means that a single commander directs and coordinates the actions of all forces toward a common objective. Cooperation may produce coordination, but giving a single commander the required authority is the most effective way to achieve unity of effort. Unified action is the synchronization, coordination, and/or integration of the activities of governmental and nongovernmental entities with military operations to achieve unity of effort. (See JP 1 for details.) The joint nature of unified action creates situations where the commander does not directly control all organizations in the AO. In the absence of command authority, commanders cooperate, negotiate, and build consensus to achieve unity of effort. (See FM 3-0 for details.)

UNITY OF EFFORT VICE UNITY OF COMMAND

1-24. Uniting the diverse capabilities necessary to achieve success in full spectrum UO requires focusing those capabilities toward a common goal. Where military operations typically demand unity of command, the challenge for military and civilian leaders is to forge unity of effort among the many organizations involved in UO. Unity of effort is the coordination and cooperation toward common objectives, even if the participants are not necessarily part of the same command or organization—the product of successful unified action. (See JP 1 for details.)

1-25. Unity of effort is fundamental to successfully incorporating all the elements of combat power, influence, and nonmilitary capabilities available to the BCT commander in a collaborative approach to full spectrum operations. At the BCT level, unity of effort is typically associated with stability operations. During stability operations, considerations for offensive and defensive actions remain, but many of the activities and actions center on nonmilitary actors and agencies. Frequently, many groups, particularly nongovernmental organizations, participate in unified action at their own discretion. Their roles are often defined by competing interests and governed by differences in policy. In the case of nongovernmental organizations, their activities are driven by humanitarian principles and may have goals separate from the U.S. government or the international community.

LINES OF EFFORT

1-26. A line of effort is a line that links multiple tasks and missions using the logic of purpose—cause and effect—to focus efforts toward establishing operational and strategic conditions. Lines of effort are essential to long-term planning when positional references to an enemy or adversary have little relevance. In operations involving many nonmilitary factors, lines of effort may form the only way to link tasks, effects, conditions, and the desired end state. Lines of effort help commanders visualize how military capabilities can support the other instruments of national power. They prove particularly invaluable when used to achieve unity of effort in operations involving multinational forces and civilian organizations, where unity of command is elusive, if not impractical. (See FM 3-0 for details.)

LINES OF OPERATION AND LINES OF EFFORT

1-27. A line of operations is a line that defines the directional orientation of a force in time and space in relation to the enemy and links the force with its base of operations and objectives. Lines of operations connect a series of decisive points that lead to control of a geographic or force-oriented objective. Operations designed using lines of operations consist of a series of actions executed according to a well-defined sequence. Major combat operations are typically designed using lines of operations. These lines tie offensive and defensive tasks to the geographic and positional references in the operational area. Commanders synchronize activities along complementary lines of operations to achieve the end state. (See FM 3-0 for details.)

1-28. Lines of operations and lines of effort bridge the broad concept of operations across to discreet tactical tasks. They link objectives to the end state. Continuous assessment gives commanders the information required to revise and adjust lines of operations and effort. Subordinate commanders reallocate resources accordingly. Commanders may describe an operation along lines of operations, lines of effort, or a combination of both. An operational approach using both lines of operations and lines of effort reflects the characteristics and advantages of each. With this approach, commanders synchronize and sequence actions, deliberately creating complementary and reinforcing effects. The lines then converge on the well-defined, commonly understood end state outlined in the commander's intent. (See FM 3-0 for details.)

OPERATIONAL VARIABLES

1-29. The operational environment is a composite of the conditions, circumstances, and influences that affect the employment of capabilities and bear on the decisions of the commander. (See JP 3-0 for details.) Understanding the urban environment is essential to the successful execution of operations. Operational variables describe not only the military aspects of an operational environment but also the population's influences on it. As BCT and battalion commanders better understand their operational environment (including the capabilities of their own and enemy forces), they more skillfully employ and integrate their combined arms teams to create the conditions that lead to the desired end state.

1-30. Operational variables are fundamental to developing an understanding of the operational environment necessary to plan at any level and in any situation. The degree to which each operational variable provides useful information depends on the situation and echelon. For example, social and economic variables often receive close analysis as part of enemy and civil considerations at brigade and higher levels. The BCT commander and staff refine the information about the operational variables and develop mission variables, focusing on those which provide mission-relevant information.

1-31. Urban operations include PMESII-PT variables. Included within these variables are the enemy, friendly, and neutral capabilities and actions and interactions that are relevant to a specific operation. An operational environment is more than just military capabilities. It is a combination of the interrelated variables and the links among them. (See FM 3-0 for details.)

MISSION VARIABLES

1-32. Operational variables are relevant to planning; however, they may be too broad for tactical planning. Upon receipt of a mission, BCT and battalion commanders and staff narrow their focus to six mission variables—mission, enemy, terrain and weather, troops and support available, time available, and civil considerations (METT-TC). Mission variables are those aspects of the operational environment that directly affect a mission.

1-33. Incorporating the analysis of the operational variables into the mission variables emphasizes the operational environment's human aspects and affects all of the mission variables. Incorporating human factors into mission analysis requires critical thinking, collaboration, continuous learning, and adaptation. It also requires analyzing local and regional perceptions. (See FM 3-0 and FM 3-90.5 for details.)

COMMAND POSTS

1-34. The BCT and battalion commanders organize their staffs into CPs that provide staff expertise, communications, and information systems to aid the commander in planning and controlling operations. All CPs have the responsibility to conduct the six basic functions of information management:

- Collect relevant information.
- Process information from data to knowledge.
- Store relevant information for timely retrieval to support mission command.
- Display relevant information tailored for the needs of the user.
- Disseminate relevant information.
- Protect knowledge products, data, and information.

1-35. While each echelon and type of unit organizes CPs differently, two types of CP cells exist:

- **Integrating.** Integrating cell group personnel and equipment to integrate the warfighting functions according to planning horizon.
- **Functional.** Functional cells group personnel and equipment according to warfighting function. (See FM 3-90.6 for details.)

COMMAND POST POSITIONING

1-36. The main CP is positioned to maintain communications with subordinate units and control of the operation. Urban areas are good locations for CPs because they provide cover and concealment, access to electricity and other services, and good access and egress routes. However, they can also put indigenous populations at risk and provide enemy units covered and concealed positions to monitor and attack the CP.

1-37. Position the main CP—

- Avoiding key terrain features, such as hilltops and crossroads.
- On ground that is trafficable even in poor weather.
- Where the enemy least affects the main CP operations.
- Where the main CP can best control operations and coordinate with adjacent, higher, and HN security forces if applicable.
- Where the main CP can achieve the best line of sight communications (digital and voice).
- Using buildings and terrain to mask signals from the enemy.
- Using terrain for passive security (cover and concealment).
- Colocating with tactical units for mutual support and local security.
- Near an existing road network out of sight from possible enemy observation.

1-38. In contiguous AOs, the BCT main CP is echeloned with lower and higher CPs and usually locates behind battalion CPs and out of enemy medium artillery range if practical. In noncontiguous AOs, the BCT main CP usually locates within a subordinate battalion's AO to facilitate greater security, access to lines of communications, and freedom to maneuver and reposition. Urban operations can present a commander with both possibilities. The mission variables determine how the BCT positions their CPs.

1-39. In full spectrum UO, visualizing the operational environment requires commanders to move themselves and their CPs forward to positions that may be more exposed to risk. Thus, commanders modify their mission command network and system capabilities to make them smaller, reduce their signature, and increase their mobility. Because of the greater threat to mission command networks and systems, security efforts may be more intense.

1-40. However, BCT and battalion commanders may not be able to dispersed forces from positions forward. Commanders and their staffs may be forced by the urban terrain to rely on semi-fixed CPs, develop decision points with criteria for execution, rely on subordinate leader initiative, and position themselves at the point of decision within limits of acceptable risk. Detailed leader reconnaissance of the AO by commanders, their staff, and their subordinates before the mission can compensate for this challenge.

1-41. Digital and analog communications have important line of sight issues. Buildings in urban environments affect wave propagation, which can degrade communications. Line of sight constraints within the urban environment are three-dimensional and should be addressed from all directions, both vertically and horizontally. Failure to anticipate interference adversely affects UO.

1-42. Unmanned aircraft systems can assist in overcoming many ground-based line of sight restrictions. The use of satellite and landline communications may also mitigate many line of sight problems. Digital, satellite, and burst transmission systems have proven effective in the urban environment. Some of these systems have the added capability of allowing real-time imagery of selected targets to be passed to the user.

SECTION III – UNDERSTAND

1-43. The BCT commanders should weigh U.S. domestic and international considerations during the planning, preparation, and conduct of UO. Urban operations include joint forces; interagency cooperation; multinational forces; nongovernmental organizations; and, when conducting permissive operation, the HN. Each of these forces and organizations may have different goals and objectives. Key considerations when conducting UO are—

- Clearly define and understand command relationships.
- Establish personal relationships with multinational force commanders, HN security force commanders, and local political leaders.
- Determine the mission requirements, establish task organization, and train/rehearse combined arms forces and integrated multinational forces before conducting operations.
- Integrate liaison elements into integrating processes and cells.
- Employ liaison elements at the higher headquarters, critically augmenting headquarters with subordinate headquarters to facilitate situational understanding, decision making, and flexibility in execution.
- Fully integrate planning and intelligence efforts. Aggressively seek out gaps in information and the means to answer information requirements.
- Organize the staff into integration cells (current operations, future operations, and future plans cells) tailored across the BCTs CPs to best support decision making and situational awareness.
- Focus the following staff integration processes on the urban environment early. (See FM 5-0 for details.)
  - Intelligence preparation of the battlefield.
  - Targeting.
  - Reconnaissance and surveillance synchronization
  - Composite risk management.
  - Knowledge management.

INTELLIGENCE PREPARATION OF THE BATTLEFIELD

1-44. Intelligence preparation of the battlefield (IPB) is a systematic process of analyzing and visualizing the mission variables of enemy, terrain, and weather, and civil considerations in a specific area of interest and for a specific mission. By applying IPB, commanders gain the information needed to selectively apply and maximize operational effectiveness at critical points in time and space. The four steps of the IPB process are—

- Define the operational environment.
- Describe environmental effects on operations.
- Evaluate the threat.
- Determine threat COAs.

1-45. The IPB process is useful at all echelons and remains constant regardless of the operation or environment. To successfully conduct urban IPB, a higher level of detail is required than in other environments. This is mainly due to the three distinguishing characteristics that comprise the urban environment: terrain, society, and supporting infrastructure.

1-46. Civil considerations along with the characteristics of the urban environment provide a useful structure to focus IPB efforts. Understanding their interdependence provides the commander a better understanding of the urban area.

1-47. As part of the initial planning process, civil affairs units conduct an area assessment that provide commanders with essential information about the environment. (See FM 41-10 for details.) Commanders should integrate this initial assessment into the overall urban-focused IPB process.

1-48. Intelligence preparation of the battlefield in support of UO follows the doctrinal principles and four-step IPB methodology as described in FM 2-01.3 but differs from IPB done in conventional operations in its focus. When conducting IPB to support UO, discuss the following:

- A comprehensive assessment of urban construction during terrain analysis. What materials are used? What are the designs and dimensions? What is the street and building pattern? (See appendix A for details.)
- An investigation of urban infrastructure. What are its components? Who supports it and who is supported by it? What is necessary to sustain the population?
- A study of populations, including demographic details, cultural norms, and perceptions, to understand the indigenous culture.
- The underlying natural terrain on which the man-made terrain is superimposed.
- Identify and evaluate the enemy.
- COA development for both friendly and enemy forces, to include how the actions undertaken by one element in an AO can affect other elements or actions within the same area or beyond it. The interconnectedness of an urban area produces intentional and unintentional consequences for every act, and the commander and staff should attempt to anticipate all the consequences that may impact the mission.

ANALYZE THE ENVIRONMENT

1-49. A terrain analysis involves the study and interpretation of natural and man-made features of an urban area, their effects on operations, and the effects of weather and climate on these features. The degree of detail in the analysis varies depending on the mission variables. During the evaluation, identify aspects that might favor one type of operation.

1-50. An appreciation of civil considerations (the ability to analyze their impact on operations) enhances several aspects of operations, such as the selection of objectives; location, movement, and control of forces; use of weapons; and protection measures.

1-51. Individually or collectively, people can affect UO positively or negatively or can have a minimal affect on operations. In stability operations, BCT forces work closely with civilians of all types. Many different kinds of people can be living and operating in and around an AO. As with organizations, people may be indigenous or introduced from outside the AO. An analysis of people should identify them by their various capabilities, needs, and intentions. When analyzing people, commanders should consider historical, cultural, ethnic, political, economic, and humanitarian factors.

1-52. The languages used in the region impact UO. The languages used in the AO must be identified so language training, communication aids, (such as phrase cards), and task organizing of both military and civilian translators can begin. Translators are crucial for collecting intelligence, interacting with local citizens and community leaders, and developing products for inform and influence and cyber/electromagnetic activities.

INFRASTRUCTURE ASSESSMENT

1-53. The basic infrastructure services evaluated depend on the situation, mission, and commander's intent. An infrastructure assessment is typically performed by engineers, but it may be accomplished by others when an engineer is not available depending on the expertise available and the desired type and quality of information required. Leaders should also consult other nongovernmental, governmental, and HN agencies in the area to determine if there are extenuating circumstances that may influence the assessment. While an infrastructure assessment is designed to support the resolution of the immediate challenges, it normally sets the conditions for a successful transition. Some primary assessment considerations are—

- **Sewage.** What is the status of the system? What health and environmental risks exist?
- **Water.** What potable water sources are available? Are they adequate? Have they been tested?
- **Electricity.** What is the status of generation facilities, to include availability of generators? What is the status of the transmission infrastructure? What critical facilities, to include hospitals, government buildings, and schools, are not having their needs met? What is the availability of fuel for transportation, heating, and cooking? Is there an adequate system of distribution?
- **Academics.** What schools are in need of repair and rebuilding? Is there a sufficient amount of teachers? Are education supplies available?
- **Trash.** Is there a system in place for removing waste? What hazardous waste streams are being generated that may have detrimental impacts on health and the environment? What is the ultimate disposal system for trash?
- **Medical.** Are medical services available and operational? Does an emergency service exist? Do emergency services use radio communications? If so, which frequencies do they use? Are services available for animals?
- **Safety.** Is there a police and fire service?
- **Other.** Additional assessment considerations include—
  - *Transportation networks.* Are roads, bridges, and railroads trafficable? Is the airport operational? Do helicopter landing sites exist and are they useable? Can they sustain the local, humanitarian assistance traffic?
  - *Fuel distribution.* Is there a commercial and residential fuel distribution system available?
  - *Housing.* Are the homes structurally sound and habitable? Do they include basic utilities?
  - *Explosive hazards.* Are ordnance hazards observed?
  - *Environmental hazards.* Are environmental hazards observed?
  - *Communications.* Is the telephone network available and operational? Is there access to radio and newspaper? Which frequencies are locally used and required? Are there other uses of the electromagnetic spectrum that may impact operations?
  - *Places of worship.* Are there adequate facilities to support religious activities for all groups?
  - *Attitude.* Are local people and community leaders supportive? Is there ethnic tension?

EVALUATE THE ENEMY

1-54. The BCT must be ready to evaluate enemies employing varying combinations of technology and presenting challenges of varying intensity. Not all enemies are purely military in nature. No matter who the enemy is, it is still important to portray as accurately as possible how they normally execute operations, how they have executed operations in the past, and what they are capable of doing given the current situation.

1-55. By developing cultural awareness, groups and individual members of a population can be categorized as enemies, adversaries, supporters, and neutrals. (See FM 3-0 for details.) One reason land operations are complex is that all four categories are intermixed, often with no easy means to distinguish one from another. Given the vast number of subpopulations that exist in any urban area, enemy identification is an important portion of this evaluation, as are their capabilities and activities. Enemy capabilities should be evaluated in terms of how buildings, public utilities, infrastructure, and the city residents can be used as part of their dynamic arsenal. Courses of action developed for the enemy should include all of these elements.

COURSES OF ACTION

1-56. Based on the mission variable, the intelligence staff officer depicts the enemy based on the commander's guidance. At a minimum, the staff determines likely objectives and the desired end state. The commander and staff need to develop a plan that is optimized to one of the COAs, while allowing for contingency options should the enemy choose another COA.

1-57. To ensure that the full set of available enemy COAs is identified, the staff should consider the—

- COAs that the enemy believes are appropriate to the current situation and the enemy's likely objectives. This requires an understanding of the enemy's decision-making process as well as an appreciation for how the enemy perceives the current situation.
- Enemy COAs that could significantly influence the unit's mission, such as diverting combat power to cover increasing protection requirements.
- Enemy COAs that may go outside the boundaries of known enemy doctrine or tactics.
- Enemy COAs indicated by recent activities and events. To avoid surprise from an unanticipated COA, consider all possible explanations for the enemy's activity in terms of possible enemy COAs.

URBAN MAPPING

1-58. Developing and disseminating standardized urban mapping products enhances the effectiveness of BCT operations in urban areas. Commonly, these products are based on aerial photographic products from UAS reconnaissance overflights or satellite imagery. Using digital systems, these products can be enhanced with graphic overlays showing unit AOs, building numbering systems, key building sites, and terrain features. Mapping products can then be distributed through hard-copy reproduction or digital broadcasting. When tactically and technically feasible, the BCT gains access to city planner or civil engineer maps that provide detailed information on the urban area.

1-59. The BCT conducts initial map and aerial photograph reconnaissance to pinpoint key terrain and other important locations that can be identified in the AO. These areas include—

- Power generation, communication, and water treatment facilities.
- Restricted or protected areas designated by the ROE.
- Avenues of approach.
- Safe havens, including—
  - Hospitals.
  - Police stations.
  - Embassies.
  - Other (friendly) facilities.

- Hazardous areas, including—
  - Construction sites.
  - Industrial areas.
  - Dangerous intersections.
  - Bridges.
  - Criminal areas.
- Major terrain features, including—
  - Historical, cultural, or religious sites.
  - Parks.
  - Airports and train stations.

IMPROVING THE URBAN OPERATIONS SKETCH

1-60. Urban operations sketches are critical to facilitate control in tracking elements with greater detail and in obtaining precise location updates throughout operations. Urban sketches are confirmed and updated during the planning and throughout execution of operations. The BCT reconnaissance units can provide overlays and sketches of urban areas. They can assess and map urban entry routes for maneuver units.

1-61. Urban sketches include a reference system to identify buildings and streets. Naming conventions should be simple, allowing for ease of navigation and orientation in the urban environment (for example, odd-numbered buildings on the left side of streets, even-numbered buildings on the right). Street names should not be used as references because signs can be missing or can be changed to confuse friendly forces.

1-62. Because most maps do not provide the necessary level of detail to meet these important operational considerations, the reconnaissance squadron usually creates overlays to enhance situational awareness. These overlays categorize sections of the urban area by ethnicity, religious affiliation, and other prevailing characteristics that can affect UO. Prior to reconnaissance handover or battle handover, the reconnaissance squadron consolidates sketches and overlays to create an urban map with overlays for the BCT. Figure 1-4 is an example of a UO sketch with overlay information added to show infrastructure, facilities, and building usage.

TARGETING CONSIDERATIONS

1-63. Targeting is the process of selecting targets and matching the response to them, taking account of operational requirements and capabilities.

TARGETING PROCESS

1-64. The targeting process (decide, detect, deliver, and assess) and the subset (find, fix, finish, exploit, analyze, and disseminate) is one of the integrating processes and continuing activities that commanders and staffs use during the operations process to synchronize the warfighting functions in accordance with the commander's intent and concept of operations. As the military decision-making process is conducted, targeting becomes more focused based on the commander's guidance and intent. The staff recommends to the commander the asset for detecting targets, the means in which to deliver the desired effect(s), and the assets used to assess the engagement's effectiveness.

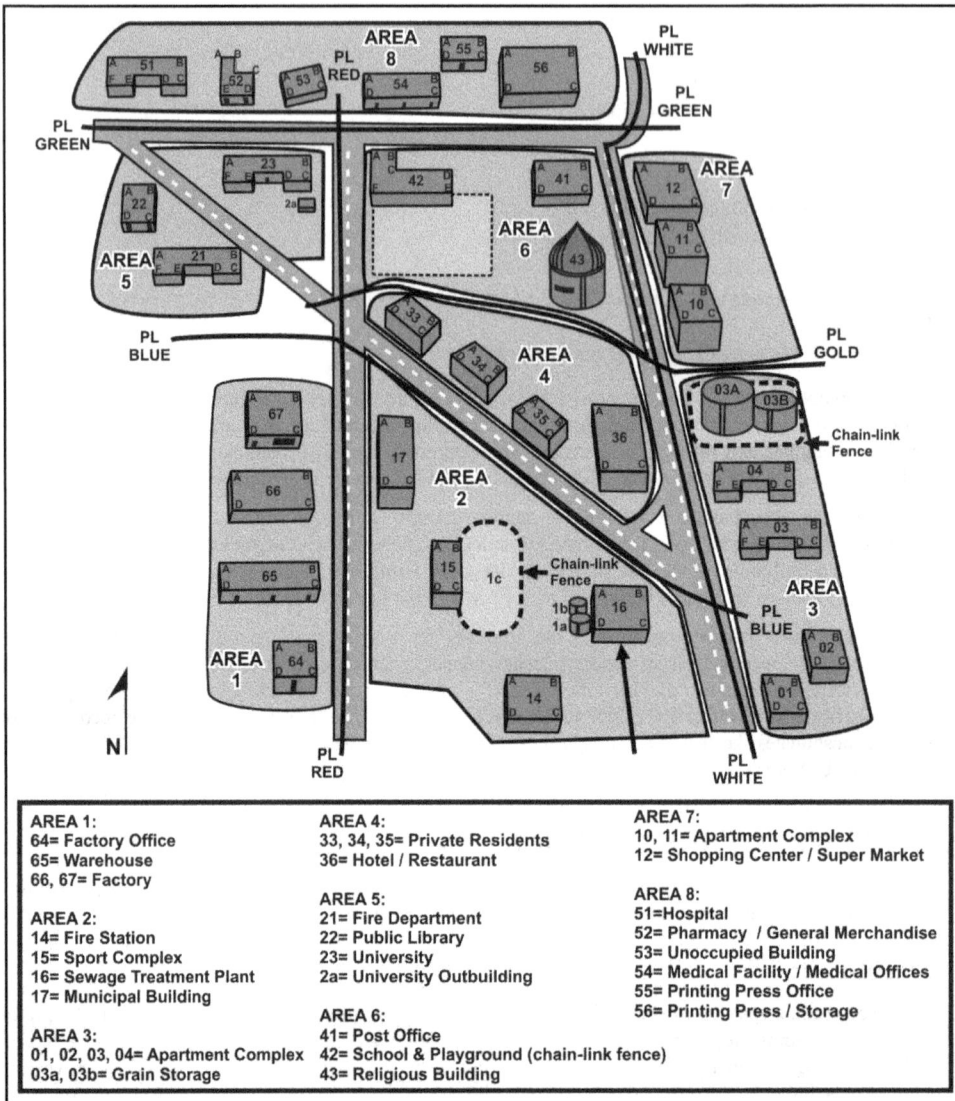

Figure 1-4. Example urban operations sketch

AREA 1:	AREA 4:	AREA 7:
64= Factory Office	33, 34, 35= Private Residents	10, 11= Apartment Complex
65= Warehouse	36= Hotel / Restaurant	12= Shopping Center / Super Market
66, 67= Factory		
	AREA 5:	AREA 8:
AREA 2:	21= Fire Department	51=Hospital
14= Fire Station	22= Public Library	52= Pharmacy / General Merchandise
15= Sport Complex	23= University	53= Unoccupied Building
16= Sewage Treatment Plant	2a= University Outbuilding	54= Medical Facility / Medical Offices
17= Municipal Building		55= Printing Press Office
	AREA 6:	56= Printing Press / Storage
AREA 3:	41= Post Office	
01, 02, 03, 04= Apartment Complex	42= School & Playground (chain-link fence)	
03a, 03b= Grain Storage	43= Religious Building	

TARGETING CHALLENGES

1-65. Targeting challenges are met by innovatively integrating the reconnaissance capabilities of snipers, UAS and aerial observers, and MI surveillance units with the BCT reconnaissance units. More artillery systems may be needed to ensure responsiveness (rather than the weight) of fires. Positioning numerous artillery systems reduces the dead space and permits units to establish more direct sensor-to-shooter links.

1-66. The three-dimensional urban terrain makes identification, reporting, and targeting of enemy locations more difficult for forces accustomed to acquiring and engaging targets in primarily two dimensions. Enemies are likely to use decoys to cause erroneous assessments of their capabilities, strength, and disposition. They also attempt to use these decoys to absorb expensive and limited terminally guided munitions and cause misallocation of other critical resources.

1-67. Target acquisition and target engagement in UO faces several other challenges, to include—

- Difficulty penetrating increased cover and concealment using sensors and reconnaissance.
- Acquiring targeting information and tracking targets throughout the depth of the urban area.
- Short exposure times due to cover and concealment, requiring firing systems to act rapidly on targeting data.
- Difficulty conducting battle damage assessment.
- Vertical structures interrupting line of sight and creating corridors of visibility along streets.
- Limited space to place battery or platoon positions with the proper unmasked gun line. This may mandate positioning in sections while still massing fires on specific targets.
- Limited use of unguided Multiple Launch Rocket Systems (MLRS) due to their destructive capabilities and the potential for collateral damage. However, commanders may use them to effectively isolate the urban area from outside influence.
- Heightened concerns for collateral damage, which require commanders to pay particular attention to their targeting process. Ten-digit grid coordinates may not be sufficient for accurately identifying targets as buildings may be connected to each other. Target locations may need to include the street address, number of stories, shape, color, or other distinguishing characteristic essential for ground and air forces to achieve targeting precision.
- Greater concerns for the safety and health (environmental matters) of the urban populace and the protection of critical infrastructure and cultural structures.
- The mix of munitions used by indirect fire systems changing somewhat in urban areas. Units are likely to request more terminally guided munitions for artillery systems to target small enemy positions, such as snipers or machine guns, while limiting collateral damage.

BRIGADE COMBAT TEAM ROLE

1-68. The BCT develops a synchronized scheme of maneuver and schemes of fires. The BCT staff recommends for the commander's approval FS tasks with the desired effects and the allocation of FS units. The BCT's role in FS planning includes—

- Setting conditions, to include fires, for the main effort battalion to conduct the BCT decisive operation.
- Providing protection to the BCT through both a proactive and reactive counterfire fight.
- Integrating refinements from subordinates of the fires support and other plans.
- Integrating the movement of artillery units with the scheme of maneuver.
- Clearly specifying priority of fires and the conditions that will change the priority of fires.

BATTALION ROLE

1-69. The BCT allocates FS to battalions to facilitate the BCT plan. Therefore, the battalion needs to understand the BCT scheme of fires, its synchronization with the BCT scheme of maneuver, and the battalion's role in the execution of the BCT scheme of fires. The battalion's role in FS planning includes—

- Developing a battalion scheme of fires.
- Requesting special munitions for preplanned targets (for example, smoke and terminally guided munitions).
- Integrating and refining BCT targets for the close fight.
- Submitting new targets to support the battalion commander's concept of operations.
- Ensuring that the battalion mortars are integrated into the scheme of fires and that their movement is synchronized with the scheme of maneuver.
- Incorporating bottom-up refinement from the companies.
- Forwarding the battalion scheme of fires and target refinements to the BCT.
- Conducting rehearsals.
- Ensuring primary and alternate observers are assigned to each preplanned target.

RECONNAISSANCE AND SURVEILLANCE SYNCHRONIZATION

1-70. To perform reconnaissance and surveillance synchronization, the intelligence officer (in collaboration with the operations officer and the entire staff) identifies requirements for collection, recommends collection assets and capabilities, prepares the reconnaissance and surveillance synchronization tools, and maintains reconnaissance and surveillance synchronization as operations progress.

1-71. Synchronization is comprised of a wide variety of intelligence and staff functions; planning, collection, processing and exploitation; analysis and production; dissemination and integration; and evaluation and feedback. It should focus on the commander's requirements. The process is not a linear or even cyclical operation, but rather it represents a network of interrelated, simultaneous actions that can, at any given time, be driven by and drive other activities.

1-72. The purpose of this staff function is to place all reconnaissance units (including surveillance and MI discipline) and supporting resources into a single plan in order to capitalize on the different capabilities. The plan synchronizes and coordinates reconnaissance and surveillance missions within the overall scheme of maneuver. A good reconnaissance and security plan fits into and supports the overall operations plan or order. It positions and tasks reconnaissance units so they can collect the right information, sustain or reconstitute for branches or sequels, or shift priorities as the situation develops. Effective synchronization focuses on meeting the commander's information requirements through reconnaissance and security tasks integrated into the orders process.

1-73. Planning consists of two significant staff processes reconnaissance and surveillance synchronization and reconnaissance and surveillance integration. Synchronization of planning is achieved by developing requirements and synchronization tools. Reconnaissance and surveillance synchronization is the responsibility of the intelligence officer and his staff. The operations officer is responsible for reconnaissance and surveillance integration with the support of the intelligence officer.

1-74. At each level, the intelligence officer, operations officer, and staff may use the following reconnaissance and surveillance synchronization steps to develop, refine, and synchronize the reconnaissance and security plan:

- Analyze information requirements and intelligence gaps.
- Evaluate available assets, internal and external, to the organization.
- Determine gaps in the use of those assets.
- Recommend reconnaissance units controlled by the BCT to collect on the CCIR.
- Submit requests for information for adjacent and higher collection support.

1-75. Reconnaissance and surveillance synchronization ensures that reconnaissance units, intelligence reach, and requests for information successfully report; produce; and disseminate information, combat information, and intelligence to support decision making. The intelligence officer, in coordination with the operations officer and other staff elements as required, synchronizes the entire collection effort. This effort includes assets the commander controls and those of adjacent and higher echelon units and organizations. It also uses intelligence reach to answer the CCIR and other requirements.

COMPOSITE RISK MANAGEMENT

1-76. Accept risks to create opportunities. Operational adaptability assists commanders to create training and organizational climates that promote calculated, disciplined risk-taking focused on winning rather than preventing defeat. A key aspect of mission command includes identifying risks, deciding how much risk to accept, and minimizing the effects of accepted risk by establishing control measures to mitigate those risks. Composite risk management is the primary process for identifying hazards and controlling risks during operations. Effective integration is critical during all UO to identify and mitigate hazards. (See FM 5-19 for details.)

KNOWLEDGE MANAGEMENT

1-77. Knowledge management exists to help commanders make informed, timely decisions during operations. All leaders need to understand the processes and procedures associated with the systems available to share information and acquire knowledge. Information systems provide detailed information that facilitates situational understanding and mission command. Even with the most advanced information systems, higher headquarters often has difficulty understanding the situation on the ground. Knowledge management is further complicated in UO when the terrain includes a population in a condensed space with complex infrastructure and sociocultural considerations.

SECTION IV – SHAPE

1-78. Shaping operations create and preserve conditions for the success of decisive operations. Shaping operations establish conditions for the decisive operation through effects on the enemy, population, and terrain. Key considerations in shaping the urban environment are—

- Isolation of the AOs.
- Inform and influence and cyber/electromagnetic activities.
- Brigade combat team continuing activities focused on the urban environment. (See FM 5-0 for details.)
  - Reconnaissance operations (including surveillance and MI discipline collection).
  - Security operations.
  - Protection.
  - Liaison and coordination.
  - Terrain management.
  - Information management.
  - Airspace integration.
- Unified action.

ISOLATION

1-79. Critical urban shaping operations may include actions taken to achieve or prevent isolation. Successful UO effectively isolate the urban area for a period of time of either short duration or long duration that requires commitment of resources for an extended period. Isolation limits the enemy's ability to conduct operations effectively by minimizing one or more of these capabilities. Isolation alone rarely defeats an enemy. However, it complements and reinforces other effects of defeat mechanisms by isolating the enemy from sources of physical and moral support. The two types of isolation are described below.

PHYSICAL

1-80. In offensive UO, physical isolation prevents the enemy from receiving information, supplies, and reinforcement and from withdrawing or breaking out. Physical isolation, however, is difficult to achieve. When accomplished, physical isolation inhibits the enemy's freedom of movement and access to support. At the BCT and battalion level, forces isolate and attack decisive points often using a cordon technique. In stability operations, physical isolation may be more subtly focused on isolating less obvious decisive points, such as a hostile civilian group's individual leaders or the population from the enemy's influence. In many operations, physical isolation may be temporary and synchronized to facilitate a decisive operation elsewhere.

PSYCHOLOGICAL

1-81. Psychological isolation is difficult to assess but is a vital enabler of disintegration. Psychological isolation is a function of physical action and other forms of inform and influence and cyber/electromagnetic activities, particularly deception and military information support operations. Psychological isolation denies the enemy political and military allies. Important indicators are the breakdown of enemy morale and alienation of a population from the enemy.

INFORM AND INFLUENCE AND CYBER/ELECTROMAGNETIC ACTIVITIES

1-82. Under mission command, staffs apply the science of control to support the commander's tasks by conducting inform and influence and cyber/electromagnetic activities. This task not only focuses on the enemy, but it expands to focus on all audiences within the information environment—friendly, neutral, adversary, and enemy. Information systems are everywhere with pervasive news and opinion media. Such systems expose individual actions that can have immediate implications. Staffs integrate the task—conduct inform and influence and cyber/electromagnetic activities—into the staff process. (See FM 3-0 for details.)

1-83. Inform and influence activities is defined as the integrating activities within the mission command warfighting function that ensures themes and messages designed to inform domestic audiences and influence foreign friendly, neutral, adversary, and enemy populations are synchronized with actions to support full spectrum operations. Inform and influence activities incorporate components and enablers expanding the commander's ability to use other resources to inform and influence.

1-84. Cyber/electromagnetic activities seize, retain, and exploit advantages in cyberspace and the electromagnetic spectrum. The result enables Army forces to retain freedom of action while denying freedom of action to enemies and adversaries, thereby enabling the overall operation. The electromagnetic spectrum is essential for communication, lethality, sensors, and self-protection. Given the Army's dependence on cyberspace as well as the electromagnetic spectrum, commanders fully integrate cyber/electromagnetic activities within the overall operation.

RECONNAISSANCE OPERATIONS

1-85. The BCT conducts reconnaissance in urban areas to gain critical information. It needs to have clear and detailed reconnaissance guidance from the BCT commander to begin planning for UO. To be successful, the reconnaissance effort should be comprehensive and synchronized. Success requires integrating all reconnaissance units (including surveillance and MI discipline), assets, and resources. These units, primarily the reconnaissance squadron, then deploy and execute early with clear reconnaissance guidance (focus, tempo, and engagement criteria) and an integrated plan that supports insertion, infiltration, fires, communication, exfiltration, extraction, resupply, cueing and mixing reconnaissance, surveillance, and security units. This is embodied in the reconnaissance and security plan. The plan should be flexible and conform to the changing information requirements of the commander. Commanders should also ensure they task organize to meet the mission requirements and assign tasks within the capabilities of the unit. (See FM 3-20.96 for details.)

PLANNING CONSIDERATIONS

1-86. In planning for UO, the commander considers the following tasks when developing a planning checklist for reconnaissance in the urban environment:

- Develop human intelligence collection plan.
- Determine reconnaissance and security objectives.
- Plan infiltration and exfiltration routes.
- Synchronize aerial and ground reconnaissance plans.
- Coordinate for FS.
- Develop communications and sustainment plan.
- Continue improvement of UO sketch.

1-87. The commander considers the following during the military decision-making process:

- Enemy situation, including—
    - Type and capabilities of likely enemy weapon systems, night vision devices, and communications systems.
    - Enemy COAs, including a situational template depicting composition, known and templated dispositions, and potential engagement area (EA).

- Civil considerations, including—
    - High population densities, which may make covert reconnaissance difficult.
    - Locations of government offices, political party headquarters, and nongovernmental organizations.
    - Compositions and dispositions of regional and local military, paramilitary, and law enforcement and public safety organizations.
    - Locations of police stations, armories or barracks, encampments, weapons holding areas, and staging areas.
    - Factions, key leaders, locations, compositions, and dispositions of known friendly, neutral, and belligerent elements. Include recent trends in public opinion, intensity levels of current and past disturbances, and effects from the use of lethal force against civilians if required.
    - Description of uniforms and insignia and capabilities of vehicles and equipment (both enemy and friendly).
    - Locations of power generation and transformer facilities, water treatment plants, and food distribution points.
    - Locations of communications networks and media outlets.
- Terrain and weather considerations, including effects on—
    - Effective ranges of weapons systems, target designators and acquisition systems, and night vision devices.
    - Aviation units (including UAS) for reconnaissance, transport, resupply, casualty evacuation, or FS.
    - Maneuverability.
- Friendly force considerations, including—
    - Missions of adjacent and follow-on forces.
    - Missions of reconnaissance and security units and other elements operating within the BCT AO but not under BCT control.
    - Reconnaissance objectives of higher headquarters and follow-on forces.
    - CCIR of higher headquarters and follow-on forces.
- BCT commander's reconnaissance focus, tempo, and engagement criteria, including guidance for adjusting tempo and engagement criteria during reconnaissance.

RECONNAISSANCE OBJECTIVES

1-88. From the understanding gained through IPB, the BCT commander identifies reconnaissance objectives. The information requirements given to subordinate units may be complex, detailed, and extensive. The ability of the commander to understand the urban environment and accurately assess information regarding the terrain and the presence of friendly, enemy, and noncombatant personnel is vital in developing reconnaissance objectives.

1-89. The considerations for developing information requirements in the urban environment are unique, placing greater demand on human and signals intelligence sources. In developing objectives, units should weigh the assigned information requirements against the time available to accomplish the mission. The following items are samples of information requirements that can help the BCT define its reconnaissance focus:

- What is the enemy's most likely and most dangerous COA?
- Where are the enemy's CPs located?
- What is the status of key lines of communications leading into and within the urban area?
- What are the likely enemy withdrawal routes and choke points?
- Are there obstacles impeding movement along the routes to and from assembly areas?
- Would isolation cause the enemy to withdraw from the urban area?
- Has the enemy force had any training in UO?
- What are the potential vulnerabilities to the infrastructure facilities?
- Where are cross-mobility corridors located within the urban area?
- Where are cultural, political, or symbolic facilities located?

- How do locals (by faction) view friendly forces and U.S. efforts in general?
- Is the population pro-U.S., neutral, or pro-enemy?
- Where does the enemy's logistical support come from?
- What are the locations of diplomatic embassies and missions in the urban area?
- What are the locations of U.S. citizens (if any) within the urban area?
- Is the enemy indigenous to the urban area or from outside the area?

SECURITY OPERATIONS

1-90. Security operations provide early and accurate warning of enemy action, giving the protected force time and maneuver space to react. By the nature of their design, all units are inherently involved in security in some capacity regardless of the specific mission they are conducting. All reconnaissance efforts assist in providing information that enhances the security of the force.

1-91. In the BCT, the reconnaissance squadron is given missions intended to specifically provide reconnaissance and security for other forces. Depending on the urban terrain restrictions, these missions can be executed by either motorized reconnaissance units or dismounted reconnaissance units.

SECURITY PLANNING GUIDANCE

1-92. Effective security operations require the BCT commander's guidance concerning focus, tempo, and engagement and displacement criteria. This guidance answers basic questions the squadron and battalion commander need to know in order to plan and execute their missions and to provide their own guidance to subordinate leaders. (See FM 3-20.96 for details.)

FOCUS

1-93. The focus of the security operation allows the commander to determine the specific critical tasks that need to be accomplished and the priority in which they need to be accomplished. Security operations are enemy-, terrain-, event-, or population-oriented. The focus should be defined around what must be protected and the expected results.

1-94. Named areas of interest provide a method of focusing the BCT's security effort. They link most likely enemy activities to terrain where those activities may occur. Using named areas of interest as a guide, subordinate commanders can position their units to provide the most effective observation. For example, they can emplace observation posts (OP) to observe primary enemy avenues of approach and employ ground-based sensors along secondary approaches to develop depth and redundancy.

TEMPO

1-95. The tempo of the security operation allows the commander to establish associated time requirements that drive certain aspects of the security plan, including OPs, UAS rotation, and enablers necessary to execute the mission. Tempo can relate to depth, especially in screening missions where time is needed to properly deploy units into position to achieve the required depth. Tempo dictates whether to use short-, long-, or extended-duration OPs.

ENGAGEMENT AND DISPLACEMENT CRITERIA

1-96. Engagement criteria establish the conditions under which the security force is expected to engage the enemy. The BCT commander's expectations and knowledge of the enemy's most likely COA determine the engagement criteria.

1-97. Depending on guidance, displacement can be either event- or time-driven. Displacement criteria can be tied to engagement criteria. The commander establishes displacement criteria based on what can, cannot, or will not be destroyed because of tactical considerations. The commander defines what events will trigger the screen to displace.

INFORMATION MANAGEMENT

1-98. Information management disseminates timely and protected relevant information to commanders and staffs. Information management helps commanders develop situational understanding. It also helps them make and disseminate effective decisions faster than the enemy. Urban areas can overload the information system with information. Urban operations across the spectrum of conflict can generate large volumes of information before, during, and in transitions between UO. The volume of information can easily overwhelm commanders and CPs and the information conduit connecting the two. Staffs need to create products (visual or textual) that present information for their commanders to know and help their commanders understand the urban environment.

JOINT, INTERAGENCY, INTERGOVERNMENTAL, AND MULTINATIONAL CONSIDERATIONS

1-99. In UO, many organizations operate in the area as long as possible before combat or as soon as possible after combat. Therefore, coordinating with these organizations sharing the urban AO is essential to achieving synchronization. However, effective synchronization is challenging, time-consuming, and manpower intensive.

1-100. Unified action includes joint integration that extends the principle of combined arms to operations conducted by two or more service components. Brigade combat teams and battalions may operate as part of an interdependent joint force, which makes them more effective than they would be otherwise.

1-101. Overall, establishing a close relationship with other agencies and the urban civilian population is often a major, positive factor in successful mission accomplishment, particularly in stability operations. Commanders that develop a direct and personal relationship with the leaders and staff of other agencies can often avoid conflict, win support, foster trust, and help eliminate the "us versus them" mentality that can frustrate cooperation among Army forces and civilian organizations.

1-102. Properly integrating multinational forces into BCT UO requires a thorough understanding of both the urban environment and the nature of individual national forces. Such understanding also includes the foreign force's doctrine and military capabilities, strengths, and weaknesses. Combining this understanding with effective mission command and an assessment of the urban environment results in effective multinational UO.

1-103. The staffs of larger headquarters (divisions or higher) normally have the breadth of resources and experience to best conduct the necessary synchronization. They can effectively use or manage the organizations interested in the urban area and mitigate their potential adverse effects on UO. However, the density of the urban environment often requires that BCTs and below coordinate and synchronize their activities with other agencies and the local civilian leadership (formal and informal) simply because of their physical presence in the units' AOs.

1-104. BCT and battalion commanders should understand the respective roles and capabilities of civilian organizations. Civilian organizations have different organizational cultures and norms. Some may be willing to work with Army forces, and others may not. Personal contact, trust building, and command emphasis on immediate and continuous coordination are essential and encourage effective cooperation.

1-105. Missions assigned to multinational units should reflect the capabilities and limitations of each national contingent. Some significant factors include—
- Relative size and mobility.
- Intelligence collection assets.
- Long-range fires and targeting capabilities in urban areas.
- Special Operations Forces capabilities.
- Organic sustainment capabilities.
- Training for operations in urban environments.
- Willingness and ability to cooperate directly with troops of other nationalities.

1-106. Some foreign forces, as part of their normal capabilities, are adept at police functions that enable them to operate with little training in a law enforcement role. Other forces specialize in small-unit, light Infantry patrolling. These forces may be ideal in stability operations. In contrast, a foreign force comprised of conscripts and trained primarily in conventional warfare techniques may best work as a reinforcing force or may require extensive training before mission execution in an urban environment.

HOST NATION SECURITY FORCES

1-107. Establishing or reestablishing competent HN security forces is fundamental to providing lasting safety and security of the HN and its population. Based on the requirements of the urban environment, the BCT can be augmented with enabling assets and capabilities to support security force assistance. Brigade combat teams can support security force assistance across the spectrum of conflict and can operate in both nonpermissive and permissive environments. (See FM 3-07, FM 3-07.1, and FM 3-24.2 for details.)

1-108. Most nations have some cultural obstacles to developing a professional military that is responsive and accountable to the HN population. Part of the challenge is to design a professional military that minimizes these culture obstacles. Most challenges arise from the differing perspectives of the U.S. and HN. Common cultural challenges include—
- Nepotism.
- Denial of negative results or errors in the interest of public image.
- Corruption, such as unofficial entitlements and bribery.
- Influence from competing loyalties (ethnic, religious, tribal, and political allegiances).

1-109. Developing HN security forces is a complex and challenging mission. Success can only be obtained if the mission approach has the same deliberate planning and preparation, energetic execution, and appropriate resourcing as the combat aspects of full spectrum UO.

1-110. Host nation security forces need to be trained and tactically proficient before they are deemed ready to conduct operations on their own. Brigade combat teams and battalions can be responsible for the mentoring, training, and augmenting of their HN counterparts. When conducting security force assistance tasks fails to prepare HN security forces to take the lead, unity of effort suffers at many levels.

INDIRECT SUPPORT

1-111. Indirect support emphasizes HN self-sufficiency. It builds strong national infrastructures through economic and military capabilities. Examples include security assistance programs, multinational exercises, and exchange programs. Indirect support reinforces HN legitimacy and primacy in addressing internal problems by keeping U.S. military assistance inconspicuous.

DIRECT SUPPORT

1-112. Direct support uses BCTs or battalions to assist the HN civilian populace or military forces directly. Direct support includes operational planning assistance, civil affairs activities, intelligence and communications sharing, logistics, and training of local military forces. It may also involve limited operations, especially in self-defense. Security force assistance is conducted according to certain imperatives. Like the principles of war, these imperatives, if followed, give the operation the best chance for success:
- Understand the operational environment.
- Provide effective leadership.
- Build legitimacy.
- Manage information.
- Ensure unity of effort.
- Sustain the effort.

SECTION V – ENGAGE

1-113. Within the BCT commander's concept of operations, the proportion and role of offensive, defensive, and stability tasks vary based on several factors. Changes in the nature of the operation, the tactics used, and where the environment falls on the spectrum of conflict affect the mix and focus. Some combinations may be sequential, but others occur simultaneously. Differing combinations of the elements of full spectrum operations characterize UO.

OFFENSE

1-114. The modular BCT's unique combined arms and organic warfighting functional capabilities enable it to conduct offensive operations with greater precision and speed than that of past organizations. Surprise, concentration, audacity, and tempo characterize successful offensive UO. The BCT commander sustains the initiative by aggressively committing his forces against enemy weaknesses. Attacks by BCTs are force-oriented or terrain-oriented and facilitate the defeat of the enemy or the continuation of the attack. The BCT commander extends the attacks in time and space by engaging the enemy in depth and destroying key elements of the enemy force. (See chapter 2, FM 3-90, FM 3-90.5, and FM 3-90.6 for details.)

1-115. Offensive UO are based on offensive doctrine modified to conform to the urban terrain. Urban combat imposes a number of demands that are different from other operating environments, such as combined arms integration at company level, fires, maneuver, use of special equipment, engagements among the population, and confined operational environment. As with all offensive operations, the commander needs to retain his ability to find and then fix the enemy and maneuver against him. Offensive UO can be more methodical and have a slower pace and tempo than operations in other environments. Conversely, the commander may choose to accept risk and apply a scheme of maneuver that accelerates the pace and tempo of the attack in an urban area if the mission variables support that COA.

1-116. The BCT commander selects the form of maneuver based on his analysis of the mission variables. An operation may contain several forms of offensive maneuver. The five forms of maneuver also apply to UO:

- Envelopment.
- Turning movement.
- Infiltration.
- Penetration.
- Frontal attack.

1-117. As part of offensive UO, the BCT may conduct or participate in movements to contact, attacks, exploitations, and pursuits. The BCT may participate in a division pursuit or exploitation by conducting a movement to contact or an attack. The BCT's reconnaissance squadron and other reconnaissance and security units do not negate the need to conduct a traditional movement to contact. However, the actual techniques used during movement to contact may be modified to fit the capabilities found within each of the BCTs and to conform to the urban environment.

1-118. At the battalion level, offensive UO takes the form of either a deliberate or hasty operation, such as a movement to contact or attack. The battalion may also receive the mission to conduct special-purpose attacks, such as a raid, demonstration, spoiling attack, or counterattack. The battalion should also be prepared to conduct different missions simultaneously. For example, a battalion may establish checkpoints in one section of a city and simultaneously clear enemy in another section.

DEFENSE

1-119. The static and mobile elements of the defense combine to deprive the enemy of the initiative, contain enemy forces, and seek every opportunity to transition to the offense. During defensive UO, the BCT and battalion commander seeks to—

- Avoid being isolated by the enemy.
- Defend key and decisive terrain, institutions, or infrastructure.
- Use offensive fire and maneuver to retain the initiative.

1-120. Battalions serve as the primary maneuver elements or terrain-controlling units for the BCT in all types of defensive operations. They can defend AOs or positions, or they can serve as security forces or reserves as part of the BCT-coordinated defense. The three types of defensive operations are area defense, mobile defense, and retrograde. An area defense is the type most often used for defending an urban area. Each of the defensive operations contain elements of the others and usually contain both static and maneuver aspects. (See FM 3-90, FM 3-90.5, and FM 3-90.6 for details.)

1-121. The reconnaissance squadron and, in some instances, a maneuver battalion conduct security operations and counterreconnaissance missions and patrols (avoiding isolation) in the security area. The maneuver battalions conduct local security and counterreconnaissance to compliment the reconnaissance squadron's efforts and assigns battle positions (BP) or AOs to company teams (defending). Additionally the battalion commander considers consolidating or reorganizing and preparing for follow-on missions (transitioning). Battalions defending in urban areas should prepare their positions for all-round defense. They should constantly patrol and use OPs and sensors to maintain effective security. Companies should employ aggressive security operations that include surveillance of surface and subsurface approaches. They should take special measures to control enemy combatants who have intermixed with the local population and civilian personnel who may support the enemy.

STABILITY

1-122. Stability operations encompass various military missions, tasks, and activities conducted outside the U.S. in coordination with other instruments of national power to maintain or reestablish a safe and secure environment and provide essential governmental services, emergency infrastructure reconstruction, and humanitarian relief. (See JP 3-0 for details.) By their nature, stability operations are typically conducted in urban areas. Stability operations can be conducted in support of an HN or interim government or as part of an occupation when no government exists. (See FM 3-07 for details.)

1-123. The BCT is designed for combined arms combat. However, as a versatile and flexible force, it can also conduct stability operations effectively. Often, the BCT must focus on simultaneous combat and stability tasks. The objective of stability operations may be more difficult to define than offensive or defensive UO. Nonetheless, the objectives must be clear from the beginning. Objectives should contribute to the operation's purpose directly, quickly, and effectively.

CHARACTERISTICS

1-124. Stability operations establish a safe and secure environment and facilitate reconciliation among local or regional adversaries. They can also help establish political, legal, social, and economic institutions and support the transition to legitimate local governance.

1-125. The responsibility for providing for the basic needs of the people normally rests with the HN government or designated civil authorities, agencies, and organizations. When this is not possible, military forces provide essential civil services to the local populace until a civil authority or the HN can provide these services. In this capacity, military forces perform specific functions as part of a broader response effort, supporting the activities of other agencies, organizations, and institutions.

1-126. Success in stability operations depends on military forces seizing the initiative. Immediate action to stabilize the urban area and provide for the immediate humanitarian needs of the people begins the processes that lead to a lasting peace. Failing to act quickly may create a breeding ground for dissent and possible recruiting opportunities for enemies or adversaries. Understanding is vital to retaining the initiative. Commanders should remain responsive to a dynamic environment while anticipating the needs of the local populace. Stability operations cannot succeed if they only react to enemy initiatives.

1-127. Stability operations are conducted among the people and within the lens of the media. Therefore, during stability operations, effective information tasks (inform and influence and cyber/electromagnetic activities) are inseparable from initiative. These activities enhance the success of each primary stability task, reinforcing and complementing actions on the ground with supporting messages.

1-128. Unity of effort in stability operations is often the operational norm. It helps to achieve a cooperative environment that focuses effort toward a common goal, regardless of individual command or organizational structures. The mechanisms for achieving unity of effort are maximized when a legitimate, functioning HN government exists. However, if the state has failed through military action or other socioeconomic factors, a transitional authority should assume responsibility for governing.

CIVIL SUPPORT

1-129. See FM 3-28 for details on civil support operations.

SECTION VI – CONSOLIDATE

1-130. Consolidation includes those activities that ensure the enemy is neutralized and that the BCT or battalion/squadron is positioned to continue operations or transition to a new mission. Consolidation facilitates repositioning, reorganizing, or resupplying subordinate units as required.

1-131. Consolidation considerations include—

- Sustainment actions.
- Security of lines of communications.
- Route clearance operations by engineers and explosive ordnance disposal.
- Route improvement (creating routes, trails by engineers, gap crossing and bridging efforts).
- Area clearance operations by engineers.
- Repositioning forces.
- Reorganization (task organization changes).

SUSTAINMENT CHARACTERISTICS

1-132. The nature of the urban environment creates distinct demands on sustainment units and operations. Urban operations are sustainment intensive, demanding large quantities of materiel and support for military forces and noncombatants displaced by operations. Thorough preparation is critical in developing an adaptable UO sustainment plan.

1-133. Though the infrastructure of an urban environment may be a source of valuable resources (such as supply systems, services, personnel, and facilities), BCT sustainment planners need to know the potential enemy and protection requirements that urban populations may present. Enemy forces, criminals, gangs, or riotous mobs may disrupt sustainment operations. When developing an urban sustainment plan, BCT planners consider—

- Commander's intent and concept of operation.
- Transportation infrastructure (air, rail, waterways, pipelines, subway).
- Telecommunications and information system posture.
- Traffic pattern and flow.
- Selection of main and alternate supply routes.
- Local resources with sustainment value.
- Local population sentiments (friendly and nonfriendly).
- Contracting, bartering, and trading capabilities.
- Increased consumption of small-arms ammunition and explosives.
- Increased consumption of terminally-guided munitions.
- Decreased consumption of certain large-caliber and area-type munitions.
- Increased consumption of nonlethal munitions.
- Increased aerial delivery requests.
- Transportation difficulties resulting from rubble.

SUSTAINMENT FUNCTIONS

1-134. Sustainment is the provision of logistics, personnel services, and health service support necessary to maintain and prolong operations until mission accomplishment.

- Logistics tasks include maintenance, transportation, supply, field services, distribution management, contracting, explosive ordnance disposal, and related general engineering.
- Personnel services tasks include human resources support, financial management support, legal support, religious support, and band support.
- Health service support tasks consist primarily of three support tasks—combat casualty care, MEDEVAC (air and ground), and medical logistics.

REORGANIZATION

1-135. Reorganization is the measures taken to maintain the BCT's combat effectiveness or return it to a specified level of combat capability. All units within the BCT undertake reorganization activities during full spectrum operations to maintain combat effectiveness. Reorganization tasks usually include—

- Replace or shift reconnaissance and security forces.
- Reestablish chains of command, fill key staff positions, and ensure command channels are operational.
- Treat and evacuate casualties.
- Redistribute ammunition, supplies, and equipment.
- Recover and repair damaged equipment.
- Reposition CP facilities, communications assets, logistics, and FS units.
- Conduct resupply and refueling operations.

SECTION VII – TRANSITION

1-136. Transitions require planning and preparation well before their execution to maintain the momentum and tempo of operations. Transitions occur when the BCT moves from one phase of the operation to another. Transitions can include the BCT—

- Changing its focus from one element of full spectrum operations to another.
- Conducting a relief in place or transition of authority to follow-on U.S., unified action, HN, or nongovernmental organizations and forces.

1-137. Transitioning from one full spectrum operation to another requires mental and physical agility on the part of the commanders, staffs, and units involved as well as accurate situational assessment capabilities. BCT and battalion commanders consider more than the enemy's forces and other combat capabilities. They use their experience, professional knowledge, and understanding of the situation to visualize the operational environment as current operations transition to future UO. The commander considers the higher commander's concept of operations, friendly capabilities, and the enemy situation when making this decision.

Chapter 2
Offensive Urban Operations

The offense is the decisive form of maneuver; this is true for UO as well. Offensive UO present unique challenges to the attacker and opportunities to the enemy defending the urban terrain. Successful offensive UO rely on understanding the enemy and urban environment, shaping the conditions for the offense, and isolating the enemy from supporting forces. Attacking in a UO requires mission command (mission orders), leader initiative, combined arms teams, task organized and augmented with Army and joint warfighting functional capabilities.

SECTION I – CHARACTERISTICS

2-1. The primary purpose of the offense is to defeat, destroy, or neutralize an enemy force. A commander may also take offensive actions to deceive or divert the enemy, deprive the enemy of resources or decisive terrain, develop intelligence, or fix the enemy. Even in the defense, offensive action may be required to destroy an attacker and exploit success. The key to a successful offensive operation is to identify the decisive point, choose a form of maneuver that avoids the enemy's strength, and mass overwhelming combat power at the decisive point.

2-2. The BCT uses mission command with mission orders, maneuver, and situational understanding to properly position forces and destroy the enemy as he reacts to threats from multiple directions. In all operations, including UO, the BCT organizes its forces for decisive, shaping, and sustaining operations.

2-3. Success in offensive operations depends on the proper application of the fundamental characteristics of the offense—surprise, concentration, tempo, and audacity. Flexibility is a key attribute of the BCT due to its ability to receive and control both Army and joint augmentation to support its ability to maneuver mounted and dismounted.

2-4. Force ratios and combat power considerations determine appropriate objectives and the number of attack axis the BCT develops. Based on mission variables, offensive UO can consist of limited, short distance movement and maneuver to seize a building or a series of buildings in order to gain a foothold. It could also require an extended penetration to attack or seize multiple objectives.

2-5. Reasons for conducting offensive UO are as follows:
- Urban areas contain critical industrial or economic facilities that need to be controlled.
- Urban areas contain critical transportation infrastructure (such as bridges, railways, and road networks) that provide an advantage to the side that controls them.
- Use of port or airfield facilities should be denied to enemy forces.
- The political importance of an urban area, such as a capital, justifies its liberation or capture.
- Attacking an urban area could have a decisive psychological impact on the enemy or significantly motivate the friendly population within the city.

2-6. Reasons for not conducting offensive UO are as follows:
- Friendly objectives lay beyond the urban area, a bypass of the urban area exists, or speed or time is essential.
- An urban area exerts no substantial threat or its threat can be contained.
- Sufficient force is not available to attack, clear, and then hold the urban area, or the attack cannot be logistically supported.
- An urban area is declared an open city to prevent civilian casualties or to preserve cultural or historical sites.

Note. An open city, by the law of land warfare, is a city that cannot be defended or attacked. A defender must immediately evacuate an open city and cannot distribute weapons to the city's inhabitants. An attacker assumes administrative control of the city and must treat its citizens as noncombatants in an occupied country. The presence of large numbers of noncombatants, hospitals, or wounded personnel may also affect the commander's decision not to attack an urban area.

SECTION II – SEQUENCING

2-7. Properly planned and executed offensive UO involve multiple tasks. Depending on the mission variables, they may be conducted simultaneously or sequentially. During offensive operations, the BCT or battalion commander's intent normally includes—

- Developing a detailed reconnaissance and security plan to develop the situation; maintain contact with adjacent, forward, or flank forces; or secure an exposed flank of the BCT or battalion main body.
- Synchronizing fires, inform and influence and cyber/electromagnetic activities, and nonlethal capabilities.
- Isolating key terrain to dominate the urban area.
- Using combat power to destroy HPTs.
- Using close combat, when needed, against decisive points.
- Transitioning to stability, defensive, or other offensive UO.

2-8. Offensive operations in urban areas follow the same sequence as operations conducted in other environments. (See FM 3-90 for details.) The sequence for conducting offensive UO is—

- Gain and maintain enemy contact.
- Disrupt the enemy.
- Fix the enemy.
- Maneuver.
- Follow-through.

GAIN AND MAINTAIN ENEMY CONTACT

2-9. The commander uses all available sources of information to find the enemy's location and dispositions to ensure friendly forces are committed under optimal conditions. The terrain, infrastructure, and society of the urban environment enhance the enemy's ability to deceive and confuse information collection to verify the enemy's positions, strength, disposition, and intent. To determine the enemy's intent, the BCT must develop the situation through action. This may include reconnaissance and maneuver forces to gain contact and fight for information. Situational awareness becomes clearer as the BCT's reconnaissance (surveillance and MI discipline collection) and security elements conduct actions on contact to rapidly develop the situation in accordance with the commander's plan and intent.

DISRUPT THE ENEMY

2-10. Once contact is made, the commander brings overwhelming fires onto the enemy to prevent the enemy from conducting either a spoiling attack or organizing a coherent defense. The canalizing effect of urban terrain and the three-dimensional compressed AO typically result in short range acquisition and engagement ranges. The attacking force is required to reposition rapidly and integrate reconnaissance (air, sensor, and ground), mobility (engineer breaching and protected platforms), and fires (close air support, close combat attack, artillery, and mortars) to shape the conditions for fixing and defeating the enemy. In the UO, the isolation of enemy forces from mutually supporting forces or withdrawal routes are also key considerations for fixing and disrupting the enemy's ability to maneuver.

FIX THE ENEMY

2-11. The security force commander does not allow enemy security and main body forces to maneuver against the friendly main body. In an urban environment, the fixing force can be the reconnaissance squadron augmented with combat forces, but it is typically a maneuver battalion that has the combat power and ability to maneuver to fix the enemy for the main effort attack. The BCT uses Army and joint FS units (including mission command networks and systems) to fix an enemy force in its positions by directly attacking enemy maneuver elements and command systems and emplacing situational obstacles.

2-12. A primary purpose for fixing the enemy is to isolate the objective of the maneuver force conducting the BCT's decisive operation to prevent the enemy from maneuvering to reinforce or support the enemy force or terrain that is the objective. The commander normally allocates the bulk of his combat power to the force conducting his decisive operation. Therefore, fixing operations are (by necessity) shaping operations that illustrate economy of force as a principle of war and use a minimum amount of force.

MANEUVER

2-13. BCT maneuver forces deploy rapidly to deliver the assault before the enemy force can deploy or reinforce its engaged forces. In the canalized and condensed urban environment, battle handover and passage of lines are critical enabling operations that require positive control of forces and situational awareness during these transition points. Typically, these transitions are conducted face-to-face between combined arms units. In the urban environment, firepower, mobility, protection, and Infantry-centric combined arms teams determine the success of the attack. Commanders should integrate augmenting Army and joint fires at the lowest level. In all cases, the commander makes every effort to retain the initiative and prevent the enemy from stabilizing the situation by conducting violent and resolute attacks.

2-14. Offensive maneuver seeks to achieve a massing of effects at the decisive point or at several decisive points if adequate combat power is available. In offensive UO, the ROE, effects of urban terrain on observation systems, munitions, structures, population, and key infrastructure present a challenge to the commander in determining the application of combat power to achieve his intent.

FOLLOW-THROUGH

2-15. After seizing the objective or defeating the enemy, the commander has two alternatives–exploit success and continue the attack or transition to another mission or operation. At BCT and below, the unit maintains contact with the enemy and attempts to exploit its success within its capabilities and, when the situation permits, conducts consolidation and reorganization to continue the attack or transition.

SECTION III – TASK ORGANIZATION CONSIDERATIONS

2-16. Task organization is driven by tasks and missions that a commander assigns to his subordinate forces. It includes configuring subordinate forces to accomplish the commander's intent and follows the established priority of support. It includes allocating assets and resources and establishing a command or support relationship. (See FM 3-0 and FM 5-0 for details.) In offensive UO, the commander allocates his available forces against identified mission requirements, which typically include—

- Reconnaissance and security force.
- Support force.
- Breach force.
- Assault force.
- Other unique considerations (clearing force, reserve force, outer or inner cordon forces, fixing force, line of communication security force, detainee holding area force).
- Sustainment.

2-17. The BCT commanders should select the right subordinate force for the mission and balance it with appropriate attachments. BCT commanders do not direct how to organize the small tactical combined arms teams, but they ensure that battalions and companies have the proper balance of forces from which to form these teams. Successful offensive UO require small-unit combined arms teams, with Infantry as the base of this force. Commanders decide how to task organize Armor, aviation, engineer, MI, air defense, and mechanized Infantry elements to accomplish the tactical task.

2-18. Brigade combat teams conducting offensive UO may require additional resources, to include—

- Linguists.
- Human intelligence specialists.
- UAS.
- Engineering units. Task organization of a unit executing the decisive operation may require a one-to-one ratio of engineer units to maneuver units.
- A tailored and dedicated support battalion or group to assist in providing anticipated support to a displaced and stressed civil population.
- Civil affairs augmentation to deal with nongovernmental organizations and civilian government issues.

SECTION IV – UNDERSTAND

2-19. The basic fundamentals of the offense do not change in an urban environment. Considerations vary depending on the situation and scale of the operation. However, no set rules exist. All UO are unique.

PLANNING CONSIDERATIONS

2-20. In UO, the defender usually has several key advantages over the attacker. For example, the—

- Attacker is often canalized by the urban terrain and has limited maneuverability.
- Defender can increase the man-made and natural obstacles found in the urban terrain.
- Enemy may not have the same policies to minimize collateral damage and civilian casualties as U.S. forces.
- Attacker may have to clear every building and every room, while the defender can selectively defend selected buildings and rooms.

2-21. The plan for offensive UO should be flexible and promote disciplined initiative by subordinate leaders. Develop a simple scheme of maneuver, issue a clear commander's intent, and develop plans to execute likely maneuver options that may occur during execution. Commanders should visualize the urban AO and employ the right force mix at the right place and time to achieve the desired effect.

2-22. When developing his concept, the commander anticipates where he is likely to meet the enemy and then determines how he intends to develop the situation that leads to an attack under favorable conditions. The commander should attempt to visualize this process during his mission analysis and take into account his active and passive responses to enemy contact. The commander focuses on determining the task organization and formation that best retains freedom of action on contact and supports his concept against known or anticipated enemy forces.

WARFIGHTING FUNCTION CONSIDERATIONS

2-23. As a combined arms force, the BCT integrates warfighting functions to increase the effects of combat power through complementary and reinforcing capabilities.

MOVEMENT AND MANEUVER

2-24. The BCT and battalion commander develop plans for the maneuver options of attack, report and bypass, defend, and retrograde based on the division commander's intent and the situation. They define the conditions in terms of enemy and friendly strengths and dispositions that are likely to trigger the execution of each maneuver option. They identify likely locations of engagements based on known or suspected enemy locations. The commander states the bypass criteria for the advance guard. He needs to recognize the loss of tempo created by fighting every small enemy force encountered with the lead element. The advance guard may attack small enemy forces that it can quickly destroy without losing momentum, but it is best that the advance guard bypass larger or more stubborn enemy forces and allow their engagement by the main body.

2-25. Potential danger areas (likely or known enemy defensive locations, EAs, OPs, or obstacles) require close planning considerations. The staff should carefully plan actions for moving through these danger areas quickly and securely.

2-26. Maintaining the mobility of the battalion in offensive operations is critical. The maneuver battalion needs to plan and allocate mobility and potential countermobility resources to the security force, advance guard, and main body. Engineer task organization is based on supporting breaching (or gap crossing) operations with minimal engineer units. These units should be under battalion control so they can transition to a breach in support of a deliberate attack if needed.

2-27. Based on the mission variables, engineer teams may join the reconnaissance and security forces to reconnoiter obstacles. The security force should have enough firepower, protection, and mobility resources to cover its own movement and to complete the reconnaissance mission. The advance guard needs resources to conduct breaching (and potentially gap crossing) operations and may also be task organized with countermobility units. The maneuver battalion commander may plan situational obstacles as part of the countermobility effort to support the security forces and the advance guard, to attack an enemy's vulnerability or specific COA, or to secure the unit's flanks. Key considerations for the scheme of engineer operations are—

- Task organize engineer forces well forward to support reconnaissance, breaching complex obstacles, and clearing or gap crossing operations.
- Ensure the reconnaissance and security plan integrates the collection of known or templated obstacles and other terrain information and is focused to verify critical information.
- Maintain the flexibility to consolidate engineers to breach complex obstacles.
- Develop and adjust obstacle locations and triggers for execution based on the battalion's movement and the enemy situation.
- Develop plans for the handover of marked obstacles, lanes, and bypasses.
- Plan for adjustment of the breach (or gap crossing) location.
- Immediately disseminate information on obstacles including supporting platforms and units.
- Support assaulting forces with engineers to breach enemy protective obstacles.
- Ensure adequate guides, traffic control, and lane improvements to support movement of follow-on forces and sustainment traffic.

2-28. Effective direct fire control requires the rapid acquisition of the enemy and massed fires to achieve decisive results in the close fight. BCT and subordinate leaders need to know how to apply the following principles of direct fire during offensive UO:

- Mass the effects of fire.
- Destroy the greatest threat first.
- Avoid target overkill.
- Employ the best weapon for the target.
- Minimize friendly exposure.
- Prevent fratricide.
- Plan for extreme limited visibility conditions.
- Develop contingencies for diminished capabilities.

2-29. The purpose of these direct fire principles is not to restrict the actions of subordinates. Applied correctly, they help the maneuver battalion accomplish its primary goal in any direct fire engagement; for example, to acquire first and shoot first. They give subordinates the freedom to act quickly upon acquisition of the enemy.

INTELLIGENCE

2-30. The BCT plays a major role in reconnaissance and surveillance synchronization and integration based on the assets available and its links to division and higher reconnaissance and security assets. The maneuver battalion is one of several elements executing the BCT offensive plan, and its reconnaissance plan should be integrated, synchronized, and coordinated with the BCT reconnaissance squadron and other elements executing the BCT plan.

2-31. The first priority is to determine enemy locations, strengths, and actions. Potential enemy objectives, use of key terrain, avenues of approach and routes, EAs, population, and obstacles are among the items that should be identified early and incorporated into the reconnaissance and security plan. Various elements within the BCT conduct reconnaissance operations include the following:

- **Reconnaissance Squadrons.** Reconnaissance squadrons of the HBCT, IBCT, and SBCT are organized to conduct reconnaissance missions throughout the BCT's AO. By leveraging the Army Battle Command System, MI multidiscipline collection capabilities in the military intelligence company (MICO), and air/ground reconnaissance capabilities in complex terrain, the reconnaissance squadron can develop the situation by focusing on all categories of threats in a designated AO. This allows the BCT commander to maintain understanding and visualization of the changing urban environment to better inform his decisions on movement, maneuver, and engagement of the enemy at a time and place of his choosing.
- **MI Company.** The MI company integrates and analyzes information across the other warfighting functions' reconnaissance and surveillance reporting to develop intelligence products in response to priority intelligence requirements. The MICO also has human and signals intelligence collection capabilities and affords the BCT commander intelligence reach and access to higher and adjacent force products and intelligence that can impact the BCT's operations.
- **Reconnaissance Platoon.** The reconnaissance platoon satisfies the battalion's CCIR. It is the element that can be committed the quickest. Scouts reconnoiter areas of interest and link with the BCT reconnaissance squadron. They confirm and identify enemy locations, orientations, and dispositions.
- **Sniper Teams.** Once the enemy has been located, the sniper teams maintain contact through observation or deny enemy access to key terrain through controlled precision fires.
- **Unmanned Systems.** Unmanned systems to include both UAS and unattended ground sensors, can prevent enemy units from surprising the main body. After making contact, UAS and unattended ground sensors can maintain contact with ground reconnaissance elements, reconnoiter elsewhere, or move to another vantage point.

2-32. Digitally linking subordinate commanders with information sources (geospatial intelligence and signals intelligence sensors, human intelligence, and reconnaissance) helps to develop a common operational picture essential to their situational understanding of the urban environment. The IPB process guides this assessment. As operations progress, additional reconnaissance and security units may become available, to include UAS, long-range reconnaissance and security units, and counterfire radar. As these units are employed, they are linked into the net of sources sharing information and further refine a common situational understanding of the environment.

2-33. BCT staffs need to track the battalion's use of UAS and consider their impacts on airspace management within the BCT AO. They should also be alert for enemy attack aviation and UAS during movements through intersections, choke points, bridges, and other restrictive urban terrain.

FIRES

2-34. Priority of fires shifts as the operation progresses. The security for an Army attack aviation element under operational control of the BCT typically has priority of fires during the approach march and initial shaping operations. Priority targets are allocated to the security force and the advance guard and will target, depending on the commander's scheme of maneuver and priority HPTs, enemy air defense artillery, command and control, artillery, engineer and maneuver forces. The nature of urban terrain makes massed enemy targets less likely, and restrictive ROE may inhibit some specific munition types or methods of engagement. The BCT positions field artillery units to provide continuous indirect fires to support the shaping and decisive operations. Army attack helicopters and close air support may be available to detect; disrupt; fix; or interdict enemy security, main battle area (MBA), and counterattack forces. Given the

BCT's emphasis on proactive counterfires and the restrictive urban terrain, the battalion/squadron may need to rely on its organic mortars.

2-35. Based on the mission variables, battalion mortars may be placed under the operational control of the advance guard to provide responsive fires and obscuration to support initial actions on contact, or they may be controlled by the battalion commander or FS officer in support of the entire battalion effort. In either case, it is likely that the security force and advance guard receive initial mortar priority of fires.

2-36. The following are key considerations for the FS plan in UO:

- Position FS units to support the reconnaissance effort.
- Use deception fires to deceive the enemy as to the location of the main effort.
- Facilitate responsive and decentralized fires through a clear understanding of the essential tasks for FS for each phase of the operation. This understanding is critical to the success of the FS plan. Upon contact, the battalion shifts control of all available fires to the observer who is in the best position to control fires against the enemy.
- Plan targets based on known or suspected enemy locations and danger areas and to support future operations. Refine targets based on the reconnaissance effort as the operation progresses.
- Maximize the use of priority targets along the axis of advance. Plan triggers to put these targets into effect, and cancel them based on the movement of the battalion.
- Plan fires in support of the approach to the objective. These fires engage enemy security forces, destroy bypassed enemy forces, and screen friendly movement.
- Plan suppressive and obscuration fires at the point of penetration and in support of breaching operations.
- Ensure immediate responsive FS to the lead elements by assigning priority of fires to the security force or the advance guard.
- Synchronize the movement and positioning of artillery, mortars, and military information support units with the tempo of the battalion and the FS requirements.
- Position observers and forward air controllers effectively and maximize the use of lead maneuver forces to call for fires since they often have the best view of the enemy. Observers should understand the essential tasks for FS for each phase of the operation.
- Synchronize fires on the objective to achieve the effects of suppression, neutralizing or destroying critical enemy forces that can most affect the battalion's closure on the objective.
- Plan fires beyond the objective to support an attack or defense.
- Use indirect fires and close air support to delay or neutralize repositioning enemy forces and reserves.

MISSION COMMAND

2-37. Offensive UO quickly devolve into small-unit tactics of squads, platoons, and companies seizing their objectives. The compartmented effect of the urban terrain and the obstacles to controlling small units, especially once they enter close combat inside buildings or underground, often restricts the ability of the BCT and battalion commander ability to influence operations. Commanders can influence the actions of subordinates by clearly identifying the decisive points leading to the center of gravity; using mission orders; developing effective task organizations; synchronizing their decisive, shaping, and sustaining operations; and managing transitions.

PROTECTION

2-38. Protection tasks, such as security operations, operations security, and information protection, keep or inhibit the enemy from acquiring accurate information about BCT forces. Commanders and staffs plan and implement survivability and other protection measures that deny the enemy the ability to inflict damage as the BCT maneuvers. This includes the use of combat formations and movement techniques. It may involve the use of electronic warfare systems, minefield plows and rollers, and modifications to the ROE. This may also include the conduct of countermobility missions to deny the enemy maneuver and thereby provide additional protection to friendly maneuvering forces.

2-39. Protection has five broad forms.

- **Deterrence.** The posture of an individual, formation, or structure can have a deterrent effect on threat decision making and result in protection.
- **Prevention.** The ability to neutralize, forestall, or reduce the likelihood of an imminent attack before it occurs. Prevention can be achieved through deliberate action or as an effect.
- **Active Security.** Dynamic activities with the organic ability to detect, interdict, avert, disrupt, neutralize, or destroy threats and hazards while maintaining the freedom of action can provide protection to the overall operation or force.
- **Passive Defense.** Achieved from survivability positions, fortifications, and physical barriers that are designed to protect forces and material from identified threats and hazards.
- **Mitigation.** The ability to minimize the effects or manage the consequence of attacks and designated emergencies on personnel, physical assets, or information, reserve the potential, capacity, or utility of a force or capability, have a protective quality.

SECTION V – SHAPE

2-40. Shaping operations establish conditions for the decisive operation through effects on the enemy, population (including local leaders), and terrain. They may occur throughout the urban AO and involve any combination of forces and capabilities.

RECONNAISSANCE AND SECURITY

2-41. The fundamentals discussed in chapter 1 of this manual also apply to offensive UO.

SNIPER OPERATIONS

2-42. During offensive UO, snipers help the commander accomplish the mission by—

- Obtaining information.
- Depriving the enemy of resources.
- Deceiving or diverting the enemy from the main effort.
- Keeping the enemy from regrouping or repositioning.
- Conducting preemptive attacks to gain the initiative.
- Disrupting enemy offensive actions.

2-43. In a movement to contact, snipers infiltrate enemy areas and engage them from unexpected directions. The teams should move out well in advance of the projected movement. This allows them to move at their own pace so they remain undetected. It also allows them to engage any targets that threaten the advance. The teams may use normal stalking methods, or they can be inserted by ground vehicle, helicopter, parachutes, or boats. The best way to employ snipers in a hasty attack is to let them operate on their own initiative with their supported unit. Their precision fire reduces delays during the hasty attack.

2-44. In a deliberate attack, snipers can be effectively employed near the FS element. Their accuracy and optics allow them to reduce enemy targets in the midst of friendly forces. During a deliberate attack, the unit should take care to avoid drawing enemy attention to the sniper team's position. The team may also be deployed forward of the FS element to support the attack with accurate selective rifle fire or deployed with a cutoff force with the same task. If time permits, they infiltrate behind the enemy positions to disrupt counterattacks or withdrawal and to harass enemy reinforcements. (See FM 3-22.10 for details on sniper operations.)

BATTLE HANDOVER AND PASSAGE OF LINES

2-45. Battle handover is a coordinated operation to sustain continuity of the combined arms fight and to protect the combat potential of both forces involved. Battle handover is usually associated with the conduct of a passage of lines.

BATTLE HANDOVER

2-46. Battle handover may occur during either offensive or defensive operations. In the offense, it is situation-dependent and often initiated by a fragmentary order. Battle handover in the offense usually occurs when one unit passes through or around another unit. Standing operating procedures (SOP) containing clear, simple, standardized procedures and control measures enhance a unit's ability to coordinate and synchronize actions quickly without experiencing a corresponding loss in momentum.

PASSAGE OF LINES

2-47. Units usually conduct passage of lines when at least one mission variable does not permit the bypass of a friendly unit. A passage of lines is a complex operation requiring close supervision and detailed planning, coordination, and synchronization between the commanders of the unit conducting the passage and the unit being passed. It involves the transfer of responsibility for fighting an enemy force from one unit to the other.

2-48. Passages of lines occur in the offense and defense and under two basic conditions. A forward passage of lines occurs when a unit passes through another unit's position while moving towards the enemy. A rearward passage of lines occurs when a unit passes through another unit's position while moving away from the enemy. (See FM 3-90, FM 3-90.5, and FM 3-90.6 for details.)

2-49. A passage of lines may be conducted to—

- Continue an attack or counterattack.
- Envelop an enemy force.
- Pursue a fleeing enemy.
- Withdraw covering forces or MBA forces.

2-50. As part of division operations, the BCT may be a stationary unit assisting the passage of another force, or the BCT may be the moving force conducting the passage through another force. As part of BCT operations, the BCT may be the controlling headquarters for the passage of lines between two subordinate forces. Digital systems enable BCTs to share and rapidly disseminate information. Digital systems enable BCTs to adapt the traditional TTPs for passage of lines and to economize collaborative planning and coordination measures. Assured communications enhances this process and allows a more rapid and common understanding of the passage during execution.

2-51. In a forward passage of lines, conducted as part of a BCT attack, both the stationary and passing battalion commanders should be aware of the passing unit's objective. This awareness is especially important if the stationary battalion needs to provide supporting fires.

BREACHING OPERATIONS

2-52. Breaching is a synchronized, combined arms operation under the control of a maneuver commander. A BCT requires engineer augmentation to conduct a brigade-level combined arms breaching operation. Whenever possible, a unit should bypass obstacles, enabling it to maintain the momentum of the operation. Commanders should ensure that conducting the bypass provides a tactical advantage without exposing the unit to unnecessary danger. The BCT plans a brigade-level breaching operation when the—

- Enemy's strength is beyond a battalion's capability to conduct a breaching operation successfully.
- Subordinate battalion has failed in its attempt to breach an obstacle.

2-53. The BCT needs to obtain accurate, real-time information on the composition, size, location, orientation, and overwatch of enemy obstacles throughout the depth of the urban AO. The reconnaissance squadron usually obtains this information as part of its assigned reconnaissance and security efforts. If a breaching operation is an integral part of a decisive operation, engineer reconnaissance teams can augment the reconnaissance squadron or other units to collect enemy obstacle information. Timely and accurate enemy obstacle information, made available early in the planning process, enables greater precision in the decision to bypass or breach and the selection of bypass or breach site locations. The BCT needs to identify multiple bypass routes that best support the scheme of maneuver and avoid unwanted enemy contact. (See FM 3-34.2 for details on breaching operations.)

2-54. The breaching tenets (intelligence, breaching fundamentals, breaching organization, mass, and synchronization) apply to breaching operations in urban terrain. However, the application of these tenets is different from a breaching operation conducted in open terrain. Consider the following when breaching in urban terrain:

- **Intelligence.** Intelligence is critical when conducting breaching operations in restricted urban terrain. The commander must identify how the enemy is using the terrain to minimize the risk of surprise. Forces used to collect intelligence on obstacles should be able to recommend reduction methods to reduce the obstacle. It is essential that the breach force knows the location and types of obstacles and the composition of any complex obstacle. With this information, the breach force commander can ensure that the assets necessary to reduce the obstacle are available and placed in the right order in the movement formation. The ability of the breach force to move reduction assets within the formation may be extremely limited.
- **Breaching Fundamentals.** The breaching fundamentals are suppress, obscure, secure, reduce, and assault (SOSRA). These fundamentals always apply, but the relative importance of each may vary based on the mission variables.
- **Breaching Organization.** A commander organizes his forces to accomplish the breach quickly and effectively. This requires him to organize support, breach, and assault forces with the necessary assets to accomplish their roles.
  - *Support.* Support force eliminates the enemy's ability to interfere with a breaching operation by isolating the reduction area, suppressing the enemy, using obscurants, and neutralizing the enemy's ability to bring fires on the breach force.
  - *Breach.* Breach force provides additional suppression and obscurants, reduces the obstacle, secures the far side of the obstacle, and secures and marks the breaching lanes.
  - *Assault.* Assault force destroys the enemy and seizes terrain on the far side of the obstacle.
- **Mass and Synchronization.** The commander masses combat power against an identified area of enemy weakness or creates one by fixing the majority of the enemy force and isolating a small portion to affect the breach. Breaching operations require precise synchronization of the breaching fundamentals by support, breach, and assault forces. Synchronizing requires detailed planning, rehearsals, swift execution, and individual initiative by small-unit leaders.

GAP CROSSING OPERATIONS

2-55. A gap crossing operation normally requires special equipment or materials that are limited or not organic to the BCT. Engineer planners should highlight the need for augmentation of additional assets early in the planning process. Regardless of the type of crossing, the planning requirements and engineer technical support are similar. (See FM 3-34.22 for details.) The three types of gap crossing operations are described below.

DELIBERATE

2-56. A BCT can conduct a deliberate crossing. However, in most cases, a division or higher organization provides command and control for the crossing because it involves more than one BCT. Deliberate crossings usually involve gaps greater than 20 meters and normally require support bridging. A deliberate crossing (wet or dry) is conducted when a hasty crossing is not feasible or has failed.

2-57. A deliberate gap crossing is characterized by a—
- Significant contiguous obstacle.
- Strong enemy resistance.
- Necessity to clear entry and exit crossing points of enemy forces.

2-58. A deliberate gap crossing involves—
- Centralized planning and control by the division or BCT.

- Thorough preparations, including the time to perform extensive reconnaissance and rehearsals.
- Massing of forces and crossing equipment.

HASTY

2-59. A hasty crossing is preferable to a deliberate crossing because there is no intentional pause to prepare. A hasty crossing (wet or dry) is possible when enemy resistance is weak and the gap is not a significant obstacle. The BCT may seize existing fords or bridges or use organic or expedient crossing means.

2-60. Hasty crossings are typically for, but are not limited to, gaps 20 meters or less in width and can be overcome by self-bridging assets (organic or augmented) within the BCT. They are normally done through tactical bridging (armored vehicle-launched bridge, joint assault bridge, Wolverine, or rapidly emplaced bridge system). The SBCT has four organic rapidly emplaced bridge systems, each capable of spanning 13 meters and crossing vehicles up to military load classification 40 (caution crossing). Neither the HBCT nor IBCT has organic gap crossing capability, so they require augmentation.

COVERT

2-61. A covert crossing is used to overcome gaps (wet or dry) without being detected by the enemy. It is used when surprise is essential to infiltrate across a gap and when limited visibility and gap conditions present an opportunity to complete the crossing without being seen. Common crossing means to facilitate a covert crossing include rope bridges, Infantry foot bridges, boats, fording and swimming, or aerial insertion.

2-62. The covert crossing is normally accomplished by a battalion-size element or smaller (dismounted or in wheeled vehicles), as a BCT is typically too large to maintain the level of stealth necessary to conduct a successful covert crossing. While a covert crossing can precede a deliberate or hasty crossing by a like-size or larger element, it is planned and conducted as a separate operation.

SECTION VI – ENGAGE

2-63. Some forms of maneuver have greater application in UO than others. Success belongs to commanders who imaginatively combines and sequences these forms throughout the depth, breadth, and height of the urban environment. This is true at all command levels within the BCT.

MOVEMENT TO CONTACT

2-64. In an urban area where the enemy situation is vague, BCTs often conduct a movement to contact to establish or regain enemy contact and develop the situation. A movement to contact occurs as both sides try to establish their influence or control over a contested urban area.

2-65. The situation determines whether the movement to contact or its specific technique, the search and attack, is appropriate. The search and attack technique works well when a smaller enemy has established a noncontiguous defense. This operation is characterized by robust reconnaissance, and rapidly concentrated combat power to fix and defeat or destroy enemy resistance once located.

2-66. A meeting engagement often results from a movement to contact. It occurs when the BCT is partially deployed for battle and makes contact with and engages an enemy at an unexpected time and place. In an urban meeting engagement, the unit that reacts most quickly and decisively will likely win. Rapid and accurate decision making depends on understanding the nature of the urban area and its operational impact. This permits accurate decision making regarding where to attack, where to defend, and how to allocate resources. Situational understanding enhanced by digital information system that provide an accurate common operational picture also facilitates the rapid reaction of BCT units and a synchronized response. This reaction and response allow BCT forces to seize the initiative and dominate the enemy.

ATTACK

2-67. All forms of attack consist of the following critical events, which units control by using phasing and graphic control measures:

- Moving from the assembly area to the line of departure.
- Maneuvering from the line of departure to the probable line of deployment.
- Occupying support-by-fire positions.
- Conducting the breach.
- Assaulting the objective.
- Consolidating on the objective.
- Exploiting success or pursuing a withdrawing enemy.
- Actions of echelon reserves.

2-68. The attack is the most likely offensive UO that the BCT conducts. The BCT usually executes deliberate attacks. In an urban environment, units larger than battalion size rarely conduct hasty attacks. Hasty attacks are common below company level as units use their initiative to take advantage of tactical opportunities. However, larger units will conduct hasty attacks when enemy defenses are disrupted or unprepared to take advantage of an unexpected situation and to prevent the enemy from establishing or reestablishing a coherent defense.

2-69. Battalions and below conduct hasty attacks as a result of a movement to contact, a meeting engagement, or a chance contact during a movement; after a successful defense or part of a defense; or in a situation where the unit has the opportunity to attack vulnerable enemy forces. When contact is made with the enemy, the commander immediately deploys; suppresses the enemy; attacks through a gap, flank, or weak point; and reports to his higher commander. The preparation for a hasty attack is similar to a deliberate attack, but time and resources are limited to what is available. The hasty attack in an urban area differs from a hasty attack in open terrain because the terrain makes command, control, communications and massing fires to suppress the enemy difficult.

2-70. A deliberate attack is a fully synchronized operation employing all available assets against the enemy. It is necessary when enemy positions are well prepared, when the urban area is large or severely congested, or when the element of surprise has been lost. Deliberate attacks are characterized by precise planning based on detailed information thorough reconnaissance, preparation, and rehearsals. Attacking the enemy's main strength is avoided and combat power is focused on the weakest point of his defense. Battalion and below conduct deliberate attacks of an urban area in the phases listed below. (See chapter 5 for a complete discussion.)

- **Phase 1.** Reconnoiter the objective.
- **Phase 2.** Move to the objective.
- **Phase 3.** Isolate the objective.
- **Phase 4.** Secure a foothold.
- **Phase 5.** Clear the objective.
- **Phase 6.** Consolidate and reorganize.
- **Phase 7.** Prepare for future missions.

EXPLOITATION

2-71. BCT commanders should consider focusing exploitation attacks on urban areas. An enemy defeated in an attack will attempt to rally units, reinforce, and reorganize. With its information and communications capability, transportation network, and defensive attributes, the urban area is an ideal environment to reestablish a disrupted defense. By establishing urban centers as the objectives of the exploitation, commanders deny the enemy the sanctuary needed to reorganize and reestablish his defense. A successful exploitation to seize an urban area works efficiently because the attack preempts the defense and denies the enemy the full advantages of urban terrain.

PURSUIT

2-72. The pursuit is designed to destroy enemy forces attempting to escape. It focuses on the enemy and not on the urban area. When conducting a pursuit, BCT units move through undefended urban areas and, if possible, bypass those areas in which enemy forces successfully take refuge. The enemy will likely attempt to use urban areas to disrupt the pursuit and permit the enemy main body to escape. Commanders can prevent escape by denying enemy forces time to establish defensive positions that cannot be bypassed. The agility of Army aviation forces for attack, reconnaissance, and transportation is essential to execute a successful pursuit around and through urban areas.

SECTION VII – CONSOLIDATE

2-73. The BCT should be prepared to conduct sustainment operations in both contiguous and noncontiguous AOs.

SUSTAINMENT

2-74. The BCT may be required to provide command and control to subordinate battalions and elements over extended distances. This could include securing lines of communications and deploying battalions individually in support of operations in the BCT's area of influence or area of interest or outside of the BCT's AO. However, sustainment units should be able to secure and sustain themselves.

2-75. To maintain momentum and freedom of action, coordination should be continuous. During offensive UO, certain requirements present special challenges. The most important materiel and services are typically fuel (Class III Bulk) and ammunition (Class V), major end items (Class VII), movement control, and MEDEVAC. Based on planning assessments, commanders direct the movement of these and other support to meet anticipated requirements.

2-76. Commanders should understand that maps quickly become outdated due to the constantly changing urban environment and the effects of full spectrum operations. Aerial imagery can provide more up-to-date route information and can minimize re-routing sustainment units down streets that may not have been cleared of possible IEDs or enemy.

2-77. Another challenge in planning for and sustaining offensive UO is the lengthened lines of communications. Widely dispersed forces and congested road networks increase stress on transportation systems. As a result, a combination of ground and aerial delivery may be planned to accommodate the distribution. Distribution managers and movement control units synchronize movement plans and priorities according to the commander's priority of support. Distribution should be closely coordinated and tracked to ensure delivery of essential support. The routing function of movement control is an essential process for coordinating and directing movements on main supply routes or alternate supply routes and regulating movement on lines of communications to prevent conflict and congestion. Sustainment planners must also consider vehicle size and weight when establishing routes.

CONSOLIDATION

2-78. Consolidation may consist of rapidly repositioning BCT forces and security elements, reorganizing the maneuver force, or organizing and improving the position for defense. Actions taken to consolidate gains include—

- Conducting reconnaissance.
- Establishing security.
- Eliminating enemy pockets of resistance.
- Positioning forces to enable them to conduct a hasty defense by blocking possible enemy counterattacks.
- Adjusting the fires plan.

REORGANIZATION

2-79. Any reorganization actions not completed during the conduct of offensive UO are accomplished during consolidation. These actions include—

- Redistributing supplies, ammunition, and equipment.
- Matching operational weapon systems with crews.
- Forming composite units by joining two or more attrited units to form a single, mission-capable unit.

- Replacing key personnel.
- Recovering, treating, and evacuating casualties (including civilians and EPWs), and damaged equipment.
- Resupplying as time permits.
- Revising communication plans.
- Placing the BCT CPs in position to conduct further operations and control the consolidation.

SECTION VIII – TRANSITION

2-80. BCT and battalion commanders ensure smooth transitions by planning for post-offensive operations early. They should begin planning for transition simultaneously with planning for offensive operations. Commanders should consider the feasibility of relinquishing control of urban areas to civil government, law enforcement, or nongovernmental organizations even before offensive operations are complete. During the conduct of UO, transition operations are closely synchronized with the execution of the attack. The BCT or battalion can transition to the defense or to stability missions.

2-81. As the unit transitions from an offensive focus to a defensive focus, the commander—
- Maintains contact with the enemy, using a combination of reconnaissance and surveillance units to develop the information required to plan future actions.
- Establishes a security area and local security measures.
- Redeploys fires (to include mortars) to ensure the support of security forces.
- Redeploys forces based on probable future employment.
- Maintains or regains contact with adjacent units in a contiguous AO and ensures that units remain capable of mutual support in a noncontiguous AO.
- Transitions the engineer effort by shifting the emphasis from mobility to countermobility and survivability.

2-82. Transitioning to stability operations is often accompanied by a transition in roles from supported to supporting. The commander should focus on meeting the immediate essential service and civil security needs of the population within the AO in coordination with any existing HN government and nongovernmental organizations.

2-83. Transitioning during the mission can be more challenging than transitioning at the end of the mission. Soldiers may have difficulty transitioning from stability to offense and defense and back again multiple times during UO. Soldiers may apply the TTPs of offensive UO directly to the stability missions with potentially disastrous results. Commanders may not have the luxury of permanently designating specific units to conduct civil-military and humanitarian support tasks and may need to rely heavily on preparatory training and strong unit leadership to mitigate potential difficulties.

Chapter 3

Defensive Urban Operations

Defending the urban area denies the enemy resources; infrastructure; and control of significant political, cultural, or religious sites. The purpose of the defense is to force or deceive the enemy into attacking under unfavorable circumstances, defeat or destroy his attack, and regain the initiative for the offense. The urban environment provides the defender unique advantages based on the density of buildings, infrastructure, and three-dimensional aspects of the AO. While conducting an urban defense, the defender should also consider the surrounding areas that support the urban area and their level of importance to the defense and the defeat of the enemy's attack. This may include power systems, water treatment or water source systems, or access to lines of communications. While the urban defense provides advantages, the defender must not become isolated or lose the ability to maneuver his forces in and around the urban area to defeat the attacker. As with all operations, the BCT's defense of an urban area is not an isolated unit action. It includes other BCTs and brigades in a unified action environment.

SECTION I – CHARACTERISTICS

3-1.   While the offense is the most decisive type of operation, the defense is the strongest. The inherent strengths of the defense include the BCT's ability to occupy positions before the attack and to use the available time to prepare defenses. Preparations end only when the BCT retrogrades or begins to fight. The defender can study the urban terrain and select defensive positions that mass the effects of fires on likely approaches. He combines natural and man-made obstacles to canalize the attacking force into his EAs.

3-2.   Reasons for defending urban areas are—
* Urban areas may dominate avenues of approach.
* Restrictive terrain may canalize movement into urban areas.
* Urban areas contain critical industrial or economic complexes that must be protected.
* Urban areas contain critical transportation infrastructure (such as bridges, railways, and road networks) that provide an advantage to the side that controls them.
* Friendly forces must retain use of port or airfield facilities.
* The political importance of an urban area, such as a capital, justifies its defense.
* Retention of the urban area affects critical enemy operations in the surrounding area.
* Urban areas are excellent for economy of force as defending in urban terrain typically requires fewer forces.

3-3.   Reasons for not defending urban areas are—
* The location of the urban area does not support the defensive plan by being too far forward or back in a unit's defensive AO or not near an enemy's expected avenue of approach.
* Nearby terrain is not defended and allows the enemy to bypass the urban area.
* The danger of fire or toxic contamination from structures, such as refineries or chemical plants, outweighs the defensive benefits.
* Nearby terrain dominates the urban area. This applies mainly to smaller urban areas, such as a village. It is often better to defend from the dominating terrain rather than the urban terrain.
* An urban area is declared an open city.

3-4. Defensive UO provide BCT commanders great opportunities to use the environment's characteristics to their advantage. The defense may be contiguous or noncontiguous depending on the size of the area to be defended and the availability of forces. A contiguous urban defense offers greater security and interior lines of communications, while a noncontiguous defense allows the commander to focus his combat power on strongpoint or perimeter defenses of key terrain, infrastructure, or the population. The five general characteristics of the successful urban defense are described below.

PREPARATION

3-5. The BCT and battalion commander determine likely enemy avenues of approach and schemes of maneuver. They identify EAs, the location and integration of obstacles, and the integration of Army and joint fires; assign missions; and determine task organization requirements accordingly. Additional defensive preparations include—

- Conducting a detailed reconnaissance of the AO in order to determine the shaping efforts necessary to attrite, disrupt, and defeat the enemy attack.
- Establishing a priority of support, a main effort, and a no later than time to be prepared to defend.
- Identifying contingencies and requirements to move, transport, or secure civilians in the area.
- Designating a reserve and a plan to regenerate the reserve once committed.
- Conducting rehearsals, to include employing the reserve and counterattack forces.
- Positioning forces in depth.
- Designating, prioritizing, and preparing survivability positions.

SECURITY

3-6. Security is inherent in all operations. In an urban defense, the BCT identifies the security area force and its orientation, depth, and duration. The scheme of maneuver for the BCT's urban defense is either contiguous or noncontiguous. In either case, there is a need for security and a dedicated security force. The commander describes the purpose of the security area and force in terms of the effect on the enemy, the requirement for preparation and MBA tasks for the force being secured, and disengagement and withdrawal criteria. Typically, the reconnaissance squadron, augmented with some maneuver forces and MI collection capabilities, is the BCT's security force. The other BCT units also integrate into the security of the defense by conducting local, area, and convoy security for forces in their AO as outlined in the reconnaissance and security plan and overlay.

DISRUPTION

3-7. The urban terrain and defense lends itself to disrupting and blunting the enemy's attack. The use of man-made structures, rubble, situational obstacles, and fires in the security area and MBA causes the enemy to be compartmentalized and inhibits their ability to mass fires and forces against defenders. The BCT combines fires, obstacles, unexpected defensive positions, electronic warfare attack, and counterattacks at all levels. Repositioning forces; aggressive protection measures; employment of roadblocks, ambushes, and checkpoints; performing inform and influence activities; and performing cyber/electromagnetic activities combine to disrupt the attack.

MASSING EFFECTS

3-8. The BCT and maneuver battalions shape and decide the battle by massing (focusing, distributing, and shifting) the effects of combat power (direct fire, Army and joint fires, and obstacles). Effects should be synchronized around EAs in time and space. They should be rapid and unexpected to break the enemy's offensive tempo and disrupt his attack.

3-9. The commander employs reconnaissance and security forces (typically the reconnaissance squadron) to shift the effects of fires and maneuver forces so that they are continually refocused to achieve disruptive, destructive, and decisive effects upon the enemy's attack.

3-10. Using EAs remains vital to massing effects in an urban defense. Engagement areas should be identified early in the preparation phase and assigned to a combined arms element that has the combat power to defeat the anticipated enemy force. Mission variables dictate the size and type of EAs, but commanders must prioritize the resources to develop them and the support for each within the available time for preparation. Commanders and staffs consider the following factors during the EA development process for the urban defense:

- Canalized and compartmentalized effect of urban terrain.
- Masking of fires and direction of fires for Army and joint fires (close air support, close combat attack, artillery, and mortars).
- Acquisition and observation distances for optical and electromagnetic spectrum systems.
- Use of remote and unmanned systems to add to the commander's situational understanding.
- Engagement distances for direct fire systems.
- Three-dimensional aspect of the terrain to acquire and engage the enemy.
- Integration of blocking, turning, and disrupting obstacles inside and outside of structures.
- Mobility and gap crossing requirements for repositioning forces.
- Number of available direct fire units.
- Number of available Army and joint fires units.
- Proficiency of observer and firing unit.
- Enemy's direction of attack and likely objectives.
- Trigger and intercept points.
- Terrain analysis.
- Anticipated enemy actions.
- Amount of time the enemy is expected to remain inside the EA.

FLEXIBILITY

3-11. The BCT gains flexibility through sound preparation, disposition in depth, retention of reserves, and effective command and control. The defense is characterized by rapid simultaneous and collaborative planning with flexible execution. Contingency planning also permits flexibility. The urban terrain and defense lends itself to adaptability and changes to the scheme of maneuver. The BCT and battalion's plan should allow for subordinate leader initiative to adjust their defensive actions within the commander's intent. The availability of existing structures affording good defensive positions and requiring little improvement adds to the flexibility of the BCT defense. The defender also has interior lines of communications and can reposition quickly to reinforce or conduct local counterattacks to retain the integrity of the defense and gain the initiative.

SECTION II – SEQUENCING

3-12. The following general sequence of operations applies to defensive UO and may occur sequentially or simultaneously. (See FM 3-90 for details.)

GAIN AND MAINTAIN ENEMY CONTACT

3-13. The security force, typically the BCT reconnaissance squadron, gains enemy contact first. The positioning of the squadron in depth, focused on enemy avenues of approach and named areas of interest, provides the BCT time and space to occupy defensive positions or reposition forces based on the enemy's actions. The security forces focus their efforts on identifying committed enemy unit locations and capabilities, determining the enemy's intent and direction of attack, and gaining time to react. Military intelligence collection assets, unattended ground sensors, and UAS working with ground and air reconnaissance forces maintain contact with enemy forces and either engage, hand-off to maneuver forces, or continue to observe and report.

DISRUPT THE ENEMY

3-14. The urban terrain and defense is well-suited to disrupt the enemy's attacking forces command and control and tempo. The commander executes shaping operations (information operations, counterattacks, and employment of Army and joint fires against HPTs) to disrupt the enemy within the BCT AO. After making contact with the enemy, the commander seeks to disrupt the enemy's plan, the enemy's ability to control forces, and the enemy's combined arms team. Once the process of disrupting the attacking enemy begins, it continues throughout a defensive operation.

FIX THE ENEMY

3-15. By fixing the enemy, the BCT ensures that it does not become isolated, and it allows the commander to maneuver or reposition his forces to complete the destruction of the enemy. The urban terrain and the organization of the urban defense allow the commander to create separation in time and space between attacking enemy echelons. He can use that separation to fix and defeat smaller forces while denying the attacker to mass his forces against a portion of the defense. The commander does everything possible to limit the options available to the enemy.

MANEUVER

3-16. In the defense, the decisive operation occurs in the MBA. Rather than large avenues of approach and EAs, the urban MBA can have several smaller and in depth EAs that focus on narrower avenues of approach. These afford the defender more flexibility in repositioning and defeating the attacker through a series of engagements to slow and then stop their attack. Once the attack has culminated, the urban terrain lends itself to multiple counterattack options for the commander. Army and joint fires employed to attack HPTs in depth create separation between forces, isolating portions of the attacker's force. This allows counterattacking forces to engage and defeat smaller elements and secure key terrain and lines of communications structures, further isolating the enemy force and causing it to fight in more than one direction.

FOLLOW-THROUGH

3-17. The purpose of defensive UO is to retain terrain and create conditions for a counteroffensive that regains the initiative. The defense does this by causing the enemy to sustain unacceptable losses short of any decisive objectives, which allows the commander to transition to an attack. A defense could also result in a stalemate with both forces left in contact with each other.

3-18. During this follow-through period, time is critical. Unless the commander has a large, uncommitted reserve prepared to quickly exploit or reverse the situation, the commander should reset the defense, generate combat power for offensive action, and maintain contact with the enemy. Time is also critical to the enemy, who uses it to reorganize, establish a security area, and fortify positions.

SECTION III – TASK ORGANIZATION CONSIDERATIONS

3-19. When determining task organization, the commander should consider all phases of mission execution. The commander ensures the task organization maximizes the available warfighting functions. The BCT and battalion commander organizes his force to accomplish reconnaissance, security, MBA, reserve, and sustaining operations. He has the option of defending forward or defending in depth.

3-20. When the commander defends forward within an AO, he organizes his force to commit most of his combat power early in the defensive effort. To accomplish this, forces are deployed forward or counterattacks are planned well forward in the MBA. If the defense is conducted in depth, the commander uses security forces and forward MBA elements to identify, define, and control the depth of the enemy's main effort while holding off secondary thrusts. This allows the conservation of combat power, strengthening of the reserve, and a better resourced counterattack.

3-21. The commander analyzes the forces and assets available, paying particular attention to the engineer and FS units. Engineer and FS allocations should be defined in terms of capability. FS analysis should include the number of targets to be engaged, the point in the battle in which to engage the targets, and the expected result.

3-22. The BCT commander may change task organization to respond to the existing or projected situation. Whenever possible, the commander ensures that changes in task organization take place between units that have previously trained or operated together. The commander's purpose in task organization is to maximize the ability of subordinate commanders to generate a combined arms effect consistent with the concept of operations. Commanders and staffs work to ensure the distribution of capabilities to the appropriate components of the force to weight the decisive operation.

SECTION IV – UNDERSTAND

3-23. The BCT commander defending in the urban area assesses many factors. His mission statement and guidance from higher commanders help him focus his assessment. The mission variables guide the commander's assessment. Of these, the impacts of the enemy and environment (to include the terrain, weather, and civil considerations) are significant to the commander's understanding of defensive UO.

PLANNING CONSIDERATIONS

3-24. When planning defensive UO, the BCT and battalion commander consider threat and urban environment characteristics.

THREAT

3-25. The commander conducts defensive planning, particularly his allocation of forces, based on his initial assessment of the enemy's intentions. This assessment determines whether the commander's primary concern is preventing isolation by defeating enemy efforts outside the area or defeating an enemy attacking the urban area directly. It also clarifies threats to sustainment operations and helps shape how he arrays his forces.

URBAN ENVIRONMENT CHARACTERISTICS

3-26. Understanding the defensive qualities of the urban environment, as in any defensive scenario, is based on mission requirements and on a systemic analysis of the terrain in terms of observation and fields of fire, avenues of approach, key terrain, obstacles, and cover and concealment (OAKOC). It is also based on potential CBRN and fire hazards that may be present in the urban area.

3-27. Units occupy less terrain in urban areas than in more open areas. Commanders shape the urban battle according to the type of defense they are attempting to conduct. If conducting an area defense or retrograde, they use shaping actions like those for any defensive action. Important shaping actions that apply to all defensive UO include—

- Performing inform and influence activities.
- Performing cyber/electromagnetic activities.
- Preventing or defeating isolation.
- Separating attacking forces from supporting resources.
- Creating a mobility advantage.
- Applying economy-of-force measures.
- Effectively managing the urban population.
- Planning counterattacks.

3-28. In most cases, defending force commanders are in the urban area before combat. This time gives them the chance to manage civilians. Consequently, they can better manage and protect the population (a legal requirement) and gain more freedom of action for their forces.

3-29. Resources devoted to population management are carefully weighed against availability; mission requirements; and possible collateral damage affecting tactical, operational, or strategic success. Moving the population allows defending forces to more liberally apply fires, emplace obstacles, and relieve units of requirements to continue life support for civilians while executing operations.

WARFIGHTING FUNCTION CONSIDERATIONS

3-30. When integrating warfighting functions into the combined arms defensive UO scheme of maneuver, the BCT and battalion commander consider movement and maneuver, intelligence, fires, mission command, and protection.

MOVEMENT AND MANEUVER

3-31. During the MBA engagement, the BCT and maneuver battalions shift combat power and priority of fires to defeat the enemy's attack. This may require—

- Adjusting AOs and missions of subordinates.
- Repositioning forces.
- Shifting the main effort.
- Committing the reserve.
- Modifying the original plan.

3-32. In defensive UO, countermobility operations can greatly influence guiding enemy forces into an EA. An understanding of the urban transportation system, city design, and construction characteristics is necessary to conduct effective countermobility operations. Demolitions can have important implications for creating impassable obstacles in urban canyons and clearing fields of fire where necessary. Careful engineer planning can make the already restrictive terrain virtually impassable to mounted forces. Demolitions should be executed to deny the enemy avenues of approach and access to structures that may be used as support-by-fire positions.

3-33. The speed and mobility of aviation can help maximize concentration and flexibility. During preparation, aviation can provide aerial reconnaissance and fires. Throughout the AO, aviation forces can conduct interdiction against HPTs, enemy concentrations, and moving columns and can disrupt enemy centers of gravity. The division will likely employ attack reconnaissance helicopter units to attack follow-on echelons before they can move forward to the close battle. Aviation forces may conduct security of an open flank in conjunction with ground forces.

3-34. Attack reconnaissance helicopters routinely support the security area force and mass fires during the MBA fight. Synchronization of aviation units into the defensive plan is important to ensure aviation units are capable of massing fires and to prevent fratricide. Detailed air-ground integration and coordination are essential to ensure efficient use of aviation units.

ENGAGEMENT AREA DEVELOPMENT

3-35. The critical planning piece for both maneuver and FS during defensive UO is EA development. Commanders position defensive systems toward avenues of approach. The following steps, some of which can and should be done concurrently, represent a way to build an EA:

- Identify all likely enemy avenues of approach, to include subsurface and supersurface routes.
- Determine likely enemy concept of operations.
- Determine where to kill the enemy.
- Plan and integrate obstacles.
- Emplace weapons systems (includes preparation of fighting positions).
- Plan and integrate direct and indirect fires.
- Rehearse the execution of operations in the EA.

INTELLIGENCE

3-36. Intelligence preparation of the battlefield helps the commander define where to concentrate combat power, where to accept risk, and where to plan potential decisive actions. The BCT commander studies patterns of enemy operations and the enemy's vulnerability to counterattack, interdiction, electronic warfare, air attacks, and canalization by obstacles.

3-37. To aid in the development of a flexible urban defensive plan, IPB should present all feasible enemy COAs. The essential areas of focus are—

- Available reconnaissance units, to include aerial and ground sensors, snipers, and joint forces.
- Urban terrain and weather.
- Enemy force size and likely COAs with associated decision points.
- Locations of enemy CPs.
- Enemy vulnerabilities and high-value targets (HVT).
- Location of enemy indirect fire weapon systems and units.
- Location, numbers, and intentions of civilian population.

3-38. The intelligence plan must address the continuation of collection and analysis efforts throughout the defensive operation because it is unlikely that the commander has complete knowledge of the enemy's intentions, capabilities, and dispositions.

FIRES

3-39. Considerations for developing the FS plan are—

- Allocate initial priority of fires to the forward security force.
- Plan targets along enemy reconnaissance mounted and dismounted avenues of approach.
- Engage approaching enemy formations at vulnerable points along their route with indirect fires and close air support (if available).
- Plan the transition of fires to the MBA fight.
- Plan deceptive fires to channel enemy forces into EAs.
- Develop clear triggers to adjust FS coordination measures, identify priority of fires, and integrate echelon of fires in support of defensive plan.
- Ensure integration of fires in support of obstacle effects.
- Ensure integration of fires with the maneuver battalion counterattack plans and repositioning contingency plans.
- Integrate the emplacement of scatterable mines into the countermobility and counterattack plans.

MISSION COMMAND

3-40. Defending an urban AO is a typical mission for BCTs and battalions. This mission allows the commander to distribute forces to suit the urban terrain and plan an engagement that integrates direct and indirect fires. The commander has freedom of maneuver within assigned boundaries but must prevent enemy penetration of the rear boundary. The commander ensures that the defensive plans of subordinate units are compatible and control measures, such as contact points and phase lines, are sufficient for flank coordination when assigning AOs. The defensive plan should address what happens when it succeeds and transitioning to other full spectrum operations.

3-41. Defensive operations are often difficult to conduct because they may occur against an enemy who has the initiative. Because the enemy has the initiative, the commander may have to frequently shift his shaping operations to contain the enemy's attack until he can seize the initiative. This may require him to adjust subordinate unit AOs, repeatedly commit and reconstitute his reserve, and modify the plan. The commander may change task organization to respond to the existing or projected situation.

3-42. To break through the MBA, the enemy often attacks along the boundaries of defending units that can be identified. Therefore, it is extremely important for commanders at every echelon to ensure that the plan for their part of the defense is properly coordinated within their units as well as with flanking and supporting units. This coordination is best done by personal visits to subordinate commanders on the ground. Planning considerations requiring attention in the coordination process are—

- Commander's intent and concept of operations.

- Scheme of maneuver to be applied by flanking and supporting units.
- Selection of boundary locations that do not increase coordination problems.
- Mutual support planning.
- Reconnaissance and security plans.
- Location and composition of security forces.
- Obstacles and demolition plans.
- Fire plans, to include employing antitank systems, illumination, and smoke.
- Air defense coverage areas.
- Communications, to include compatibility with HN and multinational forces.

Note. Because CPs tend to be more stationary in the defense, the commander should place them in hardened areas or protective terrain and reduce their electronic signature. They need to remain capable of rapid relocation.

PROTECTION

3-43. Protection plans are essential during defensive UO and require a deliberate and detailed approach to ensure that combat power is focused where it is most needed. Air and missile defense support to the BCT may be limited. Units should expect to use their organic weapons systems for defense against enemy air threats. Commanders should plan for CBRN reconnaissance at likely locations for enemy employment of CBRN agents and hazards.

3-44. Due to the three-dimensional aspects of the urban terrain, individuals and small elements are more likely to become isolated, missing, or captured. This is especially true if the BCT conducts noncontiguous defensive operations. The BCT staff must plan how to use combinations of immediate and deliberate recoveries to regain control of these personnel. It may also be possible for the isolated, missing, or captured personnel to conduct their own unassisted recovery operation. (See FM 3-50.1 for details.)

3-45. In defensive UO, commanders protect forces and critical assets by conducting area security operations. BCT forces conducting area security in the defense can deter, detect, or defeat enemy reconnaissance while creating standoff distances from enemy direct and indirect fire systems. Area security operations can also protect the rapid movement of combat trains or protect sustainment assets until needed.

SECTION V – SHAPE

3-46. The size and complexity of the urban area prevent defending forces from being strong everywhere. Shaping operations designed to engage the enemy on terms that are advantageous to the defense are described below.

ISOLATION

3-47. Failure to prevent isolation of the urban area can rapidly lead to the failure of the entire urban defense. In planning the defense, commanders should anticipate the enemy's attempt to isolate the urban area. Commanders may defeat this effort by allocating sufficient defending forces outside the urban area to prevent its isolation. Using military deception can also mislead the enemy regarding defensive disposition and organization in and outside the urban area.

DISRUPTION

3-48. Commanders use fires, conduct inform and influence activities, and conduct cyber/electromagnetic activities to separate enemy forces from attacking the urban area. The purpose of this shaping action is the same as for any conventional area defense. It aims to allow defending BCT forces to defeat the enemy piecemeal as they arrive in the urban area without support, already disrupted by fires and attacks on their communications systems. This separation and disruption of the enemy also sets the conditions for a mobile defense if division or corps commanders choose to execute that type of defense. These operations also prevent the enemy commander from synchronizing and massing his combat power at the decisive point in the close battle.

MOBILITY

3-49. Well-conceived mobility operations in urban terrain can provide defending forces mobility superiority over attacking forces. This is achieved by carefully selecting routes between primary, alternate, and subsequent positions and moving reserves and counterattack forces. These routes are reconnoitered, cleared, and marked before the operation. They maximize the cover and concealment characteristics of the terrain. Using demolitions, lanes, and innovative obstacles denies the defense of these same routes.

ECONOMY OF FORCE

3-50. Economy of force enables the defending force to mass effects at decisive points. Forces execute security missions and take advantage of obstacles, mobility, and firepower to portray greater combat power than they actually possess. They prevent the enemy from determining the actual disposition and strength of the friendly defense. Security forces in an economy-of-force role take position in parts of the urban area where the enemy is less likely to attack.

COUNTERATTACKS

3-51. Counterattacks as a shaping tool have two applications: retaining the initiative and separating forces. However, opportunities for effective counterattacks are brief. Thus, timing is critical. Commanders should understand the effect of the urban environment on time-distance relationships. Otherwise, the timing of the attack may be upset and the operation desynchronized.

RECONNAISSANCE AND SECURITY

3-52. The fundamentals discussed in chapter 1 of this manual also apply to offensive UO. (See FM 3-20.96 for details.)

SNIPER OPERATIONS

3-53. Snipers play a vital role in the commander's planning and help the BCT maintain an offensive posture while in the defense. In the defense, the sniper team can—

- Augment the fires of maneuver elements.
- Cover avenues of approach, obstacles, dead space, and key terrain features.
- Provide final protective fires if necessary.
- Deter enemy infiltration attempts.
- Operate as an extension of patrols.

3-54. During defensive UO, sniper teams work outside the forward edge of battle area (FEBA) to provide early warning and disruption and, if possible, cause the enemy to deploy prematurely. In the defense, sniper teams—

- Move out at night.
- Build hide positions that overwatch likely avenues of approach.
- Provide early warning of impending attacks (day or night), probes, or infiltrations.
- Reduce targets of opportunity.
- Collect information.

BATTLE HANDOVER AND PASSAGE OF LINES

3-55. Battle handover may occur during either offensive or defensive operations. During defensive operations, it is usually planned and coordinated in advance to facilitate execution and usually involves a rearward passage of lines. (See FM 3-90, FM 3-90.5, and FM 3-90.6 for details.)

SECTION VI – ENGAGE

3-56. BCT forces organize defensive UO around a—

- Security area.
- Main battle area.
- Reserve.

SECURITY AREA

3-57. The BCT establishes a security area with the reconnaissance squadron before the maneuver battalions move into the AO to provide early warning and reaction time, deny enemy reconnaissance efforts, and protect the MBA. However, maneuver battalions should still provide their own internal security, especially in a noncontiguous AO.

3-58. Usually, the forward security mission is executed as a guard or screen. If the division attaches an additional maneuver battalion to the BCT, it may be employed as a BCT-controlled security force. Two general options for organizing the security force are—

- Forward defending maneuver battalions establish their own security areas.
- Maneuver battalions provide security forces that operate with the reconnaissance squadron under the BCT's direct control.

3-59. The division commander defines the depth of the BCT's security area. The BCT's security area extends from the FEBA to the BCT's forward boundary. Depth in the security area provides the MBA more reaction time and allows the security force more area to conduct security operations and engage enemy forces. A shallow security area may require more forces and assets to provide the needed reaction time. The BCT commander should clearly define the objective of the security area, tasks of the security force, expected results, disengagement and withdrawal criteria, and follow-on tasks. He identifies specific avenues of approach and named areas of interest the security force covers. Security forces also assist the rearward passage of lines of any division or corps security forces at the battle handover line.

3-60. Throughout the preparation phase of defensive UO, security operations continue without interruption. Security forces may be assigned screen or area security missions. Reconnaissance elements may be positioned to screen and guard along likely enemy avenues of approach, reinforced in depth.

3-61. If the maneuver battalion commander organizes his own security force, he chooses from three basic options:

- Use the reconnaissance platoon only as a screening force.
- Use the reconnaissance platoon with maneuver elements, mortars, or a company team (or in combination) in a counterreconnaissance task.
- Use a company team with or without the reconnaissance platoon and mortars in a counterreconnaissance task.

3-62. The security area is largely the domain of the BCT's reconnaissance squadron for shaping the AO and setting favorable conditions for the close fight. The maneuver battalion may execute some engagement tasks in the security area to support its own or the BCT's defensive scheme. Actions that take place during the security area engagement are—

- Execution of planned indirect fires on primary enemy avenues of approach.
- Execution of situational obstacles to disrupt the enemy and to force him to commit his engineer units.
- Execution of a delay through the security area and into the MBA to—
  - Take advantage of restrictive avenues of approach.
  - Set the conditions for a counterattack.
  - Avoid a decisive engagement until favorable conditions have been set.

- The maneuver battalion assumes battle handover and control of the FEBA fight from the security force as it completes its rearward passage of lines.
- As security area engagements transition into the MBA, security area forces withdraw through the MBA defense, conduct a counterattack, or occupy reserve positions.

MAIN BATTLE AREA

3-63. The MBA is where the commander intends to defeat, disrupt, or neutralize the enemy's attack. The BCT's MBA extends from the FEBA to the forward maneuver battalion's rear boundary. The commander selects his MBA based on the higher commander's concept of operations, IPB, initial reconnaissance and security results, and his own assessment of the situation. The BCT commander delegates responsibilities within the MBA by assigning boundaries to subordinate battalions. If the commander does not assign boundaries to subordinate battalions, the BCT is responsible for terrain management, security, clearance of fires, and coordination of maneuver within the entire AO. The commander may control his forces by assigning AOs, BPs, or strongpoints.

3-64. The BCT and its maneuver battalions deploy the bulk of their combat power in the MBA. The FEBA marks the foremost limit of the areas in which the majority of ground combat units deploy, excluding the areas in which security forces are operating. Organization of the MBA varies according to the type of defense. As in all operations, commanders promote freedom of action by using the least restrictive control measures necessary to implement their tactical concepts.

3-65. If the reconnaissance squadron can bring sufficient firepower to shape the enemy in the security area, an MBA engagement may not occur. In this event, the BCT can rapidly transition into a counterattack. An MBA engagement is a combined arms fight, integrating both direct fire and indirect fires reinforced with obstacles and organic mortars.

3-66. Combining all available fires with maneuver, obstacles, and reserve elements, the commander seeks to destroy the enemy in designated EAs or force his transition to a retrograde or hasty defense. The BCT specifies control measures to coordinate and focus the defensive operation.

RESERVE

3-67. The commander's defensive plan should be able to succeed without using the reserve. However, the most likely mission of the reserve is to conduct a counterattack in accordance with previously prepared plans. Commanders use their reserves primarily to conduct local counterattacks to restore the integrity of the defense or to exploit opportunities.

DEFENSIVE TASKS

3-68. The BCT may conduct an area defense, be part of a mobile defense, or conduct retrograde operations in an urban environment.

AREA DEFENSE

3-69. An area defense may include both urban areas and open maneuver areas and is best suited to take advantage of distinct urban area characteristics. It concentrates on denying enemy forces access to designated terrain for a specific time rather than destroying the enemy outright. Although an urban area defense does not directly seek to destroy or defeat attacking enemy forces, it does aim to terminate the enemy's attack. The urban area defense is often effective at exhausting enemy resources and shaping conditions for a transition to offensive UO. The urban area may also be used as a strongpoint to force enemy movement in a different direction or to fix enemy forces as part of a large, mobile defense taking place in the AO outside the urban area. (See FM 3-90, FM 3-90.5, and FM 3-90.6 for details.)

MOBILE DEFENSE

3-70. As part of a mobile defense, BCTs may conduct UO as part of the fixing force or striking force. Infantry and SBCTs can be especially effective as part of the fixing force to slow and disrupt the enemy's advance by retaining key terrain within urban areas. At the same time, HBCTs maneuver as part of the striking force to engage the enemy's flanks and rear. The overall commander may also decide to accept risk by leaving friendly forces to conduct defensive UO behind enemy lines to defend choke points and block key transportation centers.

3-71. A mobile defense can operate in an urban area under specific conditions. It focuses on destroying or defeating the enemy through a decisive attack by a striking force and requires the defender to have greater mobility than the attacker. This is accomplished by effectively using the terrain and correctly task organizing the defensive force. The principles of applying the mobile defense in the urban area remain the same: a small fixing force stops the enemy and limits any ability to maneuver while a striking force quickly maneuvers and counterattacks to destroy him. A key consideration for commanders is to retain the mobility advantage of the striking force within an urban area while adequately supporting the fixing force.

3-72. An urban mobile defense seeks to entice an enemy force into the depths of the urban area where it begins to lose mobility options. Defending commanders can attempt to shape the battlefield so that the attacker commits significant resources into an urban area where his maneuver capabilities are reduced. The urban environment can help defending forces achieve a mobility advantage over an attacker in a broader sense. (See FM 3-90, FM 3-90.5, and FM 3-90.6 for details.)

RETROGRADE

3-73. The urban environment enhances the defending force's ability to successfully conduct retrograde operations. (See FM 3-90, FM 3-90.5, and FM 3-90.6 for details.) Retrograde operations are described below.

Withdrawals

3-74. The cover and concealment afforded by the urban environment facilitates withdrawals in which friendly forces attempt to break contact with the enemy and move away. The environment also restricts enemy reconnaissance, limits observation, and presents deceptive action opportunities.

Delays

3-75. The urban environment's natural cover and concealment and its compartmented effects facilitates delays. Delays can effectively draw the enemy into the urban area for subsequent counterattack or as an integral part of a withdrawal under pressure. Compartmented effects force the attacking enemy to move on well-defined and easily interdicted routes and limit the enemy's ability to flank or bypass delaying positions. Delaying units can quickly displace from one position to another.

Retirements

3-76. A retirement is a retrograde operation in which a force that is not in contact with the enemy moves to the rear in an organized manner. Typically, another unit's security force covers the movement of one formation as the unit conducts a retirement.

SECTION VII – CONSOLIDATE

3-77. At the conclusion of defensive UO, the BCT may pause to consolidate and reorganize before the next operation. If required, the commander decides the best time and location that facilitates future operations and provides active security. The BCT should maintain a high degree of security when performing consolidation and reorganization activities.

CONSOLIDATION

3-78. The BCT may need to consolidate to reorganize, avoid culmination, prepare for an enemy counterattack, or allow time for movement of adjacent units. Consolidation is planned for every mission. Actions during consolidation are—
- Eliminate pockets of enemy resistance.

- Establish security consistent with the threat.
- Establish contact with adjacent friendly units.
- Prepare defensive positions.
- Position air defense units to maintain coverage.
- Clear obstacles or improve lanes to support friendly movement and reorganization activities.
- Plan and prepare for future operations.
- Destroy captured enemy equipment and process EPWs.
- Maintain contact with the enemy and conduct reconnaissance.

3-79. The BCT maintains contact with the enemy by redirecting reconnaissance and security units, directing small-unit patrols, and possibly conducting limited objective attacks. In some situations, the BCT may leave a small force to control key terrain or complete clearing the objective while the remainder of the BCT begins an attack.

REORGANIZATION

3-80. The BCT and maneuver battalion S-4s ensure that the sustainment plan is fully coordinated with the rest of the staff. They coordinate with the S-3 to ensure that supply routes support the full depth of the defense without interfering with maneuver or obstacle plans. Coordination with the S-3 provides engineer and potential military police (MP) support to keep supply routes open. The S-4 coordinates with the CBRN officer to ensure appropriate routes are designated for contaminated equipment. In addition, the S-4 coordinates with the forward support company for the possible use of prestocked classes of supply (Class IV and Class V).

3-81. Enemy actions and the maneuver of forces complicate forward area medical operations. Health services support considerations for defensive operations are—

- Medical personnel have much less time to reach the patient, complete vital emergency medical treatment, and remove the patient from the battle site.
- The enemy's initial attack and the maneuver battalion's counterattack produce the heaviest patient workload. These are also the most likely times for enemy use of artillery and CBRN weapons.
- The enemy attack can disrupt ground and air routes and delay evacuation of patients to and from treatment elements.
- The depth and dispersion of the defense create significant time-distance problems for evacuation units.
- The enemy may exercise the initiative early in the operation, which could preclude accurate prediction of initial areas of casualty density. This fact makes effective integration of air assets into the MEDEVAC plan essential.

3-82. As the situation allows, all units undertake reorganization to maintain combat effectiveness. More extensive reorganization is usually conducted after the BCT defeats an enemy attack. Typical reorganization tasks are—

- Establish and maintain security.
- Destroy or contain enemy forces that still threaten the BCT.
- Establish security consistent with the threat. This may include moving forces, adjusting boundaries, changing task organization, and coordinating adjacent units.
- Replace or shift reconnaissance and security units, and refocus the plan as needed.
- Reestablish the BCT chain of command, key staff positions, and CPs lost during the battle.
- Treat and evacuate casualties.
- Redistribute ammunition, supplies, and equipment as necessary.
- Conduct emergency resupply and refueling operations.
- Recover and repair damaged equipment.
- Submit required logistics and battle reports by FM or digital communications.

- Process EPWs and detainees as required.
- Repair and emplace additional obstacles, and improve and construct additional fighting positions.
- Repair and restore critical routes within the BCT AO to assure mobility of the force.
- Reposition CPs, communications assets, logistics, and FS units for future operations.

SECTION VIII – TRANSITION

3-83. During the planning for any operation, the BCT commander and staff should discern from the higher headquarters' operation order what the follow-on missions are and how they intend to achieve them. At the conclusion of a defensive UO, the BCT can transition to another defensive operation, an offensive operation, or stability operations. The commander considers the higher commander's concept of operations, friendly capabilities, and the enemy situation when making this decision.

3-84. If a defense is successful, the commander anticipates and seeks the opportunity to transition to the offense. The BCT commander can use two basic techniques when transitioning to the offense:

- Attack using forces not previously committed to the defense.
- Conduct offensive actions using the currently defending forces.

3-85. If the defense is unsuccessful, the commander needs to transition from a defensive posture into retrograde operations. The commander must be careful to avoid being successfully targeted by enemy deception operations designed to tempt the BCT to abandon the advantages of fighting from prepared defensive positions.

3-86. The commander conducts any required reorganization and resupply concurrently while transitioning to another mission. Subordinate commanders and staff should anticipate new task organizations. Transitions also require a flexible and responsive sustainment effort. The brigade support battalion and forward support company commanders and sustainment staffs must anticipate and plan for transitions so that the required supplies are available when needed.

PART TWO

Company and Platoon

Chapter 4

Urban Operations

Urban combat is characterized by small units maneuvering in canalized streets and inside compartmentalized structures. The inherent strengths and limitations of both Infantry and Armor units are accentuated in urban terrain. It is difficult for these units to compensate for their limitations when working separately. Only when task organized to conduct operations as combined arms teams can these forces decisively accomplish their mission.

SECTION I – ORGANIZATION

4-1.   The maneuver companies within BCTs have similar organizations. The main differences are the means of transportation to and on the battlefield, the protection afforded by vehicles, the weapons mounted on the vehicles, and the organic supporting units available to them.

4-2.   This section covers only the combat units that a maneuver company may expect to have attached, on its flank, or in direct support. (See the specific unit manuals for details.) In particular, this section briefly discusses the—

- Maneuver battalions within the three BCTs.
- Maneuver companies and platoons within each battalion.
- BCT reconnaissance troops.

4-3.   Each battalion has three or four maneuver companies. The Infantry battalion has a weapons company. Each battalion headquarters and headquarters company contains a scout platoon, a heavy mortar platoon, and a sniper squad. Each maneuver company has three maneuver platoons. Table 4-1, table 4-2, table 4-3, and table to 4-4 compare the differences between similar units in each of the BCTs.

Table 4-1. Maneuver battalions within brigade combat teams

Battalion Type	Headquarters Company Combat Units	Maneuver Companies	Weapons Company
Infantry	Scout Platoon Heavy Mortar Platoon Sniper Squad	Three Infantry	Weapons company with four assault platoons
Combined Arms	Scout Platoon Heavy Mortar Platoon Sniper Squad	Two Mechanized Infantry Two Armor	None
Stryker Infantry	Scout Platoon Heavy Mortar Platoon Sniper Squad	Three Stryker Infantry	None

Table 4-2. Headquarters and headquarters company combat units

Unit	Scout Platoon	Heavy Mortar Platoon	Sniper Squad
Infantry Battalion	Three squads with six men each	Four 120-mm mortars* Four 81-mm mortars* Transported by wheeled vehicles and trailers	Three sniper teams Ten men
Combined Arms Battalion	Three sections with a total of three cavalry fighting vehicles and five wheeled vehicles	Four 120-mm mortars Four tracked carriers	Three sniper teams (Ten men)
Stryker Infantry Battalion	Three teams with a total of four Stryker reconnaissance vehicles	Four mounted 120-mm mortars* (mounted only) Four 81-mm mortars* (dismounted use) Four Stryker mortar carriers	Two sniper teams Seven men
* Platoon only has crews to man four mortars.			

Table 4-3. Maneuver companies

Unit	Platoons	Squads per Platoon	Major Weapons per Platoon	Mortar Section
Infantry Company	Three Infantry	Three rifle One weapons	Two medium machine guns Two Javelins	Two 60-mm
Mechanized Infantry Company	Three with four BFVs each	Three rifle	Three medium machine guns Three Javelins Four BFVs	None
Armor Company	Three with four tanks each	Two sections of two tanks	Four tanks mounting— 120-mm cannon One heavy machine gun Two medium machine guns	None
Stryker Company	Three with four Stryker ICVs each	Three rifle One weapons	Four ICVs Three medium machine guns Three Javelins	Two 120-mm* Two 60-mm*
	One MGS with three vehicles	NA	Three MGS mounting— 105-mm cannon One heavy machine gun One medium machine gun	
* Section only has crews to man two mortars.				

Table 4-4. Reconnaissance troops, weapons company, and antitank company

Unit	Platoons	Mortars
IBCT Motorized Reconnaissance Troop	Three reconnaissance platoons	Two 120-mm
IBCT Dismounted Reconnaissance Troop	Two dismounted reconnaissance platoons with a sniper team	Two 60-mm
HBCT Reconnaissance Troop	Two scout sections with three tracked and five wheeled vehicles	Two 120-mm
SBCT Reconnaissance Troop	Three reconnaissance troops	Two 120-mm

IBCT CONSIDERATIONS

4-4.   Infantry units can operate effectively in most terrain and weather conditions. Because of their rapid deployability and mobility, they are effective in high-tempo operations. In such cases, they can wrest the initiative early, seize and hold ground, and mass fires to stop the enemy. They are particularly effective in urban terrain, where they can infiltrate and move rapidly to the rear of enemy positions.

CAPABILITIES

4-5. In UO, the IBCT Infantry company can—

- Engage targets with small-arms fire under almost all conditions. Infantry small-arms fire within a building can eliminate resistance without seriously damaging the structure.
- Physically clear and occupy buildings.
- Provide its own fires with an organic mortar section.
- Move stealthily into position without alerting the enemy. Soldiers can move over, around, or through most urban terrain regardless of the amount of damage to buildings and have excellent all-round vision.
- Participate in air assault operations.
- Participate in airborne operations (airborne and Ranger companies).
- Participate in amphibious operations, to include crossings and patrols.

4-6. Operational capabilities of the IBCT weapons company in UO include—

- Precision direct fires of missile systems and the destructive effects of the heavy machine guns provide excellent support to Infantry in an urban environment.
- Thermal sights on close combat missile systems can detect enemy activity through darkness and most smoke.
- Mounted patrols can monitor large areas of a city while making their presence known to the entire populace.
- Mobile firepower of weapons company vehicles can add security to resupply convoys.
- Armored weapons company vehicles can resupply Infantry units and evacuate casualties.

LIMITATIONS

4-7. In UO, the IBCT company—

- Lacks heavy supporting firepower, protection, and mobility. Protection and mobility limitations can be mitigated to a degree when augmented with mine resistant ambush protected (MRAP) vehicles. (See appendix B and TC 7-31 for details.)
- Possesses limited sustainment assets.
- Is vulnerable to enemy armor, artillery, and air assets.
- Is vulnerable to enemy CBRN attacks with limited decontamination capability.

4-8. Operational limitations of the IBCT weapons company in UO include—

- If isolated or unsupported by Infantry, vehicles are vulnerable to enemy close-in attack, heavy machine guns, and light or medium antiarmor weapons.
- Improvised barricades, narrow streets and alleyways, or large amounts of rubble can block vehicles.
- Leaders and gunners usually require accurate target identification from forward Infantry units.
- The minimum arming distance for close combat missile systems may reduce effectiveness in close terrain. Hanging wires and other debris may also limit effectiveness.
- Restrictive terrain may limit the crew's ability to clear the backblast area for Improved Target Acquisition System (ITAS) firing.
- Close combat missile systems usage may be limited by the brief target exposure time for moving vehicles.
- Heavy weapons may cause unwanted collateral damage and can destabilize certain structures.

HBCT CONSIDERATIONS

4-9. The maneuver companies within the combined arms battalion are highly capable of conducting UO. They provide their own suppressive fires either to support maneuver or repel enemy assaults. The maneuver companies within a combined arms battalion are routinely task organized into company teams consisting of a mix of mechanized Infantry and tank platoons. Each mechanized Infantry platoon is equipped with four Bradley fighting vehicles (BFV), and each tank platoon is equipped with four M1 tanks. Each HBCT also has reconnaissance troops assigned to the reconnaissance squadron.

CAPABILITIES

4-10. In UO, the mechanized Infantry platoon can—
- Assault enemy positions.
- Use 25-mm cannon and 7.62-mm machine gun fire to effectively suppress or destroy enemy infantry.
- Block dismounted avenues of approach.
- Breach makeshift roadblocks and rubble, walls, gates, and buildings.
- Engage close targets located at high elevations.
- Detect concealed targets using day and night enhanced optics.
- Conduct mounted or dismounted patrols and operations.
- Establish strongpoints to deny the enemy important terrain or flank positions.
- Overwatch and secure tactical obstacles.
- Operate in a CBRN environment.

4-11. In UO, the tank platoon—
- Is fully protected against antipersonnel mines, fragments, and small-arms weapons.
- Dominates large expanses of open area with their long-range sights and weapons, allowing Infantry to operate in more restrictive terrain and visual dead space. Armored vehicle thermal sights detect activity in daylight, darkness, and through smoke.
- Delivers both devastating close-in direct fires and accurate long-range fire beyond the range of Infantry small-arms weapons with the 120-mm main gun.
- Engages simultaneous targets in multiple directions from protected positions using the main gun and the commander's and loader's weapons.
- Projects a psychological presence with their firepower that aids friendly forces in deterring violence. Mounted patrols can monitor large areas of a city while making their presence known to the entire populace, both friendly and unfriendly.
- Has excellent mobility along unblocked routes.

LIMITATIONS

4-12. Operational limitations of the mechanized Infantry platoon in UO include—
- Increased maintenance requirements.
- Increased fuel requirements.
- Road and bridge weight classifications that may limit access in unimproved urban areas.
- Loud noise signature.
- Limited crew situational awareness.
- No organic mortars.

4-13. In UO, tanks and their crews—
- Have limited visibility to the sides and rear and no visibility to the top with hatches closed.
- Have good all-round vision but are susceptible to enemy small-arms fire and fragmentation without transparent gun shields in place.
- Have difficulty acquiring and identifying close-in targets without exposing the vehicle commander or having dismounted Soldiers direct the vehicle.
- Cannot elevate or depress their main guns enough to engage targets very close to the vehicle or high up in nearby buildings. (See figure 4-1.)
- Can cause excessive collateral damage and may destabilize basic structures with main gun ammunition.
- Are vulnerable to close-in enemy light and medium antiarmor weapons, especially those fired from above ground level.
- Require Infantry Soldiers to provide security.

- Have an increased noise signature.
- Can be blocked by narrow streets and alleyways. The main gun may prevent the turret from rotating if it encounters a solid object, such as a wall or post.

SBCT CONSIDERATIONS

4-14. The Army organized the SBCT in response to the need for a force that can deploy rapidly to a crisis area anywhere in the world. Each SBCT Infantry company has three platoons equipped with Infantry carrier vehicles (ICV), an MGS platoon, and a headquarters section. The ICV is a fully mobile system capable of operating in conjunction with Infantry and other elements of the combined arms team.

INFANTRY CARRIER VEHICLE CAPABILITIES AND LIMITATIONS

4-15. The SBCT company team combines the effects of the Infantry squads; the weapons squad; and the direct fires of the ICV, to include Javelin fire-and-forget antitank missile fires. Protection is afforded by the vehicle and the ability of the vehicle to protect the Soldiers from small-arms fire and fragmentation before dismounting.

4-16. In UO, the ICV-equipped company team can—

- Use the mobility of the ICV to transport the Infantry squads to a position of advantage under the protection of the vehicle. Infantry can move stealthily into position without alerting the enemy.
- Operate in a mounted or dismounted role and conducts mounted or dismounted patrols and operations in support of security operations.
- Destroy, suppress, or fix personnel with direct fires and destroys tanks and fighting vehicles with close combat missile system fires out to 2000 meters (Javelin).
- Provide its own fires with an organic mortar section.
- Conduct sniper operations with its organic sniper team.
- Block dismounted avenues of approach.
- Protect obstacles and prevent enemy breaching operations.
- Establish strongpoints to deny the enemy key terrain or flank positions.
- Conduct assault breaches of obstacles.
- Clear danger areas and prepare positions for mounted elements.
- Move over terrain not trafficable by other wheeled vehicles with the Infantry squads. Infantry can move over or around most urban terrain regardless of the amount of rubble or damage to buildings. Infantry small-arms fire within a building can eliminate resistance without seriously damaging the structure.

4-17. Operational limitations of the ICV-equipped company team in UO include—

- ICVs that are vulnerable to enemy antiarmor fires.
- Infantry squads that are vulnerable to small-arms and indirect fires.
- The pace of dismounted offensive operations that is limited to the foot speed of the Soldiers.
- ICVs that pose a variety of difficulties in water-crossing operations, including the requirement for either adequate fording sites or a bridge with sufficient weight classification.
- Infantry firepower that is predominately small-arms and shoulder-fired munitions.
- Dismounted Infantry movement that is slow.

MOBILE GUN SYSTEM CAPABILITIES AND LIMITATIONS

4-18. In UO, the MGS platoon—

- Is fully protected against antipersonnel mines, fragmentation effects, and small-arms fire.
- Has excellent mobility along unblocked routes.
- Has armored vehicle thermal sights that detect activity in daylight, darkness, and through smoke.
- Projects a psychological presence with their firepower.

- Can monitor large areas of a city with mounted patrols while making their presence known to the entire populace, both friendly and unfriendly.
- Delivers both devastating close-in direct fires and accurate long-range fire beyond the range of Infantry small-arms weapons with the 105-mm main gun.

4-19. In UO, the MGS platoon—

- Has limited visibility to the sides and rear and no visibility to the top. Exposed crews have good all-round vision but are susceptible to enemy small-arms fire and fragmentation. Target acquisition and identification is difficult unless the vehicle commander is exposed or dismounted Soldiers direct the vehicle.
- Cannot elevate or depress the main gun enough to engage targets very close to the vehicle or high up in nearby buildings. Main gun fire may cause significant collateral damage and even destabilize basic structures. The length of the MGS main gun may prevent the turret from rotating if the main gun encounters a solid object, such as a wall or post. (See figure 4-1.)
- Is vulnerable to close-in enemy light and medium antiarmor weapons, especially those fired from above ground level.
- Can be blocked by improvised barricades, narrow streets and alleyways, or large amounts of rubble.

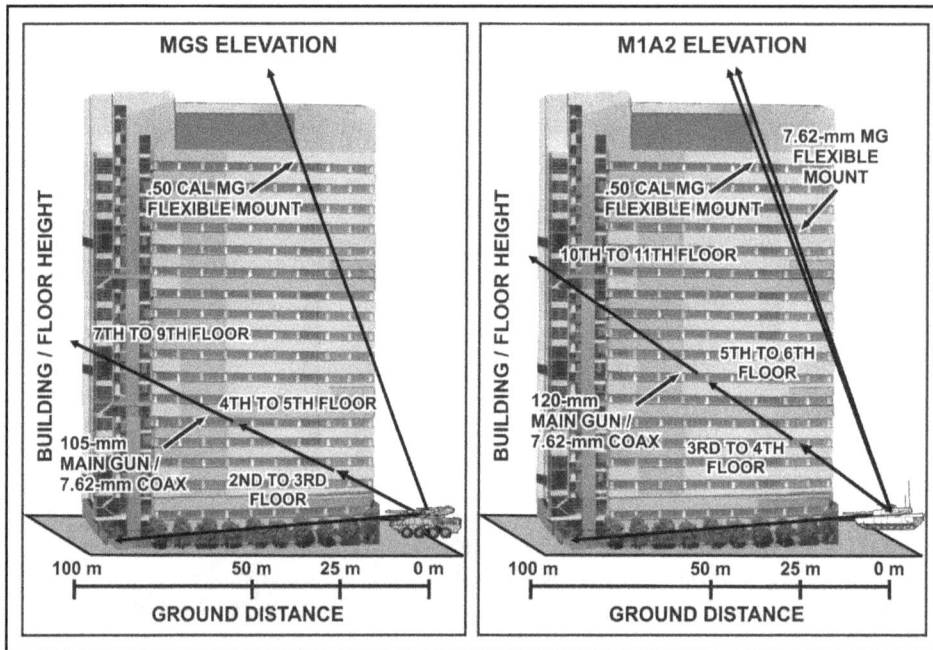

Figure 4-1. Main gun elevation and depression

SECTION II – MISSION COMMAND

4-20. Mission command enhances the company commander's ability to make sound and timely decisions. Success in operations demands timely and effective decisions based on applying judgment to available information and knowledge. Commanders and staff members make countless decisions throughout an operation under constantly changing conditions. They use the mission variables, in combination with the operational variables, to refine their understanding of the situation and to visualize, describe, and direct operations.

TASK ORGANIZATION

4-21. Based on an analysis of the mission variables, the company commander determines the decisive, shaping, and sustaining operations. The commander also determines the requirements for the assault, breach, support, security, and reserve forces. The commanders should task organize to obtain the right mix of forces, capabilities, and expertise to accomplish a specific mission by integrating elements that are attached, placed under operational control, or placed in direct support.

4-22. When task organizing tanks within the company team the following guidelines apply. These guidelines also apply to MGS, BFVs, and ICVs.

- Tanks should be used as sections. Single tanks may operate in support of Infantry. However, tanks should operate as sections. If using tanks to shield squads and teams from building to building as part of the maneuver plan, the leader of the forward element needs to control the tanks.
- If the company commander is controlling the tanks, he needs to move forward to a position where he can effectively employ the tanks in support of the Infantry.
- Task organization should support the span of control. If the company commander is going to control the tanks, then there is no reason to task organize the tanks by section under Infantry platoons.

TROOP-LEADING PROCEDURES

4-23. Troop-leading procedures begin when the leader receives the first indication of an upcoming mission and continue throughout the operational process of planning, preparing, executing, and assessing. The troop-leading procedures comprise a sequence of actions that help leaders use available time effectively and efficiently to issue orders and execute tactical operations. Some actions may be performed simultaneously.

4-24. The troop-leading procedures are not a hard and fast set of rules. They are a guide that should be applied consistent with the situation and experience of the commander and his subordinate leaders. The standard Army planning process embedded within the troop-leading procedures consists of a series of interrelated subprocesses. (See FM 5-0 for details on each process.)

COMPOSITE RISK MANAGEMENT

4-25. Integration of composite risk management at each level of command allows small-unit leaders to conduct parallel planning. (See FM 5-19 for details.)

MISSION COMMAND

4-26. Urban operations require centralized planning and decentralized execution. Therefore, effective vertical and horizontal communications are critical. Leaders should trust the initiative and skill of their subordinates. This philosophy of directing operations encourages and assists subordinates in taking action consistent with the intent and concept of higher headquarters. Mission command requires a clear understanding by subordinate elements of the unit's purpose. At the same time, it provides them with the freedom to react to enemy actions without further guidance. The underlying guidelines of this mission command philosophy are described below.

EXPECT UNCERTAINTY

4-27. The commander must understand the urban environment. Urban operations are dynamic, and the enemy is uncooperative. Communications may be degraded by the urban terrain, and the chaos of battle may prevent the company commander from knowing what is happening beyond the reach of his own senses. The situation the unit anticipates during the planning phase inevitably changes before and during execution.

ALLOW MAXIMUM FREEDOM OF ACTION FOR SUBORDINATES

4-28. Given the expected battlefield conditions, leaders at every level should avoid placing unnecessary limits on their Soldiers' freedom of action. The leader at the point of decision should have the knowledge, training, and freedom necessary to make the correct choice in support of the commander's intent. This concept should be emphasized at every opportunity and at every level of leadership.

4-29. When Soldiers expect the commander to make every decision or initiate every action, they may become reluctant to act. To counter this tendency, the commander should plan and direct operations in a manner requiring minimal intervention. He operates on the principle that some loss of precision is better than inactivity.

4-30. However, the commander should be prepared to provide subordinates with the criteria and guidance for making decisions when required for synchronization. During the planning process, he should identify those few critical decisions that are required during the battle and then determine the criteria for initiation of actions associated with these decisions. Examples include the use of engagement criteria, trigger lines, and disengagement criteria. The commander then disseminates the decision criteria throughout the company team.

4-31. The commander should keep in mind that changing conditions and unexpected situations require him to make decisions continuously once the battle begins. His preparations related to critical decisions allow him and his subordinates to react more effectively when changes become necessary.

4-32. Soldiers win battles. Their leaders can only place them in a position where they are able to seize the opportunity to do so. Subordinates are successful on the battlefield only if their commanders and leaders have fostered the necessary confidence and initiative before the battle begins.

OPTIMIZE PLANNING TIME FOR SUBORDINATES

4-33. The company commander should ensure that the timelines he develops for mission planning and preparation provide adequate troop-leading time for subordinate leaders.

ENCOURAGE CROSS TALK

4-34. Subordinate leaders do not always require guidance from the commander to address a change in the situation. In some instances, because of their position on the battlefield, two or more subordinates working together may have the clearest view of what is happening. Thus, they may be better suited than the commander to develop a tactical solution. This type of problem solving, involving direct coordination between subordinate elements, is critical to mission command. In addition to its obvious impact on mission accomplishment, it empowers subordinates to take decisive action and teaches them the value of close cooperation in achieving the unit's overall purpose.

4-35. Company commanders should also ensure that there is clear communication with adjacent units and understanding of each other's mission. This coordination may be with multinational or HN forces.

COMMAND AND LEAD WELL FORWARD

4-36. The commander positions himself where he can best fight his company team and make critical decisions to influence the outcome of the fight. This position is normally with the main effort to allow the commander to exert his leadership and to shift or refocus the main effort as necessary. He should be far enough forward to effectively control the battlefield using all available resources, to include visual observation, radio reports, and information provided over digital systems. The team executive officer (XO) is normally with the supporting effort and should be able to rapidly assume command if needed.

INFORMATION SYSTEMS

4-37. The complexities of the urban environment can restrict the application of communication technology. Structures and a high concentration of electrical power lines normally degrade FM and digital communications in urban areas. Typically, very high frequency radios are easily blocked and overall communication ranges reduced in urban areas. Many buildings are constructed so that radio waves will not pass through them. Companies may not have enough radios to communicate with subordinate elements as they enter buildings and move through urban canyons and defiles.

4-38. Consider the following to minimize the adverse effects of the urban environment on information system:

- Mission command versus detailed command.
- Restrictive control measures and shortened graphic control measures.
- Internal retransmission stations.
- Command post location.
- Location of key leaders.

4-39. Radios should be carefully located to maximize their effectiveness. Retransmission stations and remote antennas on taller structures maximize the communications range. Ground units attempting to communicate with aircraft or other ground units should use the upper end of the very high frequency band and high power switches on radios. Commanders should set limited objectives covering a small area and plan for the frequent relocation of retransmission stations. If time and mission variables permit, make maximum use of the civilian telephone system.

4-40. Visual signals may be used, but are often ineffective due to the screening effects of buildings and walls. If used, visual signals should be understood by all elements of the company team. Increased noise in urban areas makes the effective use of sound signals difficult.

4-41. Urban communications infrastructure and systems can serve as an alternate or backup means of communications for both friendly and enemy forces and can be secured with off-the-shelf technologies. Adversaries may make use of commercial systems intertwined with legitimate civilian users, making it undesirable to prevent use of these assets. Army forces can use these systems to influence public opinion, gain intelligence, support deception efforts, or otherwise support information activities.

COMPANY INTELLIGENCE SUPPORT TEAM

4-42. The company intelligence support team describes the effects of the weather, enemy, terrain, and local population upon UO to—

- Aid the commander in his decision making by bringing a fused intelligence picture down to the company.
- Assist the battalion by providing a flow of bottom-up intelligence.

4-43. The company intelligence support team—

- Manages the company's lethal and nonlethal targeting.
- Supervises the synchronization of the company's security plan.
- Manages the patrol prebrief and debrief for the company.
- Manages detainee operations.
- Manages tactical site exploitation information.

4-44. Key tasks of the company intelligence support team include—

- Collecting data and conducting pattern analysis.
- Collecting and analyzing patrol debriefs.
- Collecting biometric data.
- Tracking and analyzing all significant activities.
- Generating analytical, assessment, and mission summary products for the commander.
- Conducting local intelligence analysis, forecasting enemy actions, and preparing the threat situation template.
- Maintaining updated intelligence boards for outgoing patrols.
- Conducting predictive analysis and maintaining a predictive analysis board identifying likely enemy activities.

- Recommending company priority information requirements and specific information requirements to the commander.
- Providing deception recommendations to the commander.

SECTION III – UNDERSTAND

4-45. Across the spectrum of conflict in urban areas, powerful combined arms teams produce the best results. Companies conducting UO need to accomplish many Infantry-specific tasks. However, operations conducted by pure Infantry units have often proven to be unsound. Appropriately tasked-organized combined arms teams, integrating all available warfighting function capabilities, are needed to conduct successful full spectrum UO. Considerations based on the mission variables should include interpreters, military information support operations units, UAS and other aviation assets, HN forces, multinational forces, and sniper teams.

4-46. Below are the considerations that apply for company-size combined arms teams.

CHANGING CONDITIONS

4-47. Company teams may find themselves executing missions in changing conditions during UO, from stability operations to combat operations and vice versa. The mission variables and the ROE determine this change. Changes to the ROE are made at echelons higher than company, but they require that units modify the way they fight in urban areas. Companies select different tactics and techniques based on the conditions they face.

SMALL-UNIT BATTLES

4-48. Units conducting UO often become or feel isolated, making combat a series of small-unit battles. Soldiers and squad or team leaders must have the initiative, skill, and courage to accomplish their missions while isolated from their parent units. A skilled, well-trained defender has tactical advantages over the attacker in this type of combat. The defender may occupy strong covered and concealed static positions and conduct ambushes, whereas the attacker must be exposed in order to advance. Greatly reduced line of sight ranges, built-in obstacles, and compartmented terrain may require the commitment of more troops for a given AO. While the defense of an urban area can be conducted effectively with relatively small numbers of troops, the troop density required for an attack in urban areas may be greater than that for an attack in open terrain.

PERSONNEL RECOVERY

4-49. Company commanders should incorporate personnel recovery planning into all full spectrum UO. Personnel recovery guidance should synchronize the actions of commanders and staffs, recovery forces, and isolated individuals. In order to synchronize the actions of all three, commanders develop personnel recovery guidance based on command capabilities to conduct recovery operations. This requires understanding the complex, dynamic relationships among friendly forces, enemies, and the environment (including the populace). (See FM 3-37 for details.)

4-50. At company level, personnel recovery guidance becomes isolated Soldier guidance. Isolated Soldier guidance is a specific directive to individual Soldiers that defines the events that constitute being isolated and the actions to take during an isolating event.

SNIPERS

4-51. Snipers are especially useful in urban areas. They can provide long- and short-range precision fires and can help with company- and platoon-level isolation efforts. Snipers also provide valuable precision fires during stability operations. Along with engaging assigned targets, snipers are a valuable asset to the commander for providing observation along movement routes and suppressive fires during an assault.

COORDINATION

4-52. Coordination between all elements task organized to the company team should be close and continuous. Continuous coordination should also be maintained with reconnaissance elements, adjacent units, and any HN and multinational forces. The complexity of situations and intense noise are barriers to close coordination and mission command for which commands must plan.

SECTION IV – SHAPE

4-53. Tactical enabling operations executed during full spectrum UO are specialized missions planned and conducted to achieve or sustain a tactical advantage. The fluid nature of the battlefield increases the frequency with which the Infantry company plans and executes the below enabling operations.

RECONNAISSANCE AND SECURITY

4-54. Because of its composition and capabilities, the reconnaissance troop is ideally suited to conduct the reconnaissance in urban areas. Leaders and Soldiers should understand the situation at regional, local, and neighborhood levels. Commanders should learn how the urban area operates and how to identify sources of power or influence. Examples of this information include the—

- Formal and informal political power structure.
- Police, secret police, and intelligence agencies.
- Religious leaders.
- Criminal organizations.
- Military and paramilitary structures.
- Key terrain.

4-55. The most important and potentially most confusing factors to reconnaissance units that influence the complexity of UO are noncombatants and the human dimension. Furthermore, man-made features significantly affect systems and units and, thus, tactics and operations.

RECONNAISSANCE

4-56. The reconnaissance troop conducts reconnaissance of the urban area to gain information on the objective and provide timely, accurate, and actionable information to the squadron. Depending on the time available, the troop develops the urban situation progressively from the surrounding area toward the city. The commander refines objectives and routes as he gains and analyzes information. Using data obtained from sensors (such as Prophet, UAS, or aerial reconnaissance), assets conduct aerial reconnaissance of routes and objective areas. Unmanned aircraft systems focus on entry points to develop the enemy situation, such as obstacles, ambush positions on rooftops, or movement of enemy personnel and vehicles as friendly units approach.

4-57. The troop orients on the objective by occupying or observing key terrain and enemy avenues of approach. Reconnaissance platoons use their sensors and optics to conduct long-range surveillance and to locate enemy positions and vehicles prior to forces entering the urban area. The commander compiles and analyzes the information gathered by the platoons. He then assesses the AO according to the mission and intent of the squadron commander. The assessment includes, but is not limited to, the—

- Enemy composition and activity.
- Areas of vulnerability to friendly forces.
- Key terrain.
- Approach routes for mounted and dismounted forces.
- Entry points or points of penetration.
- Support positions for direct and indirect fire assets.
- Civilian disposition.
- Density and composition of the urban area.

- Hazard areas (such as fuel storage, natural gas lines, and chemical production sites).
- Key infrastructure (communication facilities, water treatment facilities, religious or culturally sensitive sites.)

4-58. The result of the reconnaissance troop's effort occurs when the commander can provide answers to two critical questions for the squadron.

- Is it essential to conduct operations in the urban environment?
- If so, how can the squadron or higher headquarters employ combat power in the most efficient manner?

SECURITY

4-59. The troop performs security missions to provide the BCT with early and accurate warning during UO. This prevents the main body from being surprised and preserves the combat power of the maneuver force for decisive employment. Critical information includes the size, composition, location, direction, and rate of movement of the enemy. Terrain information focuses on obstacles, avenues of approach, and key terrain features that affect movement. The intent is to provide information that gives the commander reaction time and the maneuver space necessary to effectively fight the enemy.

4-60. Current trends stress the likelihood of conducting operations in noncontiguous, extended AOs, possibly creating significant gaps. Despite continual evolution of sophisticated sensors and collection assets, situational awareness is never perfect. This is true especially in periods of limited visibility or adverse weather. Uncertainty will always be present in the urban AO.

4-61. The troop may conduct or support any of the five primary forms of security during UO (screen, guard, cover, area security, and local security). During the conduct of security operations, reconnaissance elements may—

- Call for and adjust indirect fires.
- Identify, isolate, and prevent enemy forces from escaping within unit capabilities.
- Identify, interdict, and provide early warning of enemy reinforcement of the urban area within unit capabilities.
- Perform counterreconnaissance.

MOVEMENT AND MANEUVER

4-62. Combined arms teams work together to provide mutual support and bring the maximum combat power available to bear on the enemy. ICVs, BFVs, MGS, M1 tanks, and vehicle-mounted weapons are powerful systems for supporting assault forces to isolate the objective area and secure a foothold.

4-63. Reconnaissance and maneuver forces locate and identify targets for the supporting Armor elements to engage. As the maneuver force moves to clear the urban area, supporting elements remain in initial support-by-fire positions.

4-64. When possible, supporting elements should move to subsequent positions where their direct fires can prevent enemy armor or mechanized reinforcement from attacking the objective and can engage those enemy forces withdrawing from the objective.

MOBILITY

4-65. The engineer company is tailored to fight as part of the combined arms team. It focuses on mobility but also provides limited countermobility and survivability engineer support.

4-66. An engineer platoon may be task organized to a company based on the mission variables. However, the engineer platoon lacks organic sustainment assets and has minimal combat systems. Thus, it usually requires augmentation or external support to conduct continuous operations over a sustained period of time.

4-67. The engineer platoon may also require some augmentation to conduct combined arms tasks, such as breaching buildings. The engineer platoon may receive augmentation from its engineer company or other units as required. In this role, the engineer platoon may conduct covert breaches, route reconnaissance, and obstacle reduction. It may also identify potential enemy counterattack routes to establish countermobility measures, such as scatterable mines, to protect the force.

INFORMATION TASKS

4-68. Information efforts aimed at influencing non-Army sources of information are critical in UO. Because of the density of noncombatants and information sources, the media, the public, multinational partners, neutral nations, and strategic leadership are likely to scrutinize how units plan and conduct UO. Properly conducted IPB results in a focused reconnaissance and security plan that produces timely, accurate, predictive, and actionable intelligence. A method to confirm or deny an intelligence assessment in UO is the conduct of persistent surveillance by reconnaissance units.

4-69. While information tasks are planned at levels above the brigade, tactical units conducting UO may often be involved in the execution of inform and influence and cyber/electromagnetic activities. See chapter 1 for additional information on inform and influence and cyber/electromagnetic activities.

FIRES

4-70. Even under the most favorable conditions, synchronizing fires and maneuver is difficult enough. If not properly planned and prepared for, its attainment becomes decidedly less likely. In UO, the procedures for obtaining precision fires are the same for offensive, defensive, and stability operations. Successful targeting enables the commander to synchronize intelligence, maneuver, fires, and SOFs by attacking the right target with the best system at the right time. (See FM 3-09.31 for details.)

4-71. Collateral damage estimates and precision targeting are necessary in UO. Specially trained and certified FS teams using precision strike suite for SOFs determines, refine, and transmit precise coordinates to strike units for precision strike munitions more quickly and easily.

4-72. The approval process, based on the political sensitivity of engaging UO targets in certain situations, can reside at command levels higher than the requesting commander. The targeting team should completely understand this process, the target details, and the commander's intent.

4-73. Guidance to the FS coordinator does not have to be any different than the guidance given to the subordinate maneuver commanders. Give appropriate doctrinally stated—

- **Tasks.** Tasks describe targeting effects against a specific enemy formation's function or capability.
- **Purposes.** Purposes describe how targeting effects contribute to accomplishing the mission within the intent.

4-74. The initial planning guidance for FS becomes the basis for the scheme of fires and the fires paragraph. Synchronization in the plan depends largely on the commander's ability to issue planning guidance that causes development of integrated COAs.

4-75. Consider the following when deciding what to issue for FS guidance:

- Preferred FS system for the engagement of HPTs.
- Guidance for fires. Consider stating the task as an effect on the enemy.
- Developing a specific task and purpose for each FS asset (field artillery, mortars, close air support) during each phase of the operation.
- Employment of FS teams retained under battalion control and any BCT combat observation and lasing teams allocated to maneuver battalions.
- Special munitions, such as illumination use, smoke and white phosphorus, ground- and air-launched terminally guided munitions, and scatterable mines.
- Synchronization of counterfire or counterbattery responsibilities planned by the battalion FS coordinator with the BCT or the counterfire headquarters.
- Suppression or destruction of enemy air defense guidance.
- FS coordination measures.

- Protected target list, to include ROE guidance.
- Guidance for final protective fires, minimum safe distances, and risk estimate distances.
- Commander's engagement criteria on the size and type of unit fires should engage at select points in the operation.

PROTECTION

4-76. Air defense units may operate in and around the company AO. However, the company is unlikely to receive task-organized air defense units. It relies on disciplined, passive air defense measures and the ability to engage aerial platforms actively with organic weapons systems. Soldiers should be familiar with air defense units, capabilities, operational procedures, and self-defense measures.

4-77. CBRN weapons can cause casualties, destroy or disable equipment, restrict the use of terrain, and disrupt operations. They may be used separately or in combination to supplement conventional weapons. The company should be prepared to fight on a CBRN-contaminated battlefield. CBRN detection and decontamination units within the company are limited. To survive on a contaminated battlefield, the company should practice the fundamentals of CBRN defense, avoidance, protection, and decontamination. (See FM 3-11.4 for details.)

AIR-GROUND INTEGRATION

4-78. Operations should be integrated so that air and ground forces can work simultaneously to achieve a common objective. Integration maximizes combat power through synergy of both forces. The synchronization of aviation operations into the ground commander's scheme of maneuver may require the integration of joint or multinational aviation units, to include helicopters, UAS, and fixed-wing aircraft.

4-79. If available, digital transmission of information, such as coordinates, is faster and more accurate. Voice communications are necessary to verify information and to clarify needs and intentions. The minimum information required by the Army aviation team to ensure accurate and timely support includes the—

- Situation, including locations of friendly forces, ground tactical plan, enemy situation, known enemy air defense artillery in the AO, mission requests, and tentative EA coordinates.
- BCT- and battalion-level graphics update via the Maneuver Control System, Aviation Mission Planning Software, or radio communications, updating critical items (such as limit of advance, fire control measures, and maneuver graphics).
- FS coordination information, to include location of direct support artillery and organic mortars, call signs, and frequencies.
- Ingress and egress routes in the AO, to include passage points into the AO and air route to the holding area or LZ.
- Call signs and frequencies of the battalion in contact, down to the company in contacts. Air-ground coordination should be done on command frequencies to provide situational awareness for all elements involved.
- Global Positioning System (GPS) and Single-Channel Ground and Airborne Radio System (SINCGARS) time coordination. Ensure that all units are operating on the same time.

SECTION V – ENGAGE

4-80. The complexity of urban environments requires the combination of offensive, defensive, and stability operations as part of unified action to defeat the enemy and establish the conditions that achieve the commander's end state.

OFFENSE

4-81. Like all offensive operations, offensive UO are designed to impose the commander's will on the enemy. Offensive operations in an urban environment aim to destroy, defeat, or neutralize an enemy force.

However, the purpose may be to achieve some effect relating to the population or infrastructure of the urban area. No matter the purpose, commanders should use a combined arms approach for successful offensive UO.

4-82. Urban offensive success depends on the following operations, of which two or more usually occur simultaneously:

- **Decisive.** Decisive operations are attacks at a series of decisive points that conclusively determine the outcome of UO.
- **Shaping.** Shaping operations create the conditions for decisive operations. In UO, much of the shaping effort focuses on isolation.
- **Sustaining.** Sustaining operations in offensive UO ensure freedom of action. They occur throughout the AO and for the duration of the operation.

DEFENSE

4-83. Company forces defend urban areas to defeat an attack, gain time, economize forces, protect infrastructure, protect a populace, and shape conditions for offensive or stability UO. Usually two or more of these purposes apply to the urban defense. Defensive UO provide commanders opportunities to turn the environment's characteristics to the advantage of Army forces. Urban areas are ideal for defensive operations and enhance the combat power of defending units.

4-84. Urban defensive success depends on synchronizing the following simultaneous operations as one action:

- **Decisive.** Decisive operations may not be effective if those tasks are not integrated into the overall mission plan.
- **Shaping.** Shaping operations vary greatly depending on the type of defense and create the conditions for decisive operations.
- **Sustaining.** Sustaining operations ensure freedom of action, secure lines of communications, and establish movement control.

STABILITY

4-85. Stability operations are complex and demanding. The company team in a stability operation must master a variety of skills. The tasks that may be conducted at the company level during stability operations are—

- Establish and occupy a lodgment area or forward operating base.
- Negotiate.
- Monitor compliance with an agreement.
- Enforce cessation of hostilities.
- Establish observation posts.
- Establish checkpoints.
- Search.
- Patrol.
- Escort a convoy.
- Open and secure routes.
- Conduct reserve operations.
- Control crowds.

4-86. All UO, especially stability operations, are subject to influence from the civil population and nonmilitary organizations. Commanders who can understand and cope with the complexities of stability operations gain insights that directly apply to executing any UO.

4-87. Urban stability operations may complement urban offensive and defensive operations or may dominate the overall operation. Companies may need to conduct offensive and defensive operations to defend themselves or destroy enemy seeking to prevent the decisive stability mission.

4-88. Commanders should expect to operate in a fluid environment. They must learn, adapt, and live with ambiguity. They cannot expect to operate in a political vacuum. They should expect to work alongside both governmental and nongovernmental leaders and organizations. Commanders should expect to show restraint with a keen sensitivity to political considerations and to foreign cultures.

4-89. Soldiers cannot become too complacent or too eager to rely on the use of force to resolve conflict. They should remain calm and exercise good judgment under considerable pressure. This balance is the essence of stability operations and the fundamental aspect that ensures mission success. Proactive leaders that communicate and enforce the ROE are instrumental in achieving this mindset. (See FM 3-07 for details.)

PLANNING CONSIDERATIONS

4-90. The commander acquires and develops intelligence for stability operations much the same as other operations. The principle difference is in its focus. At lower echelons, political, economic, linguistic, and ethnic factors assume greater relevance to the mission.

4-91. Initial considerations for stability operations are—
- Implement the five stability tasks.
- Maintain a constant, forward presence with the population.
- React to the ambush of patrols and fire on helicopters.
- Use countersniper operations, especially at roadblocks, outposts, and sentry posts.
- Avoid overreaction to enemy activity.
- Emphasize countermeasures against explosive hazards (to include IEDs and mines).
- Control access to weapons, uniforms, and other supplies the enemy may use.
- Acquire and disseminate timely, accurate, relevant, and predictive intelligence.
- Protect industry and public services from attack and sabotage.
- Prevent riots, protests, and other large population incidents.
- Ensure the population has the basic level of essential services.
- Develop relationships with host nation officials.

TASK ORGANIZATION

4-92. Because of the unique requirements of stability operations, the company is usually task organized with a variety of units. This includes some elements with which the company does not normally work, such as linguists, counterintelligence teams, military information support operations teams, and civil affairs teams. Unless the commander is conducting battlefield circulation, the company CP is likely located within the forward operating base during platoon-level shaping operations.

4-93. In conducting stability operations, the company commander organizes his forces for the type of mission to be performed, integrating attached units to accomplish the mission. The company organization should enable the unit to meet changing situations. Thus, the commander should consider which resources to allocate to platoon or squads and which to maintain control of at the company headquarters. Task organization and support arrangements change frequently during long-term stability operations. Commanders should frequently shift the support of engineers, medical units, and aviation units from one area or task to another.

SHAPING OPERATIONS

4-94. Although not considered stability tasks, inform and influence and cyber/electromagnetic activities are fundamental to stability operations. Inform and influence and cyber/electromagnetic activities are integrated in each stability operation and primary stability task to complement and reinforce the success of operations. These activities should be carefully sequenced with other tasks and supported with thorough risk assessments. Exploiting or ceding the initiative within the information domain is often a matter of precise timing and coordination. Combined with broad efforts to reduce the drivers of conflict and build HN capacity, inform and influence and cyber/electromagnetic activities are essential to achieving decisive results.

4-95. Commanders should implement appropriate security measures to protect the force. Offensive measures, to include aggressive patrolling and offensive actions taken against identified enemy forces, are usually the most effective. Aggressive intelligence gathering and analysis greatly increases the commander's situational understanding. As the commander's situational understanding increases, he can more aggressively and accurately identify, deter, capture, or destroy enemy elements. Defensive survivability measures include the establishment of various CPs, effective base camp security procedures, and protection against IEDs and unexploded ordnance.

SECTION VI – CONSOLIDATE

4-96. During UO, the terrain and nature of operations create unique demands on the company sustainment system. Solutions to these challenges require innovative techniques and in-depth planning.

GUIDELINES

4-97. The following guidelines for sustainment exist regardless of UO conditions:
- Preconfigure resupply loads and push them forward at every opportunity.
- Provide supplies in required quantities as close as possible to the location where they are needed.
- Protect supplies and sustainment elements from the effects of enemy fire by seeking cover and avoiding detection.
- Disperse and decentralize sustainment elements with proper emphasis on communication, command, control, security, and proximity of main supply route for resupply.
- Plan for carrying parties and litter bearers.
- Plan for and use host nation support and civil resources when practical.
- Position support units as far forward as the tactical situation permits.

SOLDIER'S LOAD

4-98. The Soldier's load is a crucial concern for all leaders. This is especially true during UO, where physical and mental stresses are combined with the need to carry additional ammunition and water. Urban combat places additional physical stress on Soldiers, partly because of the additional weight they carry.

4-99. The company commander should be directly involved in load planning and management. He must weigh the needs of the mission, based on the mission variables, against the physical reality of what a Soldier can carry into the fight.

TYPES

4-100. The Soldier's load is divided into three major types—combat load, sustainment load, and contingency load. The combat load is the minimum mission-essential equipment as determined by the commander. This includes only what is needed to fight and survive immediate operations.

4-101. The combat load is further broken down into two levels—fighting load and approach march load. The fighting load is what the Soldier carries once contact has been made with the enemy. It consists of only essential items the Soldier needs to accomplish his task during the engagement.

MANAGEMENT TECHNIQUES

4-102. Soldiers usually carry more than the recommended 48-pound fighting load during urban combat, which fatigues Soldiers and creates a greater amount of physical exertion. Commanders should be aware of this fact and manage loads accordingly. (See FM 21-18 for details.) Key load management techniques for UO are—
- Distribute loads throughout the unit. Have the assault element carry only the items necessary to accomplish the mission (usually ammunition and water). Designate individuals in the support element to bring additional ammunition, medical supplies, and water forward as the tactical situation permits.
- Designate individuals to perform breaches and modify ammunition loads accordingly. Rotate

these individuals when they tire or after they have made numerous breaches.

● Rotate the assault element after each intermediate objective is secured as the tactical situation permits. Try to maintain fresh assault troops to the maximum extent possible.

● Use additional transportation units to carry loads.

● Avoid unnecessary movement and displacements to conserve the Soldiers' stamina.

● Closely supervise precombat inspections to ensure Soldiers carry only necessary items.

SECTION VII – TRANSITION

4-103.   Urban operations of all types are resource intensive. Thus, commanders should plan to conclude UO quickly yet consistent with successful mission accomplishment. The end state of all UO ultimately transfers control of the urban area to another agency or returns it to civilian control. This requires the successful completion of the mission and a thorough transition plan.

4-104.   Transitions between the different elements of full spectrum operations are difficult and may create unexpected opportunities for both friendly and enemy forces during execution. Commanders must quickly recognize such opportunities, developing transitions as branches during the planning process and acting on them immediately as they occur. Flexibility in transitioning contributes to a successful operation.

4-105.   The transition plan may include returning control of the urban area to another agency a portion at a time as conditions permit. For companies, transition may include changing missions from combat operations to stability operations or vice versa. It may also include providing training and assistance to HN security forces.

Chapter 5

Offensive Urban Operations

Urban offensive operations, like all operations, are arranged using the organization of decisive, shaping, and sustaining operations (FM 3-06). The company commander maneuvers his forces to advantageous positions before contact. Protection tasks, such as security operations, operations security, and information protection, inhibit the enemy from acquiring accurate information about the composition and location of the company team. Contact with enemy forces before the decisive operation is deliberate, designed to shape the optimum situation for the decisive operation. The decisive operation is a sudden action that capitalizes on subordinate initiative. The company team executes violently without hesitation to break the enemy's will or destroy him.

SECTION I – CHARACTERISTICS

5-1. All offensive operations, including those in urban areas, contain the characteristics of surprise, concentration, tempo, and audacity. Commanders consider and incorporate these characteristics in their offensive UO plans. (See FM 3-0 for details.)

SURPRISE

5-2. Army forces can achieve offensive surprise at two levels—operational and tactical. The goal is to attack the urban area before the enemy expects or from a direction or in a manner he does not expect. At lower tactical levels, forces achieve surprise by attacking asymmetrically. An asymmetric method attacks the enemy so he cannot respond effectively. Attacking from unexpected or multiple directions achieves surprise by leveraging Army information system and superior synchronization of combat power and capabilities.

CONCENTRATION

5-3. In UO, the attacking force creates a major advantage by concentrating the effects of combat power at the point and time of its choosing. The environment hinders repositioning forces rapidly. Successful UO need synchronized air and ground maneuver with overwhelming effects from fires at decisive points on the urban battlefield.

TEMPO

5-4. Tactical tempo is important in urban combat. Because of the complex terrain, defending forces can rapidly occupy and defend from a position of strength. Once offensive operations are initiated, the defender cannot be allowed to set the tempo of the operation. Creating and operating at a tempo faster than an opponent can maintain favors forces that are better led, trained, prepared, and resourced.

AUDACITY

5-5. In an urban attack, a thorough understanding of the physical terrain can mitigate risk. The terrain's complexity can be studied to reveal advantages to the attacker. Well-trained Soldiers who are confident in their ability to execute offensive UO foster audacity.

SECTION II – SEQUENCING

5-6. The sequence for conducting offensive UO is—
- Gain and maintain enemy contact.
- Disrupt the enemy.
- Fix the enemy.
- Maneuver.
- Follow through.

5-7. Depending on the mission variables, the sequence of offensive operations may be conducted simultaneously or sequentially. However, it is not the only way to conduct offensive operations. Normally the first three of these steps are shaping operations, while the maneuver step is the decisive operation. The follow-through step is normally a sequel or a branch to the plan based on the revised situation. (See chapter 2 for a complete discussion.)

SECTION III – TASK ORGANIZATION CONSIDERATIONS

5-8. A flexible and well-rounded task organization is critical for successful offensive UO. The task organization of a company team conducting offensive UO varies according to the specific nature of the urban area and objective. The actual task organization is determined by the mission variables.

5-9. Whereas task organization is normally done no lower than platoon level, UO may require task organization of squads and sections. The company team may face a number of unusual organizational options, such as a tank section working with an Infantry platoon. Additionally, task organizations change as the mission transitions from offensive to defensive or stability operations.

ELEMENTS

5-10. The four organization elements common to an urban attack are described below.

SUPPORT

5-11. The support element provides immediate suppressive fire, enabling the assault element to close with the enemy and to provide any other required support. Normally, most mounted elements of the unit are task organized in the support force. This allows the company team commander to employ the firepower of the fighting vehicles while reducing their vulnerability to enemy short-range weapons and explosive devices. The support force isolates the AO and the actual entry point into the urban area, allowing assault forces to secure a foothold.

5-12. The support element may conduct additional tasks, such as—
- Conducting resupply.
- Conducting casualty evacuation.
- Handling prisoners of war.
- Securing areas cleared by the assault element.

5-13. The tactical situation dictates whether or not additional elements need to be task organized to conduct specific supporting missions. An example of an additional element is a security element. If created, this element is responsible for securing cleared rooms, floors, and stairs as the platoons continues to clear the rest of a building. However, this seriously affects the available combat power of the assault element and is best accomplished by follow-on forces or as a modification to the support element's mission.

BREACH

5-14. Breaching provides the assault element with access to an urban objective. At the company team level, breaching is normally conducted by a separate element or integrated into the assault element. However, a separate breaching element may be created, and a platoon may be given this mission and task organized accordingly.

5-15. A separate breach element often executes breaches along a route and the initial breach into a building, while an integrated breach element often executes breaches from room to room. Inherent with breaching is the marking of cleared lanes, especially lanes through exterior obstacles. Additional training and preparation time is often required for thermal, ballistic, and explosive breaching methods. Using engineers can reduce this additional training requirement. Mechanical breaching does not require much training or preparation but is often not as efficient and effective as the other methods.

ASSAULT

5-16. The assault element kills, captures, or forces the withdrawal of the enemy from an urban objective. At company level, the assault element should be reinforced with engineers and possibly armored vehicles for transportation and shielding from enemy small-arms fire. The assault element should be prepared to first breach into a building and gain a foothold and then breach into individual rooms.

5-17. Building and room clearing is typically conducted at the platoon and squad level. A common technique is to designate one squad as an assault squad with one clearing team and one support team. The clearing team clears the room or hallway, while the support team provides close-in security for the clearing team, prepared to assume the duties of the clearing team.

RESERVE

5-18. If designated, the reserve should be mobile, well forward, and prepared to become the assault element. The size of the reserve is METT-TC dependent. At company level, the reserve normally consists of a squad. At platoon level, the reserve normally consists of a fire team. To be effective, the reserve should be in position to rapidly deploy. This often means moving directly behind the assault element. Typically, the reserve is called upon to—

- Exploit an enemy weakness or friendly success.
- Clear a bypassed enemy position.
- Secure the rear or a flank.
- Defend against an enemy counterattack.
- Maintain contact with adjacent units.
- Attack from another direction.
- Conduct support by fire or attack by fire as needed.

COMPANY

5-19. As part of a battalion-level attack, the company is normally tasked as either an assault or support element with the company mortars remaining under company control. Armored vehicles and specialty attachments are task organized based on the mission variables.

- As the battalion assault element, the company typically organizes into two assault platoons, a support platoon, a breach element, and a reserve squad.
- As the battalion support element, the company typically organizes into three support platoons, with tanks or other supporting elements attached to the platoons.

5-20. For a company-level attack, the company is normally task organized similar to its organization as a battalion assault element. The mission variables are the driving force in determining the best mix of Infantry, tanks (or MGS), engineers, and other augmenting forces at the company and platoon level. While actual command and support relationships vary, Infantry and tanks (or MGS) are often task organized down to the platoon level. To be effective, units and leaders must understand the capabilities and limitations of these attached elements and should rehearse with them prior to operations.

5-21. At the company level, the tank (or MGS) platoon either remains as a maneuver platoon or is task organized to support Infantry platoons. Tanks should not operate in elements smaller than sections as their tactics, training, and communication systems are designed to work at section level and higher. This is also true for the MGS if supporting an Infantry platoon other than a Stryker Infantry platoon. When task organized, the tank or MGS leader recommends to the attached leader the optimal employment of his unit.

The five basic techniques of task organizing a tank or MGS platoon into an Infantry company are described below.

TANK OR MOBILE GUN SYSTEM PLATOON PURE UNDER COMPANY CONTROL

5-22. In this technique, the tank (or MGS) platoon leader is responsible for maneuvering their tanks (or MGS) in accordance with the company commander's intent.

5-23. Advantages of this technique are—
- Tank platoon leader controls and maneuvers tanks.
- Excellent for support-by-fire, attack-by-fire, overwatch, counterattack, or reserve missions.
- The company has a maneuver platoon.
- Tanks may still operate in two tank sections.

5-24. Disadvantages of this technique are—
- Tank and Infantry maneuver is difficult to synchronize, especially for the close-in fight.
- Tank platoon leader lacks knowledge of Infantry, Stryker, and BFV platoon tactics and techniques.
- Tank platoon is not capable of clearing a building without Infantry support.
- Company commander is responsible for effectively employing the tanks and should be well forward. When not employed, their firepower goes unused.
- Difficult for the tank (or MGS) platoon to effectively support more than one Infantry, Stryker, or BFV platoon at a time.

INFANTRY SQUADS UNDER TANK OR MOBILE GUN SYSTEM PLATOON CONTROL

5-25. In this technique, the company commander places one or more Infantry squad (typically one squad per section) under the operational control of the tank or MGS platoon leader.

5-26. Advantages of this technique are—
- The company has another maneuver platoon.
- Tank platoon leader controls and maneuvers his tanks.
- Excellent for support-by-fire, attack-by-fire, overwatch, counterattack, or reserve missions.
- Excellent protection against the close-in antiarmor threat.
- May still operate as two tank sections.

5-27. Disadvantages of this technique are—
- Tank and Infantry maneuver is difficult to synchronize, especially for the close-in fight.
- Requires time for platoon and tank section combined planning and rehearsals.
- Tank platoon has limited ability to clear buildings.

TANK OR MOBILE GUN SYSTEM SECTIONS UNDER INFANTRY PLATOON CONTROL

5-28. In this technique, tanks or MGS are broken down into two sections, with each section supporting an Infantry platoon. The MGS platoon, consisting of three vehicles, may breakdown into one section and one vehicle. The single MGS vehicle operates in accordance with the technique of tanks or MGS operating individually under platoon control.

5-29. Advantages of this technique are—
- Allows for the continuous close-in support of two Infantry, Stryker, or BFV platoons.
- Tank rate of movement matches the Infantry, Stryker, or BFV platoon movement.

5-30. Disadvantages of this technique are—
- Requires time for platoon and tank section combined planning and rehearsals.
- Infantry platoon leaders are burdened with the responsibility of maneuvering tanks (or MGS).

TANK OR MOBILE GUN SYSTEM SECTIONS SPLIT UNDER COMPANY AND PLATOON CONTROL

5-31. In this technique, tanks or MGS are broken down into two sections, with one under company control and the other under platoon control. The MGS platoon, consisting of three vehicles, may breakdown into one section and one vehicle. The single MGS vehicle operates in accordance with the technique of tanks or MGS operating individually under platoon control.

5-32. Advantages of this technique are—
- Allows for the continuous close-in support of one Infantry, Stryker, or BFV platoon.
- Tank platoon leader controls and maneuvers a section of his tanks.
- Supports limited support-by-fire, attack-by-fire, overwatch, counterattack, or reserve missions.
- Tank rate of movement matches the Infantry, Stryker, or BFV platoon movement.
- Company commander retains a tank (or MGS) platoon as a maneuver element.

5-33. Disadvantages of this technique are—
- Tank and Infantry maneuver is difficult to synchronize, especially for the close-in fight.
- Requires time for platoon and tank section combined planning and rehearsals.
- Company commander is responsible for effectively employing the tanks. When not employed, their firepower is unused.

TANK OR MOBILE GUN SYSTEM OPERATING INDIVIDUALLY UNDER PLATOON CONTROL

5-34. In this technique, individual tanks or MGS support Infantry platoons. The MGS platoon, consisting of three vehicles, breaks down into one vehicle per platoon, while the tank platoon, at four vehicles, usually places one tank with the company headquarters element. This is the least preferred method, except for the MGS if operating with the platoons of their assigned company.

5-35. Advantages of this technique are—
- Each platoon has one tank for close in support.
- Tank rate of movement matches the Infantry, Stryker, or BFV platoon movement.

5-36. Disadvantages of this technique are—
- Requires time for combined planning and rehearsals.
- Infantry leaders are burdened with responsibility of maneuvering a tank (or MGS).
- Individual tanks or MGS are dependent on their supporting Infantry unit for sustainment.

PLATOON

5-37. As part of a company-level attack, a platoon is normally tasked as an assault or support element. As a company assault element, the platoon typically organizes into two assault squads, with two assault teams each, and attaches their machine guns and armored vehicles (if any) to the company support element. As a company support element, the platoon typically organizes into three support squads, with machine guns, armored vehicles, and antiarmor weapons attached. The attached machine guns provide the support element with added firepower for increased lethality.

5-38. For platoon-level operations, platoons typically use four elements: breach, assault, support, and reserve (figure 5-1). Based on the actual breaching requirements, the breach element may be integrated into the assault element or may be an attached vehicle or engineer element. However, due to the abundance of urban obstacles, the assault, support, and reserve teams should all be prepared to breach urban obstacles. While the mission variables determine their size and composition, the elements should maintain unit integrity as much as possible.

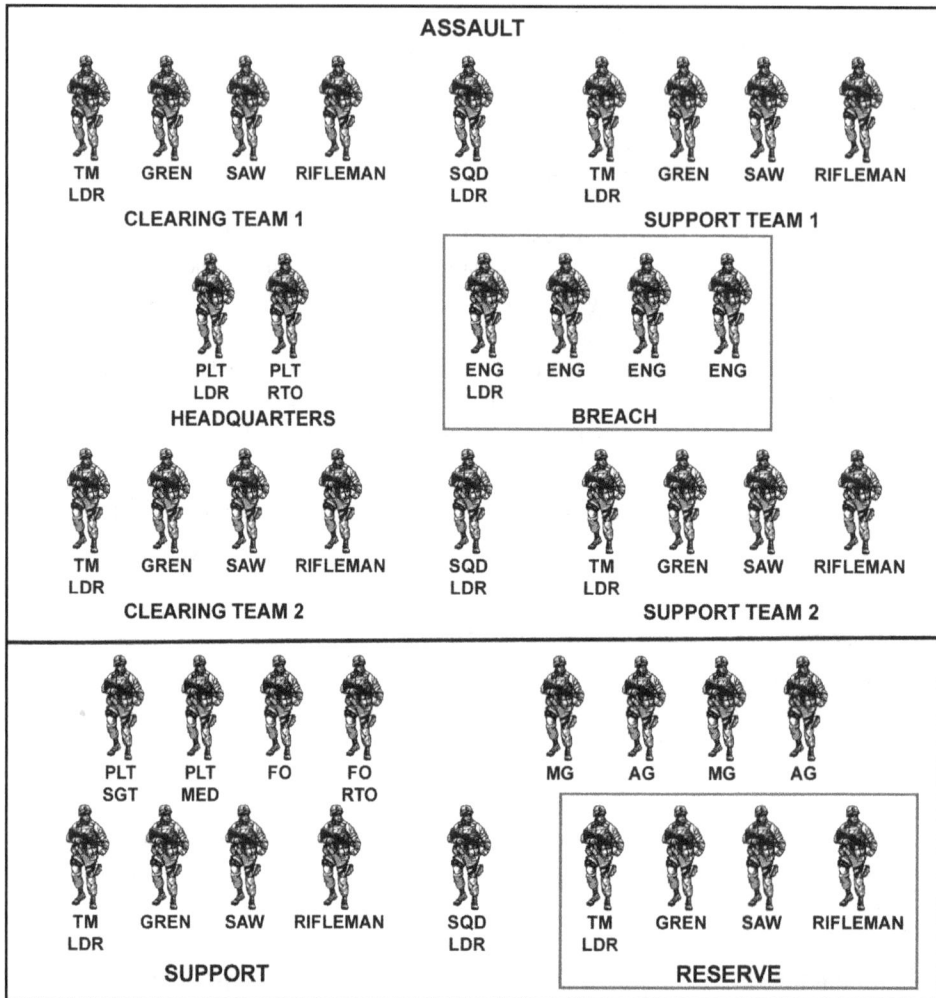

Figure 5-1. Platoon task organization

SECTION IV – UNDERSTAND

5-39. The urban operational construct provides a structure for developing considerations unique to offensive UO. The considerations vary depending on the situation and scale of the operation. Some considerations applicable to major operations that include an urban area apply at the tactical level. However, no set rules exist.

5-40. All UO are unique. Issues addressed at the operational level in one situation may be addressed in a new situation only at the tactical level. Under the right circumstances, a consideration may become an operational issue, a tactical issue, or a combination of the two. The following identifies some planning and execution issues that commanders conducting major operations should address.

5-41. The first requirement, and a continuing requirement throughout the conduct of offensive UO, is the assessment and understanding of the situation. Commanders should base this understanding on detailed information regarding the particular urban area.

5-42. The enemy usually dominates or controls most of the urban area during the planning phase of offensive operations. Thus, achieving an accurate understanding of the urban environment is difficult. A comprehensive reconnaissance effort can provide a clearer picture of the AO.

RECONNAISSANCE AND SECURITY

5-43. The intelligence collection from reconnaissance and security units within the urban AO may lead to decisive ground operations. This effort, and the understanding it supports, continues as long as the urban area remains in the AO.

5-44. Simultaneously, multiple intelligence sources contribute to the database/data file. The database/data file sources collect, process, store, display, and disseminate the relevant information on large urban areas through open and classified resources. These information sources include—

- Historical research.
- Travel brochures that include cultural information and recent maps.
- Classified debriefings of diplomats, businesses, Department of Defense personnel, and allies.
- Maps and special geospatial intelligence products of the urban area.
- Previous intelligence assessments of the country, government, and population.
- Appropriate economic, political, cultural, and infrastructure subject matter experts not in the commander's AO.

5-45. The gathering and analysis of human intelligence assists commanders in understanding ethnic, cultural, religious, economic, political, and other societal and infrastructural facets of the environment.

ASSESSMENT

5-46. In offensive UO, the tactical commander's assessment focuses on defeating the enemy in the urban area within the constraints of the environment. To be efficient and effective, offensive UO focus on that which is decisive. Decisive points for an urban attack depend primarily on the mission within the urban area. They can vary widely in composition and size. Since commanders only focus on the essential, they may determine the decisive point to be a single building; an entire system within the urban infrastructure, such as communications and information; or a limited subsystem of the transportation and distribution infrastructure, such as a single airfield. Sometimes the decisive point is the enemy military capability. Decisive points relate directly to the enemy's center of gravity and to mission success. Some decisive points related to the urban enemy's center of gravity may be physically located outside the urban area.

5-47. To gain specifics on enemy dispositions within the urban area requires a reconnaissance capability to see into the depths of the area and an intelligence capability to determine the enemy's likely defensive COA. With this information, commanders can determine decisive points and apply combat power discretely against them. Effective offensive UO require detailed situational understanding of an area of interest that extends well beyond the perimeter of the urban area.

5-48. Commanders should also assess the collateral damage risks that their operations may include. This assessment helps to initially determine the viability of a COA. However, commanders should reassess their COAs at frequent intervals in offensive UO based on known information to determine if the original evaluations remain valid. This reassessment minimizes potential collateral damage from a change in mission or COA. Many aspects of the environment can change during mission execution.

5-49. The urban environment's unique aspects can significantly impact the COA chosen by Army forces and the enemy. Commanders should assess these effects in planning, but they should also verify and monitor these effects as forces execute offensive missions. In particular, commanders need to confirm the civilian population's locations, beliefs, and actions and to monitor any changes. They will need to validate terrain considerations and monitor the effects of any changes due to rubble and other damages.

SECTION V – SHAPE

5-50. When conducting enabling operations in support of offensive UO, units may conduct the following operations. This section discusses techniques and procedures unique to offensive UO that are applicable to these specialized operations.

RECONNAISSANCE OPERATIONS

5-51. Reconnaissance patrols collect information and confirm or disprove the accuracy of information previously received. They identify enemy locations, reconnoiter specific locations, locate leaders, and gather information. Reconnaissance patrols provide the commander with timely, accurate information on the enemy, population, and terrain. This information is vital in making tactical decisions. Leaders ensure that no pattern is established that would allow an enemy force to ambush reconnaissance units.

5-52. The four forms of reconnaissance are zone, area, route, and reconnaissance in force. Zone, area, and route reconnaissance are normally conducted with a focus on the population, infrastructure, enemy, and terrain. (See FM 3-20.96 for details on reconnaissance operations and reconnaissance fundamentals.)

5-53. Using his sources, the company commander identifies—
- Best approach route into the urban area.
- Locations or obstacles to avoid.
- Information sources within the urban area.
- Any other specific areas of interest.

5-54. After analyzing the commander's mission and intent, the commander determines how to gain the information required within the AO. The company uses a combination of stealth, human intelligence, and imagery intelligence, when available, to develop the urban situation. The use of tactical questioning is an invaluable skill in validating the information from the populace.

5-55. The information-gathering process is conducted progressively from outside the urban area to inside the urban area. As information is gained from the outer ring of the AO, the focus of the collection plan is updated, and reconnaissance objectives within the urban area are refined. The urban situation can change quickly, leading to compromise or attack. Thus, it is essential that reconnaissance units continuously maintain situational awareness. The company continues to collect and corroborate information as it approaches the urban area. Although reconnaissance elements can use stealth during limited visibility, the human density within an urban area makes it difficult for these units to remain undetected.

5-56. The considerations for developing information requirements in the urban environment are unique, placing greater demand on human and imagery intelligence sources. In developing its objectives, the company should weigh the assigned information requirements against the time available to accomplish the mission. The following are samples of information requirements that can help the company commander define reconnaissance objectives:
- What is the enemy's most likely and most dangerous COA?
- Where are the enemy's CPs located?
- What is the status of key lines of communications leading into and within the urban area?
- What are the likely enemy withdrawal routes and chokepoints?
- Are there obstacles impeding movement along the routes to and from assembly areas?
- Would isolation cause the enemy to withdraw from the urban area?
- Has the deployed enemy force had any training in UO?
- What are the potential vulnerabilities to the infrastructure facilities?
- Where are cross-mobility corridors located within the urban area?
- Where are cultural, political, or symbolic facilities located?
- How do locals (by faction) view friendly forces and U.S. efforts in general?
- What are the locations of diplomatic embassies and missions in the urban area?
- What are the locations of U.S. citizens (if any) within the urban area?
- Is the enemy indigenous to the urban area or from the outside the area?

SECURITY OPERATIONS

5-57. The five forms of security are screen, guard, cover, area security, and local security. Of these, screen, guard, and cover missions entail deployment of progressively higher levels of assets and provide increasing levels of security for the main body. Area security preserves a commander's freedom to move his reserves, position FS units, conduct inform and influence and cyber/electromagnetic activities, and provide for sustainment operations. (See FM 3-20.96 for details on security operations in general to include security fundamentals.)

5-58. The company team can conduct a screen on its own. It participates in area security missions as part of a larger element. The company team always provides its own local security. Local security includes OPs, local security patrols, perimeter security, and other measures taken to provide close-in security.

5-59. When assigned to conduct a screen mission, the company team may be task organized with additional maneuver, mobility, sustainment, intelligence, and protection units. At minimum, attachments include a reconnaissance platoon and an additional mortar section or platoon. The time by which the screen must be set and active influences the company team's method of deploying to the security area as well as the time it begins the deployment. The company commander uses a thorough analysis of the mission variables to determine the appropriate methods and techniques to accomplish reconnaissance.

5-60. Area security operations require the company to deal with a unique set of enemy considerations. For example, the array of enemy forces (and the tactics that enemy commanders use to employ them) may differ from those for any other tactical operation the company conducts. Additional enemy considerations that can influence company security operations are—

- Presence or absence of specific types of forces on the battlefield, including—
  - Insurgent elements that may be external to the enemy force.
  - Enemy reconnaissance elements of varying strengths and capabilities.
  - Enemy security elements, such as disruption forces, including enemy stay-behind elements or other bypassed enemy elements.
- Possible locations where the enemy will employ his tactical units, including—
  - Reconnaissance and infiltration routes.
  - OP sites for surveillance or indirect fire observers.
- Availability and anticipated employment of other enemy units, including—
  - Surveillance devices, such as radar devices or UAS.
  - Long-range rocket and artillery units.
  - Helicopter and fixed-wing air strikes.
  - Elements capable of dismounted insertion or infiltration.
  - Mechanized forward detachments.

5-61. Route security is a type of area security that aims to prevent an enemy from destroying, seizing, or hindering traffic along a route. It also prevents the enemy from interfering with the route itself by emplacing obstacles on or destroying portions of the route. Because of the nature of this mission, long routes may be extremely difficult to secure. However, commanders should identify and enforce measures to reduce the effect of enemy forces on the routes. These measures include establishing mutually supporting combat outposts that can respond to enemy activity and conducting security patrols along the route. Combat outposts are typically established at critical chokepoints along the route or on high ground overlooking the route.

5-62. Establishing and maintaining local security in UO is important because of the short ranges, three-dimensional aspect of the terrain, and the closeness of enemy forces. Local security prevents a unit from being surprised and is an important part of maintaining the initiative. Maintaining local security is an inherent part of all operations and includes establishing OPs, conducting patrols, and establishing specific levels of alert and stand-to times.

BREACHING OPERATIONS

5-63. Breaching operations are the employment of tactics and techniques to advance a force to the far side of an obstacle despite the presence of hostile forces. They are conducted when the company cannot bypass the obstacles with maneuver. (See FM 3-34.2 for details on urban breaching operations and chapter 7 for breaching interior obstacles.)

5-64. Understanding breaching theory is the first step to understanding breaching tactics. Units should always try to bypass enemy obstacles. If the situation demands that the obstacles be reduced, units should try to bypass the obstacles, destroy or repel the defending enemy forces, and then reduce the obstacles. Only as a last resort should commanders try to breach into an obstacle that is actively defended.

OBSTACLES

5-65. Obstacles can exist naturally (existing), be man-made (reinforcing), or be a combination of both. In urban terrain, obstacles can vary from standard linear obstacles blocking an avenue of approach to a closed door hindering movement into a building or room. The commander and breach element should prepare a breach plan based on analyses of available information pertaining to specific obstacles encountered.

5-66. Two general categories of urban obstacles are exterior and interior. When breaching exterior or interior urban obstacles against a defending enemy, the breaching fundamentals of SOSRA apply. However, the application varies based on the mission variables.

Exterior

5-67. Exterior obstacles hinder movement between buildings and along roadways. Treat them similarly to obstacles encountered in rural areas. Additional considerations in urban terrain include the—

- Three-dimensional aspect of the surrounding urban terrain to establish overwatch positions.
- Availability of urban debris, such as concrete and vehicles.
- Restricted ability to use the ground as an anchor point.
- Ability to use concrete structures to anchor the flanks of the obstacles.

Interior

5-68. Interior obstacles hinder entry into a building or room or movement within the building.

ENTRY

5-69. Begin by identifying the desired entry point, and determine if breaching is necessary. To determine the best primary and alternate points of entry and the method of breaching, analyze the design, construction, and material makeup of the structure to be entered and any visible obstacles. Only consider an entry point open and not requiring a breach if it is clearly open and large enough for a Soldier to enter unhindered. After identifying specific entry points, examine each entry point design, construction, and material makeup to determine the best primary, secondary, and tertiary breaching method to conduct.

INTERIOR MOVEMENT

5-70. Hallway and stairwell obstacles are constructed with available building materials and possibly augmented with concertina wire. It is often best to bypass them and secure the far side or adjacent stairwell first and then breach the obstacle using standard fundamentals. Often, a grappling hook can reduce the obstacle from a safe distance and avoid Soldier exposure at the breach point.

OTHER TACTICAL ENABLING OPERATIONS

5-71. The fluid nature of the modern battlefield increases the frequency with which the company conducts tactical enabling operations that are described below.

LINKUP

5-72. A linkup is an operation that entails the meeting of friendly ground forces (or their leaders or designated representatives). The company conducts linkup activities independently or as part of a larger force. Within a larger unit, the company may lead the linkup force. (See FM 3-90 for the details.)

5-73. Linkup may occur in, but is not limited to, the following situations:

- Advancing forces reaching an objective area previously secured by air assault, airborne, or infiltrating forces.
- Units coordinating a relief in place.
- Cross-attached units moving to join their new organization.
- Unit moving forward with a fixing force during a follow-and-support mission.
- Unit moving to assist an encircled force.
- Units converging on the same objective during the attack.
- Units conducting a passage of lines.

RELIEF IN PLACE

5-74. A relief in place is an operation in which one unit replaces another unit and assumes the relieved unit's responsibilities. The primary purpose for a relief in place operation is to maintain the combat effectiveness of committed units. (See FM 3-90 for details.) A relief in place may also be conducted to—

- Reorganize, reconstitute, or re-equip a unit that has sustained heavy losses.
- Rest units that have conducted sustained operations.
- Establish the security force or the detachment left in contact during a withdrawal operation.
- Allow the relieved unit to conduct another operation.

PASSAGE OF LINES

5-75. A passage of lines is the movement of one or more units through another. This operation becomes necessary when the moving unit(s) cannot bypass the stationary unit and must pass through it. The primary purpose of the passage is to maintain the momentum of the moving elements. A passage of lines may be designated as either forward or rearward. The headquarters ordering the passage of lines is responsible for planning and coordination. However, specific coordination tasks are normally delegated to subordinate commanders. (See FM 3-90 for details.)

SECTION VI – ENGAGE

5-76. Company combined arms teams should expect to receive similar types of offensive missions in urban terrain that they receive in other terrain. Common company, platoon, and squad missions in UO are described below.

HASTY ATTACK

5-77. Company teams conduct hasty attacks—

- As a result of a movement to contact, a meeting engagement, or a chance contact during a movement.
- After a successful defense or part of a defense.
- In a situation where the unit has the opportunity to attack vulnerable enemy forces.

5-78. The hasty attack in an urban area differs from a hasty attack in open terrain because the terrain makes command, control, communications, and massing fires to suppress the enemy difficult. In urban areas, incomplete intelligence and concealment may require the maneuver unit to move through, rather than around, the friendly unit fixing the enemy in place. Control and coordination become critical to reduce congestion at the edges of the urban area. (See FM 3-90 and FM 3-21.10 for details.)

DELIBERATE ATTACK

5-79. A deliberate attack is characterized by sufficient time to prepare a detailed plan. The commander conducts a phased deliberate attack by performing the actions below.

RECONNOITER THE OBJECTIVE

5-80. This involves conducting a reconnaissance of the objective as the tactical situation permits. If available, UAS provides accurate real-time reconnaissance of the objective. It also involves making a map reconnaissance of the objective and all the terrain that affects the mission. Additionally, units should analyze aerial imagery, photographs, or any other detailed information about the buildings or other urban terrain for which the unit is responsible. Human intelligence (HUMINT) collected by reconnaissance and surveillance units should be considered during the planning process.

MOVE TO THE OBJECTIVE

5-81. Urban movement should take into account the three-dimensional aspect of the urban area. It may involve moving through both open and urban terrain. Movement can involve moving through buildings, down streets, in subsurface areas, or a combination of all three. If possible, move along covered and concealed routes and as rapidly as possible without sacrificing security.

5-82. Ideally, units should conduct the first phases of an urban attack when visibility is poor. Soldiers can exploit poor visibility to cross open areas, gain access to rooftops, infiltrate enemy areas, and gain a foothold. If the attack must occur when visibility is good, units should consider using smoke to conceal movement. The formation of an attack depends on the width and depth of the AO to be cleared, the character of the area, anticipated enemy resistance, and the formation adopted by the next higher command.

5-83. Plan all routes to the entry point in advance. Select the best route during the leader's reconnaissance. The route should allow the assault element to approach the entry point from the enemy's blind side if possible. Once inside the building, the priority tasks are to cover the staircases and to seize rooms that overlook approaches to the building. These actions are required to isolate enemy forces within the building and to prevent reinforcement from the outside.

ISOLATE THE OBJECTIVE

5-84. Units achieve isolation by physically occupying terrain and dominating access to the area through direct and indirect fires. It involves seizing terrain that dominates the objective so that the enemy cannot resupply, reinforce, or withdraw its defenders. Depending on the tactical situation, units may occupy positions that isolate an objective by infiltration and stealth (figure 5-2).

5-85. Ideally, the individual objective building as well as the city block or even the complete city is isolated. The intent, at the tactical level, is to completely dominate the area leading to the points of entry to protect assaulting troops entering the building from effective enemy fire. Isolating an urban objective is often critical to successfully assaulting an urban objective. Additionally, moving quickly to isolate an urban objective ensures the defender has little time to react. Isolating an objective psychologically affects the enemy, who must either fight his way out or remain in place until another force fights their way in.

5-86. Consider using military information support operations teams to communicate appropriate messages to the enemy and to direct the civilian population to move to a designated safe area. These actions should be coordinated with the overall military information support operations plan for the BCT and should not sacrifice surprise. Engineers or other augmenting units may reinforce the company based on the ROE and mission variables.

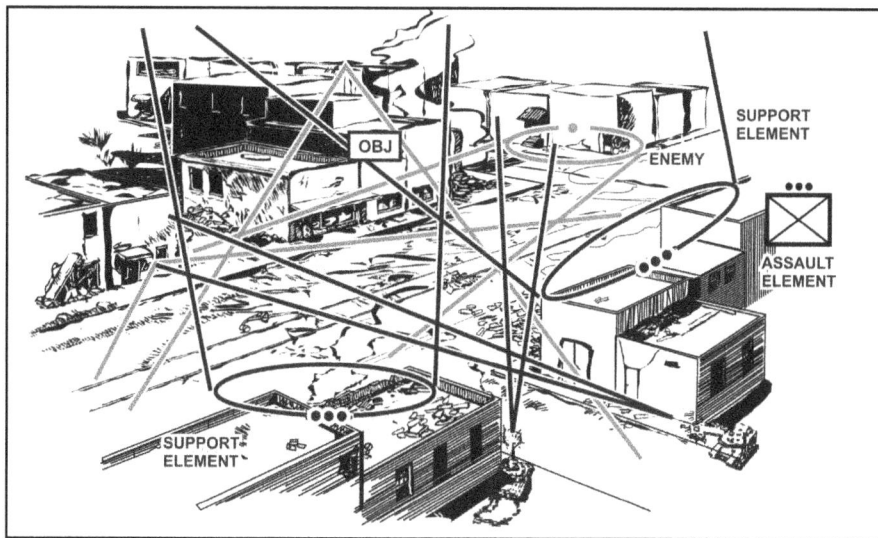

Figure 5-2. Infantry platoon, with tanks in support, isolating the objective

SECURE A FOOTHOLD

5-87. Concealed by smoke and supported by direct-fire weapons, an assaulting platoon assaults the first isolated building and secures a foothold. Securing a foothold involves seizing a position from which to continue the assault through the objective. The size of the foothold is METT-TC dependent and is usually identified as an intermediate objective. A large building is used as a foothold into an urban area, while a specific room is assigned as a foothold into a large building.

5-88. Typically, a squad or platoon conducts the actual assault of an individual building. This is the focus of an attack and is done as soon as possible after isolating the objective. The assault element's first objective is to secure a foothold in the building. This is best accomplished using obscuration and suppressive fires. Leaders should closely coordinate the assault with their supporting fire so that suppressive fire is shifted at the last possible moment. Once inside, a squad or team clears the foothold room and then enters and clears additional rooms as directed. When exiting a cleared building, friendly troops should notify supporting elements using the radio or preplanned signals.

5-89. The assault force, regardless of size, should quickly and violently execute the assault and subsequent clearing operations. Leaders must maintain momentum to deny the enemy time to organize a more determined resistance. Enemy obstacles may slow or stop forward movement. Assaulting forces must rapidly create a breach in an obstacle or redirect the flow of the assault over or around the obstacle.

SUPPRESS THE OBJECTIVE

5-90. The support element provides suppressive fire while the assault element is systematically clearing the building. It also provides suppressive fire on adjacent buildings to prevent enemy reinforcements or withdrawal. Armored vehicles are useful in providing heavy, sustained, accurate fire. Suppressive fire may consist of firing at known and suspected enemy locations or, depending on the ROE, may only include firing at identified targets or returning fire when fired upon. The support element destroys or captures any enemy trying to exit the building and should also deal with civilians displaced by the assault.

5-91. The support element covers mounted avenues of approach with antiarmor weapons and dismounted avenues of approach with automatic weapons. It also suppresses enemy fires and neutralizes enemy positions to enable the breach team and assault element to move into position. Bradley fighting vehicles, tanks, machine guns, and other direct FS weapons fire on the objective from covered positions consistent with the ROE. The gunners should use a series of positions and displace from one to another to gain better fields of fire and to avoid being targeted by the enemy. Direct FS tasks can be assigned as follows:

- Mounted and ground-mounted machine guns fire along streets and into windows, doors, mouseholes, and other probable enemy positions.
- BFVs, tanks, and antitank weapons fire at enemy vehicles, especially tanks.
- All vehicle-mounted weapon systems conduct countersniper operations due to their range and target acquisition capability.
- BFVs, ICVs, tanks, and shoulder-launched munitions engage targets protected by urban structures.
- BFVs, tanks, and MGS create breaches with their main guns.
- Riflemen engage targets of opportunity.

EXECUTE A BREACH

5-92. Units may have to conduct a breach to enter a building, rooms, or stairwells. If engineers are attached to the unit, they should support all breach operations. Depending on the mission variables, urban breach operations vary from opening doors to reducing a deliberate obstacle preventing access to a door. Breaching also includes the deliberate opening of a wall to gain entry to a building. The ROE influence the decision to use mechanical, thermal, ballistic, or explosive breaching methods.

CLEAR THE OBJECTIVE

5-93. Before determining to what extent the urban area should be cleared, commanders should consider the mission variables. The ROE affect the tactics and techniques that units select to move through the urban area and clear individual buildings and rooms. When the commander's concept is based on speed or when conducting a hasty attack, a battalion may be directed not to clear its entire AO. However, bypassing buildings increases the risk of attack from the rear or flank. The commander may decide to clear only those parts necessary for mission success if an objective must be seized quickly or if resistance is light or fragmented.

5-94. If the area has large open areas between buildings, the commander clears only those buildings along the approach to the objective or only those necessary for security. A unit's mission may be to systematically clear an area of all enemies. For example, a company may be assigned their own AO within the battalion's AO to conduct systematic clearing. As a result, one or two platoons may attack on a narrow front against the enemy's weakest area. They move through the area, clearing from room to room and building to building. The other platoon supports the clearing units and is prepared to assume their mission.

Clear the Entry Floor

5-95. The assault element clears each room on the entry floor. Their objective is to kill, capture, or force the withdrawal of all enemy personnel. Squads and teams perform room clearing. The squad leader controls the maneuver of the fire teams as they clear hallways, stairways, and rooms. The platoon leader alternates the squads as required, maintains momentum, and ensures resupply of ammunition and water.

5-96. Units should ensure that they carry enough room marking equipment and plainly mark cleared rooms from the friendly side as per unit SOP. Also, if the operation occurs during limited visibility, the markings must remain visible to friendly units. The support element should understand building, floor, and room markings to ensure they do not engage cleared rooms and floors. Maintaining situational awareness concerning the location of the assault elements and which rooms and floors have been cleared is a key control function for the company commander. If necessary, consolidate unit radios, giving priority to the squads and platoons clearing rooms.

Clear the Building

5-97. After clearing and securing the entry floor, units proceed to clear all floors, to include the basement. If entry is not made from the top, consider rapidly clearing and securing the stairwell and then clearing from the top down. Clear any basements as soon as possible, preferably at the same time as the ground floor. Basement clearing procedures are the same as for any floor, but important differences do exist.

Basements may contain entrances to tunnels, such as sewers and communications cable tunnels, that should be cleared and secured to prevent enemy infiltration back into cleared areas.

CONSOLIDATE AND REORGANIZE

5-98. Consolidation is the process of organizing and strengthening a newly captured position so that it can be defended. Consolidation action (many occurring simultaneously) provide security to facilitate reorganization. Rapid consolidation after an engagement is extremely important in an urban environment. The assault force in a cleared building must be quick to consolidate in order to repel enemy counterattacks and to prevent the enemy from infiltrating back into the cleared building. After securing a floor, selected members of the assault force are assigned to cover potential enemy counterattack routes to the building. Priority must be given to securing the direction of attack first.

5-99. Reorganization includes all measures taken by the commander to maintain the combat effectiveness of his unit or return it to a specified level of combat capability. Reorganization actions (many occurring simultaneously) prepare the unit to continue the mission.

PREPARE FOR FUTURE OPERATIONS

5-100. The commander anticipates and prepares for future missions and prepares the chain of command for transition to defensive and or stability missions.

5-101. After seizing an objective, the most likely on-order mission is to continue the attack. During consolidation, the unit continues troop-leading procedures in preparation for any on-order missions assigned by a higher headquarters. The commander uses available combat information and intelligence products to adjust contingency plans and support the next mission.

SPECIAL-PURPOSE ATTACKS

5-102. A company team could possibly receive a mission to conduct a raid, ambush, or spoiling attack. It can use both support and attack-by-fire positions during these types of attacks. Its mobility is an advantage. However, any attachments should be equally mobile. The commander selects weapons based on a detailed analysis of the mission variables. (See FM 3-21.10 for details.)

MOVEMENT TO CONTACT

5-103. Units execute a movement to contact when the tactical situation is not clear or when the enemy has broken contact. The purpose of a movement to contact is to gain or reestablish contact with the enemy. (See FM 3-21.10 and FM 3-21.20 for details.)

5-104. Understanding the composition of the expected enemy force and the composition of the urban terrain itself is important to developing the movement to contact concept. Upon contact with the enemy, the commander's aim is to achieve a five-to-one force advantage and to isolate the enemy force. To achieve this, the commander should use multiple avenues of approach that are mutually supporting. The approach-march objective (or at least intermediate objectives) should be key nodes within the urban area that ensure both flexibility in movement and gain control of key terrain.

TASK ORGANIZATION

5-105. A company team is a well-rounded element for an urban movement to contact. Due to their speed and firepower, a task-organized company with tanks, BFVs, MGS, or Strykers is preferable to an Infantry-only unit. While dismounted Infantry and tanks can also execute an urban movement to contact, their inherent lack of rapid mobility is a limiting factor.

EXECUTION

5-106. Use travelling overwatch or bounding overwatch along urban routes. In open areas where rapid movement is possible due to terrain, a tank section (if available) should lead. In closer terrain, the Infantry should lead while overwatched by tanks. Additional Infantry and tanks should move on a parallel street. Plan artillery fire along the complete route. Ensure engineers accompany the lead platoon to help clear obstacles and mines on the main route.

5-107. Movement to contact operations in urban terrain are characterized by alternating periods of rapid movement to quickly cover distances and much slower movement for security. The speed of movement depends on the urban terrain and enemy situation. Between danger areas, the company moves with the Infantry mounted, or rapidly on foot, when contact is not likely. Due to the canalization caused by streets, the main body should move on a minimum of two avenues of approach, typically adjacent, to maintain their maneuverability.

Approach March

5-108. Conducting a movement to contact using the approach march is common in rural terrain. It is also common for fast-moving urban situations when contact with the enemy is desired and a general understanding of the location is known.

Search and Attack Technique

5-109. The search and attack technique is a decentralized movement to contact requiring multiple, coordinated patrols (squad, platoon, or company size) to—
- Destroy enemy forces.
- Protect friendly forces.
- Deny an area to the enemy.
- Collect information.

5-110. The search and attack technique is effective when knowledge of the enemy is unclear and contact is required. Use this technique against an enemy that is operating in dispersed elements, is disorganized, or is incapable of massing strength against friendly forces; for example, dispersed regular forces, urban insurgents, or irregular forces. (See FM 3-21.10 and FM 3-21.20 for details.)

5-111. Tracking an enemy in urban areas is difficult due to the nature of the terrain and the presence of a population. In urban areas, leaders rely on all available intelligence, a thorough knowledge of their AO, UAS and air reconnaissance, and information from their own unit and adjacent units.

CORDON AND SEARCH

5-112. A cordon and search is an operation to seal (cordon) off an area that units then search for persons, items, and information of potential intelligence value. Effective cordon and search operations possess sufficient forces to effectively cordon and thoroughly search a target area. Cordon is given to a unit to prevent withdrawal from or reinforcement to a position. It is a form of isolation.

5-113. Cordon implies occupying or controlling terrain, especially mounted and dismounted avenues of approach. Search implies the physical and visual inspection of an area. Both the object of the search and the physical area of the search influence the type and degree of the search.

METHODS

5-114. The two basic methods of executing a cordon and search are the cordon and knock/ask method and the cordon and kick method. These two methods reflect variances of aggressiveness towards the occupants of the target location. Based on the enemy situation template and identified operational risk, actual cordon and search operations lie somewhere between these two variances. Table 5-1 shows sample variances to cordon and search operations based on level of entry.

Table 5-1. Sample variances of cordon and search methods

CORDON AND KNOCK / ASK (PERMISSIVE)				CORDON AND KICK (NON-PERMISSIVE)			
INVITED IN	ASK	DICTATE	DEMAND	JUST ENTER	KICK-IN	SHOOT-IN	EXPLODE-IN
ESCALATING LEVEL OF VIOLENCE ──────────►							──────────►

5-115. In both methods, units establish the cordon with as much speed and surprise as possible to isolate the objective. What differs is the aggressiveness of the cordon personnel and the actions of the search personnel. Regardless of the method selected, the potential for combat still exists, and all units should be prepared to react to contact or a changing situation in accordance with the ROE.

Cordon and Knock/Ask

5-116. The cordon and knock, as the name implies, uses a less intrusive entry into the search area. Unit personnel physically knock on the door before entering. Use this method when the surrounding population is viewed as friendly or at least not hostile, no resistance is anticipated, and minimal disruption and inconvenience to the occupants is desired. Depending on the situation, units may give the occupants the opportunity to exit the search area before search forces enter.

5-117. A variation of the cordon and knock is the cordon and ask. The cordon and ask seeks permission either directly from the occupants or from the local authorities. If this permission is denied, no entry takes place except in accordance with the rule of law.

5-118. The cordon and knock and the cordon and ask require some degree of integration with HN security force or HN authorities to obtain the agreement by the occupants of the target to the subsequent search. At a minimum, a sufficient number of translators (preferably one with each element) is required.

Cordon and Kick

5-119. The cordon and kick uses some level of intrusive entry into the search area. The intent is to rapidly breach barriers to gain entry into the targeted search area. It typically uses speed and surprise to allow the unit to quickly gain control of the foothold and possible search area. This action allows units to maintain the initiative over a potentially unknown enemy force operating in the search area. Intrusive entry ranges from a Soldier simply opening a door without occupant permission to mechanical breaching to explosive breaching. Mounted units can use vehicles to breach or provide mechanical breach assistance.

5-120. Since the agreement by the occupants for entry and for execution of the subsequent search is not a requirement, the cordon and kick does not explicitly require integrated HN security forces or HN authorities. However, if an established relationship with a HN exists, it is always preferred to have HN leadership approval or direct support. Commanders assume risk by foregoing these considerations as any benefits gained may be offset by losses with the HN government or population.

PLANNING CONSIDERATIONS

5-121. Establishing the cordon requires detailed planning, effective coordination, and meticulous integration and synchronization of available units to achieve the desired effects. The commander must consider both lethal and nonlethal effects. Each subordinate cordon position, such as a traffic control point or blocking position, should have a designated leader and a clearly understood task and purpose. Key planning considerations are—
- Develop a simple cordon and search plan.
- Employ a selective or systematic search of the objective area.
- Allocate sufficient time to conduct the search of the area, to include time to conduct site exploitation and tactical questioning.
- Establish disciplined and standardized search SOPs to ensure searches are thorough, priority intelligence requirement focused, and of minimal risk to Soldiers.

- Reconnoiter the objective area to identify the relative size and location of buildings, entry points, cordon position, and avenues of approach. Useful analytical tools include aerial photographs, maps, and material from local emergency services.
- Seek to conduct operations during limited visibility and early morning hours to achieve surprise and maximize the presence of the targeted individuals. Proven techniques for success often involve searchers returning to a searched area after the initial search to surprise targeted individuals who either returned or remained undetected during the initial search.
- Plan to counter the belligerent's propaganda. Belligerents often have an information plan focused on the cordon and search operation. Commanders should seek to anticipate this plan and negate it or, at a minimum, mitigate the operational risk of it.

Cordon

5-122. Develop plans for establishing a cordon. Typically, the security element rapidly surrounds the area while the search element simultaneously moves in. Ideally, surround the entire area at once, covering any gaps with observed fire. A cordon that prevents egress of individuals from the search area and outside support into the search area is critical to success. Based on the mission variables, units often establish an—

- **Outer.** Outer cordon to isolate the objective from outside reinforcements or disruptions.
- **Inner.** Inner cordon to prevent individuals from leaving outside of the search area.

5-123. Both cordon elements should maintain 360-degree security. If applicable, cordon all subsurface routes. Typically cordons include checkpoints and roadblocks to block, canalize, or divert traffic.

5-124. To cordon and search a small urban area (village) surrounded by rural terrain, use the same general techniques. However the outer cordon is typically composed of unit BPs or OPs on dominant terrain, with roadblocks on the roads leading into the urban area (village). Executing the cordon during periods of limited visibility often aids in the establishment and security of the cordon.

5-125. Develop plans for handling detained personnel. Soldiers normally provide security and accompany police and intelligence forces who identify, question, and detain suspects. Under police supervision, Infantry may conduct searches and assist in detaining suspects. However, their principal role is to reduce any resistance that may develop and provide security for the operation, keeping use of force to a minimum.

Search

5-126. A search can orient on people, materiel, structures, or an area of terrain. A company or platoon is normally the largest element required to perform a search as part of a cordon and search operation. Search of an urban area varies from a few, easily isolated buildings to a large well-developed urban city. A large-scale search of an urban area is normally conducted at battalion task force level or higher and should be a combined police and military operation. Leaders should divide the urban area to be searched into clearly defined AOs. Number each individual building, and assign specific search teams to specific buildings.

5-127. Search teams thoroughly search the houses, yards, buildings, and underground and underwater areas that compose the designated search area. Consider using mine detectors to locate metal objects underground or underwater and canine search teams to locate hidden persons or other objects. Consider all enemy material found to be booby trapped until inspection proves it is safe. All search elements should be prepared to handle male and female personnel, key equipment, hazardous materials (biohazards or other toxic elements), and ordinance and to record key events.

5-128. Individual Soldiers should be trained in tactical site exploitation methods. Tactical site exploitation consists of the actions taken to ensure that documents, material, and personnel are identified, collected, protected, and evaluated in order to facilitate follow-on actions. It focuses on actions taken by Soldiers and leaders at the point of initial contact. When conducted correctly, tactical site exploitation can provide further intelligence for future operations, answer information requirements, and provide evidence to keep detainees in prison. The Soldier should not focus his total attention on the specific requirements of the search. Rather, he should be aware of anything unusual and worth reporting and further investigation.

5-129. Searches should be planned in detail yet simple in execution and should be rehearsed and executed quickly. Leaders should ensure that any physical reconnaissance does not compromise the operation. Prior to conducting the search, leaders should understand the limits of their search authority and the ROE, which is usually given in fragmentary or operation orders. Misuse of search authority can adversely affect the outcome of the overall mission. Therefore, lawfully conduct and properly record the seizure of contraband, evidence, items of potential intelligence value, supplies, or other items during searches to ensure future value. Proper use of authority during searches gains and maintains the respect and support of the people. Basic personnel considerations for any search include—

- Detailed instructions that include lists of prohibited items.
- Understanding of search restrictions and special considerations, to include searching—
  - Religious institutions.
  - Females with female Soldiers.
  - Historical, cultural, or governmental sites neither authorized nor deemed hostile.
- Augmentation with trusted individuals who speak and read the local language.
- Host nation security forces or local interpreters.
- Necessity to maintain communication and report location.
- Respect for personal property.

5-130. Searches cause considerable inconvenience and sometimes fear to both the affected individuals and nearby residents. If possible, conduct searches with minimal inconvenience to the populace. As much as tactically possible, keep the local population informed that the search contributes to their safety and security. However, it is important to balance the level of inconvenience to the local populace. It should discourage belligerents and their sympathizers from remaining in the locale and encourage the local population to provide information on them. The level of inconvenience should not be so great as to turn the local population toward active or passive support of the belligerents.

5-131. Communication about the search should begin during the actual search and continue after the search by follow-up patrols. Follow-up patrols can aid in mitigating some of the negative aspects of the search. They can also see if missed individuals have returned to the searched area. Follow up patrols that include military information support operations organizations, provide a critical capability to conduct consequence management, reinforce messages, and collect additional information, particularly if the populace was affected by the search.

TASK ORGANIZATION

5-132. The typical cordon and search organization includes a command element, a security element, a search element, and a reserve element, each with a clear task and purpose (figure 5-3).

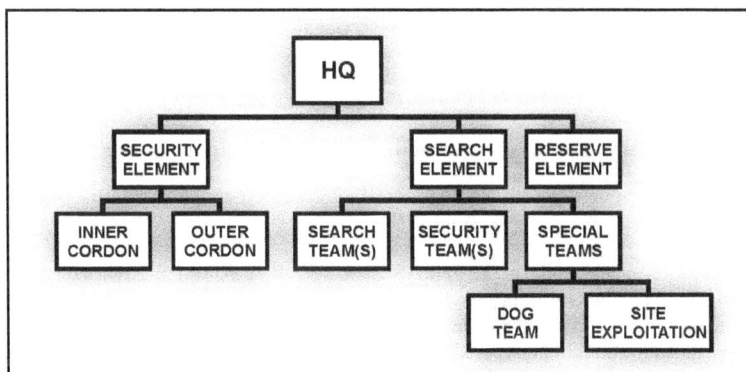

Figure 5-3. Typical organization for cordon and search operations

5-133. The size and composition of the cordon and search force is based on the size of the area to be cordoned, the size of the area to be searched, and the suspected enemy situation. Host nation security forces that are dependable and competent, especially police forces, are extremely valuable in urban search operations.

5-134. Assets employed during the cordon and search may include—
- Interpreters.
- Host nation or multinational forces.
- Human intelligence collection teams.
- Law enforcement professionals.
- Technical intelligence teams.
- Special advisors.
- Attack reconnaissance aviation.
- Signals intelligence enablers.
- Measurement and signature intelligence enablers.
- Military working dog teams.
- Biometrics collection efforts.
- Tactical military information support operations teams.
- Civil affair teams.

5-135. Units often receive additional assets to assist them in a cordon and search based on availability and the mission variables. These assets may be included as teams in the security element or the search element, or they may remain independent and on call. They may also be internal or external to the battalion and can include MP, engineer, civil affairs, military information support operations organizations, MI, or artillery units that form—
- Mine detection teams.
- Demolition teams.
- Interrogation teams.
- Documentation or biometric teams (uses a recorder with a camera).
- Scout dog teams.
- Military information support operations and civil affairs augmentation teams.
- Detainee and EPW teams.
- Tunnel reconnaissance teams.
- Escort parties.
- Transportation teams.

Command Element

5-136. An overall commander controls the unit conducting the cordon and search. He identifies the subordinate element leaders.

Security Element

5-137. The security element surrounds the area while the search element moves in. This force should have enough combat power to cordon off the area.

Search Element

5-138. The search element conducts the actual search operation. A large search element often includes personnel and special equipment for processing detainees, medical screening, security, tactical questioning, recorders, site exploitation, demolitions, employment of military working dog teams, or subterranean search operations. They should be prepared to conduct site exploitation, detainee operations, and adjacent unit coordination and to engage the enemy.

5-139. Normally, a search element is organized into specific teams, such as a basic search team, a detainee team, a site exploitation team, and so on. The basic search team is a two person team consisting of one person who conducts the actual search and another person who provides immediate security to the searcher. Search personnel should be trained to operate with HN security forces and within the established ROE. Often, having basic language training or interpreters within the search element is essential to an effective search.

5-140. All search element members should be trained to use special equipment, to include—

- Biometrics tools.
- Breaching kit.
- Vehicle access tools, such as lock picks.
- Video and audio recording devices and data imaging devices.
- Markings and signaling equipment.
- Detection and recording equipment.
- Standardization of maps, imagery, and labeling conventions.

Reserve Element

5-141. The reserve element is a mobile force, typically a quick reaction force, positioned in a nearby area. Its mission is to reinforce or replace the security or search elements if they meet resistance beyond their capabilities. The reserve element should possess and maintain enough combat power to defeat the enemy forces understood to be within the AO. The commander tasks the reserve to plan, rehearse, and be prepared to execute any of the subordinate unit missions and possible additional missions, such as casualty evacuation or reinforcement. The reserve element leader focuses efforts on synchronized communications, rehearsals, battle tracking, and positioning before and during the operation.

EXECUTION

5-142. Although METT-TC analysis determines specifics, a unit typically establishes the outer cordon first, establishes the inner cordon second, and moves the search element to the objective last. Commanders should consider the value of using the opposite technique of forming the cordons following rapid movement to the objective to gain surprise. Timing is important when executing either technique. The quicker these three events are accomplished, the less time personnel on the objectives have to egress, find concealment, and destroy materials or equipment.

Position the Reserve Element

5-143. Position the reserve element or quick reaction force to ensure multiple routes allow for their rapid movement to the objective area by either ground, air, or both.

Establish the Cordon

5-144. The two techniques for emplacing the actual cordon positions are simultaneously and sequentially. give careful consideration to both as each has advantages and disadvantages. Units establishing a cordon position themselves to be able to block movement to and from the objective area. This may be by observed fire, but usually it is by physically controlling routes. Normally, occupy cordon positions rapidly just prior to the search element reaching the objective. Establishing the cordon during a period of limited visibility increases movement security but makes control difficult. Assume that the local population, as they conduct their daily business, will detect unit cordon positions soon after the unit occupies them.

5-145. Both the outer and inner cordon leaders should maintain situational understanding of their AOs as well as each other's cordon and the search element's progress. In doing so, they can anticipate belligerent activity; control direct and indirect fires, and achieve their task and purpose. The various elements of the outer and inner cordons may include—

- Vehicle-mounted platoons or sections.
- Dismounted platoons or squads.
- Interpreter(s).
- Detainee security teams.
- Crowd control teams.
- Tactical military information support operations teams.

- Observation posts.
- Traffic control points or blocking positions.
- Host nation security forces (military or police).
- Aviation units.

5-146.   The outer cordon usually focuses on traffic control points and blocking positions. The inner cordon focuses on overwatching the objective and preventing exfiltration or repositioning of persons within the search area. Figure 5-4 shows the typical establishment of an urban cordon. Figure 5-5 shows the details of an inner cordon in an urban setting.

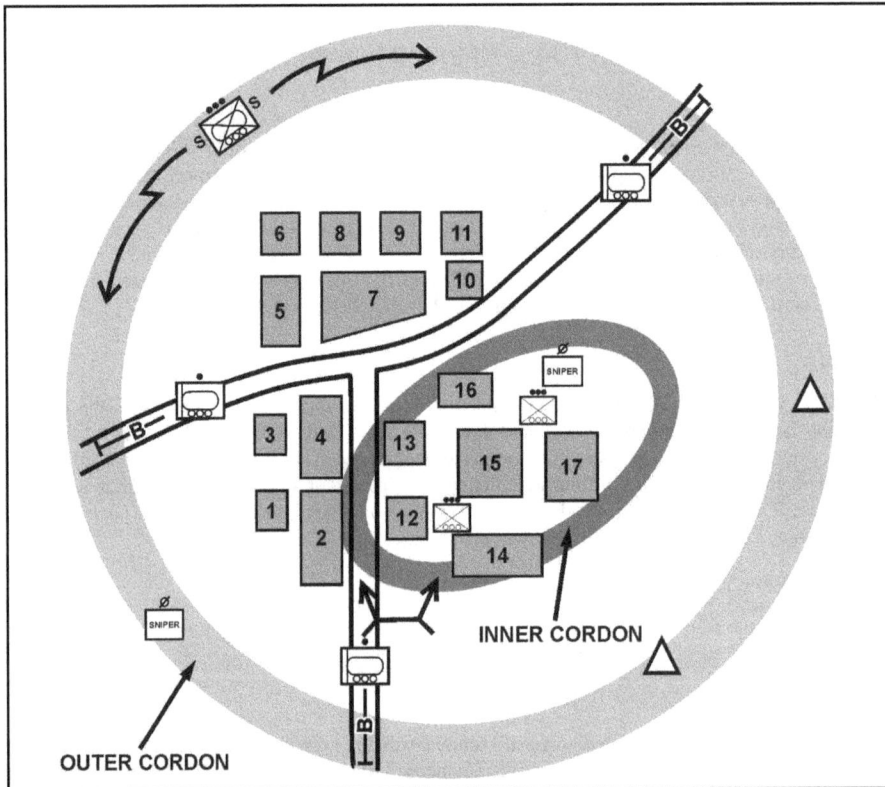

Figure 5-4. Typical urban cordon

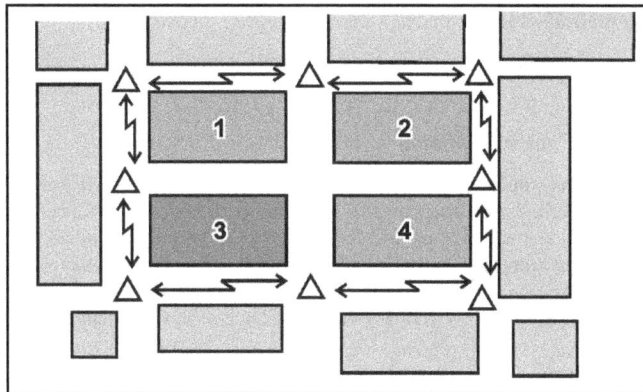

Figure 5-5. Urban inner cordon

Conduct the Search

5-147. A search should be a systematic action to ensure that personnel, documents, electronic data, and other material are identified, evaluated, collected, and protected to develop intelligence and facilitate follow-on actions. The tempo of the search operation should be slow enough to allow for an effective search but not so slow that it allows the belligerent force time to react to the search. Search teams should consider returning to an area after an initial search. This can surprise and remove belligerents who may not have been detected or may have returned.

5-148. Ensure higher command reviews and approves all search operations. The purpose of the search and the authority to search must be clear. Usually special laws regulate the search powers of military forces. Misuse of search authority can adversely affect the outcome of operations and future legal proceedings. Therefore, all searches must be lawful and properly recorded to be of value. These laws must be disseminated to the population to ensure understanding and compliance. (See FM 3-06.20 for details on searches.) Searches should have instructions for—

- **Personnel.** Personnel includes both male and female and both persons of interest and other persons.
- **Physical Items.** Physical items includes weapons, equipment, documents, computers, and cameras.
- **Information Mediums.** Information mediums includes data inside computers, cameras, and cell phones.

SEARCH OPERATIONS

5-149. A search is the deliberate examination of a person, place, area, or object using Soldiers, animals, or technological sensors to discover something or someone. Examples include searches of enemy or detained personnel, military objective areas, personnel or vehicles at a checkpoint, and lines of communications.

5-150. When conducting a search—

- Treat any objectionable material found, including propaganda signs and leaflets, as booby trapped until inspection proves it safe.
- Search underground and underwater areas thoroughly, using mine detectors to locate metal objects. Any freshly excavated ground could be a hiding place.
- Employ a graduated response technique in accordance with the mission variables. This technique uses warnings and progressive amounts of force to obtain compliance. For example, give warnings in the native language announcing that some type of force, lethal or nonlethal, will be used in a given amount of time if the occupants do not exit the building.
- Consider making announcements before entering the area to encourage inhabitants to leave peacefully. This alleviates discomfort. However, it also gives an enemy time to react.

POPULATION CONTROL METHODS

5-151. The three basic methods for controlling the population during a search of an urban area are described below.

Assemble Inhabitants in Central Location

5-152. This method moves inhabitants from their homes to a central area. It provides the most control, simplifies a thorough search, denies occupants an opportunity to conceal evidence, and allows for tactical questioning. However, this method has the disadvantage of taking the inhabitants away from their dwellings and possibly encouraging looting, which, in turn, engenders ill feelings. A specific element should control the centralized inhabitants. A military information support operations team, using a loudspeaker, can facilitate assembly by giving specific instructions to the inhabitants of the search area.

Restrict Inhabitants to Home

5-153. This method prohibits movement of civilians, allows them to stay in their dwellings, and discourages looting. Using a military information support operations team to broadcast messages in the local language facilitates clearing the streets of civilians and aids in restricting their movement. The security element must enforce this restriction to ensure compliance. The disadvantages of this method are that it makes control and tactical questioning difficult and gives inhabitants time to conceal contraband in their homes.

Control Heads of Households

5-154. In this method, the head of each household remains in front of the house while everyone else in the house is brought to one room. The security element controls the group at the central location, controls the head of each household, and provides security for the search team. When dealing with the head of a household, it is important to explain the purpose of the search using an interpreter. During the search, the head of the household accompanies the search team through the house and can open doors and containers to facilitate the search. This allows the head of the household to see it is a moral and ethical search, therefore, resulting in positive information operations.

SEARCHING HOUSES OR BUILDINGS

5-155. The object of a house search is to look for contraband and to determine if any residents are sought after adversaries. A search party assigned to search an occupied building should consist of at least one local police officer, a protective escort for local security, and a female searcher. If inhabitants remain in the dwellings, a protective escort should isolate and secure the inhabitants during the search. Forced entry may be necessary if a house is vacant or if an occupant refuses to allow entry. If a house containing property is searched while its occupants are away, it should be secured to prevent looting. Before U.S. forces depart, the commander should arrange for the community to protect such houses until the occupants return.

5-156. Make every effort to leave the house in the same condition than when the search began. In addition to information collection, the search team may use digital cameras or video recorders to establish the condition of the house before and after the search and to document all sensitive material or equipment found in the house. Before removing material, ensure that the date, time, location, the person from whom it was confiscated, and the reason for the confiscation is recorded. For a detailed search, search the walls and floors to discover hidden caches.

SEARCHING MALES

5-157. Anyone in an area to be searched can be an enemy or a sympathizer. However, to avoid making an enemy or sympathizer out of a suspect, searchers must be tactful. A search and cover team is task organized with one member providing security while the other member conducts the search. The search team should—

- Keep the individuals separated at a distance and, if possible, keep the individual isolated from the general population.
- Have the individual raise his arms and conduct a visual inspection.

- Test suspicious occupants should with explosive detection kits.
- Use a metal detection wand, if available, to quickly identify concealed weapons or other devices.
- Pat down the person being searched, starting from the head and moving systematically to the individual's feet. The searcher may need to wear protective gloves.
- Conduct tactical questioning during the search regarding information of tactical significance.

5-158. If the individual should be detained, move the individual quickly and quietly to a detainee collection point without creating friction for the other civilians in the area. Providing an explanation of the purpose or reason for the search through the use of an interpreter mitigates friction between the search team and the person being searched. Minimize escalation of posture and the nature of the search unless hostile indicators are present.

SEARCHING FEMALES

5-159. Enemy forces may use females to their advantage by using them to transport or hide contraband. To counter this, use female searchers. If a male must search females, take all possible measures to prevent perceptions of inappropriate conduct by—

- Using a metal detection wand to establish the immediate need for a more detailed search.
- Having the female raise her arms and systemically pat herself down. This enables the searcher to visually inspect for concealed weapons.
- Visually inspecting for physical attributes of a man in case the enemy is attempting to exfiltrate dressed as a woman.

5-160. If it is necessary for a male to conduct a more detailed search of the female, use the back side of the hands or ask another female from the same urban area to assist with the search. Cultural differences may make this a particularly sensitive problem, so small-unit leadership and supervision is recommended.

SEARCHING VEHICLES

5-161. Searching vehicles may require equipment such as detection devices, mirrors, tools, and military working dogs. Move and individually search occupants away from vehicles before searching the vehicle itself. A technique is to have the driver of the vehicle open all doors, the trunk, and the hood himself while under the close observation of a search team member. Immediately move the driver and all occupants to the individual search area after opening all doors. Then conduct a thorough search of a vehicle. Look under the vehicle and in the engine compartment and look for disturbances in the floorboards, seats, or side panels of the vehicle. Establish a separate vehicle search area to avoid unnecessary delays and traffic jams. An estimate of the situation determines if all or a portion of the vehicles should be searched.

AERIAL SEARCHES

5-162. UAS, rotary-wing, and even fixed-wing aircraft can act as observation platforms. Typically aircraft conduct reconnaissance of an assigned area or route in search of adversarial elements. Aerial search crews should be trained in both identifying and tracking potential enemies using terrain masking, deception, and standoff capability of aviation optics.

5-163. Rotary-wing aircraft are also an effective means of conducting mounted search patrols, specific population control measures, and security operations. Use air assault patrols during operations in which sufficient intelligence is available to justify their use or operations in which friendly ground-based operations have become predictable to adversaries. Such patrols are most effective in conjunction with ground operations.

5-164. Search teams may conduct snap checkpoints on roads to interdict adversaries mounted and dismounted movement. When the team locates a known enemy, it can instruct attack reconnaissance aviation teams to engage the enemy, or it may also choose to land and attack the enemy with a dismounted assault. This technique can be useful in open rural areas, unless an air defense threat is present.

5-165. In aerial or air-ground combined search operations, helicopters insert Soldiers in an area suspected of containing adversaries. With the helicopters overwatching from the air, Soldiers search the area, remounting and repeating the process in other areas. Leaders should plan for the evacuation of detainees, casualties, and materials by both air and ground.

SECTION VII – CONSOLIDATE

5-166. Guidelines for providing effective sustainment to company teams fighting in an urban environment are—

- Protect supplies and sustainment elements from the effects of enemy fires by preventing or avoiding detection and by using effective cover and concealment.
- Provide security for sustainment units when they are moving within the AO.
- Plan for a higher consumption rate of supplies, especially ammunition.
- Disperse and decentralize sustainment elements.
- Position support units as far forward as the tactical situation permits.
- Plan the locations of casualty collection points and evacuation sites.
- Plan for and use host nation support and civil resources when authorized and practical.

SECTION VIII – TRANSITION

5-167. Once offensive operations begin, the attacking commander tries to sense when subordinates reach, or are about to reach, their respective culminating points. Before they reach this point, the commander must transition to a focus on the defensive element of full spectrum operations.

TRANSITION TO DEFENSIVE OPERATIONS

5-168. The company commander prepares orders that include the time or circumstances under which the transition to the defense takes place, the missions and locations of platoons, and command and control measures. As the company transitions from an offensive focus to a defensive focus, the commander—

- Maintains contact and surveillance of the enemy, using a combination of reconnaissance units and surveillance assets to develop the information required to plan future actions.
- Establishes local security measures.
- Redeploys forces based on probable future employment.
- Maintains or regains contact with adjacent units in a contiguous AO and ensures that units remain capable of mutual support in a noncontiguous AO.
- Consolidates and reorganizes.

5-169. A lull in combat operations often accompanies transition. The commander cannot forget about the stability component of full spectrum operations. The civilian population in the unit's AO tends to come out of their hide positions and request assistance from friendly forces during these lulls. The commander must consider how to minimize the interference of these civilians with the company's operations while protecting the civilians from future hostile actions in accordance with international law.

5-170. The company commander should not wait too long to transition from the offense to the defense as subordinate forces approach their culminating points. Without prior planning, transitioning to defensive actions after reaching a culminating point is difficult. Initial defensive preparations are hasty, and forces are not adequately disposed for defense. Also, defensive reorganization requires more time than the enemy will probably allow.

5-171. A commander can use two basic techniques when transitioning to the defense.

- Establish a security area by having leading elements push forward to defensible terrain. The main force moves forward or rearward as necessary to occupy key terrain and institutes a hasty defense that progresses into a deliberate defense as time and resources allow.
- Establish a security area along the unit's final positions, moving the main body rearward to defensible terrain. The security force thins out, and the remaining force deploys to organize the defense.

TRANSITION TO STABILITY OPERATIONS

5-172. During major combat operations, the company commander transitions to a focus on the stability element of full spectrum operations if the company's offensive operations are successful in destroying or defeating the enemy and the situation is such that a focus on defensive operations is inappropriate. A tactical commander focuses on meeting the immediate essential service and civil security needs of the civilian inhabitants of the AO in coordination with any existing HN government and nongovernmental organizations before addressing other stability tasks. A significant change in the ROE will probably occur that must be inculcated down to the individual Soldier. A change in the task organization of the company team will also occur to introduce those capabilities required by the changes in the mission variables.

This page intentionally left blank.

Chapter 6

Defensive Urban Operations

The immediate purpose of a defensive operation is to defeat an enemy attack and gain the initiative for offensive operations. The combined arms team may also conduct the defense to—

- Gain time.
- Retain key terrain.
- Support other operations.
- Preoccupy the enemy in one area while friendly forces attack him in another.
- Erode enemy forces at a rapid rate while reinforcing friendly operations.

SECTION I – CHARACTERISTICS

6-1.   In urban terrain, the defending company takes advantage of the inherent cover and concealment. The commander considers restrictions to the attacker's ability to maneuver and observe. By using the terrain and fighting from well-prepared and mutually supporting positions, a defending company can delay, block, fix, or destroy a much larger attacking force. The defense of an urban area is organized around key terrain features, buildings, and areas that preserve the integrity of the defense and provide the company ease of movement.

6-2.   The five characteristics of a successful defense are described below.

PREPARATION

6-3.   The physical characteristics of urban areas naturally enhance the combat power of defending company teams. Urban terrain provides superb defensive positions for small units and vehicles with minimum preparation. With deliberate preparation, urban defensive positions can rapidly become strongpoints. Primary characteristics of urban terrain that enhance the defense are protection, obstacles, and concealment.

PROTECTION

6-4.   With little or no advance preparation, buildings, subsurface structures, and walls limit observation and engagement ranges. Nearly all buildings provide some ballistic protection from direct and indirect fire. Because of their height and close proximity, buildings in urban areas can mask Soldiers from indirect fire by interdicting the flight path at a point short of the intended target. Masking protects static company defenses and protects forces moving along routes bordered with tall buildings that form urban canyons. These protected routes can be used for sustainment, counterattacks, and maneuver.

OBSTACLES

6-5.   Structurally significant buildings in an urban area can create major obstacles to maneuver. These obstacles canalize maneuver into streets without any preparation by the defense. These areas then become kill zones for well-positioned company defenses. Blocking streets with obstacles can further restrict the maneuver options of the attacking force.

CONCEALMENT

6-6.   Buildings conceal the location, disposition, maneuver, and intent of the defense. The physical aspect of the urban environment enhances the defense by degrading the opposition's reconnaissance and security capabilities. Although the environment constrains defensive mobility in much the same manner as offensive mobility, the company has the time and opportunity to conduct careful reconnaissance and select and prepare routes. This gives the commander the ability to move reserves, maneuver counterattack forces, and plan sustainment without observation. Careful preparation provides the defending company a mobility advantage over attacking forces.

SECURITY

6-7.   The urban area can be an advantage or a disadvantage to the security of defending company teams. This largely depends on the populace. If the population is evacuated or supportive of U.S. forces, the environment may assist in the security of defending company elements. However, if the population is present and hostile, they may make security difficult.

6-8.   Friendly civilians in the urban area can help identify enemy forces attempting to conduct reconnaissance. Civilian activity also helps to mask defense preparations. However, a hostile element of the population may pass intelligence information to the enemy. They may assist enemy reconnaissance to infiltrate the urban area or provide guides, manpower, or resource support for enemy forces. Commanders should take measures to ensure strict control of hostile populations. If resources permit, commanders may consider removing potentially hostile civilians from the area.

6-9.   The physical aspects of the urban environment, uninfluenced by the human dimension, may assist in the security of defending company teams. The combat power of small security forces manning OPs is greatly enhanced and can restrict and monitor avenues of approach for enemy reconnaissance.

6-10.   The physical aspects of the urban environment may present some security challenges with observation. The compartmented terrain limits the field of observation from any one point. The defense may require more security forces to adequately observe the mounted and dismounted avenues to prevent infiltration. Enemy forces that successfully infiltrate are more difficult to locate. These forces gain numerous hide positions for small reconnaissance units in complex terrain.

DISRUPTION

6-11.   The urban environment helps defending company teams disrupt the attacker through compartmentalization, inhibiting detailed situational awareness, and facilitating counterattacks.

6-12.   The physical aspects of the urban area force the attacking enemy into compartmented urban canyons that make mutual support between attacking enemy columns difficult. Shifting resources from one portion of the enemy attack to another is also difficult. Physically, the urban area disrupts tactical communications, making synchronization of combat power difficult.

6-13.   Through careful planning, preparation, and rehearsals, defending company teams can facilitate rapid movement of larger forces that are normally hindered by complex urban terrain. Company teams can assemble counterattacks undetected, move them along covered and concealed routes, and achieve surprise at the point of the counterattack. Attacking forces, using the compartmented terrain, often leave forward elements in position to be isolated or expose long and vulnerable flanks to friendly counterattack and interdiction.

MASSING EFFECTS

6-14.   The restrictive nature of urban terrain reduces the attacker's maneuver options. Defenders can position forces in protected and mutually supporting positions oriented on deadly EAs. Relatively few well-positioned defenders can generate significant combat power. Without the positional advantage and the corresponding protective effects of the terrain, attacking forces often mass numbers to achieve the necessary combat power. Knowing the complex terrain permits defending companies to plan EAs that maximize the effects of their combat power.

FLEXIBILITY

6-15. The terrain of urban areas facilitates defensive flexibility because it can be quickly adapted for defensive operations with little or no preparation. The effect is similar to having multiple prepared positions on nearly every possible approach. The urban area can also permit rapid covered movement on interior lines, permitting swift movement to and occupation of strong defensive positions with little or no preparation.

6-16. The defense also has more flexibility since defenders often know and better understand the effects of urban terrain on operations. Normally, defenders do not get lost as easily, know complex lines of sight and masking effects, and best understand the ballistic characteristics of individual structures.

6-17. Defensive flexibility results from detailed planning and mental agility. Commanders develop defensive flexibility by ensuring that plans adequately address branches and sequels that include alternate and subsequent positions and emphasize counterattack options.

6-18. At company level and in smaller urban areas, mental agility allows commanders to see that the best urban defense may actually be to defend outside of the area. Such a defense mitigates the danger to the urban population and potentially reduces collateral damage. It takes advantage of long-range engagement capabilities and denies the enemy the opportunity to position themselves close to company forces or noncombatants as protection from fires. This defense may be appropriate when company teams have enough resources to defend more open terrain; when time permits deploying extensive obstacles and constructing protected positions; and when natural terrain, such as river obstacles, aids the defense.

SECTION II – SEQUENCING

6-19. Usually, the company team conducts defensive operations as part of a larger element, performing several integrated and overlapping activities. The following discusses the tactical considerations and procedures involved in each activity. This discussion shows an attacking enemy that uses depth in its operations. However, situations in which a company must defend against an enemy that does not have a doctrinal foundation are common. Unconventional enemy situations require a more flexible plan that allows for responsive and decentralized control of combat power.

6-20. A leader's reconnaissance is critical in order for the company to conduct occupation without hesitation and begin the priorities of work. The participants in the reconnaissance are the—

- Company commander.
- Platoon leaders.
- Mortar section leader.
- Fire support officer.
- Leaders of any attached elements.
- Security element.

6-21. The goal of the reconnaissance is to identify the—

- Enemy avenues of approach.
- Engagement areas.
- Sectors of fire.
- Tentative obstacle plan.
- Indirect fire plan.
- Observation post locations.
- Command post locations.

6-22. The BCT, battalion, and company establish security forces during occupation and preparation, and remaining forces begin to develop EAs and prepare BPs. Operational and tactical security is critical during the occupation to ensure the company avoids detection and maintains combat power for the actual defense. Soldiers at all levels of the company should thoroughly understand their duties and responsibilities related to the occupation. They should be able to execute the occupation quickly and efficiently to maximize the time available for planning and preparation of the defense.

6-23. Company and below defensive UO are conducted using the sequence of—

- Gain and maintain enemy contact.
- Disrupt the enemy.
- Fix the enemy.
- Maneuver.
- Follow through.

GAIN AND MAINTAIN ENEMY CONTACT

6-24. Security forces must protect friendly MBA forces to allow them to prepare their defense. These security forces work in conjunction with and compliment battalion and brigade security operations. The enemy will try to discover the defensive scheme of maneuver using reconnaissance elements and attacks by forward detachments and disruption elements. He will also try to breach the battalion's tactical obstacles.

SECURITY FORCE

6-25. The goals of the security force normally include providing early warning, destroying enemy reconnaissance units, and impeding and harassing enemy assault elements. The security force continues its mission until directed to displace. The commander may also use security forces in his deception effort to give the illusion of strength in one area while establishing the main defense in another. While conducting this type of security operation, the company may have to simultaneously prepare BPs, creating a challenging time management problem for the commander and his subordinate leaders.

GUIDES

6-26. During security operations, the company may have to provide guides to assist in the rearward passage of lines by BCT and battalion security forces and may be tasked to close the passage lanes. The company may also play a role in shaping the battlefield. The battalion commander may position the company to deny likely enemy attack corridors to enhance flexibility and force enemy elements into friendly EAs. When it is not conducting security or preparation tasks, the company normally occupies hide positions to avoid possible CBRN strikes or enemy artillery preparation.

DISRUPT THE ENEMY

6-27. The company engages the enemy at a time and place where it can maximize the lethality of direct and indirect fire systems to achieve success within the designated AO. As the enemy's assault force approaches the EA, the BCT or battalion may initiate close air support to weaken the enemy. Company forces occupy their actual defensive positions before the enemy reaches direct fire range. They may shift positions in response to enemy actions or other tactical factors.

FIX THE ENEMY

6-28. During his assault, the enemy deploys to achieve mass at a designated point, normally employing both assault and support forces. This may leave him vulnerable to the combined effects of indirect and direct fires and integrated obstacles. The enemy may employ additional forces to fix company elements and prevent them from repositioning.

6-29. Company counterattack forces may be committed against the enemy flank or rear, while other friendly forces may displace to alternate, supplementary, or subsequent positions in support of the commander's scheme of maneuver. All forces should be prepared for the enemy to maximize employment of combat multipliers, such as dismounted Infantry operations, to create vulnerability. The enemy is also likely to use artillery, close air support, and CBRN weapons to set the conditions for the assault.

MANEUVER

6-30. As the enemy's momentum slows or stops, company forces may conduct a counterattack. The counterattack may be for offensive purposes to seize the initiative from the enemy. In some cases, however, the purpose of the counterattack is mainly defensive, such as reestablishing a position or restoring control of the AO. The company may participate in the counterattack as a base-of-fire element, providing support by fire for the counterattack force or as the actual counterattack force.

FOLLOW-THROUGH

6-31. The company secures its defensive area by repositioning forces, destroying remaining enemy elements, processing EPWs, and reestablishing obstacles. The company conducts all necessary sustainment functions as it prepares to continue the defense. Even when enemy forces are not actively engaging it, the company maintains awareness of the tactical situation and local security at all times and prepares itself for possible follow-on missions.

SECTION III – TASK ORGANIZATION CONSIDERATIONS

6-32. Proper task organization is essential for successful defensive UO. The company commander allocates assets where needed to accomplish specific tasks. When developing task organization, the commander should consider all tasks being executed during an operation. Changes in task organization may be required to accomplish different tasks during mission execution.

6-33. With knowledge of the assets available and the battalion commander's intent, the company commander determines what terrain, forces, fires, and obstacles to use to accomplish the mission. Effective combined arms task organization ensures that forces are task organized with Infantry—the essential building block for all organizations conducting UO.

6-34. Urban operations often require an increased proportion of dismounted Infantry and engineer capabilities. Armor may not be required in the same proportion as Infantry. Combined arms UO are required at lower tactical levels where small, well-trained and well-led units dominate. Company level requires true combined arms capability and may include combat engineers, MI, reconnaissance, and artillery. In addition to combat engineers, explosive ordnance disposal teams, MP, CBRN personnel, and others with essential expertise to conduct mobility missions significantly reduce mobility and maneuver challenges.

SECTION IV – UNDERSTAND

6-35. The defender organizes and plans his defense by considering OAKOC, fire hazards, and communications restrictions. Commanders should give special consideration to the below paragraphs during UO.

MANEUVER

6-36. Tanks, MGS, and BFVs provide long-range fires and increased mobility. However, urban areas may restrict their mobility and make them vulnerable to enemy infantry antiarmor weapons.

FIRES

6-37. Conduct comprehensive FS planning due to the proximity of buildings to targets, minimum range restrictions, repositioning requirements, and ROE. Use indirect fires to suppress and blind enemy overwatch elements, engage enemy infantry, provide counterbattery fire, and support counterattacks.

6-38. Employ mortars to maximize the effect of their high-angle fires. Use them to engage—
- Enemy overwatch positions.
- Enemy infantry before they seize a foothold.

- Targets on rooftops.
- Enemy reinforcements within range.

MOBILITY

6-39. Usually, one engineer platoon or company supports a battalion. Engineers are employed under battalion control or attached to companies. Company commanders may be given an engineer platoon or squad to assist them in developing the survivability, mobility, and countermobility considerations of the company defense plan. Tasks that engineers can accomplish in the defense of an urban area include—

- Constructing obstacles and rubbling.
- Clearing fields of fire.
- Laying mines.
- Preparing mobility routes between positions.
- Preparing fighting positions.

AMMUNITION AND OTHER SUPPLIES

6-40. Ammunition expenditure is high when fighting in an urban area. To avoid moving around the AO with ammunition resupply during the battle, members of each occupied platoon and squad position should stockpile ammunition. Platoons should also stockpile firefighting equipment, drinking water, food, and first-aid supplies at each squad position.

SECTION V – SHAPE

6-41. Counterreconnaissance tasks are a crucial component of security operations. Counterreconnaissance is the sum of all actions taken to defeat enemy reconnaissance and security efforts. It is a directed effort to prevent visual observation or infiltration of friendly forces by enemy reconnaissance elements. The focus of counterreconnaissance is to deny the enemy any information on friendly operations by destroying, defeating, or deceiving enemy reconnaissance units and sensors in accordance with engagement criteria and the ROE.

6-42. Countering the enemy's mounted and dismounted reconnaissance elements is the first and possibly most important step in ensuring the friendly main body can successfully execute its mission. At the same time, it can be extremely difficult to identify enemy reconnaissance forces, especially when they are dismounted. The platoon may lack this capability. As a result, this task is most successfully executed when it is approached as a combined arms effort at troop and battalion task force level.

6-43. The company or troop concept of executing counterreconnaissance should address how the unit will accomplish the two aspects of counterreconnaissance: acquiring the enemy and then destroying it. At battalion and squadron level, the intelligence staff officer provides key input in this determination. He identifies the type of enemy reconnaissance elements that may be used in the area and when they are most likely to move into the area. It is especially important for the intelligence staff officer to note the locations and activities of dismounted enemy elements, which present the greatest danger to the company and the supported unit. Information from the intelligence staff officer is integrated into the operation order and is part of the unit's IPB.

6-44. The commander should discuss conduct of counterreconnaissance in the orders process, indicating in tactical terms how elements will organize and conduct the operations throughout the depth of the AO. This information should include planning considerations for the operation, including—

- Direct fire planning and coordination.
- Observation planning and coordination.
- Command and control.
- Battle handover.

6-45. In all counterreconnaissance operations, the goal is to destroy the enemy reconnaissance forces before or after they have penetrated the initial screen line. The role of the units in these operations is usually to conduct a screen mission to acquire and identify enemy reconnaissance forces. To prevent the enemy from detecting the screen, the acquiring elements of the platoon should be well hidden. In most cases, the platoon cannot be expected to have the capability to acquire, identify, and defeat the enemy reconnaissance by itself. Other elements should be tasked to fight and destroy the enemy reconnaissance elements.

6-46. Screens have certain critical tasks that guide planning but are not a fixed checklist or a sequential execution guide, to include—

- Maintain continuous surveillance of all avenues of approach that affect the main body's mission under all conditions.
- Conduct counterreconnaissance to destroy, defeat, or repel all enemy reconnaissance elements within capabilities.
- When facing an echeloned enemy force, locate and identify the lead elements that indicate the enemy's main attack as prescribed in the enemy's threat characteristics based on IPB. Determine the direction of enemy movement.
- Maintain contact and report activities of the enemy even while displacing.
- Impede and harass the enemy within capabilities while displacing to provide the protected force commander with additional time and maneuver space.
- Detect and report all enemy ground elements attempting to pass through the screen.

SECTION VI – ENGAGE

6-47. Company and below defensive UO missions support the three basic defensive tasks—area defense, mobile defense, or retrograde. Common defensive missions are described below.

HASTY DEFENSE

6-48. A combined arms team in urban terrain often conducts a hasty defense, which is characterized by reduced preparation time. Units are deployed, weapons are emplaced, and positions are prepared in accordance with the amount of time the company commander has available. All urban troop-leading procedures are the same as in other operational environments. The priorities of work are basically the same, but many take place concurrently.

6-49. Preparations for the hasty defense vary with the time available. Units should follow their established defensive priorities of work. In a hasty defense, the primary effort is to position weapons and Soldiers to destroy or channel the enemy, camouflage and conceal fighting positions, and provide as much protection as possible for the Soldiers manning them.

6-50. The company constructs positions using appliances, furniture, and other convenient items and materials and locates them back from the windows in the shadows of the room. The company places less emphasis on fortifying positions and making major alterations to the environment, delaying such activities until after it has established security.

6-51. Considerations for preparing hasty defensive positions are—

- **Positioning Crew-Served and Special Weapons.** Unless an outside position is preferable and can be protected and camouflaged, the company positions crew-served and special weapons inside buildings.
- **Emplacing Barriers and Obstacles.** To permit more time, the company establishes two belts of barriers and obstacles that are not as extensive as in a defense. The company covers all obstacles with observation and fires.
- **Preparing Positions.** The tactical SOP lists the sequence in which fighting positions are constructed. The following is an example sequence:
  - Gather available materials (such as tables, dressers, and appliances) to construct positions.
  - Construct stable firing platforms for the weapons.
  - Use the material gathered to build frontal and side protection to stop small-arms fire.
  - Do not disturb firing windows. Curtains and other aspects of the original setting are components of camouflage.

- ■ Construct alternate firing positions similar to the primary positions.
- ■ Emplace rear and overhead cover on the primary positions.
- ■ Remove fire hazards. Pre-position firefighting equipment.
- ■ Construct dummy positions in rooms above, below, and next to primary and alternate positions to draw enemy suppressive fire away from primary positions.
- ■ Walk the positions from the enemy side.
- ● **Conducting Rehearsals.** Conduct rehearsals with leaders and Soldiers, to include the orientation of the defense, unit positions, location of crew-served weapons, counterattack plans, and withdrawal plans.
- ● **Enhancing Movement.** Little time is available to enhance movement within the defense. Units should plan to use tunnels, underground routes, and routes through buildings. Removing obstructions to alternate positions and the counterattack route is priority.
- ● **Establishing and Maintaining Communications.** Check communications. Communications are primarily FM and digital. Plan and improve routes for messengers. If time is available, emplace wire as an improvement to the defense.
- ● **Improving the Defense.** As time permits, consider the following areas and prioritize them in accordance with the mission variables:
  - ■ Armored vehicle integration.
  - ■ Barrier and obstacle improvement.
  - ■ Improvement of primary and alternate positions.
  - ■ Preparation of supplementary positions.
  - ■ Additional movement enhancement efforts.
  - ■ Initiation of patrols.
  - ■ Improvement of camouflage.
  - ■ Continued rehearsals for counterattack and withdrawal.
  - ■ Sustainment considerations, including stockpiling ammunition and providing maintenance for weapons and vehicles.
  - ■ Rest plan.

AREA DEFENSE

6-52. A village is an urban area surrounded by other types of terrain. A company team may receive an area defense mission to defend a village as part of a battalion defense. The company commander establishes BPs or strongpoints within his or the battalion's AO. He coordinates and integrates his defense with battalion and other maneuver companies. Once the company commander has completed his reconnaissance, he reconnoiters the surrounding terrain and, with the information assembled, develops his plan for the defense.

6-53. One of his first decisions is whether to defend on the leading edge of the village or farther back within the confines of the village. This decision is based on the mission variables. Normally, defending on the leading edge, where the defending company can take advantage of long-range observation and fields of fire is more effective against an armor-heavy force. Defending in depth within the village to deny the enemy a foothold is more effective against a force that is primarily infantry. The company may need to coordinate with adjacent units to plan for the defense or control of the open terrain that typically surrounds a village.

6-54. Company commanders should know the type of enemy. If the enemy is mainly infantry, the greatest danger is allowing him to gain a foothold in the village. If the enemy is armored or motorized infantry, the greatest danger is direct fire that can destroy the company's defensive positions. The company commander should also consider the terrain forward and to the flanks of the village from which the enemy can direct fires against his positions.

PLATOON BATTLE POSITIONS

6-55. Platoons receive a small group of buildings in which to prepare their defense, permitting the platoon leader to establish mutually supporting, squad-size positions. This increases the area that the platoon can control and hampers the enemy's ability to isolate or bypass a platoon. A platoon may be responsible for the road through the village. The rest of the company is then positioned to provide all-round security and defense in depth.

COMPANY MORTARS AND JAVELINS POSITIONS

6-56. Mortar positions should protect the mortars from direct fire and allow for overhead clearance. Javelin positions should allow the Javelins to engage targets at maximum ranges with alternate firing points.

INFANTRY CARRIER VEHICLE AND BRADLEY FIGHTING VEHICLE POSITIONS

6-57. Leaders can position ICVs and BFVs in defilade positions behind rubble and walls or inside buildings for movement into and out of the area. However, they should first verify that the buildings selected can support the vehicle weight. ICVs and BFVs can conduct resupply, casualty evacuation, and rapid repositioning during the battle. They can also provide a mobile reserve for the company.

MOBILE GUN SYSTEM AND TANK PLATOON POSITIONS

6-58. The company commander can place the MGS or tank platoon along the leading edge of the defensive position where rapid fire will complement the Javelins. The MGS or tank platoon leader should select exact firing positions and recommend EAs. If faced by enemy infantry, the MGS or tank platoon moves to alternate positions with the protection of the Infantry. These alternate positions allow the MGS platoon to engage to the front as well as the flanks with as little movement as possible.

6-59. Positions can be selected within buildings, and mouseholes can be constructed. Leaders should first verify that the buildings selected can support the vehicle weight and are structurally sound enough to withstand firing overpressure. After they are withdrawn from the leading edge of the town, the MGS or tank platoon can provide a mobile reserve for the company.

RUBBLING

6-60. If he has the authority and the ROE permit, the company commander decides which buildings to rubble. To defeat the enemy, he should have good fields of fire, but rubbling the buildings too soon or rubbling too many may disclose his exact locations and destroy cover from direct fire.

FINAL PROTECTIVE FIRES

6-61. The company plans final protective fires to address the biggest threat to his company—the enemy's infantry. When firing final protective fires inside an urban area is necessary, mortars are more effective than artillery. Mortars have a higher angle of fall, which gives them a greater chance of impacting on the street.

BARRIERS AND OBSTACLES

6-62. The company can construct obstacles in an urban area, but the obstacles should stop enemy vehicles without interfering with the company's own movement within the urban area. The company can detonate cratering charges at key street locations on order and lay antitank and command-detonated mines on the outskirts of the urban area and along routes the company will not use. Barriers and obstacles are emplaced in multiple belts.

ENGINEERS

6-63. Supporting engineers can use C4 and other explosives to make firing ports, mouseholes, and demolition obstacles. Based upon the priority of work, the company commander orders the engineer squad leader to assist each of the Infantry platoons preparing the small urban area for defense and to execute the company obstacle plan.

6-64. The engineer squad leader's mission is to tell the Soldiers exactly where to place the demolitions and how much is needed for the desired effect. He assists in preparing the charges, emplacing and recording minefields, and preparing fighting positions.

COMMUNICATIONS

6-65. Leaders should develop a plan for redundant communication systems in case FM and digital systems become degraded. If time permits, run wire between positions and vehicles. Develop pyrotechnic signals and plan for the use of messengers.

AREA DEFENSE OF A BLOCK OR GROUP OF BUILDINGS

6-66. A company normally conducts a defense of a city block or group of buildings as part of a battalion conducting an area defense in an urban area. Company commanders may assign their platoons strongpoints, BPs, AOs, or any combination of these. The unit may have to defend a city block or group of buildings in a core periphery or residential area. This operation is conducted in accordance with the battalion's defensive scheme of maneuver.

6-67. The company commander must ensure that the defense is synchronized with the actions of security forces conducting delaying operations to the front of the company's position. The defense should take advantage of the protection of buildings that dominate the avenues of approach into the MBA. This mission differs from defense of a small urban area in that it is more likely to be conducted completely on urban terrain, without the surrounding open terrain that characterizes the defense of a small urban area. An Infantry company is particularly well suited for this type of mission since the fighting requires the enemy to move infantry into the urban area to seize and control key terrain.

6-68. A well-organized company defense in an urban area—

- Stops the attack of the enemy on streets by using obstacles and direct and indirect fires.
- Destroys the enemy by ambush and direct fire from prepared positions within defensible buildings.
- Ejects the enemy from footholds or remains in place for a counterattack.

RECONNAISSANCE AND SECURITY

6-69. Soldiers conduct reconnaissance patrols of the AO, prepare obstacles, and prepare positions. Patrols supplement OPs mainly during periods of limited visibility. The company should establish wire communications in addition to FM and digital systems. Platoons may establish an OP in order to provide spot reports concerning the enemy assaulting the company AO or BP.

EXECUTION

6-70. Engage the enemy with direct and indirect fire along avenues of approach, cover the obstacles by fire, and prepare a strong defense inside the buildings. Reserve forces should be near the front of the company AO in covered and concealed positions with a number of planning priorities. Counterattack forces should have specific instructions as to what their actions will be after the enemy assault has been repelled. The company should conduct rehearsals both day and night.

PERIMETER DEFENSE OF KEY TERRAIN

6-71. A combined arms team defends key terrain independently or as part of a battalion. It may form a perimeter defense around key terrain, such as a public utility, communications center, government center, or traffic circle that enhances movement. During the defense of key terrain, a combined arms team may also—

- Provide inner and outer security patrols.
- Establish observation posts.

- Establish checkpoints and roadblocks.
- Conduct civilian control and evacuation.
- Conduct coordination with local authorities.
- Prevent collateral damage.
- Supervise specific functions associated with operation of a facility, such as water purification tests and site inspections.

6-72. A combined arms team can defend a traffic circle or similar terrain to prevent the enemy from seizing it. This is characterized by the occupation and defense of the buildings around the traffic circle that control the avenues of approach into and out of the objective area. Armored vehicles are positioned to dominate avenues of approach. This defense may be part of conventional defensive operations or part of stability operations. In many cases, an unclear enemy situation and restrictive ROE characterize this mission. The mission variables determine how to defend the objective.

CONSIDERATIONS

6-73. Depending on the mission variables, the commander considers the following when establishing a perimeter defense:

- Artillery and attack helicopter support.
- Air defense artillery units.
- Engineer units to construct obstacles.
- Interpreters to assist in the functioning of a facility and operation of the equipment.
- Military police, civil affairs, and military information support operations units for civilian control and liaison.
- Coordination with local police and authorities.

EXECUTION

6-74. The company commander does not have to occupy the key terrain. He deploys his units in such a manner to prevent the enemy from controlling the key terrain. The company emplaces machine guns and antitank weapons to cover the dismounted and mounted avenues of approach, respectively. It uses wire obstacles to deny entry into the area and uses antitank and command-detonated mines consistent with the ROE. Obstacles are covered by fire and rigged with detection devices and trip flares.

6-75. The company is prepared to defend against a direct attack, such as a raid or sabotage. The mortar section provides all-round FS, and the antitank section engages vehicular targets. If the threat does not require the employment of mortars or antitank weapons, the commander can assign these sections other tasks.

DEFENSE OF AN URBAN STRONGPOINT

6-76. A company may be directed to construct a strongpoint as part of a battalion defense. To do so, it should be augmented with engineer support, more weapons, and sustainment resources. A strongpoint is defended until the unit is formally ordered out of it by the commander directing the defense.

6-77. A strongpoint may be part of any defensive plan. It may be built to protect vital units or installations, as an anchor around which more mobile units maneuver, or as part of a trap designed to destroy enemy forces that attack it.

6-78. Urban areas are easily converted to strongpoints. Stone, brick, or steel buildings provide cover and concealment. Buildings, sewers, and some streets provide covered and concealed routes and can be rubbled to provide obstacles. Telephone systems can provide communications.

6-79. The specific positioning of units in a strongpoint depends on the commander's mission analysis and estimate of the situation. The same considerations for a key terrain defense apply. Additional considerations are—

- Reinforce each individual fighting position (to include alternate, subsequent and supplementary positions) to withstand small-arms fire, mortar fire, and artillery fragmentation.
- Stockpile food, water, ammunition, pioneer tools, and medical supplies in each fighting position.
- Support each individual fighting position with several others.
- Plan and construct covered and concealed routes between positions and along routes of supply and communication. Use these to support counterattack and maneuver within the strongpoint.
- Divide the strongpoint into several independent but mutually supporting positions or AOs. If one of the positions or AOs must be evacuated or is overrun, limit the enemy penetration with obstacles and fires and support a counterattack.
- Construct obstacles and minefields to disrupt or canalize enemy formations, to reinforce fires, and to protect the strongpoint from the assault. Place the obstacles and mines out as far as friendly units can observe them, within the strongpoint, and at points in between where they will be useful.
- Prepare range cards for each position and confirm them by fires. Plan indirect fires in detail and register them. Also, plan indirect fires for firing directly on the strongpoint using proximity fuzes.
- Plan and test several means of internal and external communication, to include FM, digital, wire, messenger, pyrotechnics, and other signals.
- Improve or repair the strongpoint until the unit is relieved or withdrawn. More positions can be built, routes to other positions marked, existing positions improved or repaired, and barriers built or fixed.

DELAY

6-80. The intent of a delay is to trade space for time by slowing the enemy, causing him casualties, and stopping him without becoming decisively engaged. This is done by defending, disengaging, moving, and defending again. A company delay is normally conducted as part of the battalion task force's plan. The delay destroys enemy reconnaissance elements forward of the outskirts of the urban area, prevents the penetration of the urban area, and gains and maintains contact with the enemy to determine the strength and location of the main attack. Infantry companies are well suited for this operation. They can take advantage of the cover and concealment provided by urban terrain and inflict casualties on the enemy at close range.

6-81. Platoons delay by detecting the enemy early; inflicting casualties using patrols, OPs, and ambushes; and by taking advantage of all obstacles. Each action is followed by a disengagement and displacement. Displacement occurs on covered and concealed routes through buildings or underground. By day, the defense is dispersed. At night, it is more concentrated. Close coordination and maintaining awareness of the current friendly and enemy situation are critical aspects of this operation.

6-82. Delays are planned by assigning platoon BPs, platoon AOs, or both. Routes are planned to each BP or within the AO. Routes are also planned to take advantage of the inherent cover and concealment afforded by urban terrain. The company's AO should be prepared with obstacles to increase the effect of the delay. Engineers prepare obstacles on main routes but avoid some covered and concealed routes that friendly troops use for reinforcement, displacement, and resupply. When no longer needed, these routes are destroyed and obstacles are executed.

6-83. Antiarmor weapon systems and armored vehicles should position on the outskirts of the urban area in defilade positions or in prepared shelters to destroy the enemy at maximum range. They fire at visible targets and then displace to alternate positions. If available, platoons are reinforced with sensors or ground surveillance radars, which can be emplaced on the outskirts or on higher ground to attain the maximum range in the assigned AO.

SECTION VII – CONSOLIDATE

6-84. Guidelines for providing effective sustainment to units fighting in an urban environment are—

- Protect supplies and sustainment elements from the effects of enemy fires by preventing or avoiding detection and by using effective cover and concealment.
- Provide security for sustainment units when they are moving within the AO.
- Plan for a higher consumption rate of supplies, especially ammunition.
- Disperse and decentralize sustainment elements.
- Position support units as far forward as the tactical situation permits.
- Plan the locations of casualty collection points and evacuation sites.
- Plan for and use HN support and civil resources when authorized and practical.

SECTION VIII – TRANSITION

6-85. If a defense is successful, the company commander anticipates and seeks the opportunity to transition to the offense. If the defense is unsuccessful, the commander needs to transition from a defensive posture into retrograde operations.

OFFENSIVE OPERATIONS

6-86. A defending commander transitioning to a focus on the offense element of full spectrum operations anticipates when and where the enemy will reach its culminating point or require an operational pause before it can continue. The enemy force will do everything it can to keep the company team from knowing when it is becoming overextended.

6-87. The company team must be careful not to be successfully targeted by enemy deception operations designed to tempt the commander to abandon the advantages of fighting from prepared defensive positions. The commander ensures that platoons have the assets necessary to accomplish their assigned offensive missions. As the company team transitions from the defense to the offense, it—

- Establishes a line of departure for the offensive operation. This may require conducting local, small-scale attacks to secure terrain necessary for the conduct of the offensive operation or to destroy enemy forces that could threaten the larger offensive operation.
- Maintains contact with the enemy, using combinations of available reconnaissance and security units to develop the information required to plan future operations and avoid being deceived by enemy deception operations.
- Redeploys the combined arms team based on the probable future employment of each element.
- Maintains or regains contact with adjacent units in a contiguous AO and ensures that platoons remain capable of mutual support in a noncontiguous AO.
- Transitions the engineer effort by shifting the emphasis from countermobility and survivability to mobility.

6-88. The company commander should not wait too long to transition from the defense to the offense as the enemy force approaches its culminating point. Enemy forces will be dispersed, extended in depth, and weakened in condition. At that time, any enemy defensive preparations will be hasty, and enemy forces will not be adequately disposed for defense. The commander wants the enemy in this posture when the company team transitions to the offense, denying the enemy time to prepare for the defense.

6-89. A commander can use two basic techniques when transitioning to the offense:

- Attack using forces not previously committed to the defense. This technique is preferred since defending platoons or squads may still be decisively engaged. These attacking forces may come from the reserve.
- Conduct offensive actions using the currently defending forces. This technique has the advantage of being more rapidly executed and thus more likely to catch the enemy by surprise.

STABILITY OPERATIONS

6-90. A defending commander transitions to a focus on the stability element of full spectrum operations if the defense has retained decisive urban terrain, denied vital areas to the enemy, and successfully attrited the enemy as to make offensive actions unnecessary. A commander focuses on meeting the immediate essential service and civil security needs of the civilian population within the AO in coordination with any existing HN government and nongovernmental organizations before addressing the other stability tasks. A significant change in the ROE will probably occur that must be inculcated down to the individual Soldier. A change in the task organization of the company team will also occur to introduce those capabilities required by the changes in the mission variables.

Chapter 7

Urban Combat Skills

Successful UO depend on the proper employment of the platoon, squad, team, and crew. Each Soldier should be proficient in the skills discussed in this chapter, which include movement, breaching and clearing buildings, survivability, and subterranean operations.

SECTION I – MOVEMENT

7-1. Maintaining situational awareness of both the inside and outside of structures during movement in urban terrain is critical. Since a Soldier can move from one area to another by stepping through an opening, he should be constantly aware of both areas when moving through an urban area.

7-2. Movement in an urban area exposes a Soldier to all the dimensions of urban terrain. An enemy could be on the outside or the inside of any building or on any floor, to include below ground or the roof. Typical external sectors of fire orient on specific external open areas—a length of a street or a small section of a street—that is visible from either inside a nearby building or from down an adjoining side street. Typical internal sectors of fire orient on specific internal open areas—large open rooms, doorways, or hallways.

NAVIGATION

7-3. Urban areas present different navigational challenges. Normal terrain features depicted on maps may not apply. Buildings become the major terrain features, and units become tied to streets. Fighting in the city destroys buildings, rubble blocks streets, and road signs are often destroyed or removed. Navigational tools that may be available to leaders during UO include—
- **Maps.** Maps of sewers, gas lines, and electrical lines along with other information about the city infrastructure can often be provided by city utility workers.
- **Global Positioning System.** GPSs have difficulty determining locations when underground or within buildings due to line of sight challenges. They should be employed on the tops of buildings, in open areas, and down streets where obstacles do not affect line of sight readings.
- **Aerial Platforms.** Aerial platforms can assist units in navigating through urban terrain, using a laser or an infrared searchlight to identify objectives, friendly locations, or areas of unknown activity.
- **Photographs.** Photographs, especially current aerial photographs, are excellent supplements to military maps. Recent photographs show changes that have taken place since a map was made, which could include destroyed buildings, streets blocked by rubble, and even enemy defensive preparations. Whenever possible, use aerial photos or satellite imagery when the sun is directly overhead to minimize the amount of shadowing around structures.

COMMUNICATION

7-4. To ensure success and prevent fratricide, Soldiers must effectively communicate with other team members and other teams in their vicinity. However, using verbal commands may reveal the location and immediate intent of friendly forces to the enemy. Terms similar to the ones listed in table 7-1 should be a part of each Soldier's vocabulary and used as per unit SOP.

7-5. Prior to breach of an entry point or room entry, the clearing team members should communicate using visual signals to reduce the chance that the room's occupants are alerted to the presence of the team or their likely entry point. After entry, the clearing team members should find a balance between verbal and visual communication that allows them to rapidly and safely clear the room without alerting other enemy forces as to their location or intent.

7-6. If at any point a team member experiences a weapon malfunction, he has to make an immediate decision based on his location and the presence of any enemy. If near the doorway, he must clear the doorway. However, if an enemy combatant is present and presents an immediate threat, he must try to subdue or disable the enemy by any means possible. The immediate goal is to clear the other team members' fields of fire. Once the other team members have cleared their sectors of fire and eliminated any other enemy in the room, they can then assist the Soldier with the malfunctioning weapon.

7-7. If the enemy is outside the immediate danger area of the Soldier, the Soldier should clear the doorway and drop to one knee. Doing so indicates that he has experienced a weapon malfunction and prevents fratricide by ensuring that the next Soldier's fields of fire are clear. Once on a knee, the Soldier should remain there until the team leader directs him to stand up. If the kneeling Soldier corrects his weapon malfunction, he can continue to engage targets from his kneeling position. Announcing MALFUNCTION or GUN DOWN and GUN UP (when the gun is again operational) communicates with the other team members but can also alert the enemy.

Table 7-1. Example verbal commands

Term	Explanation
CLEAR	Given by an individual to report their AO is clear.
UP	Given by an individual to report they are ready to continue the mission.
ROOM CLEAR	Given by the team leader to team members, squad leaders, and follow-on teams to report the room is clear and secured.
COMING OUT (COMING IN)	Given by an individual to inform another element that they are about to exit a room or building or enter a room or building.
COME OUT (COME IN)	Given by another element to acknowledge that it is safe to exit a room or building or enter a room or building.
COMING UP (COMING DOWN)	Given by an individual to inform another element that they are about to ascend or descend stairs.
COME UP (COME DOWN)	Given by another element to acknowledge that it is safe to ascend or descend stairs.
SHORT ROOM	Given by an individual (Soldier 1 or Soldier 2) to inform other team members that the room is small and Soldier 3 and Soldier 4 should not enter.
MAN DOWN	Given by an individual to inform other team members that a Soldier is down (wounded or injured) and cannot continue the mission.
GRENADE	Given by an individual to warn others that an enemy grenade has been thrown and to take immediate action. If possible, include location of the grenade.
GO LONG	Given by the team leader to a team member to direct the team member to take up security farther into the room or farther down a hallway.
GUN DOWN	Given by an individual to inform other team members that their gun has malfunctioned.
GUN UP	Given by an individual to inform other team members that their previously malfunctioning gun is operational again.
RELOADING	Given by an individual to inform other team members that they are reloading their weapon. Follow with GUN UP when ready.

MOVING OUTSIDE BUILDINGS

7-8. Movement in urban terrain is best conducted by fire teams. Individual movement techniques should be practiced until they become habitual, allowing for rapid engagement of any exposed enemy. (See FM 3-21.75 for details on individual movement techniques in urban area.) Individual movement techniques include—

- Crossing streets and open areas.
- Moving parallel to buildings.

- Moving past windows, to include—
  - Above-knee windows.
  - Below-knee windows.
  - Full-height windows.
- Moving around corners.
- Observing around corners.
- Pie-ing around corners.
- Crossing walls.

ENTERING BUILDINGS

7-9. Once a leader decides to enter a building, the immediate goal is to secure a foothold. Entering a building and securing a foothold overlap with the task of entering and clearing a room. A foothold is the first room entered. From this secure room, units can launch operations throughout the rest of the building.

7-10. When preparing to enter and clear buildings and rooms, all Soldiers should use the high ready weapon position. (See FM 3-22.9 for details.)

7-11. The most important considerations in securing a foothold in the building are the three potential threats—

- Enemy outside the building.
- Enemy inside the building.
- Inside enemy's ability to engage friendly forces on the outside.

7-12. These three threats are key factors in selecting the building entry point and the operating conditions (surgical, precision, or high intensity). The selection of the entry point is heavily based on the mission variables, while the operating conditions influence how to breach an entry point.

7-13. To enter a building, use the following steps:

Note. Depending on the type of breach selected, a breach may be executed before or after moving to the entry point.

IDENTIFY ENTRY POINT

7-14. An entry point should be large enough for a Soldier to pass through. It is preferable that an entering Soldier be able to pass through in an unrestricted manner, in an upright position, and be rapidly followed by another Soldier. To obtain this size of an entry point a breach is often required.

7-15. The entry point is a focal point for all enemy in the room. As such, it is known as the "fatal funnel." To minimize vulnerability, pass quickly and smoothly through and then away from the entry point. Each additional Soldier successfully through and away from the entry point increases the unit's control of the room. If a Soldier falls within or near the entry point, he should stay down until the last man clears the entry point.

7-16. In high threat situations, avoid using ground-floor windows and doors except as a last resort. Consider using other means available to make breach holes for entry, to include entry from a higher floor, roof, or basement. If the threat situation warrants, the actual entry of Soldiers should be preceded by a hand grenade (fragmentation, concussion, or stun hand grenade) followed by immediate entry of the clearing team.

ENTERING THROUGH DOORWAYS

7-17. Doors can be easily booby trapped or blocked. Entering through a door that is not booby trapped or within the line of fire of enemy personnel is normally the best way to enter a room. If a door is suspected of being booby trapped or if enemy personnel may be in the room, avoid or explosively breach the door.

7-18.   Prior to entering or determining if a breach is necessary, Soldiers should trace the doorframe with their hand or barrel of their weapon while their eyes look for booby traps.

ENTERING THROUGH WINDOWS

7-19.   Entering through most windows is limited to one Soldier at a time and normally requires the use of at least one hand, leaving only one hand to hold a weapon. As such, an entering Soldier is extremely vulnerable to fire from inside the room. To enter an enemy occupied room by going through a window, use some form of distraction, such as a hand grenade. The two levels of windows are described below.

Ground-Floor Windows

7-20.   Treat ground-floor windows that can be entered in an upright position as a doorway. Enter other ground-floor windows using the assistance of other Soldiers. This allows the entering Soldier to enter by using one hand for balance and control while the other hand holds and manipulates his weapon. The two-man heel lift (figure 7-1) or the two-man supported lift technique (figure 7-2) can be used to enter a ground-floor window. After the first Soldier enters, subsequent Soldiers are lifted into the room while the first Soldier secures the room. From a secure room, additional Soldiers can be pulled into the room using the one-man lift (figure 7-3) or the two-man pull technique (figure 7-4).

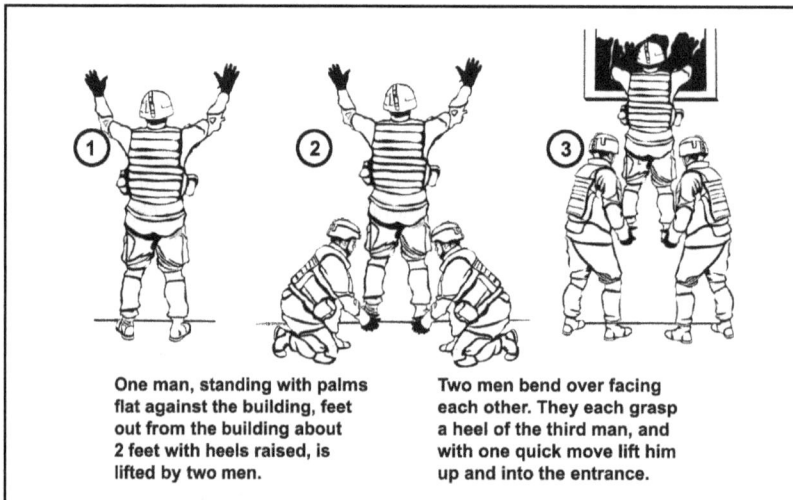

Figure 7-1. Two-man heel lift

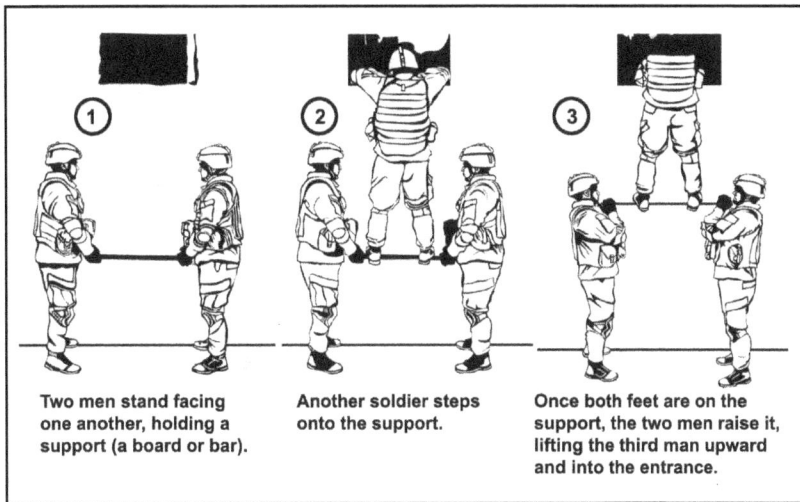

Figure 7-2. Two-man supported lift

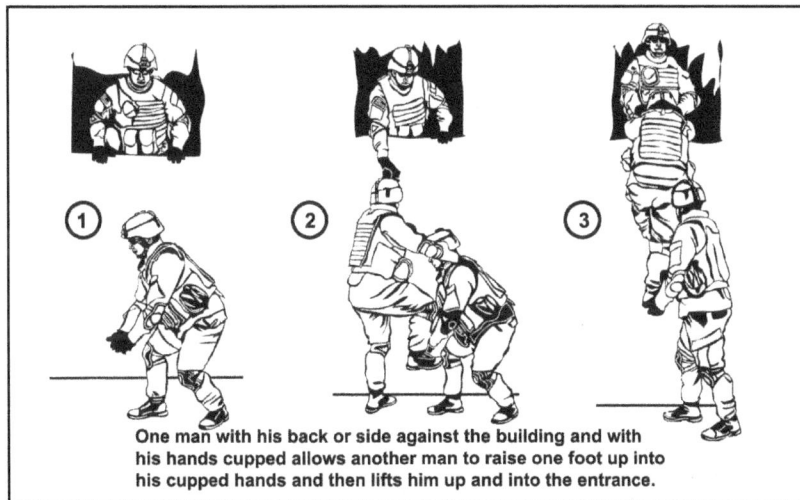

Figure 7-3. One-man lift

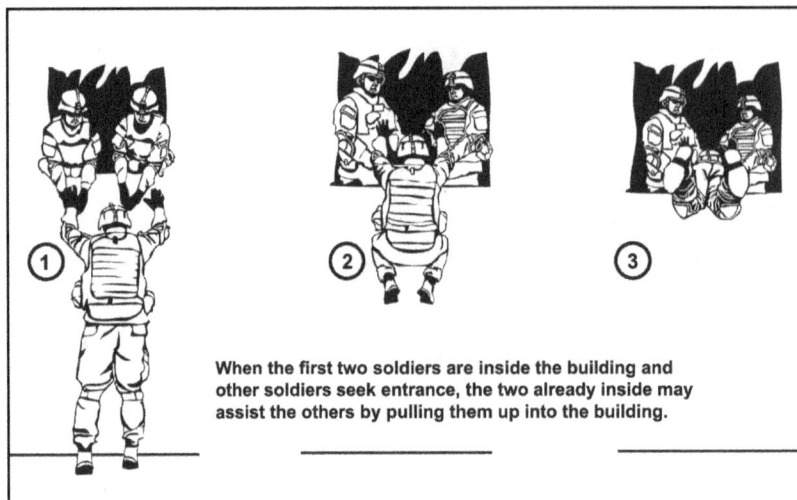

Figure 7-4. Two-man pull

Upper-Floor Windows

7-21. A Soldier scaling or rappelling to access a window is vulnerable to enemy fire. He should avoid exposing himself to fire from other windows that are not cleared. A Soldier's individual weapon should be slung over his firing shoulder so it can be quickly brought into a firing position.

7-22. Scaling using a grappling hook and rope to ascend into a building is not recommended. Scaling, especially with equipment, is extremely difficult for the average Soldier, takes a significant amount of time and energy, and exposes the climber and nearby Soldiers to enemy fire.

7-23. Rappelling can be used to descend from the rooftop or higher level floor into a lower window or to descend through a hole in the floor to a lower floor. (See TC 21-24 for details on rappelling.)

7-24. Ladders are the preferred method of entry to upper-floor windows and offer the quickest method of access. Higher level floors may be accessible with longer ladders. Units should be equipped with lightweight, man-portable, collapsible ladders as referenced in the platoon UO kit. If portable ladders are not available, material to build ladders can be obtained through supply channels. Ladders can also be built with resources available throughout the urban area; for example, lumber can be taken from inside the walls of buildings. Ladders may be used to identify obstacles and threat and entry points for the assault element. They may be used for the following:
- Gain quiet entry into a building.
- Provide overwatch security over a wall.
- Assist overwatch/snipers in gaining positions of dominance.

ENTERING THROUGH ROOFS

7-25. Many multistory buildings have a roof access that Soldiers can use to enter the building. These roof access points are typically stairs or permanently attached ladder. On buildings without roof access points or if using the established access point is not preferred, a hole can be made in the roof to gain entry. Basic hand tools can breach wood or shale-type roofs, while concrete or other durable material requires an explosive breach.

ENTERING THROUGH GROUND-FLOOR WALLS

7-26.   If doors and windows are deemed as unacceptable entry points, entry through a wall is often the best option. While it is possible to crawl through a small opening, it is preferred to use a door-size opening and enter using the same procedures as when entering through a doorway.

MOVING INSIDE BUILDINGS

7-27.   When moving inside a building, always be alert. Avoid presenting a silhouette in doors and windows, and always move with at least one other Soldier for security.

7-28.   While the mission variables affect the particulars of moving, the basic element for moving inside buildings is the four-man fire team. A four-man fire team can move throughout a building as an individual entity. However, they can only secure where they are, not where they have been.

7-29.   The members of the four-man clearing team are assigned numbers 1 through 4. The assignments of these positions often rotate as the mission variables and the experience of the clearing team change. This does not mean that all four members must enter a room, nor does it mean that more than four men cannot enter. For a standard four-man fire team, a typical breakdown is as follows:
- Rifleman is number 1. (Should not have an open bolt weapon.)
- Team leader is number 2. (May be armed additionally with a shotgun.)
- Grenadier is number 3.
- Squad automatic weapon gunner is number 4.

MOVING THROUGH HALLWAYS

7-30.   When moving through hallways, stay 12 to 18 inches away from walls. Do not rub against walls as this may alert an enemy or, if engaged by an enemy, ricochet rounds tend to travel parallel to a wall. The two basic techniques for moving through hallways are described below.

Serpentine

7-31.   Use this technique in narrow hallways (figure 7-5).
- Soldier 1 provides security to the front. His sector of fire includes any enemies who appear at the far end of the hall or from any doorways near the end.
- Soldier 2 and Soldier 3 cover the left and right sides of Soldier 1. Their sectors of fire include any enemies who appear suddenly from nearby doorways on either side of the hall.
- Soldier 4, normally carrying the M249 squad automatic weapon (SAW), provides rear security against any enemies suddenly appearing behind the clearing team.

Rolling-T

7-32.   Use this technique in wide hallways (figure 7-5).
- Soldier 1 and Soldier 2 move abreast, covering the opposite side of the hallway from the one on which they are walking.
- Soldier 3 covers the far end of the hallway from a position behind Soldier 1 and Soldier 2, firing between them.
- Soldier 4 provides rear security.

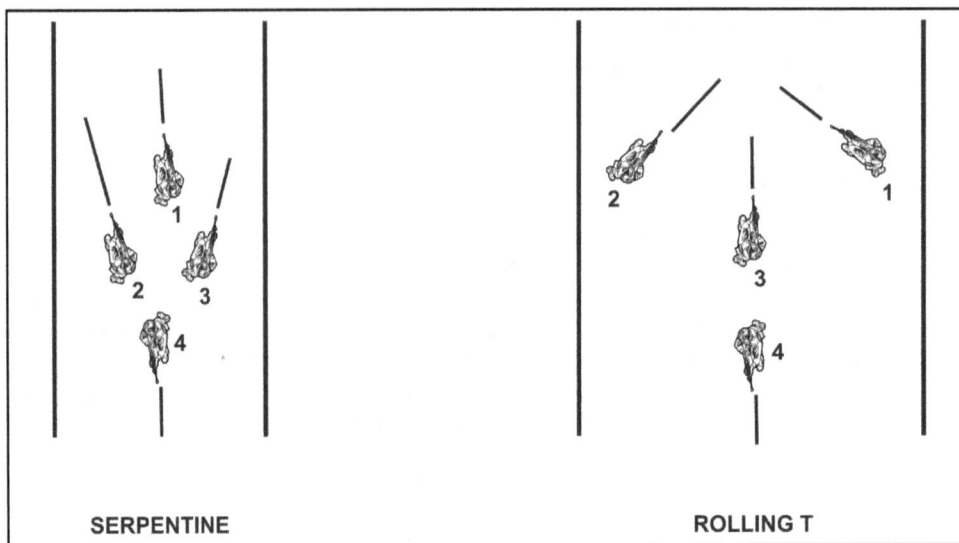

Figure 7-5. Hallway movement techniques

MOVING THROUGH INTERSECTIONS

7-33.   Hallway intersections are dangerous areas and should be approached cautiously. If the team has any left-handed Soldiers, they should clear right-hand corners. If not, right-handed Soldiers should use the left-handed firing method to minimize exposure.

7-34.   Techniques to clear intersections differ slightly based on the type of hallway intersection. The three hallway intersections are described below.

Four-Way Intersection

7-35.   The steps below depict a fire team's actions upon reaching a four-way intersection.

Assume Start Position

7-36.   Upon nearing the four-way intersection, the team configures into a 2-by-2 formation (figure 7-6).
- Soldier 1 and Soldier 2 move to the left side of the hallway.
- Soldier 3 and Soldier 4 move to the right side of the hallway.
- Soldier 1 and Soldier 3 move to the edge of their corners and assume a low crouch or kneeling position, while Soldier 2 and Soldier 4 remain standing.

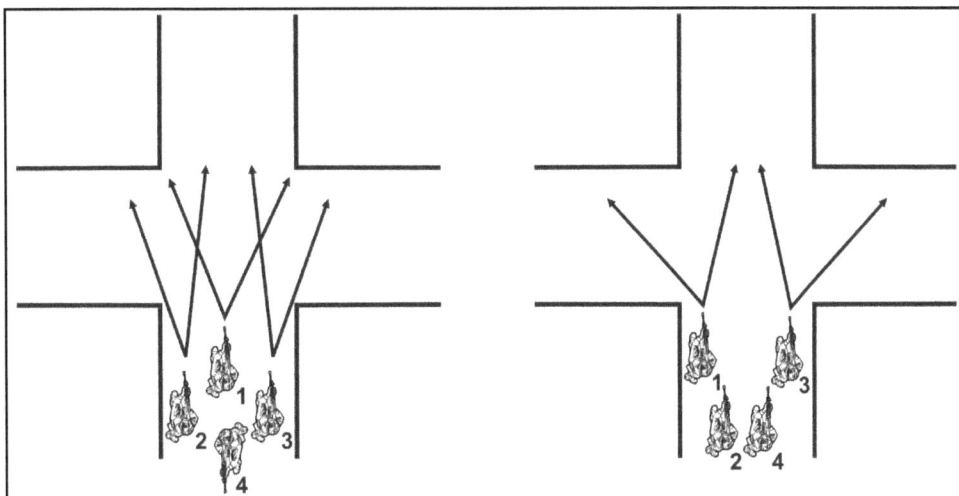

Figure 7-6. Moving through four-way hallway intersection (Step 1)

Clear Around Corners

7-37. Simultaneously execute movement on a prearranged signal. The sectors of fire for all Soldiers cover the full width of their hallway. The low and high positions prevent Soldier 2 and Soldier 4 from firing at Soldier 1 or Soldier 3, respectively (figure 7-7).

- Soldier 1 and Soldier 3 simultaneously turn left and right, respectively, and cover the hallway from their low position.
- Soldier 2 and Soldier 4 step forward and turn left and right, respectively, maintaining their high position.

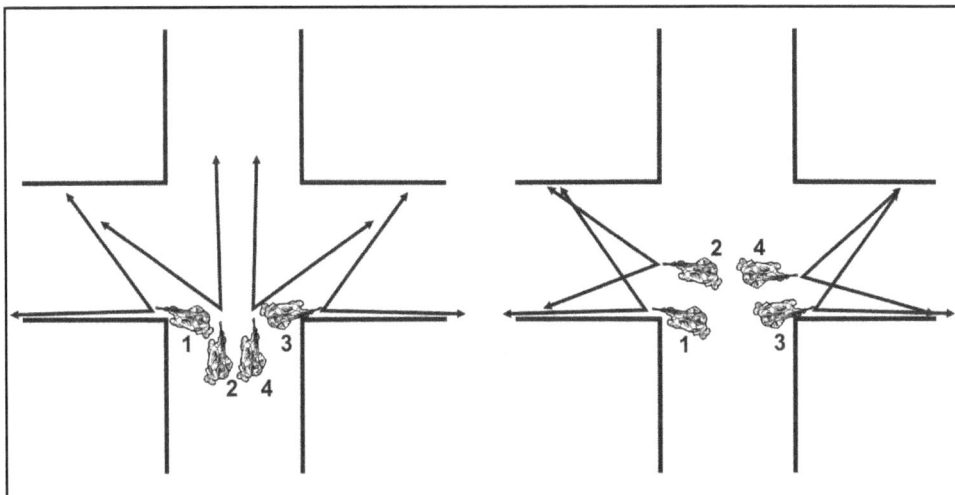

Figure 7-7. Moving through four-way hallway intersection (Step 2)

Resume Movement

7-38.   Once the left and right portions of the hallway are clear, Soldier 4 turns and secures the hallway in the original direction of movement. The fire team then resumes their hallway movement formation (figure 7-8).

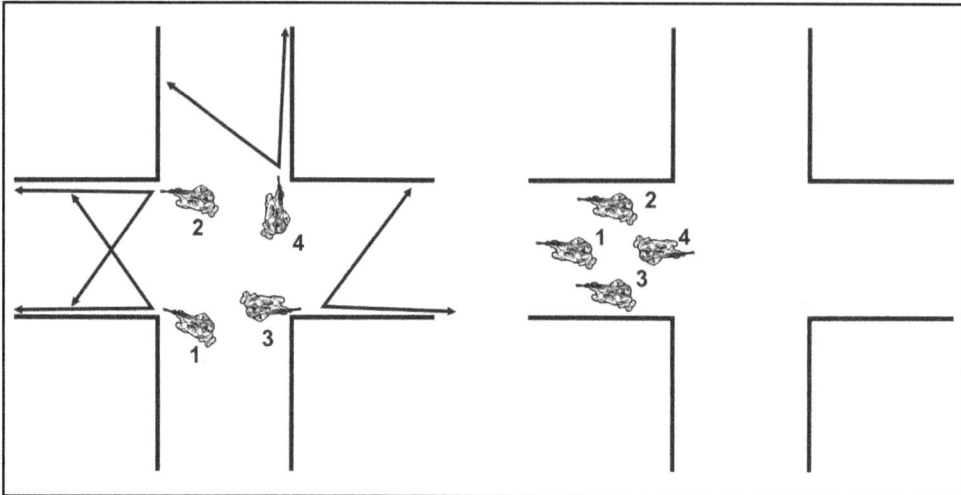

Figure 7-8. Moving through four-way intersection (Step 3)

Upright T-Intersection

7-39.   The following depicts a fire team's actions upon reaching an upright T-intersection. In an upright T-intersection, the team approaches the "T" from the base hallway.

Assume Start Position

7-40.   Upon nearing the T-intersection, the team configures into a 2-by-2 formation (figure 7-9).
- Soldier 1 and Soldier 2 move to the left side of the hallway.
- Soldier 3 and Soldier 4 move to the right side of the hallway and remain standing with their weapons in a high position.
- Soldier 1 and Soldier 3 move to the edge of their corners and assume a low crouch or kneeling position.

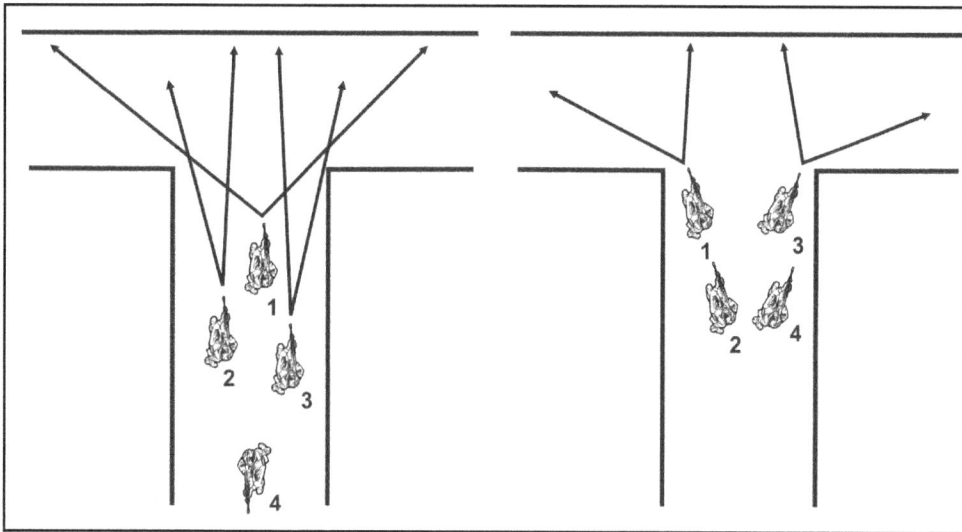

Figure 7-9. Moving through T-shaped hallway intersection from base hallway (Step 1)

Clear Around Corners

7-41.   Simultaneously execute movement on a prearranged signal. The sectors of fire for all Soldiers cover the full width of their hallway. The low and high positions prevent Soldier 2 and Soldier 4 from firing at Soldier 1 or Soldier 3, respectively (figure 7-10).

- Soldiers 1 and 3 simultaneously turn left and right, respectively, and cover the hallway from their low position.
- Soldiers 2 and 4 step forward and turn left and right, respectively, maintaining their high position.

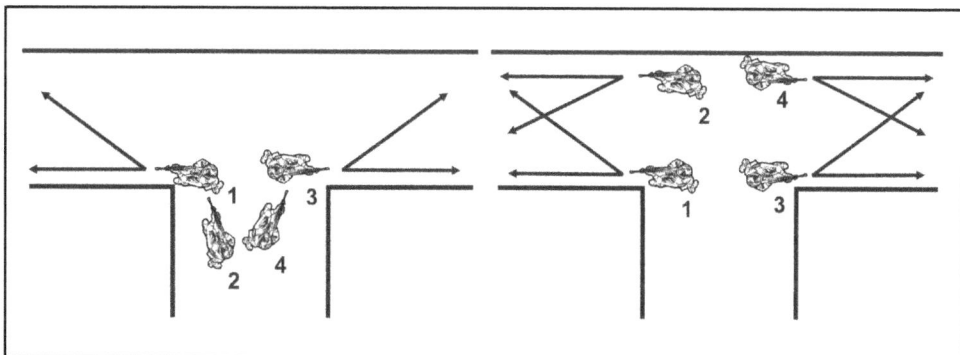

Figure 7-10. Moving through T-shaped hallway intersection from base hallway (Step 2)

Resume Movement

7-42.   Once the left and right portions of the hallway are clear, the fire team resumes their hallway movement formation (figure 7-11).

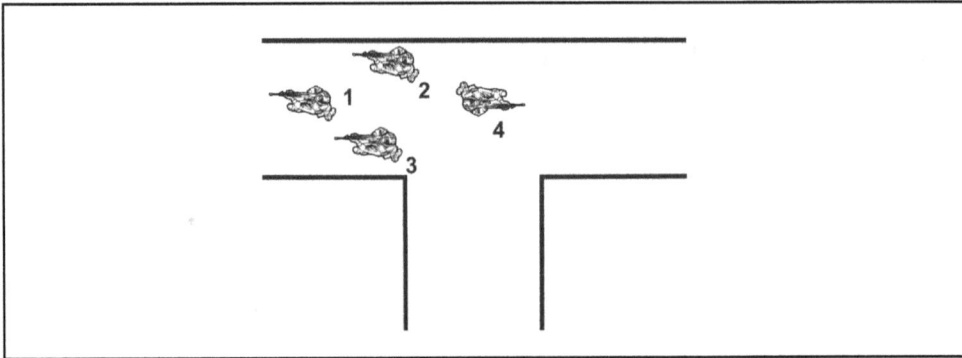

Figure 7-11. Moving through T-shaped hallway intersection from base hallway (Step 3)

Branch T-Intersection

7-43.   The following depicts a fire team's actions upon reaching a branch T-intersection. In a branch T-intersection, the team approaches the "T" from the cross of the "T."

Assume Start Position

7-44.   The team configures into a modified 2-by-2 formation (figure 7-12).

- Soldier 3 moves to the edge of the corner and assumes a low crouch or kneeling position.
- Soldier 1 moves abreast of Soldier 3 and near the right side of the hall.
- Soldier 2 moves to the left side of the hall and orients to the front.
- Soldier 4 moves to the right of Soldier 2 and maintains rear security.

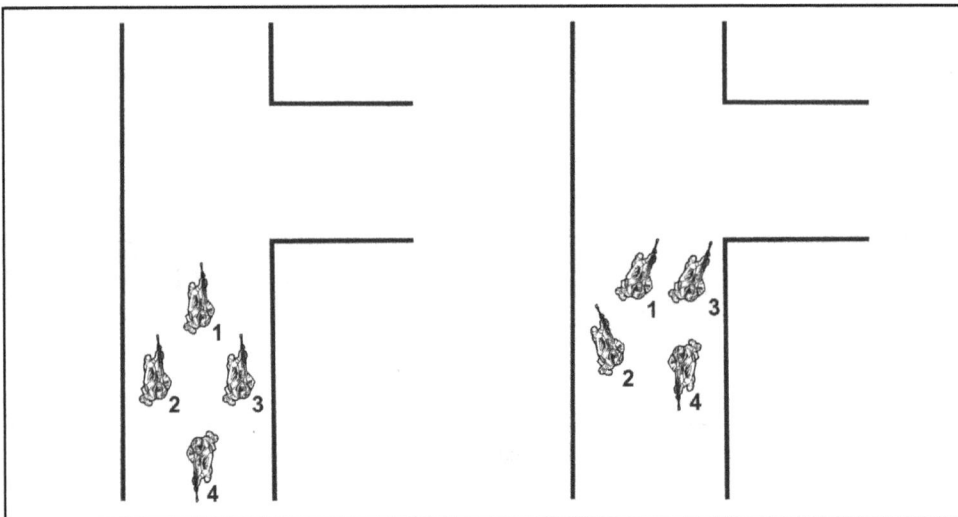

Figure 7-12. Moving through T-shaped hallway intersection from cross hallway (Step 1)

Clear Around Corner

7-45.   Simultaneously execute movement on a prearranged signal, keying in on the actions of Soldier 3. The sectors of fire for all Soldiers cover the full width of their hallway. The low and high positions prevent Soldier 2 and Soldier 4 from firing at Soldier 1 or Soldier 3, respectively (figure 7-13).

- Soldier 3 turns right around the corner keeping low.
- Soldier 1 steps forward while turning to the right and staying high.
- Soldier 2 and Soldier 4 continue their movement in the direction of travel. Their movement is continuous.

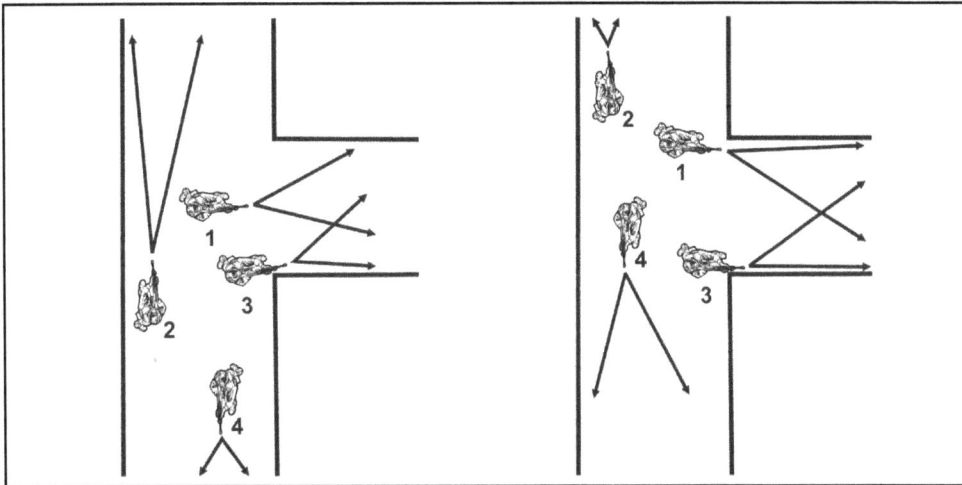

Figure 7-13. Moving through T-shaped hallway intersection from cross hallway (Step 2)

Resume Movement

7-46.   Soldier 2 and Soldier 4 continue moving across the intersection and do not stop. Their movement keys the actions of Soldier 1 and Soldier 3 (figure 7-14).

- Soldier 2 passes behind Soldiers 3. Soldier 1 then continues moving down the hallway.
- Soldier 1, as Soldier 2 passes behind, shifts laterally to his left until he reaches the far corner. Upon reaching the side of the hallway, Soldier 1 turns into the direction of travel, resumes his position in the formation, and continues moving down the hallway.
- Soldier 4 passes behind Soldier 3 and continues moving down the hallway.
- Soldier 3, as Soldier 4 passes behind, shifts laterally to his left until he reaches the far corner. Upon reaching the side of the hallway, Soldier 3 turns into the direction of travel, resumes his position in the formation, and continues moving down the hallway.

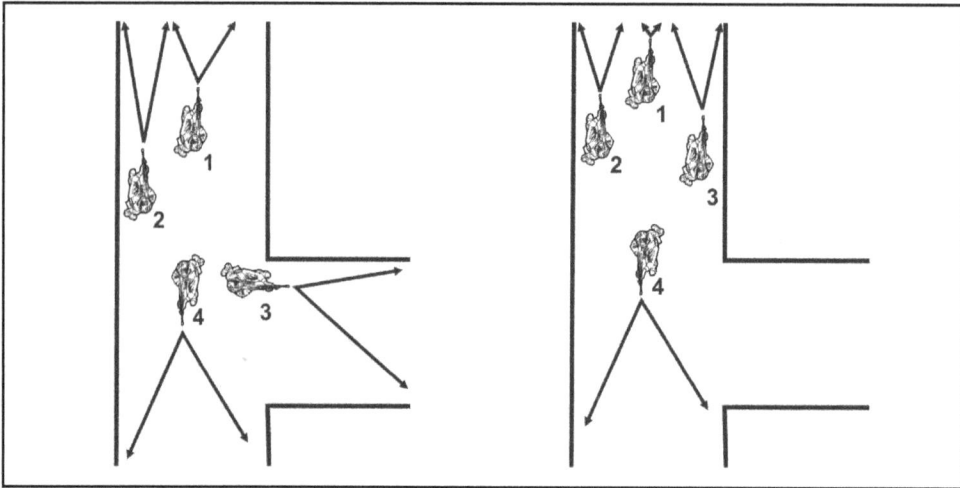

Figure 7-14. Moving through T-shaped hallway intersection from cross hallway (Step 3)

EXITING BUILDINGS

7-47.   Before exiting a building, inform nearby friendly elements to prevent fratricide and coordinate their overwatch. Unless the open area in front of the building's exit is secure, exit a building with the assumption that movement in the open exposes one to enemy fire. Before moving, identify the next covered position and then select and visually clear a route to that position. Once ready to move, a Soldier should rapidly exit the building, move along the selected route, and occupy the identified covered position.

7-48.   Depending on the threat level outside the building, additional measures, both before and during movement, may be required. These measures include other Soldiers providing overwatch or suppressive fires and the use of obscurants, such as smoke, to conceal the movement. If available, an armored vehicle may also be positioned to provide cover for part of the movement or as a final covered position.

SECTION II – BUILDING AND ROOM BREACHING

7-49.   An integral part of clearing buildings, floors, and rooms is the ability to gain access quickly to the area to be cleared. Breaching techniques for building or room entry points vary based on the mission variables; the construction of the entry point; and the availability of breaching equipment, munitions, or demolitions. Techniques range from the simple method of kicking in a door to the complex use of specialized demolitions.

7-50.   When breaching a building, Soldiers should consider the effects of the breach on the building and on adjacent buildings. This is especially true for blast-type breaches. For wood-framed buildings, the blast may cause the whole building to collapse or catch fire. For stone, brick, or cement buildings, the blast may cause part of the building to collapse.

7-51.   The presence of civilians also needs to be considered when determining how to breach a building or room. If there is a known civilian presence, consider using nonlethal means to execute the breach.

7-52.   With all breaching methods, if the enemy is suspected to be in the room or has actually fired from the room, throw a flash-bang hand grenade into the room after the breach and before entry of the clearing team. In the event a fragmentation hand grenade is thrown, you may need to wait for several minutes for the dust and debris to settle before entry. During entry, the clearing team should minimize their exposure to potential enemy fire through the fatal funnel by rapidly moving through the opening and staying close to one side of the opening. After entry, the clearing team should minimize their exposure to potential enemy fire through all openings, windows and doorways.

TASK ORGANIZATION

7-53.   The task organization of the breach and clearing team is based on the mission variables and whether the breach is distant or close-in. For distant breaches, where the breach element is located away from the breach site, the breach element and the clearing team should be separate elements. For close-in breaches, where the breach element is co-located at the breach site, breach and clearing teams may be combined. If combined, then typically Soldier 4, assisted by Soldier 3, is the breach element and Soldier 1 and Soldier 2 are the clearing element.

BREACHING FUNDAMENTALS

7-54.   Breaching an entry point follows the breaching fundamentals of SOSRA apply. Plan all five breaching fundamentals even though the breaching fundamentals of suppress and obscure typically apply only to breaching the initial foothold in a building.

- **Suppress.** Suppressing the enemy in urban terrain is done predominately by direct small-arms fire. Suppress all known or suspected enemy to allow the breach element to move to, prepare for, and breach exterior obstacles. Considerations for suppression include the three potential threats—the outside enemy, the inside enemy, and the inside enemy's ability to engage friendly forces on the outside.
- **Obscure.** Hand-emplaced smoke is the most responsive and most effective breaching obscurant. However, smoke has the potential to also degrade friendly operations. Smoke used in the interior of a building not only obscures but may become a hindrance to breathing and should be used as a last resort.
- **Secure.** Both the breaching element and the breach site must be secured. Typically, the clearing team provides close-in security, while the support force provides distant security.
- **Reduce.** Redundant breaching systems are critical during UO. The breach element is responsible for preparing equipment for use and charges for emplacement, searching for booby traps or IEDs, and verifying that the entry point can be breached as planned.
- **Assault.** The assault—the room clearing—should immediately follow the breach. The clearing team should be prepared to conduct additional breaches within the building, to include doors and interior walls and the reduction of interior obstacles in hallways and stairwells.

METHODS

7-55.   Regardless of the breaching method used, leaders should plan redundant or alternate COAs when executing a breach. The four breaching methods for urban entry points are described below.

MECHANICAL

7-56.   Mechanical breaching uses sledgehammers, bolt cutters, crowbars, picket pounders or even an armored vehicle to create a breach. Always plan mechanical breaching as a backup to a ballistic or explosive breaching. Mechanical breaching is an assumed capability within all units. The building material of the door is critical in determining the effectiveness of mechanical breaching.

7-57.   With some doors, the methods of mechanical breaching are very slow. Therefore, units should plan on an enemy reacting to the breach activity. Breaching fragile doors using a sledgehammer is effective and rapid. Sturdy doors can be breached by hooking a cable connected to a vehicle to the door. Both of these techniques minimize collateral damage and maintain the element of surprise.

BALLISTIC

7-58.   Ballistic breaching uses a projectile weapon to create a breach, to include shoulder launched munitions and close combat missiles. A ballistic breach may be directed against a wall, a door, or a window. If possible, use large caliber weapons against a wall and small caliber weapons against a door.

7-59.   Door breaches are normally executed from close distances. It is preferable to use precision fires to destroy either the latch and lock or hinges of the door. This minimizes collateral damage, quickly opens most doors, and allows for rapid entry of the room. Shooting the latch and lock of a door is easiest as it requires fewer shots and is easy to target. Whereas, shooting the hinges requires more shots, and the hinges may be hidden from the outside. Careful aim is required for both methods.

Small-Arms Weapons

7-60.   Typically, small-arms weapons, except for shotguns, have limited breaching value. Most 5.56-mm, 7.62-mm, or .50-caliber weapons produce ricochets and require numerous rounds to create a successful breach. As such, these weapons are not recommended for breaching.

Shotguns

7-61.   A shotgun can breach most interior wooden doors quickly. Metal doors and exterior wooden doors can also be breached with a shotgun but typically require additional shots. Shotgun breaching is not limited to just doors. Shotguns can also breach iron-barred windows, dislodge padlock shackles, break chain-link fences, and defeat vehicle trunk and door mechanisms.

7-62.   Because of the possibility of fragmentation, eye protection is necessary for those engaged in shotgun breaching operations. Door breachers should also consider using a balaclava to filter out the fine copper powder discharge from the round, which could be unhealthy if inhaled. Ballistic breaching using a shotgun has several advantages over other breaching techniques, to include—

- **Ease of Training.** Shotgun breaching techniques can be taught easily and quickly.
- **Repetitive Use.** Soldiers can carry enough ammunition to defeat numerous doors, and shotgun breaching is less likely to disrupt the flow of building and room clearing teams.
- **Speed.** Other breaching methods are often slow and can hinder or stop the momentum of an assault team.
- **Minimal Collateral Damage.** Demolitions or explosive rounds can weaken a building's foundation; create debris that hinders movement; and create thick, debris-filled cloud cover that obstructs sight and optic viewing.

Preparation

7-63.   The shotgun should be pistol-gripped for ease of handling, have a sling for leveraging, and equipped with a muzzle standoff device for safety. This standoff device, called a breacher, is affixed to the end of the barrel and allows for the venting of muzzle gas pressure and for the capturing of debris. When using a breacher, the shotgun is fired with the muzzle in direct contact with the target thereby eliminating any possibility of the barrel blowing up, and reducing muzzle jump and recoil. Without a breacher, the barrel is held approximately 2 inches away from the target. The goal is to maximize the blast effects and to minimize the splattering that could affect friendly troops.

7-64.   Breaching rounds are most effective when fired into a door at a 45-degree horizontal angle (from the door towards the doorframe) and at a 45-degree vertical angle (either up or down). When attempting to breach metal door with a metal doorframe, breaching rounds should be fired at a much smaller vertical angle of 15-degrees to prevent the metal from the door becoming lodged in the doorframe and jamming the door. Most shotgun ammunition can be used for breaching. Shotgun slugs pose the highest risk as they retain significant energy well after they penetrate the door. The safest shotgun ammunition is a frangible round that disperses completely upon exiting the door.

Breaching

7-65.   Most doors have hinges, a doorknob, and a locking mechanism. The two typical breaching techniques using a shotgun are the doorknob breach and the hinge breach. The doorknob breach aims to defeat the locking mechanism that secures the door, while the hinge breach aims to destroy the hinges that hold the door to the wall. For both techniques, the gunner should minimize his exposure to enemy fire through the door.

7-66.   The doorknob breach is the preferred technique as it takes the least amount of shots. However, some doors have alternate or multiple locking systems above or below the doorknob (sliding dead bolts, chain locks, bars that extend across the doorway, or floor locks with bars wedged against the doorknob). As such, even after destroying the doorknob, these locking systems may hinder or deny entry. A hinge breach is typically executed only after discovering a door has multiple additional locking mechanisms.

Doorknob Breach

7-67. The doorknob breach actually attacks the door locking mechanism, not the doorknob itself. Never target the doorknob itself (figure 7-15). A hit on the doorknob tends to bend the locking mechanism into the door frame and bind the door without destroying the locking mechanism. Before executing a doorknob breach the gunner should first turn the doorknob and attempt to open the door. If the door will not open then proceed with the doorknob breach.

7-68. To execute a doorknob breach—
- First visually inspects the door to identify the type of door (wood or metal) and if there is a visible secondary lock (such as a dead bolt lock).
- Next, the gunner chambers a round and shoots the doorknob locking mechanism by aiming at the point midway between the doorknob and the door frame using the appropriate angle of fire (45/45 for wood and 45/15 for metal).
- If there is a visible second lock (such as a deadbolt), the gunner then shoots this locking mechanism using the same procedure.
- If the initial shot does not defeat a locking mechanism, then the gunner fires an immediate second shot beside the first.
- Once the lock is defeated, the gunner immediately angles the shotgun upward, pushes or kicks in the door, and moves away from the door. The Soldier does not chamber another round in the shotgun and transitions to his primary weapon. This signals that the doorway is cleared and allows the first Soldier entry and a clear shot into the room.
- If the lock is not defeated, the gunner can either fire again at any identified additional lock or proceed to an alternate method of breaching.

Figure 7-15. Aim points for shotgun doorknob breach

Hinge Breach

7-69. A hinge breach is conducted either after a failed doorknob breach or if the door is known to have numerous locking mechanisms. A hinge breach is not fast and can require up to nine shots. Most hinges cannot be seen from the exterior side of a door. As such, targeting the hinges is accomplished by aiming at where they should be located. Most doors have three hinges, one aligned with the vertical center of the door, one approximately 8 to 10 inches from the top of the door, and one approximately 8 to 10 inches from the bottom of the door (figure 7-16).

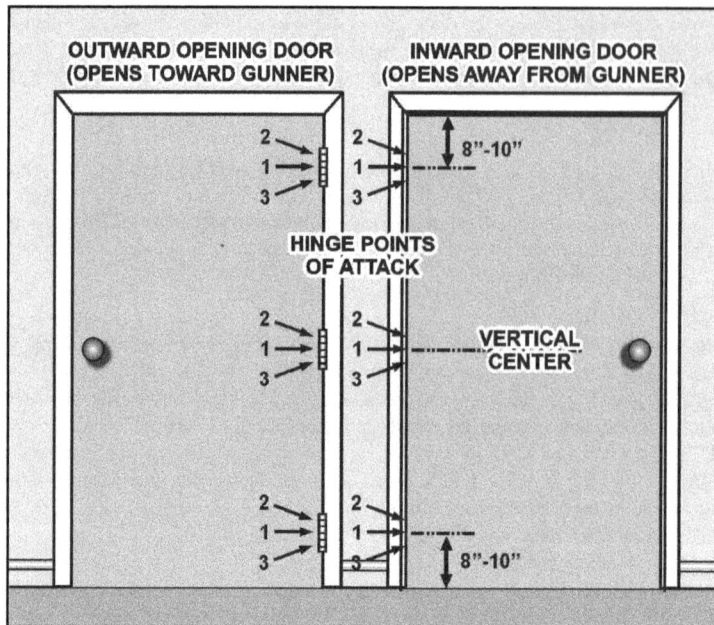

Figure 7-16. Aim points for shotgun hinge breach

7-70. On wooden doors one to two shots will normally dislodge the screws and defeat the hinge, while on metal doors two to three shots are required to dislodge all screws and defeat the hinges. To defeat the hinges of a door—

- Engage the top hinge first. Position the shotgun to eliminate the maximum number of screws holding the hinge onto the door with one shot.
- Be prepared to reengage the hinge and into the door jam. One round may not defeat a hinge; be prepared to fire follow-on shots.
- Once the top hinge is defeated, move and engage the middle hinge. Use the same technique as on the top hinge.
- Engage the bottom hinge last. In many cases defeating the two upper hinges causes the door to collapse from its own weight, pulling the lower hinge out of the door jam.
- Once the hinges have been defeated gunner immediately angles the shotgun upward, pushes or kicks in the door, and moves away from the door. This signals that the doorway is cleared and allows the first Soldier entry and a clear shot into the room.

Grenade Rifle Entry Munition

7-71. The M100 grenade rifle entry munition (GREM) is a rifle-launched entry munition mounted on a M16A2 or M4 designed to breach doors. It is an alternative to close-proximity door breaching tools, such as rams and shotguns. The assault team remains behind cover until the GREM breaches the door, thus reducing exposure time. The GREM is launched by firing a 5.56-mm cartridge (ball or tracer). It has a minimum firing range of 15 meters, a maximum firing range of 40 meters, and a maximum angle of fire of 20 degrees.

7-72. The GREM is effective against both wooden and metal doors. When used against metal doors, the GREM causes the door to buckle inward and dislocate from the doorframe. When used against wooden doors, the GREM breaks the door into several pieces upon explosion.

> *Note.* It is not recommended to use the GREM against emergency doors. Emergency doors are reinforced metal doors that open outward to allow easier and faster exit from a room. When the GREM engages and explodes against this door type, the hinges and bolts could bend and get stuck, jamming the door into its frame.

Large Caliber Weapons

7-73.   Using large caliber weapons, such as the 25-mm chain gun, 40-mm grenade launcher, 105-mm or 120-mm cannon, readily opens any door, except for the most heavily reinforced blast doors (figure 7-17). However, the collateral damage, either from penetration or explosion, can be extensive. Typically, use these weapons to create a breach and to kill or otherwise incapacitate occupants of the room.

Figure 7-17. Mobile gun system breaching building

EXPLOSIVE

7-74.   Explosive breaching uses explosives to create a breach. Explosive breaching is often the fastest and most combat-effective method. Units can use slightly modified standard Army demolitions to breach all common urban barriers. After placing the demolition charge, all personnel should move a safe distance away to covered positions. Immediately after detonation, the clearing team moves to the entry point and enters and clears the room. (See FM 3-34.214 for details on explosives and demolitions.)

MANUAL

7-75.   Manual breaching uses the foot or shoulder to force open the entry point (most commonly a door).

EXECUTING THE BREACH

7-76.   If the identified entry point is closed (such as a door) or must be created or enlarged (such as a hole in the wall), unit leaders must determine the method of breaching. Once made, use this breach as an entrance. Quick entry is required to take advantage of the effects of the blast and concussion and to prevent the enemy from reorienting on the breach.

7-77. Breaching is categorized as either a close-in breach or distant breach.

- **Close-in Breach.** Close-in breach in which the breach element is co-located at the breach site, such as mechanical breaches, ballistic breaches using small-arms weapons, and manual breaches.
- **Distant Breach.** Distant breach in which the breach element is located away from the breach site, such as ballistic breaches using large caliber weapons.

7-78. Demolition breaches usually combine elements of both close-in and distant breaches as Soldiers must first emplace demolitions and then move to a safe standoff distance.

DETERMINE STARTING POSITIONS

7-79. The starting position is the last covered position before executing the breach and entering the building. The type of breach and the enemy threat are key factors in determining the type of starting position. A starting positions is categorized as either a close-in starting position or distant starting position.

- **Close-in Starting Position.** Close-in starting position is adjacent to the entry point (figure 7-18). Use if there is no breach or no danger from secondary effects of the breach (such as an explosion, fragments, or debris), if there is no threat to the friendly side of the entry point, and if there is no danger of compromise.
- **Distant Starting Position.** Distant starting position is a covered position away from the entry point that provides protection from the enemy but allows rapid access to the entry point (figure 7-19). Use if there is a danger from secondary effects of the breach, if there is a threat to the friendly side of the entry point, or if there is a danger of compromise.

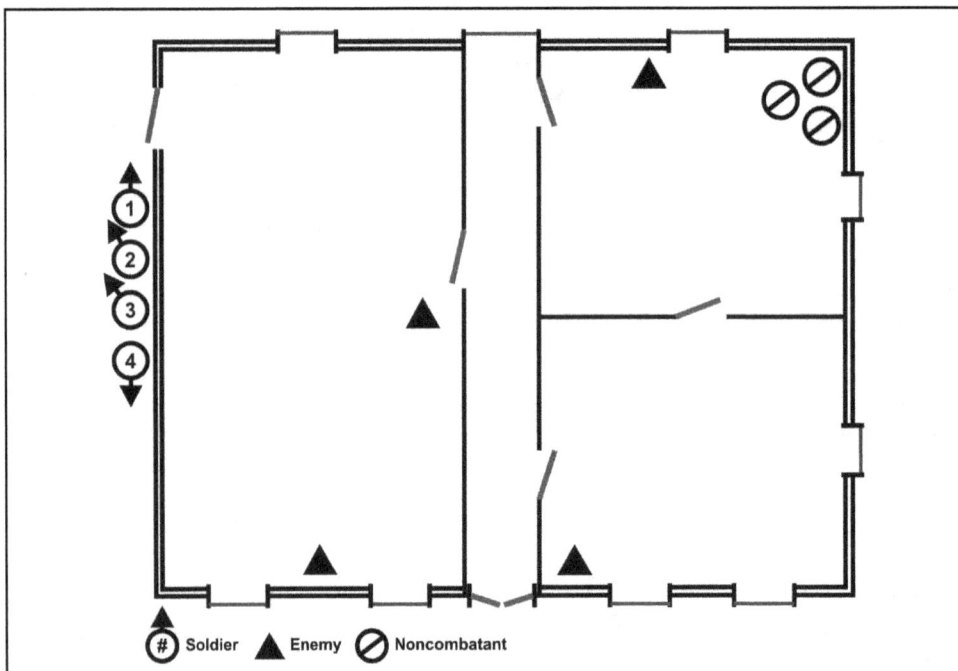

Figure 7-18. Close-in starting position

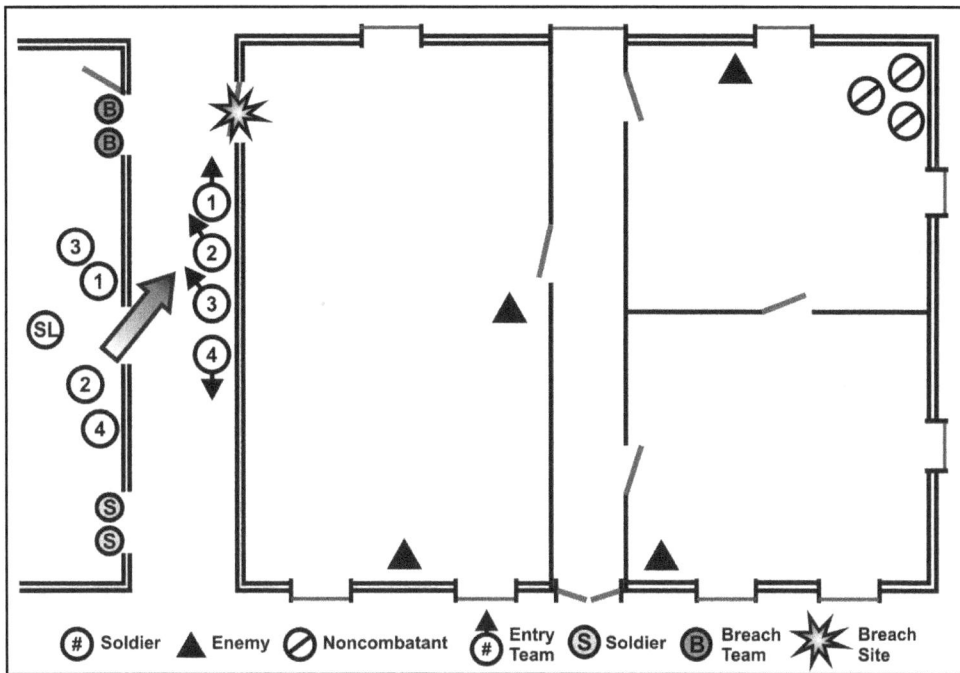

Figure 7-19. Distant starting position

MOVE TO STARTING POSITION

7-80.   After identifying the starting position and preparing for the breach and entry, which includes positioning supporting and covering forces, the breaching team (if not already there) moves into their starting position.

EXECUTE DISTANT BREACH

7-81.   The execution of the distant breach is the signal for the clearing team to move to the entry point. If a distant breach is not needed, omit this step.

MOVE TO ENTRY POINT

7-82.   Moving to a building entry point and pausing outside the entry point when exposed to enemy fire is extremely hazardous. Therefore, Soldiers must minimize the time they are exposed. When moving to the entry point, Soldiers should use all available cover and consider using smoke, suppressive fire, or diversionary measures to occupy the enemy's attention.

7-83.   Properly positioned friendly elements can suppress and eliminate enemy that attempt to engage the clearing team. Clearing team members should approach the entry point quickly, quietly, and in planned entry order. This preserves the element of surprise and allows for a quick entry and the subsequent domination of the room.

EXECUTE CLOSE-IN BREACH

7-84.   Executing a close-in breach is the signal to begin entering and clearing the foothold. If a close-in breach is not needed, omit this step.

ENTER AND CLEAR FOOTHOLD

7-85. If possible, the clearing team moves from covered or concealed positions already in their entry order. Ideally, the clearing team arrives and, unless using a hand grenade, passes through the entry point without having to stop. Once inside, they clear and secure the foothold. Entering and clearing the foothold is executed the same as entering and clearing a room. To minimize the danger of fratricide, consider the positions of friendly troops when selecting the direction of clearing additional rooms (figure 7-20).

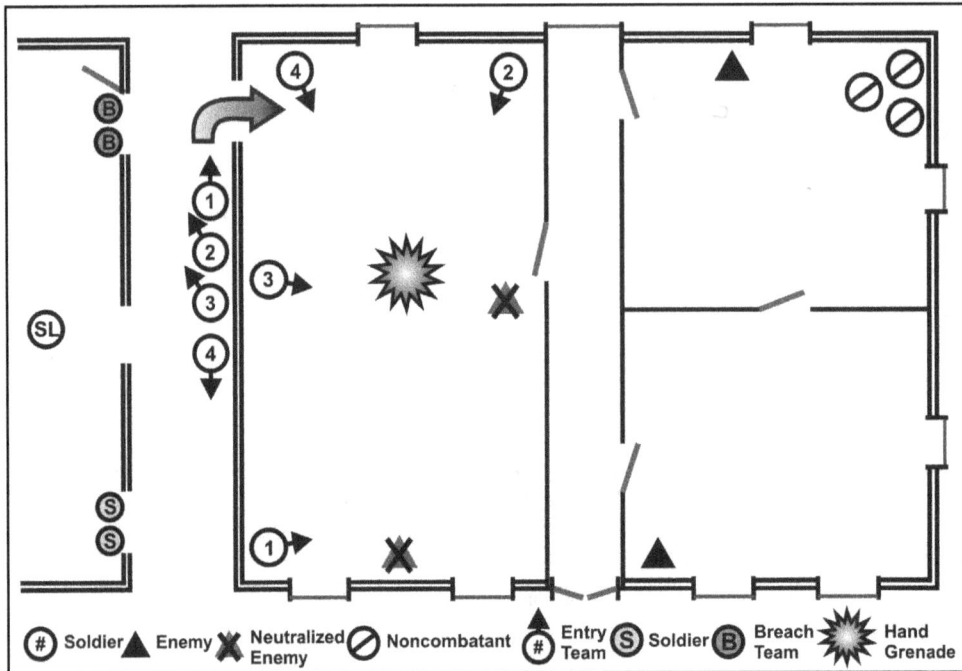

Figure 7-20. Establishing a foothold

SECTION III – ROOM CLEARING

7-86. Room clearing involves seizing control of a room and its inhabitants (both hostile and other) rapidly and methodically by eliminating the enemy, dominating the room, and controlling the situation. Typically, a squad leader or higher finalizes the plan for clearing a room. This plan—

- Identifies the room to be cleared.
- Determines the location and method of entry.
- Directs the organization of the room clearing team.
- Dictates the assault conditions (surgical, precision, or high intensity).
- Enforces the ROE.
- Positions overwatching forces, breaching elements, and supporting fires.
- Maintains control of any follow-on team.
- Determines the activity after the room is cleared.

FUNDAMENTALS

7-87. Clearing team members take the following actions while moving along confined corridors to the room to be cleared, while preparing to enter the room, during room entry and target engagement, and after contact:

- Move tactically and silently while securing the corridors to the room to be cleared.
- Carry only the minimum amount of equipment.
- Arrive undetected at the entry to the room in the correct order of entrance and prepared to enter on a single command.
- Enter quickly and move immediately to a point of domination.
- Overwhelm all enemy in the room with fast, accurate, and discriminating fires if they are clearly armed, or use combatives techniques when in doubt.
- Gain and maintain immediate control of the situation and all personnel in the room.
- Maintain security if any team members are involved in a combatives situation.
- Confirm whether enemy casualties are wounded or dead. Disarm, segregate, and treat the wounded. Search all enemy casualties.
- Perform a cursory search of the room. Determine if a detailed search is required.
- Evacuate all friendly casualties.
- Mark the room as cleared using a simple, clearly identifiable method.
- Maintain 360-degree security and be prepared to react to more enemy contact at any moment.

SURPRISE

7-88. Surprise is achieved by acting at a time or place or using a method that the enemy does not expect and, therefore, cannot effectively combat. Speed, deception, and distraction contribute to surprise.

SPEED

7-89. Speed is swiftness of action. In room clearing, it is moving as fast as one can effectively observe and shoot both through the entry point and onward to a point of domination for the room. It also includes the ability to rapidly adjust one's route and point of domination based on dynamic conditions. The key is not how fast you enter the room but rather how fast you eliminate the enemy and clear the room.

SECURITY

7-90. Maintaining security is a constant theme during tactical maneuver. Security during movement includes the actions that units take to secure themselves—proving 360-degree security. Tempo in UO does not necessarily mean speed. Offensive operations balance speed, security, and adequate firepower.

SHOCK

7-91. Shock results from applying overwhelming violence. It is a principle of high-intensity room clearing. Shock slows and disrupts an enemy and may even paralyze the enemy's ability to fight or physically stun the enemy. Surprise and speed magnify the effects of shock.

CONTROLLED VIOLENCE OF ACTION

7-92. Controlled violence of action eliminates or neutralizes the enemy while giving him the least chance of inflicting friendly casualties. It is not limited to the application of firepower. It also involves a Soldier mindset of complete domination. It is a principle of precision and surgical room clearing. Controlled violence coupled with speed increases surprise.

POINTS OF DOMINATION

7-93. Points of domination refer to designated points within a room that, when occupied, can effectively control the room through observation and fire. The corners of a room are the preferred points of domination. From any of the four corners of a typical room, one gets the smallest angle that covers the whole room. However, room layout, obstructions, and the clearing team size can effect which locations actually provide the best sectors of fire and, therefore, which are the best points of domination.

7-94.   Points of domination should not be in front of doors or windows so team members are not silhouetted to the outside of the room. No movement should mask the fire of any of the other team members. Most rooms have four points of domination based on the point of entry—the two corners on either side of the door and at least one meter to the left and to the right of the entry point. All four points are against the wall (figure 7-21).

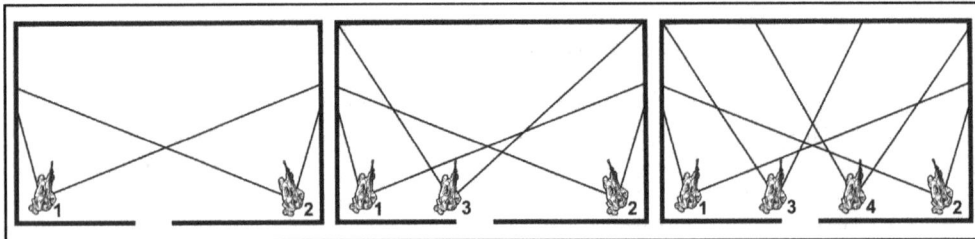

Figure 7-21. Points of domination for center entry point

7-95.   If the entry point is in the corner of a room, then using that corner as a point of domination is usually impractical as it hinders the movement and fire of the rest of the team. For rooms with corner entry points, the two points of domination on that side slide down the side wall as shown in figure 7-22.

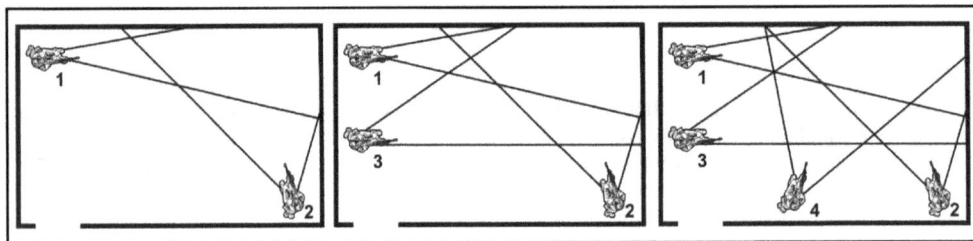

Figure 7-22. Points of domination for corner entry point

PASSING THROUGH ENTRY POINT

7-96.   Normally, the unit's SOP, the circumstances at the entry point, and the experience of the clearing team determine which technique a clearing team uses to pass through the entry point and enter a room. The major difference between these entry techniques is the route and related sectors of fire of the number 1 man. However, in each technique, a following Soldier goes in the opposite direction of the preceding Soldier. Clearing team stacks should be very tight to facilitate all team members entering the room as quickly as possible.

7-97.   When moving through a doorway, the number 1 man should push the door all the way to the wall to ensure no one is behind it. He should use his foot to push open the door and not his body, as equipment may catch on the door and slow the team's movement through the doorway. Entry techniques are discussed below.

DYNAMIC

7-98.   The number 1 Soldier selects his direction based on the enemy and obstacles observed as entering. The number 2 Soldier reads the number 1 Soldier's movement and goes in the opposite direction. Soldiers need to be prepared to go over or around furniture in rooms so that momentum is maintained and the room can be cleared and secured as rapidly as possible.

PATH OF LEAST RESISTANCE

7-99.   A door is an obstacle to entering a room. To ensure the fastest and smoothest entry possible, the clearing team should line up on the side of the door that provides the least resistance to movement during entry. If a door opens inward, the clearing team lines up on the hinge side. If the door opens outward, the team lines up on the doorknob side. The number 1 man normally takes the path of least resistance to enter the room by pushing open the door, proceeding across the doorway, and engaging any enemy as he moves to his point of domination. This allows him to clear the fatal funnel as fast as possible, which, in turn, allows the number 2 man to enter as rapidly as possible behind him.

PERSON IN THE DOORWAY

7-100.   Any person not clearly armed in the entry pathway must be forced out of the way so that the team does not get bunched up as they enter. The preferable method is to force them to the center of the room so they can be covered by fire and the team can continue to their points of domination. If this is not possible, they should be pushed into a position, such as against a wall, that allows the other members of the team to pass. The priority is for the team to clear the entry, dominate the room, and then aid the team member who is dealing with the person.

FIRE AND MOVEMENT

7-101.   Inaction or slow execution allows any hostile element time to react. Unless restricted or impeded, clearing team members stop moving only after they clear the door and reach their designated point of domination. All movement during room clearing is conducted at a brisk walk that allows Soldiers to retain their ability to fire rapid and aimed shots at appropriate targets. In addition to dominating the room, all clearing team members look for loopholes and mouseholes in the ceiling, walls, and floor. Once inside the room, avoid silhouetting or crossing in front of windows or open doors.

7-102.   Each team member must know both their sector of fire and their team members' sectors of fire, how these sectors of fire shift as they enter the room, and the final sectors of fire from the points of domination. All team members must understand that they must overwhelm all enemy as they are moving to their points of domination.

CONTROLLING THE ROOM

7-103.   By eliminating known enemy and occupying points of domination, the clearing team seizes the initiative from any remaining enemy and establishes control of the room. The clearing team must control all live noncombatants, friendly personnel, or neutralized enemy (surrendered or incapacitated). The clearing team leader or a designated team member should quickly take charge and immediately direct, through a loud commanding voice and exaggerated hand signals, the actions those personnel should take. Priority is to disarm all personnel and ensure they assume a prone position. Soldiers must confirm the casualty status of all occupants. Take note that verbal control of the room's occupants may be difficult as they may be experiencing a loss of hearing resulting from the use of explosives and firearms.

TASK ORGANIZATION

7-104.   The four-man room clearing team is the basic Army technique for room clearing. Based on the mission variables, room clearing may be conducted with two- or three-man teams. However, using fewer personnel reduces chances of success. A Soldier should never attempt to clear a room alone unless absolutely necessary.

FOUR-MAN ROOM CLEARING TECHNIQUE

7-105.   The four-man room clearing team is a warrior battle drill and is based on the standard Infantry rifle team under the overall control of the team's squad leader. The compartmentalized nature typical of buildings and rooms makes units larger than squads awkward and unmanageable. Thus, the fire team organization is the baseline from where units adapt to the specific situation.

7-106. To best use the four-man room clearing technique, a door or a door-size wall breach is needed. For other entry points, such as a window or a breach smaller than a door, other clearing techniques may work better. The following steps describe effective techniques to use when training Soldiers to the toughest possible conditions. These procedures can be trained, rehearsed, and modified as a specific situation and mission warrants.

Preparing to Enter

7-107. Identify and observe the entry point to see if the opening is large enough for entry. If the opening is too small or even nonexistent, determine a breaching method. View any closed door as being locked and assume it must be breached to gain entry. To conduct a breach, the required breaching equipment and personnel must be acquired and positioned. However, based on mission variables, most close-in breaches begin with a manual attempt to open the door. The clearing team should understand that turning the doorknob can give away the element of surprise and draw fire.

7-108. Determine whether to throw a hand grenade, and the type based on likely occupants and wall characteristics, into the room immediately prior to the clearing team entering the room. Once the decisions on breaching and hand grenade use are finalized, the clearing team and any other team (breach, overwatch, and so on) can move into position. The two options for a clearing team's starting position are lined up adjacent to the entry point (figure 7-23) or positioned near the door behind appropriate cover (figure 7-24).

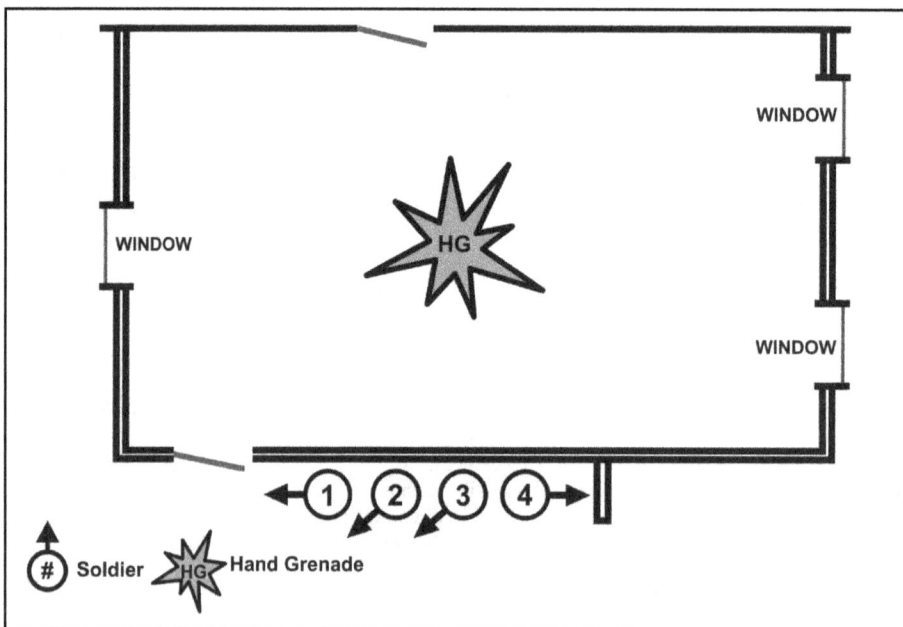

Figure 7-23. Adjacent start position

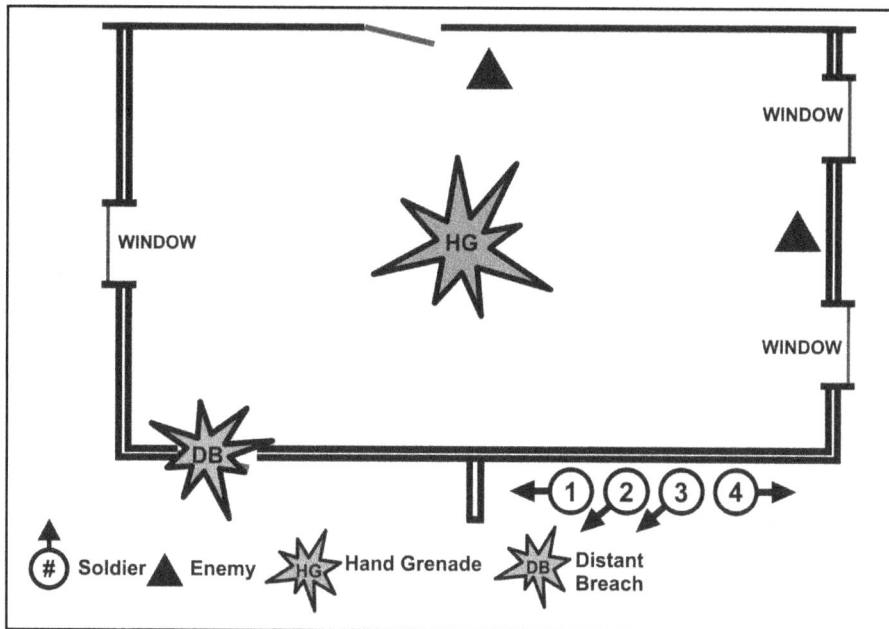

Figure 7-24. Distant start position

Entering the Room

7-109. The actions required to open or to breach the entry point, employing a lethal or nonlethal hand grenade immediately prior to entry (if appropriate), and the actual entering of the room should be a seamlessly interconnected series of events. The three conditions of entry that determine the specific actions that the clearing team takes in entering the room are described below.

Entering Through an Open Door or Existing Door-Size Opening

7-110. The clearing team moves to the start point and lines up in room entry order. This start point should be immediately adjacent to the entry point (doorway) on the side that supports the path of least resistance. If a hand grenade is to be thrown, it is readied by the number 2 man, and, on the team leader's nonverbal signal, the hand grenade is thrown into the room. If stealth is not a factor, the thrower sounds off with FRAG OUT when the grenade is thrown; otherwise, use a visual signal (figure 7-25).

7-111. Upon the team leader's signal to enter the room (or upon the explosion of the hand grenade), the clearing team moves quickly through the door. During movement, they scan their sectors of fire and overwhelm all enemy until they reach their point of domination. Upon reaching their point of domination, they cover their sector of fire and dominate the room. Clearing team members do not stop until they have cleared the door and reached their point of domination.

Entering Through a Closed Door After a Close-In Breach

7-112. The clearing team moves to the start point and lines up in room entry order. This start point should be immediately adjacent to the entry point (doorway) on the side that supports the path of least resistance. On the team leader's nonverbal signal, the team readies the close-in breach. If a hand grenade is to be used, the number 2 man readies it. Ideally, a separate breach element executes the breach, if not then Soldier 3 and Soldier 4 is the breach team. Once the breach team is ready, the team leader gives a nonverbal signal to execute the breach. Immediately after the breach, the breach team clears the doorway and, if previously deemed necessary, a hand grenade is thrown into the room. Since stealth is no longer a factor, the thrower sounds off with FRAG OUT (or STUN OUT) when the grenade is thrown (see figure 7-26).

7-113. Immediately after the breach (or upon the explosion of the hand grenade), the clearing team moves quickly through the door. They scan their sectors of fire and overwhelm all enemy until they reach their points of domination. Upon reaching their points of domination, they cover their sectors of fire and dominate the room. Clearing team members do not stop until they have reached their points of domination.

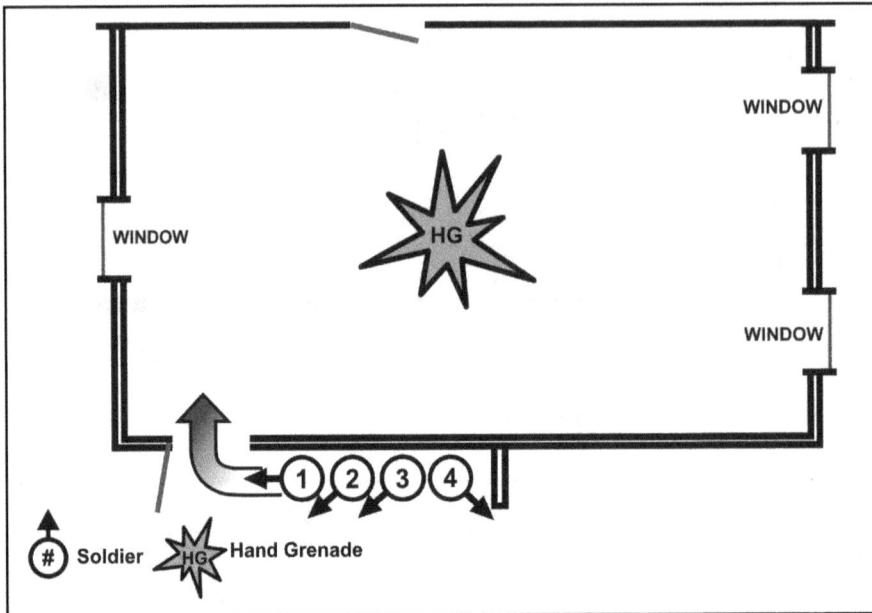

Figure 7-25. Entering through an open door

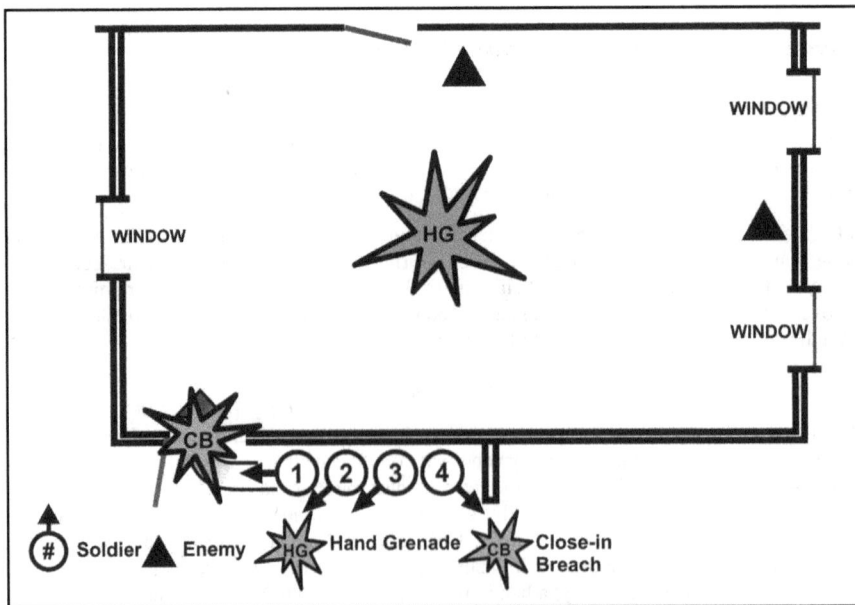

Figure 7-26. Entering after a close-in breach

Entering Through a Closed Door or a Door-Size Opening After a Distant Breach

7-114. Normally, a separate breach element executes an explosive or a ballistic breach using any weapon larger than a shotgun. The clearing team occupies a covered position, in entry order, close to the breach point, until after the breach and provides overwatch and suppressive fire, as necessary, for the breaching element. Once preparations for the distant breach are complete, the clearing team leader signals the execution of the breach and the distant breach is initiated. Immediately after the breach is made, the clearing team quickly moves from their covered positions, in entry order, to and then through the door/door-size opening. As they move, they scan their sectors of fire and overwhelm all enemy until they reach their points of domination. Upon reaching their points of domination, they cover their sector of fire and dominate the room. Clearing team members do not stop until they have reached their point of domination.

7-115. If the team must stop outside the entry point to line up or to throw a hand grenade (if previously deemed necessary), they should do so only momentarily and if throwing a grenade, they must ensure they have sufficient cover. If throwing a hand grenade, the clearing team quickly moves from their covered positions, in entry order, to the side of the opening that supports the path of least resistance. The team then assumes cover (normally against the wall). The number 2 man then readies the hand grenade and, on the team leader's signal, throws the hand grenade into the room. Since stealth is no longer a factor, the thrower sounds off with FRAG OUT (or STUN OUT) when the grenade is thrown (figure 7-27).

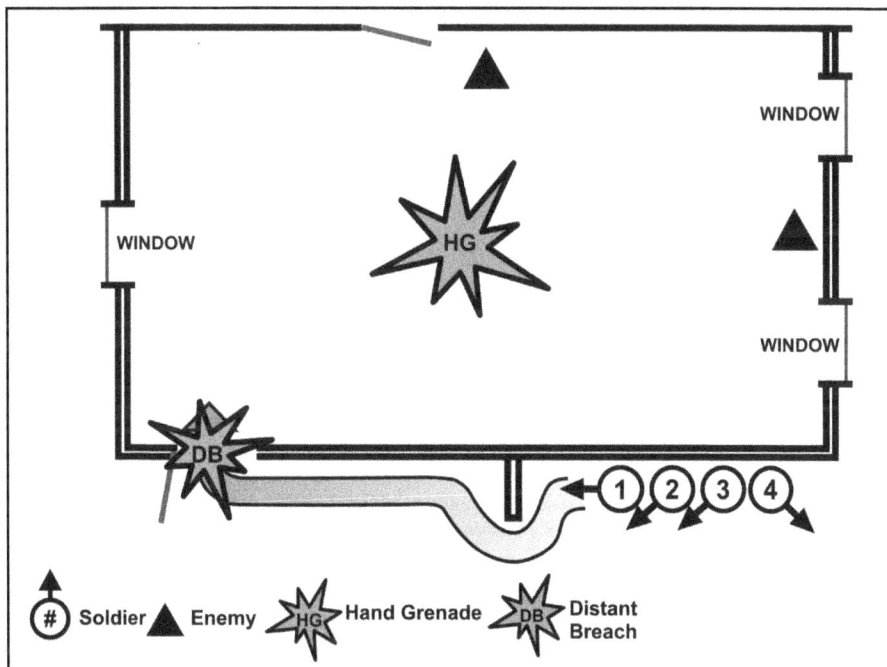

Figure 7-27. Entering after a distant breach

7-116. Upon the explosion of the hand grenade (if used), the clearing team moves quickly through the door. The team scans their sectors of fire and overwhelms all enemy until they reach their point of domination. Upon reaching their point of domination, they cover their sectors of fire and dominate the room. Clearing team members do not stop until they have cleared the door and reached their point of domination.

Clearing the Room

7-117. To effectively clear a room, each member of the team must know his sector of fire and how his sector overlaps and links with the sectors of the other team members. No movement should mask the fire of any of the other team members.

7-118. Each clearing team member moves toward their points of domination, engaging all enemy or hostile targets in their sector of fire, and clearing their path by moving any noncombatants toward the center of the room. Each Soldier's sector of fire changes, in sequence, as they enter the room and move toward their point of dominance.

7-119. On the signal, the team enters through the entry point (or breach). As team members move to their points of domination, they engage all enemy or hostile targets in sequence in their sector and move occupants not engaged by fire to the center so they can be covered by more than one team member. The direction each Soldier moves should not be rigidly preplanned unless the exact room layout is known. Each Soldier should go in a direction opposite the Soldier in front of him. Team members should stay within 1 meter of the wall as they move. If a team member finds his progress blocked by some object that will force him more than 1 meter from the wall, he should either step over it (if able) or stop where he is and clear the rest of his sector of fire from his current position. If this action creates dead space in the room, the clearing team leader should direct additional clearing actions once the other members of the clearing team have reached their points of domination. If Soldier 1 or 2 discovers that the room is very small, they can yell, SHORT ROOM or SHORT, which tells Soldier 3 or 4 (whoever is following) to stay outside the room. Clearing team members must exercise fire control and discriminate between hostile and noncombatant occupants of the room. (The most practical way to do this is to identify whether or not the target has a weapon in their hands.) Shoot without stopping, using short range marksmanship techniques. Move noncombatants toward the center or the room so more than one team member can cover them should they become hostile.

7-120. If a Soldier becomes engaged in a hand-to-hand fight, the other Soldiers should continue their actions to dominate the room before rendering support. When giving support to a Soldier so engaged, it is important that the team remain aware of the larger fight and maintain security.

7-121. If a Soldier becomes engaged in a hand-to-hand fight, the other Soldiers should continue their actions to dominate the room before rendering support. When giving support to a Soldier so engaged, it is important that the team remain aware of the larger fight and maintain security.

Opposing Corners Technique

7-122. The opposing corner technique may be used when Soldiers are experienced and the team has worked together (figure 7-28). The actions for each Soldier follow:
- Soldier 1 enters the room and eliminates any immediate threat. He can move left or right, moving along the path of least resistance to a point of domination—one of the two corners and continues down the room to gain depth.
- Soldier 2 enters almost simultaneously with the first and moves in the opposite direction, following the wall. He must clear the entry point, clear the immediate area, and move to his point of domination.
- Soldier 3 moves in the opposite direction of Soldier 2 inside the room, moves at least 1 meter from the entry point, and takes a position that dominates his sector.
- Soldier 4 moves in the opposite direction of Soldier 3, clears the doorway by at least 1 meter, and moves to a position that dominates his sector.

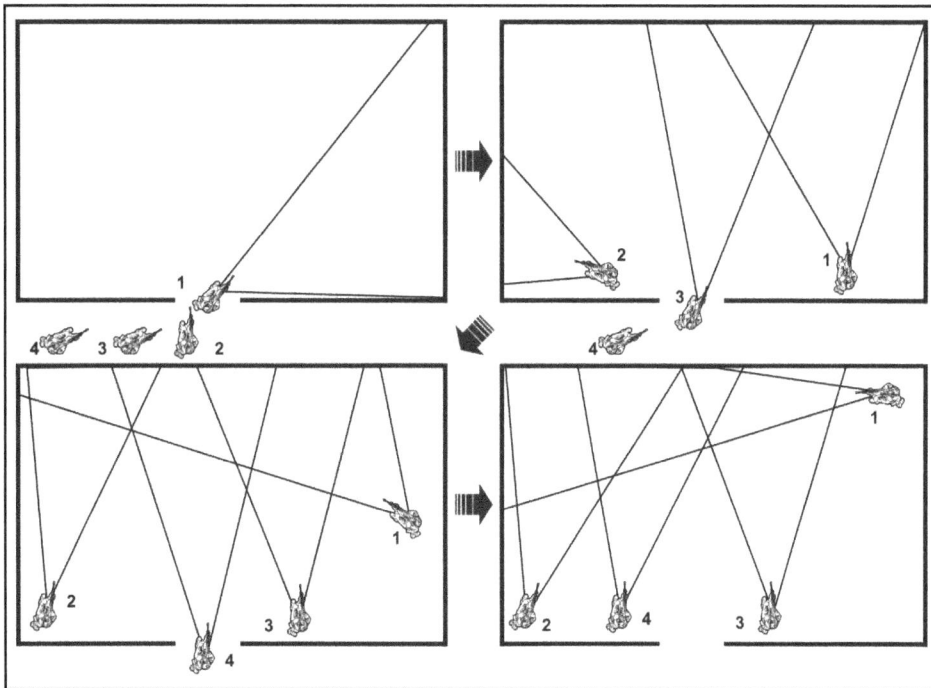

Figure 7-28. Opposing corners technique

Strong Wall Technique

7-123. The strong wall technique is used when Soldiers are inexperienced, integrating new team members, or when working with developing foreign forces. Soldier 1 has the option of going left or right and normally selects the path of least resistance to one of two near corners. In this example, Soldier 1 is going right. If Soldier 1 goes to the left, all movements and points of domination are the mirror image of those shown in the diagrams. Each Soldier covers his sector of fire directly to his front. As a Soldier turns, his sector of fire also turns with him until he reaches his point of domination position (figure 7-29).

7-124. The actions for each Soldier follow:

- Soldier 1 passes rapidly through the entry point and eliminates any immediate threat. He then clears the far wall and then the far right corner as he turns toward the near right corner, his point of domination.
- Soldier 2 passes rapidly through the entry point immediately after Soldier 1 and overwhelms any immediate threat. Soldier 2 then turns in the opposite direction of Soldier 1, clearing first the far wall and then the far left corner as he turns.
- Soldier 3 passes rapidly through the entry point immediately after Soldier 2 and overwhelms any immediate threat. Soldier 3 then turns in the opposite direction of Soldier 2, clearing first the far wall and then the far right corner as he turns.
- Soldier 4 passes rapidly through the entry point immediately after Soldier 3 and overwhelms any immediate threat. Soldier 4 then turns in the opposite direction of Soldier 3, clearing first the far wall and then the far left corner as he turns.
- Soldier 1 continues his turn and clears the near right corner, his point of domination, and the near right wall.
- Soldier 2 continues his turn and clears the near left corner, his point of domination, and the near left wall.
- Soldier 3 continues his turn and clears the right wall to the front of Soldier 1. Soldier 3 must use

extreme caution when firing toward the right wall to ensure Soldier 1 is not erroneously flagged by his weapon.

- Soldier 4 continues his turn and clears the left wall to the front of Soldier 2. Soldier 4 must use extreme caution when firing toward the left wall to ensure Soldier 2 is not erroneously flagged by his weapon.

- Soldier 1 reaches the near right corner, his point of domination, turns, and covers the far wall and far right corner.

- Soldier 2 reaches the near left corner, his point of domination, turns and covers the far wall and far left corner.

- Soldier 3 reaches the near wall (at least 1 meter to the right of the door), his point of domination, turns, and covers the far wall.

- Soldier 4 reaches the near wall (at least 1 meter to the left of the door), his point of domination, turns, and covers the far wall.

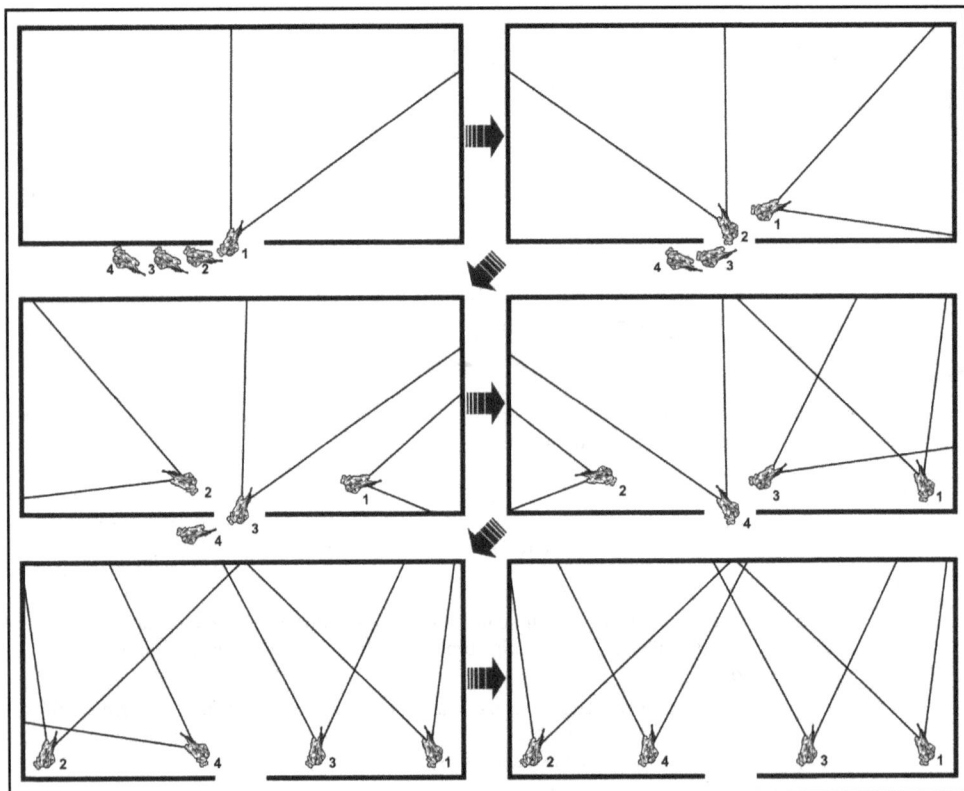

Figure 7-29. Strong wall technique

Securing the Room

7-125. On order, any member of the clearing team may move deeper into the room while being overwatched by the other team members. The team leader must control this action. Once the room is cleared, and any enemy or noncombatants secured, the clearing team leader signals to the squad leader that the room has been cleared. The squad leader then directs any further searching of the room or occupants, ensures the room is marked as per unit SOP, reports the status to the platoon leader, consolidates and reorganizes as necessary, and determines the next action of his squad.

THREE-MAN ROOM CLEARING TECHNIQUE

7-126. This technique is executed in the same manner as the four-man room clearing technique (figure 7-30). After clearing the entry point, the third man should remain close to the entry point and cover the center sector of fire.

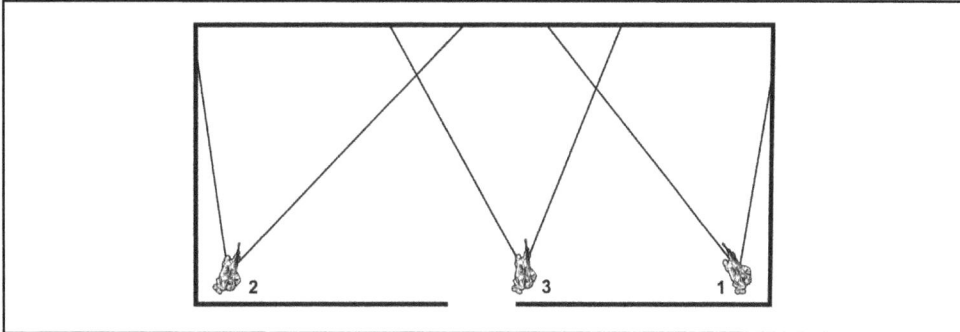

Figure 7-30. Three-man rooming clearing final positions

TWO-MAN ROOM CLEARING TECHNIQUE

7-127. This technique is executed the same as the four-man room clearing technique (figure 7-31).

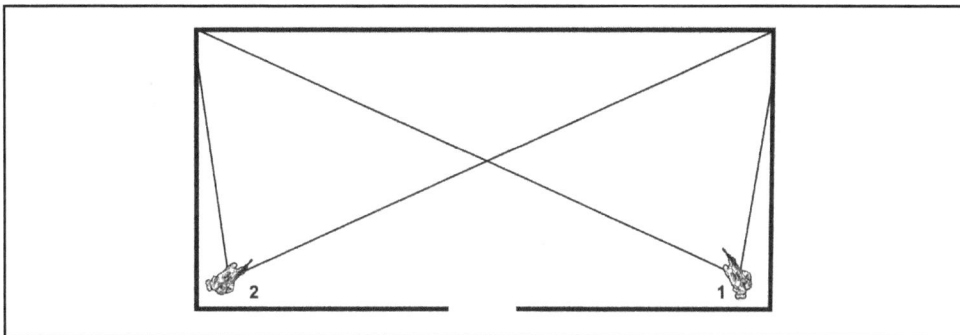

Figure 7-31. Two-man room clearing using simultaneous buttonhooks

COMPLETION

7-128. A room is cleared when the team leader designates it is cleared after receiving the report of the other members and conducting a visual scan of the whole room. The clearing team then marks the room as cleared in accordance with unit SOP. Even before a room is determined cleared by the clearing team leader, the clearing team members have often begun their next action. If the room has other doors, especially open doors, or has windows, Soldiers should evaluate the threat from the other side of those doors and windows. Even when known friendly forces are on the other side, Soldiers should not silhouette themselves. If there is a potential or a known threat from beyond other doors or windows, immediate preparation for a follow-on mission should begin. This may include a follow-on room clearing, heightened observation, or even the establishing of a defense. The clearing team maintains control of the room and the entry point until additional instructions are received from the squad leader or follow-on forces coordinate entry into the room.

SECTION IV – COMBATIVES

7-129. When you are inside a room, it is a fight and not a marksmanship contest. Given the small size of rooms in much of the world, Soldiers may be close to arms length from an enemy the second they pass through the entry point. If every room in a building can be cleared with firepower alone, there is seldom a need to send Soldiers in. Weapons may malfunction, noncombatants are not always compliant, and the enemy is not always obviously armed. Combatives is as important as close quarters marksmanship in urban operations.

WEAPONS MALFUNCTION

7-130. If a Soldier's weapon malfunctions while he is clearing a room, his actions will be dictated by how close he is to the enemy.

- In a large room, he may be far enough away that the prudent approach is to get out of the way so that someone else can engage the threat. The Soldier should bend his knee and attempt to clear his weapon while in the kneeling position. This will alert his teammates that his weapon is down and allow him to get his weapon back into the fight in the fastest possible time. It also clears the line of fire.
- In a smaller room, it is seldom advisable to kneel because of the close proximity to the enemy. Because your weapon malfunctions does not mean that the enemy's weapon has also malfunctioned. The time it takes for your teammates to clear their sectors and come to your aid may be enough to allow the enemy to bring his weapon to bear on you. The unarmed Soldier should explode into the enemy and dominate him with combatives techniques. If the enemy is armed, the Soldier must prevent him from bringing his weapon to bear. The Soldier's priority is to survive long enough for his teammates to dominate the room and come to his aid.

DELAYED COMBATANTS

7-131. It will often be unclear upon entry whether a person in the room is hostile. Take care when dealing with people who appear to be noncombatants and maintain control of the situation should they become noncompliant or hostile.

7-132. Just as a tactical unit attempts to make contact with the smallest possible element in order to maintain tactical flexibility, potential enemy should be controlled at the farthest possible range. This is best done at projectile weapons range by use of voice commands and gestures. If a Soldier must take physical control of a potential enemy, he should attempt to keep the enemy at arm's length to make it difficult for him to grasp the Soldier's equipment.

7-133. If the enemy initiates hostile action while the Soldier attempts to control him, the Soldier should attempt to maintain the farthest possible distance. This will keep the enemy from grasping the Soldier's equipment. After gaining a dominant clinch position, the Soldier has three tactical options—

- **Regain Projectile Range.** The Soldier can push the enemy away, spin, or redirect the enemy to regain projectile weapon range. The enemy should be directed toward the center of the room if possible so any fire will not endanger the Soldier's teammates.
- **Employ a Side Arm.** The Soldier can draw a bayonet, combat knife, or pistol.
- **Close the Distance.** Often the best way to gain control is to aggressively close the distance. An enemy can be forced against a wall or to the ground. If the enemy grasps the Soldier and attempts to deploy a hidden weapon, the Soldier will have difficulty regaining projectile weapon range to deploy his primary weapon. In addition, he will not have time to deploy his secondary weapon before the enemy's weapon is brought to bear. The principle concern is to survive long enough for a teammate to come to your aid.

OTHER SITUATIONS

7-134. A Soldier may also be attacked from his rear or flank, pushed against a wall, or tackled to the ground.

- If attacked from the rear, a Soldier should try to maintain a standing position. If he can remain standing, he should use combatives techniques to turn toward the enemy and fight for a dominant clinch position before executing one of the three tactical options described above.
- If pinned against a wall, the wall itself can be an aid.
- If a Soldier cannot remain on his feet and is tackled to the ground, he must protect his side arm by gaining a dominant or strong defensive position. A good position gives him several tactical options as listed below.
  - **Regain the Standing Position.** The first option is to regain the standing position. If a Soldier has managed to gain a good defensive position while being tackled, he can use the same techniques while standing to control the range and stand by escaping his hips.
  - **Employ a Side Arm.** If a Soldier can gain a dominant position controlling the enemy, he can employ a side arm such as a bayonet, combat knife, or pistol.
  - **Finish the Fight.** A Soldier may use chokes and joint attacking techniques to disable the enemy.
  - **Stall.** As a last resort, a Soldier can gain enough control to survive until one or more of his teammates can come to his aid.

SECTION V – BUILDING CLEARING

7-135. Seizing or gaining control of a building may not always require committing troops into the building and closing with the enemy. Before initiating a direct assault and exposing members of a clearing team to direct enemy contact and risking casualties, leaders should consider their range of options, which include both lethal and nonlethal actions. Lethal actions include using indirect fire, long-range vehicular fire, suppressive fire, and sniper fire. Nonlethal actions include the tactical callout, negotiations, show of force, and military information support operations.

7-136. Leaders and Soldiers should consider the task and purpose they have been given and the method they are to use to achieve the desired results. They must operate in accordance with the ROE and should be aware of the effects weapons have on the type and composition of the buildings.

CONSIDERATIONS

7-137. During UO, units encounter situations in which they must enter and clear a building. The following influence the size of the clearing force and the operational conditions for entering and clearing a building:
- Existing rules of engagement.
- Size, condition, and composition of the building.
- Strength, disposition, and conventionality of the inside and outside enemy.
- Presence, number, and status of noncombatants.

OPERATIONAL CONDITIONS

7-138. To fully clear a building, all internal and external spaces of a building should be cleared. Internal spaces include all rooms on every floor, stairs, attic areas, subterranean areas, and crawl spaces. External spaces include the roof, external stairs, and ledges. However, both the thoroughness of the clearing and the degree of force used varies according to the mission variables, especially the enemy that is expected to be present, their known capabilities, and the actions of the building's occupants.

7-139. While some situations may only require the surgical clearing of a single room, many operations necessitate the clearing of the complete building using both precision and high-intensity methods. The clearing of a complete building, even in high-intensity situations, does not require the high-intensity clearing of each and every room.

High Intensity

7-140. Under high-intensity conditions, the operational environment tends to be conventional, the enemy is robust and determined to resist, the presence of noncombatants is limited, and the existing political considerations allow for the employment of overwhelming firepower. Units may elect to destroy an entire building rather than assault it, use overwhelming suppressive or supporting fires, conduct explosive breaching, or employ fragmentation grenades to neutralize an area before entering.

Precision

7-141. Under precision conditions, the operational environment tends to be less conventional, the enemy is less robust and often mixed with noncombatants, and existing political considerations require the restrictive use of combat power. The friendly force retains the option of employing hand grenades if called for or employing overwhelming combat power if needed (and no noncombatants are present). For precision operations, the clearing team uses mechanical or other less destructive breaching methods to enter rooms.

Surgical

7-142. Surgical conditions are best employed by SOFs, specialized teams, or (in certain situations) HN special weapons and tactics teams. Often, conventional units isolate a building or area, while a SOF executes the surgical room clearing operation.

FORCE STRUCTURE

7-143. Typically, a squad is the appropriate size maneuver element to execute operations within a building on any single floor. A unit larger than a squad quickly becomes unwieldy when operating in the confined spaces of a building. Additional squads can provide supporting fire or follow and support within larger buildings. In multilevel large structures, another platoon may even be given responsibility for another floor. To simplify control, keep squads physically separated by rooms and platoons separated by floors if possible. All friendly elements within a building must maintain strong situational awareness and good communication to prevent fratricide as grenade fragments and weapon fire can penetrate walls as well as floors and ceilings.

7-144. Actual clearing operations inside a building are best conducted by the two fire teams of one squad working closely together. Typically, one team clears one room while the other team provides overwatch, covering fire, or security at the entry point. In some situations the second team may simultaneously clear a nearby room. A common technique is for the two teams of one squad to bound through rooms. This means that after one team clears one room, the other team then leaps ahead to clear the next room. Bounding continues until the floor is cleared or the squad must halt. Depending on the size and layout of the floor, a second assault squad can be used to simultaneously clear additional rooms or a stairwell.

7-145. Ultimately, to be successful, the clearing of a building should include the securing of the building to prevent enemy forces from returning to areas already cleared. This also includes, as time permits, the back clearing of key areas and rechecking of likely hiding locations. Typically, the assault force is focused on the inside, while another force is focused on the overall security of the building. This security force focuses on the outside of the building which primarily means securing all ground floor entry points. Since, ideally, the assault begins with the isolation of the building; the isolation force can achieve most of the security requirements. However, if building isolation is not achieved, or to ensure the close-in security of the ground floor, security forces should be designated to prevent entry or exit of enemy personnel. A common method of achieving this is to shift elements of the support force, as they accomplish their support tasks, to positions from which they can secure the ground floor.

METHOD FOR ENTERING AND CLEARING BUILDINGS

7-146. The goal is to gain a foothold. While a direct frontal assault can accomplish this, it also can be quite costly. As such, always look for an alternate entry points. If the building is enemy occupied, try to avoid the obvious entry as the enemy will be expecting it and, to various degrees, be ready for it.

7-147. In many instances, it is better to clear a well-defended building, especially a well-defended ground floor, from the top down as this avoids a frontal assault and bypasses the expected ground floor entry points that are often well defended and booby trapped. However, entering a building from any level other than the ground floor may be difficult, Security and speed are critical to a successful above ground entry. The exposure of Soldiers when entering a higher level must be mitigated. Use various methods to gain above ground floor access, to include ladders, drainpipes, vines, Soldier assistance, armored vehicles, adjacent roofs, windows, or walls. Additionally, consider using helicopters to gain access to the roof.

7-148. The advantages are that a unit's momentum is greater clearing down than up; grenades are easier to throw down a stairwell than up; fewer personnel are needed to secure the upper floors and roof as opposed to securing the ground floor. Also, consider that an enemy who is forced to the top of a building may be cornered and subsequently fight desperately or escape over the roof. An enemy who is forced down to ground level may elect to withdraw from the building, thus exposing himself to friendly fires from friendly forces outside.

7-149. The disadvantages of upper entry are that the means to enter a building at an upper level may not be present and, even if present, often takes additional time to reach; and the method of entry often increases the exposure risk of the assault force. These disadvantages, combined with the fact that the ground floor is by far the most accessible, mean that the most common method of gaining entry to a building remains by way of the ground floor. As such the dangers of ground floor entry can be successfully mitigated by support, suppression, security and obscuration.

SUPPORT, SUPPRESSION, SECURITY, AND OBSCURATION REQUIREMENTS

7-150. Both the operational environment and enemy situation influence the degree and type of support, suppression, security, and obscuration required. Leaders should determine where their requirements lie.

7-151. The targeted building and even nearby buildings, may require the application of overwhelming firepower on all visible apertures to suppress enemy personnel. This suppression may be necessary not only as the assault element moves to enter the building but also as the unit clears various rooms and floors, to include the roof. Obscuration may be required to provide concealment for the movement of the assault force. Additionally, the enemy and building layout may require units to physically secure numerous ground floor rooms as they clear.

7-152. All that may be required is the positioning of a few elements, such as a sniper team, to overwatch key apertures and engage identified enemy personnel. The assault element may only need to surgically clear a single floor or even a single room; while a security element may only need to control access to a single room.

SITUATIONAL AWARENESS

7-153. Leaders should be aware of the location of their subordinate units, nearby friendly units, noncombatants, the enemy, and where the enemy may move. This can only be accomplished through timely and accurate communication between all involved elements. However, synthesizing this information can be challenging.

7-154. Forces dispersed into small elements create a situation in which each element may report a single event that may be misinterpreted as two different events. Conversely, two or more separate events, reported by two or more friendly elements, may be misinterpreted as a single event. Accurate reporting is best accomplished through the use of common reference points identified and rehearsed before the operation.

7-155. Additionally, friendly units outside a building must be aware of the current location of friendly units inside a building. Often, radios become degraded the deeper a unit moves into a building. To overcome this, the positioning of a radio telephone operator near a cleared window can both improve radio communications and be used as a marking for unit progression.

7-156. A critical aspect of maintaining unit situational awareness is in the marking of cleared rooms, floors, and buildings. This is critical to ensure multiple units inside a building are aware of the progress of sister elements, and units outside a building are aware of the progress of units inside the building.

MODIFYING THE PLAN

7-157. While the mission end state remains the same, the methods to achieve that end state often change. Leaders should plan and prepare for this potential for change. Common reasons to modify the plan during its execution include updated enemy locations, changes to the exterior situation, an unexpected floor plan or characteristics of the building, the presence of noncombatants, friendly casualties, or resource shortages.

TRANSITION

7-158. If the building is to be defended, the unit transitions to defense. If the building is to be vacated, leaders should first ensure that the enemy cannot reoccupy the building and that all friendly elements are accounted for as they exit the building. Exiting is best accomplished from top to bottom through a single exit point. Units must plan the exiting of a building to prevent fratricide and avoid contact with enemy outside the building. Ensuring the building remains secured is accomplished through various means based on METT-TC. These methods include, but are not limited to, new positions that can overwatch the building, the establishment of a cleared area around the building, or the use of local security forces to secure the building.

CLEARING FLOORS

7-159. Typically, units must clear more than a single, isolated room—often a complete floor must be cleared and secured. Given the confined space inside a building, a squad-size element is the appropriate size for a maneuvering on an individual floor; however, multiple squads may be needed for large buildings, with the platoon leader controlling the overall progress.

7-160. After establishing a foothold in the building, the squad leader, based on METT-TC (especially the visible layout of the building), determines the final plan for clearing the floor. If possible, additional forces should isolate the building from outside and provide supporting fire, as needed, for the squad's advance.

7-161. As an example, the following sequences of figures illustrate the basic process of clearing a floor. Additional forces are isolating the building. Clearing a floor begins with the successful establishment of a foothold. The example below shows a squad preparing to clear the floor after successfully establishing a foothold in the building (figure 7-32).

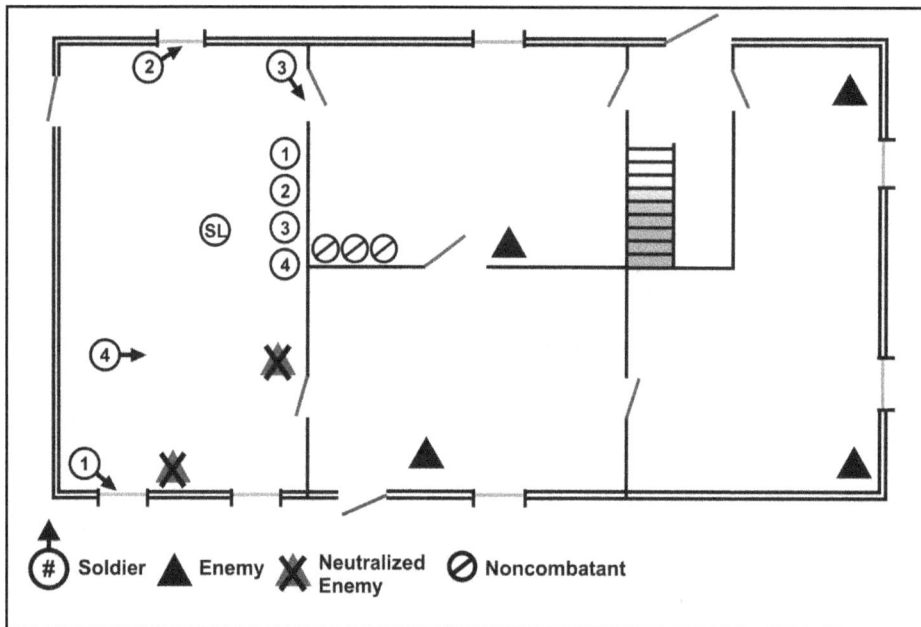

Figure 7-32. Preparing to clear a floor

7-162. Throwing a grenade into every room is not practical or always possible. However, gaining surprise is a critical advantage when entering a room. One way to accomplish this is through tactical deception. A close-in breach of one door or even the jiggling of a doorknob can provide a critical distraction while the clearing team enters through another door. In the example below, the lock and hinges of one door are shot, causing a distraction, while the clearing team enters into another room (figure 7-33).

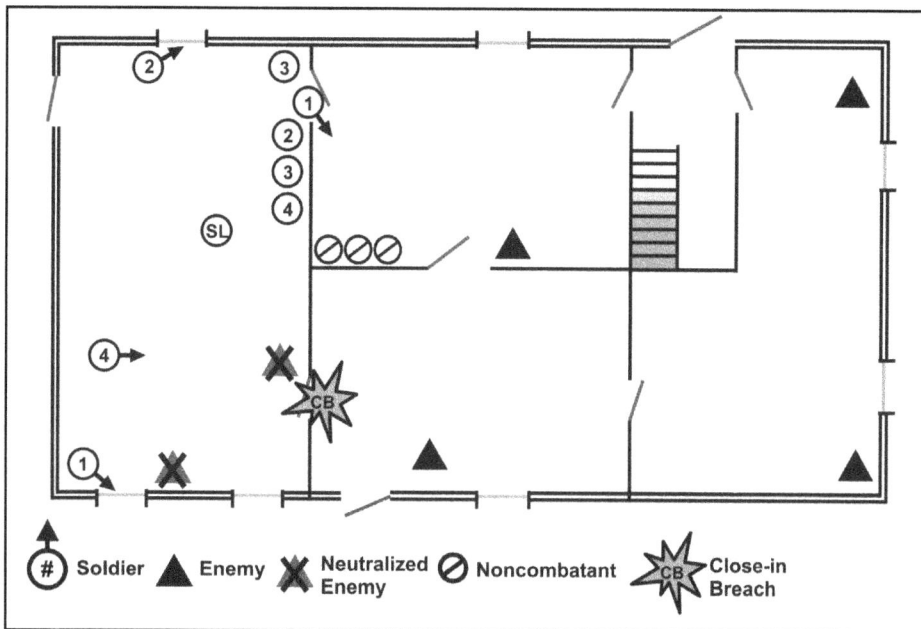

Figure 7-33. Clearing a floor (use of deception)

7-163. A requirement for success in clearing a floor is flexibility. Upon entering a room, previously unknown facts, such as the presence of noncombatants or obstacles, may be discovered. This should be relayed immediately and in-stride modifications to the room clearing plan, as per unit SOP, may be necessary. Additionally, room layout may not support the classic four points of domination. In the example shown in figure 7-34, Soldier 1 saw and announced NONCOMBATANTS, RIGHT NEAR CORNER; engaged an enemy who slipped through an open door way: announced ENEMY, RIGHT SIDE ROOM then continued making a button hook towards the left corner point of domination. Due to the position of the door and windows, Soldier 1 elects to advance slightly farther along the wall to a point of domination that provides room for Soldier 3 and does not silhouette Soldier 3 in a window or door. Soldier 2 covers and secures the noncombatants.

7-164. The position of doors and the location of Soldiers may not support the single entry line-up in all instances. When this happens, leaders should modify their basic plan to fit the situation. The entry order should always remain the same; however, the Soldiers can switch positions and, therefore, numbers as METT-TC dictates. In the example shown in figure 7-35, Soldier 4 remained covering the open doorway; the other three Soldiers in order to not cross in front of the open doorway assumed ready positions beside the side of the door nearest to them. Since enemies were known to be in the room, the decision was made to precede room entry with a hand grenade. The other team secured their room and moved the noncombatants out of the way. The squad leader continues to synchronize the two teams.

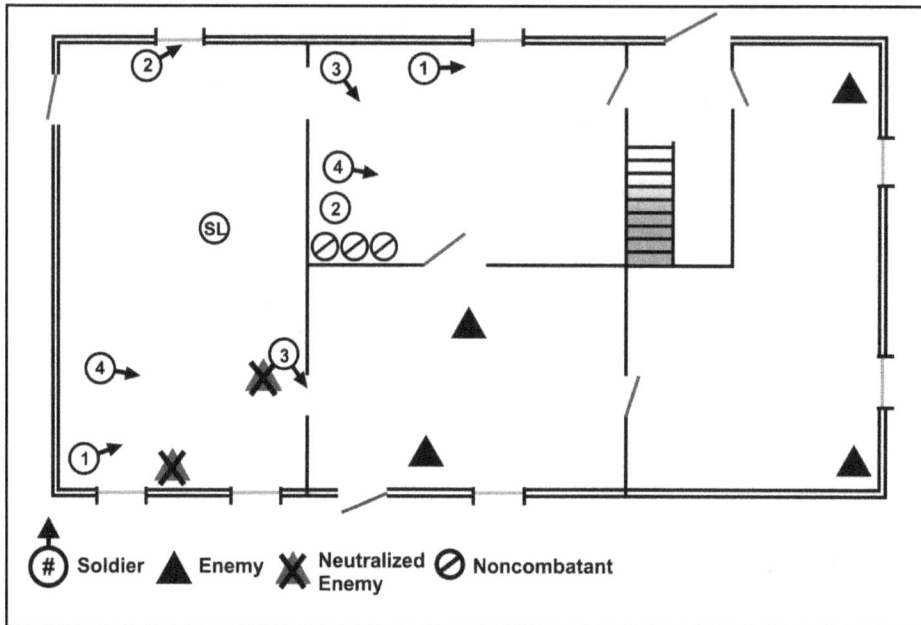

Figure 7-34. Clearing a floor (room with noncombatants)

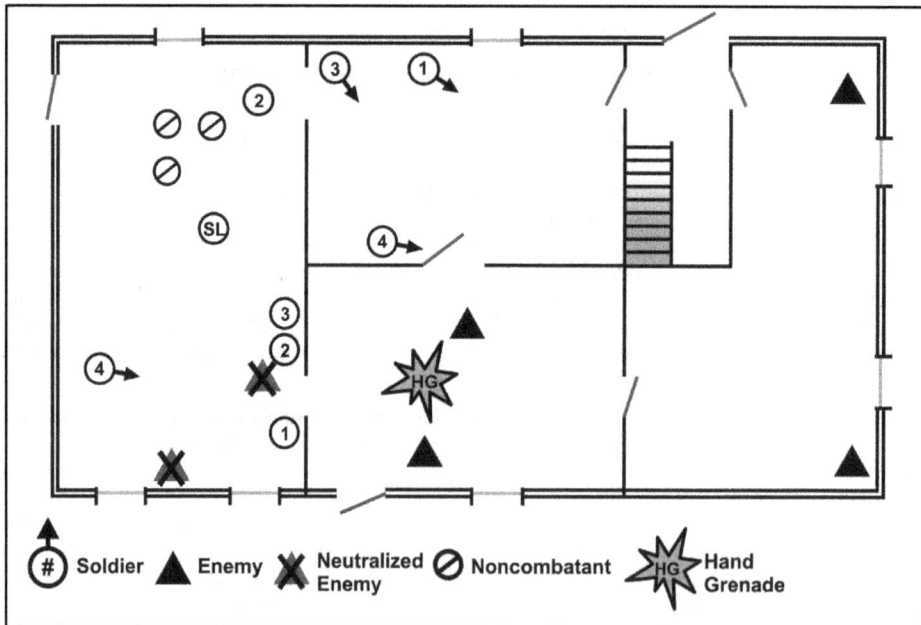

Figure 7-35. Clearing a floor (enemy-occupied room)

7-165. After the hand grenade explodes, the clearing team clears the room, reports, and moves to secure the room. The squad leader assesses the situation to determine the next step in clearing the floor and communicates this to his teams. Never leave a room or noncombatants unsecured. If there are follow-on forces, they can secure cleared rooms and noncombatants (figure 7-36).

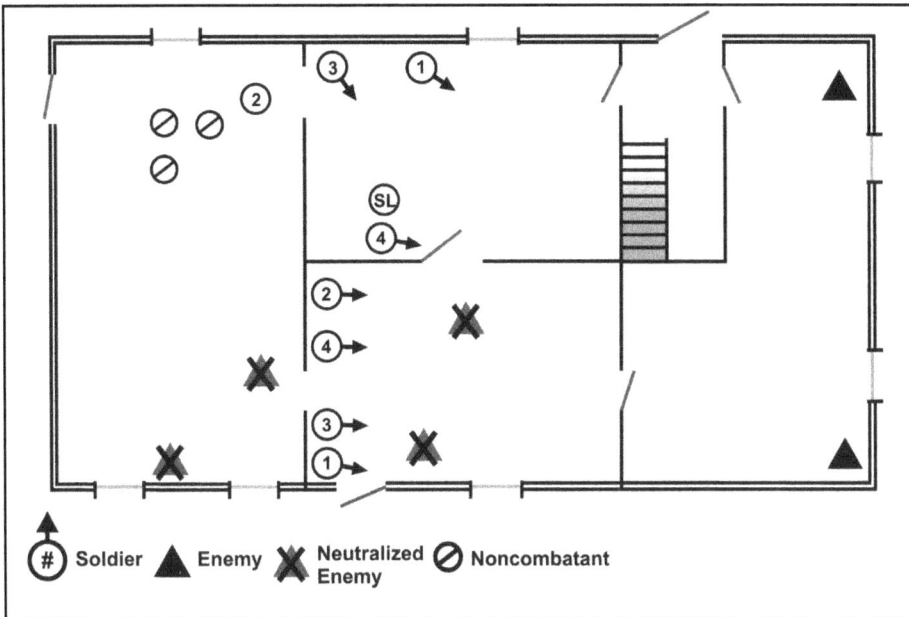

Figure 7-36. Clearing a floor (clear room and evaluate situation)

7-166. At some point, the squad leader normally bounds his teams in clearing rooms. As with all room clearing actions, bounding should be flexible, without a set pattern. One team may clear one room while the other team clears two rooms. Starting positions should also remain flexible. In figure 7-37, the clearing team completed the clearing and securing of their room. After evaluating the situation the team leader adjusted positions and directed the same team to clear the next room.

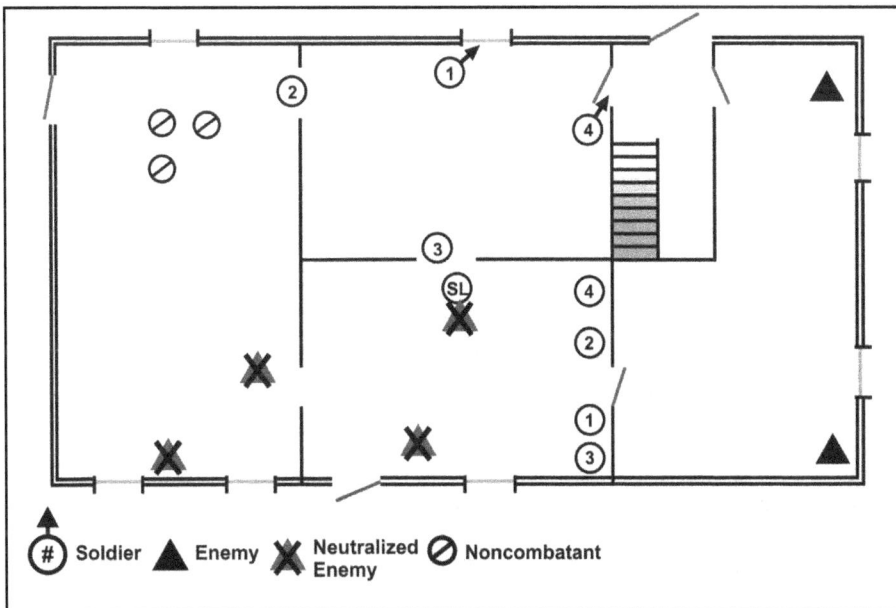

Figure 7-37. Clearing a floor (bounding)

7-167. Upon entering a room and occupying the points of domination, it may be determined that, due to the shape of the room or obstructions within the room, that there are still parts of the room that must be cleared. The clearing team leader then directs the method to clear the rest of the room (figure 7-38).

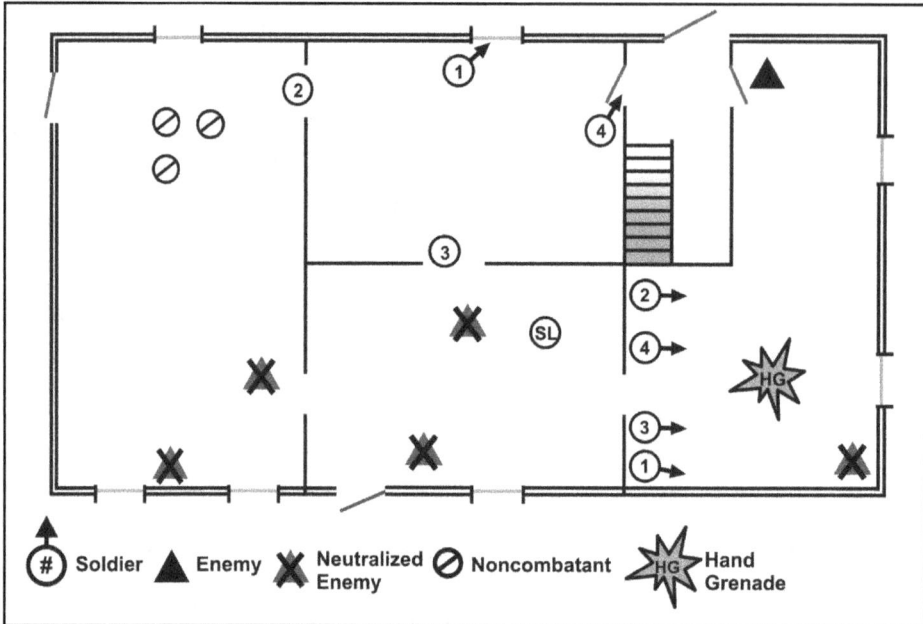

Figure 7-38. Clearing a floor (shape of rooms)

7-168. Often when additional clearing is required, it is due to a bend in the room. This corner can often be cleared just like clearing an exterior corner using the pie-ing method. Additionally, rooms may be too small for a four-man clearing team; and a two or three man clearing team is the best choice (figure 7-39).

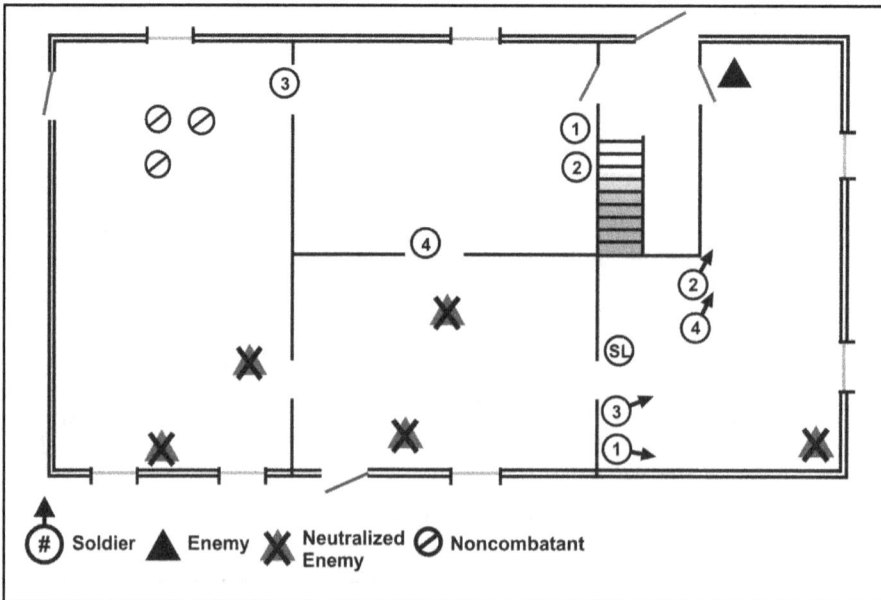

Figure 7-39. Clearing a floor (expanded room clearing)

7-169. Small rooms and stair landings are best cleared by small teams. The clearing of a complete stairwell is an operation in itself and covered later. However, units must clear and secure the stair landing on their floor (figure 7-40).

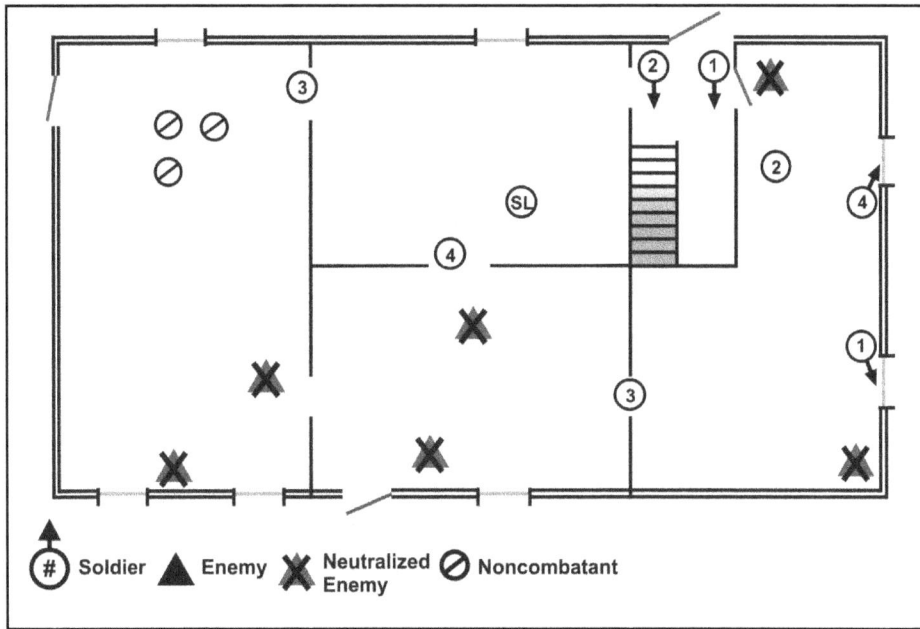

Figure 7-40. Clearing a floor (small rooms and stair landings)

7-170. Once the entire floor is secured, report the status and finalize plans for the next floor.

STAIRWELL AND STAIRCASE CLEARING

7-171. There are numerous variations to stairwell and staircase layouts, to include width, steepness, openness, location, and access. As such, leaders must evaluate each set of stairs individually. The enclosed stairwell is the most common in high-rise and multistory public buildings. An enclosed stairwell is walled off unto itself and sealed with closed doors at all entry points from the rest of the building.

7-172. When built in the interior of a building, all walls are solid; when built on the exterior of a building, the outside wall often has windows. Depending on the design, the interior stairwell gap in the center varies from negligible to a significant opening (figure 7-41 and figure 7-42).

Figure 7-41. Enclosed stairwell (small gap)

Figure 7-42. Enclosed stairwell (large gap)

7-173. Most stairwells and staircases are comparable to doorways in that they create a fatal funnel; however, in enclosed stairs, the danger is intensified by the three-dimensional aspect of the stairwell continuing both upward and downward. The layout of the stairs and the presence of any obstacles or debris can significantly affect movement.

7-174. Entering an enclosed stairwell through a door should be treated as entering a small room. Once in the stairwell, security both up and down the stairwell should be maintained. Normally, clear stairwells in conjunction with clearing a floor and by starting at either the top and working down or from the bottom and working up. Maintain security within the stairwell as other units clear the adjoining floor.

7-175. There are two concerns–entering the stairwell and clearing the stairwell. Initially, secure a stairwell by covering the entry point. Only enter a stairwell when ready to begin clearing. The clearing team should only be concerned with clearing in one direction. If both directions are not cleared, then either a separate security element covers one direction or another clearing team clears the other direction.

ENTERING AND CLEARING STAIRWELLS

7-176. If the stairs are not enclosed (that is, if the stairs can be accessed without going through a door), it is usually best to modify the plan and clear the stairs as an integral part of the room. If the stairs are enclosed (accessed by going through a door), then entering the stairwell will put Soldiers on a landing. Entering onto this landing is performed initially the same way as clearing a room. Since most stairwell landings are small, the unit should be prepared to clear and secure this landing with less than four personnel. It is important to remember that entering a stairwell ends with the landing secured and the upstairs and the downstairs directions covered. Elements are then positioned to support the clearing in one or both directions.

7-177. For an enclosed stairwell, especially one that complies with international fire safety standards, all stairwell doors are steel doors that open outward and close automatically. They are usually not lockable from the building interior side and usually automatically lock from the stair side. This means that the stairwell door should be easy to open from any floor, but it is heavy and will close if not propped open. One Soldier should be dedicated to opening and then holding the door. If the door is to be breached, a doorknob charge is recommended. Figure 7-43 shows a typical entering and clearing of a stairwell, with a non clearing team Soldier securing the open door.

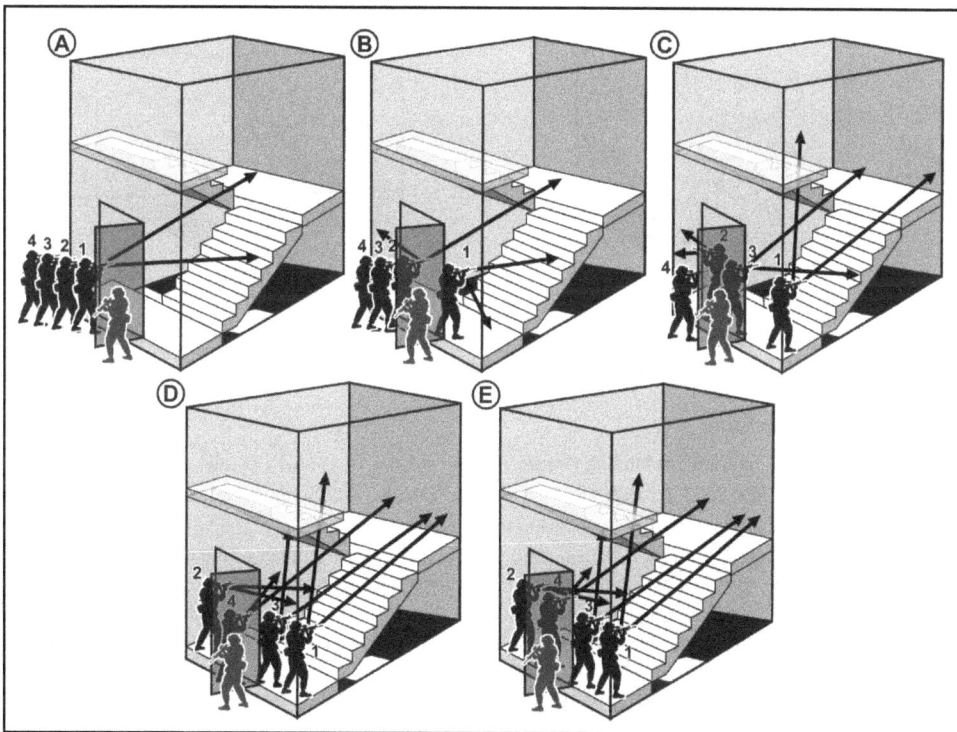

Figure 7-43. Entering and clearing up a stairwell

CLEARING STAIRS

7-178. Starting positions vary based on the actual configuration of the stairs. However, since an enclosed set of stairs is commonly found in multistory buildings, this type of stairs is used to describe the basic clearing technique. Stairs are not cleared in isolation of the rest of the building. Typically, a unit clears stairs to the next floor, emplaces security to cover the continuation of the stairs, and then clears the room or hallway adjacent to the stairwell door, thus establishing a foothold on the next floor. They then clear the rest of the floor. This process is then repeated for the rest of the building's floors.

Initial Start Position

7-179. Typically, Soldiers 1 and 2 are in points of domination at the two near corners after entering and clearing the stairwell. Soldier 3 and Soldier 4 are either just inside or outside the stairwell near the doorway. From these points of domination, the team then moves into their start positions for clearing the stairs upward or downward (figure 7-44). As soon as the stairwell clearing team moves into their start positions (numbered circles) another team (circles without numbers) should move into position to maintain security or possible clear, the stairs in the opposite direction.

- Soldier 1 moves to the wall side of the first step. Soldier 1 covers the intermittent landing straight ahead.
- Soldier 2 moves to the inward side of the first step. Soldier 2 covers the adjacent set of stairs leading to the next floor landing.
- Soldier 3 follows behind Soldier 1 to cover any window or door encountered on a landing.
- Soldier 4 moves to and covers the center opening looking up.

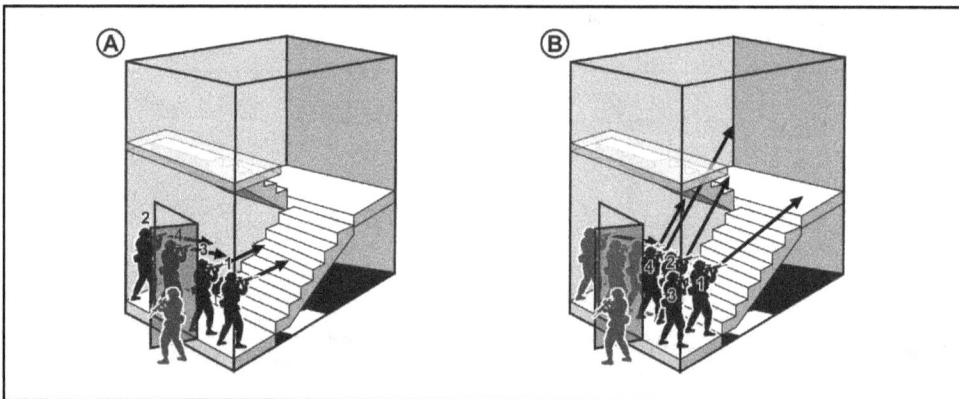

Figure 7-44. Clearing up a stairwell (starting positions)

Clear Intermittent Landing

7-180. To clear the intermittent landing (figure 7-45)—

- Soldier 1 and Soldier 2 begin by moving side-by-side, with Soldier 3 following Soldier 1.
- Soldier 1 focuses on visually clearing the intermittent landing.
- Soldier 2 focuses on the adjacent stairs until he can see the landing of the next floor. Once he can clearly see the landing, he pivots, halts, and covers the next landing.
- Soldier 1 continues past Soldier 2 and now has room to shift his coverage to the next set of stairs. Soldier 1 continues up to the intermittent landing and occupies a point of domination facing toward the next landing.
- Soldier 3 follows Soldier 1 onto the landing and covers any window or door encountered on the landing or occupies a point of domination facing toward the next landing.
- Soldier 2 and Soldier 4 slide upwards to the intermittent landing towards their start positions for the next flight of stairs.

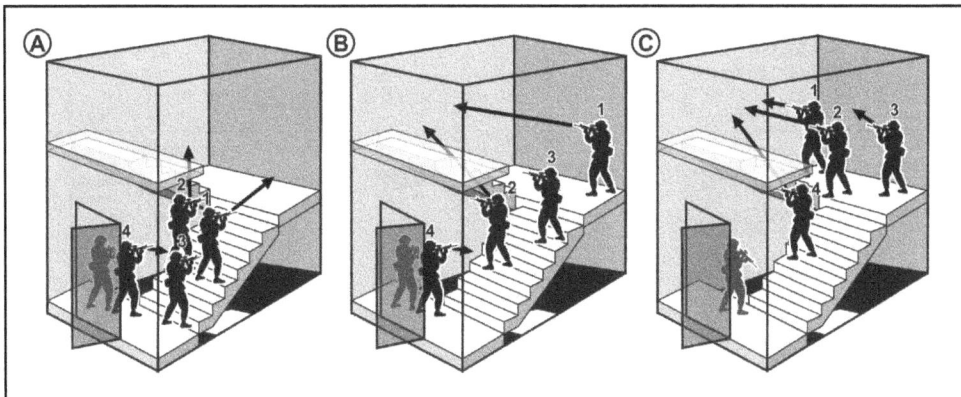

Figure 7-45. Clearing up a stairwell (clearing the intermittent landing)

Intermittent Start Position

7-181. Step 3 and Step 4 are generally a repeat of Step 1 and Step 2, respectively (figure 7-46).

- Soldier 1 moves to the wall side of the first step and covers the intermittent landing straight ahead.
- Soldier 2 moves to the inward side of the first step and covers the adjacent set of stairs leading to the next floor landing.
- Soldier 3 follows behind Soldier 1 to cover any window or door encountered on a landing.
- Soldier 4 moves to and covers the center opening looking up.

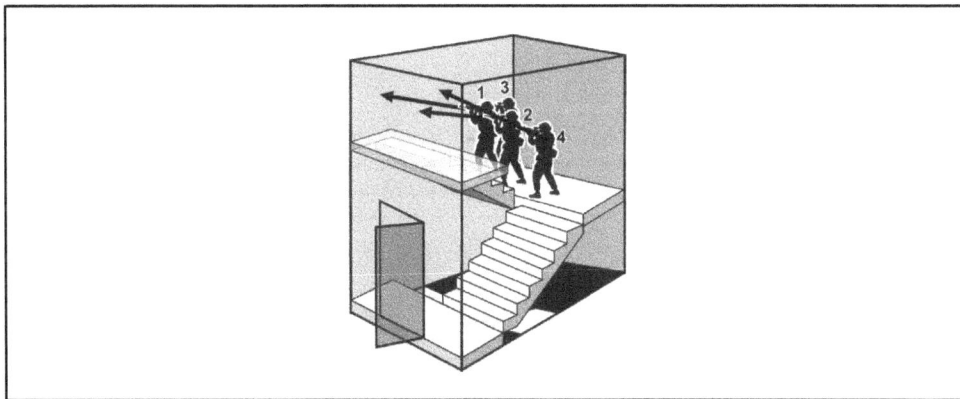

Figure 7-46. Clearing up a stairwell (intermittent landing start positions)

Clear Next Floor Landing

7-182. To clear the next floor (figure 7-47)—

- Soldier 1 and Soldier 2 begin by moving side-by-side, with Soldier 3 following Soldier 1.
- Soldier 1 focuses on visually clearing the intermittent landing.
- Soldier 2 focuses on the adjacent stairs until he can see the landing of the next floor. Once he can clearly see the landing, he pivots, halts, and covers the next landing.
- Soldier 1 continues past Soldier 2 and now has room to shift his coverage to the next set of stairs. Soldier 1 continues up to the intermittent landing and occupies a point of domination facing toward the next landing.

- Soldier 3 follows Soldier 1 onto the landing and covers any window or door encountered on the landing (cover doors from the doorknob side) or occupies a point of domination facing toward the next landing.
- The team leader signals the squad leader that the landing is secured.

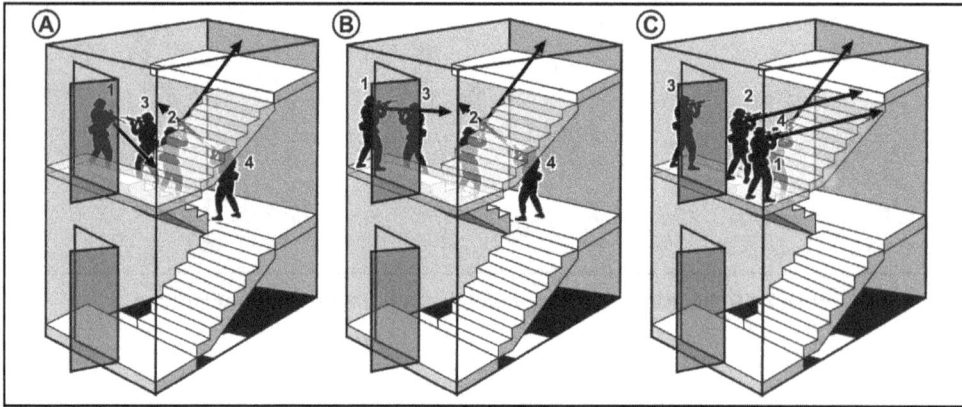

Figure 7-47. Clearing up a stairwell (clearing the next floor landing)

Evaluate Next Floor Landing

7-183. The squad leader evaluates the floor landing, the stairwell, and the access door to the floor. He communicates his assessment to the platoon leader. If the adjacent floor is secure, the squad can continue clearing to the next floor. If the adjacent floor is unsecure, the squad can—

- Leave security on the door and continue clearing the stairwell.
- Clear the adjacent room (normally a hallway) and establish a foothold on the floor.
- Clear the whole adjacent floor.
- Pass through another element that will clear the floor.

7-184. Regardless of the option chosen, the lead team should repeat step 1 and step 2 to secure the next intermittent landing and provide room for the trail team. The trail team then assumes responsibility for securing the access door. From this position, the squad can execute the selected option (figure 7-48).

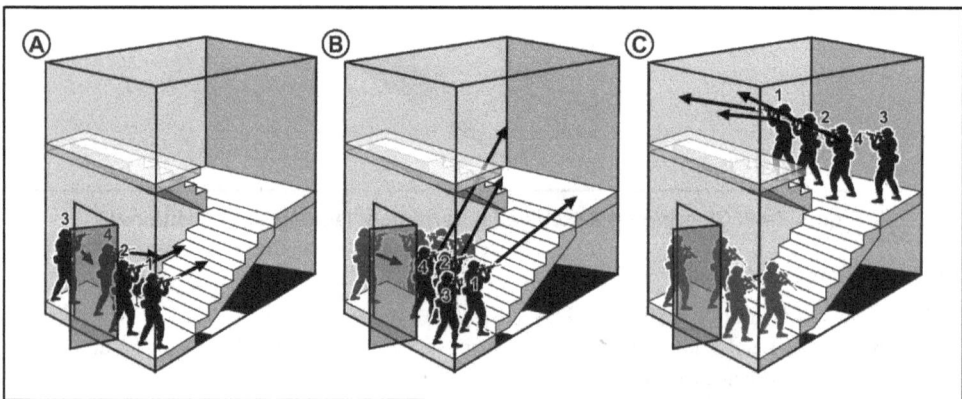

Figure 7-48. Secure landing (prepare for next activity)

7-185. Normally, a single squad cannot secure a stairwell and clear a complete floor by itself. However, if the situation does support this, a technique is to leave two Soldiers of one team to secure the stairwell and use the other two Soldiers to secure key locations on the floor as the other team clears the complete floor.

ELEVATORS AND ELEVATOR SHAFT CLEARING

7-186. An elevator and elevator shaft are potential movement routes for both friendly and enemy personnel. As such, the elevator and elevator shaft should be cleared and secured in synchronization with the rest of the building. This is best accomplished by first securing any discovered elevator doors and then securing one of the terminal ends of the elevator shaft.

CLEARING ELEVATORS

7-187. If the elevator is functioning (which is often the case during stability operations) it is usually best to clear and secure the elevator as soon as possible. This typically includes locating and securing the elevator control room which is usually located at the top of the building. If the elevator is not functioning, then the elevator will be cleared and secured after the floor where it is stopped is secured.

7-188. A four man fire team is best to clear and secure an elevator—two Soldiers to clear the elevator, one Soldier to breach the closed doors (or push the elevator button), and one Soldier to emplace a large object to prop open the elevator and elevator shaft doors. This prop will also serve to hold the elevator in place.

7-189. To clear the elevator, two Soldiers position themselves on the wall opposite the elevator, ready to clear opposite corners of the elevator. Once the doors are opened (by calling the elevator and waiting for the doors to open or by prying open both sets of doors) the clearing team uses the pie-ing method to clear the elevator. Once cleared the elevator doors are then propped open. If the situation warrants friendly use of a functioning elevator, then the prop should remain inside the elevator to be used as needed to prevent unwanted movement of the elevator.

CLEARING ELEVATOR SHAFTS

7-190. An elevator shaft becomes divided in two by the position of the elevator. As such each half of the shaft is cleared separately. It is best to visually clear from the bottom terminal upward and from the top terminal downward by having two Soldiers slowly pie their weapons upward or downward to clear the shaft from both sides of the shaft doors which have been propped open. Flashlights are often needed as the shaft is normally unlit; however, open doors on various floors can provide light. Extreme care should be taken to ensure a Soldier does not fall down the shaft and to minimize their silhouette as they clear the shaft.

SECTION VI – SURVIVABILITY

7-191. Considerations for survivability are described below.

SMOKE

7-192. Using smoke can either complement or hinder UO. If available, smoke pots, mortar and artillery smoke, or smoke generator units can employ smoke for both offensive and defensive operations. Smoke grenades can provide a hasty screen for concealing personnel movement across streets and alleys. Smoke grenades can also be used for signaling. Those launched by an M203 can mark targets for attack reconnaissance helicopters or tactical air.

7-193. Whenever smoke is employed, units should wait for the effects of the smoke to maximize prior to moving or conducting their assault, counterattack, or breaching operation. In the offense, smoke can support maneuver and deception. Smoke employed in the defense obscures enemy air and ground observation, limiting the accuracy of enemy fires and target intelligence.

7-194. Artillery-delivered white phosphorus can also be effective on enemy forces by causing casualties and fires. Leaders should consider the incendiary effects of both white phosphorus and base ejection munitions on the litter and debris of urban areas. Do not use smoke when it degrades the effectiveness of friendly forces. The use of smoke in urban areas is affected by complex wind patterns caused from buildings. Obscuration planning should include covering as much of the objective area as possible. Failure to obscure key structures provides enemy observers reference points for fire placement within the objective area. An extremely dense concentration of smoke in a closed room can displace the oxygen in the room, suffocating Soldiers even when they are wearing protective masks.

FIRING POSITIONS

7-195. Firing positions in urban terrain are no different than in any other terrain. The four basic firing positions—individual foxhole supported, prone unsupported, prone supported, and kneeling unsupported—are still valid. However, instead of digging a fighting position in the ground and then using the individual foxhole supported firing position, the existing urban terrain typically supports the building up of a fighting position. Then, uses a modified individual foxhole supported firing position, a kneeling supported firing position, or a standing unsupported firing position (FM 3-22.9 for details on firing positions and short-range marksmanship techniques).

FIGHTING POSITIONS

7-196. Buildings, street width, rubble, debris, and noncombatants all dictate the positioning and fields of fire for individual, crew-served, and key weapons in urban areas. Fighting positions are either hasty or deliberate. In all fighting positions, Soldiers should position themselves far enough back from cover to minimize the effects of secondary fragmentation.

HASTY

7-197. A hasty fighting position is normally occupied in the attack or the early stages of the defense. It is a position from which the Soldier can place fire upon the enemy while using available cover for protection from return fire. The Soldier may occupy it voluntarily or he may be forced to occupy it due to enemy fire. In either case, the position lacks preparation before occupation. Considerations for selecting and occupying individual fighting positions include—

- Make maximum use of available cover and concealment.
- Avoid firing over cover. When possible, fire around it.
- Avoid silhouetting against light-colored buildings, the skyline, and so on.
- Carefully select a new fighting position before leaving an old one.
- Avoid setting a pattern. Fire from windows that are and are not barricaded.
- Keep exposure time to a minimum.
- Begin improving your hasty position immediately after occupation.
- Use construction material that is readily available in an urban area.
- Remember that positions providing cover at ground level may not provide cover on higher floors.

7-198. Considerations when firing from specific positions include—

- When firing around corners—
  - Fire from the prone or kneeling position.
  - Use the outside shoulder to fire. For example, if firing around a left corner, use the left shoulder to fire the weapon.
- When firing behind walls, fire around the side of the wall and not over it.
- When firing through windows—
  - Fire from the sides of the window so the Soldier is protected by the wall.
  - Ensure the muzzle is inside the window.
  - Do not fire directly in front of the window.
- When firing through a hole in the wall, keep the muzzle inside.
- When firing from roofs, fire from the sides of chimneys or other protruding objects. Avoid skylining. Roofs provide good long-range fire.

DELIBERATE

7-199. A deliberate fighting position is one built or improved to allow the Soldier to engage a particular area, avenue of approach, or enemy position while reducing his exposure to return fire. Every deliberate fighting position should have an alternate position of a different type to avoid establishing a pattern. The farther back into a structure a Soldier is, the better the protection and the smaller the weapon signature.

However, the sector of fire is more limited. Examples of deliberate positions in urban terrain are described below.

Barricaded Windows or Doors

7-200. The natural firing port provided by windows and doors can be improved by barricading the window or door and leaving a small hole for the Soldier's use. Materials from the interior walls of the building or any other available material may be used for barricading. Barricade all ground-floor doors and windows, unless they are critical for friendly movement. Additionally, barricade a sufficient amount of upper-floor windows to create vertical depth and to prevent the enemy from easily identifying the overall unit position.

7-201. Avoid barricading only the windows and doors that are to be firing ports. It is better to leave two or three firing ports in each door and window. This allows Soldiers to use the other firing ports for secondary or supplementary fighting positions and increases the enemy's difficulty in locating the actual fighting positions. Firing from the bottom of the window or door gives the Soldier the advantage of the adjoining walls and makes the firing port less obvious to the enemy.

Fortified Loopholes

7-202. Creating a fortified loophole involves cutting or blowing a small hole into the wall that allows the Soldier to observe and engage targets in his sector of fire. Use sandbags to reinforce the walls below, around, and above the loophole. If the position is on the second floor or higher, place two layers of sandbags on the floor under the Soldier to protect from an explosion on a lower floor. Construct a wall of sandbags, rubble, furniture, and so on to the rear of the position to protect the Soldier from explosions in the room. A table, bedstead, or other available material can provide overhead cover for the position to prevent injury from falling debris or explosions above the position.

7-203. Hide the loophole through camouflage by knocking other holes in the wall and by removing various pieces of nearby siding. Varying their height and location makes them hard to pinpoint and identify. Dummy loopholes, knocked off shingles, or holes cut that are not intended to be used as firing positions aid in the deception. Loopholes located behind shrubbery, under doorjambs, and under the eaves of a building are also hard to detect.

7-204. Because of the angled firing position associated with loopholes, prepare secondary and supplementary positions using the same loophole (figure 7-49). This procedure allows the individual to shift their fire onto an area that was not previously covered by small-arms fire.

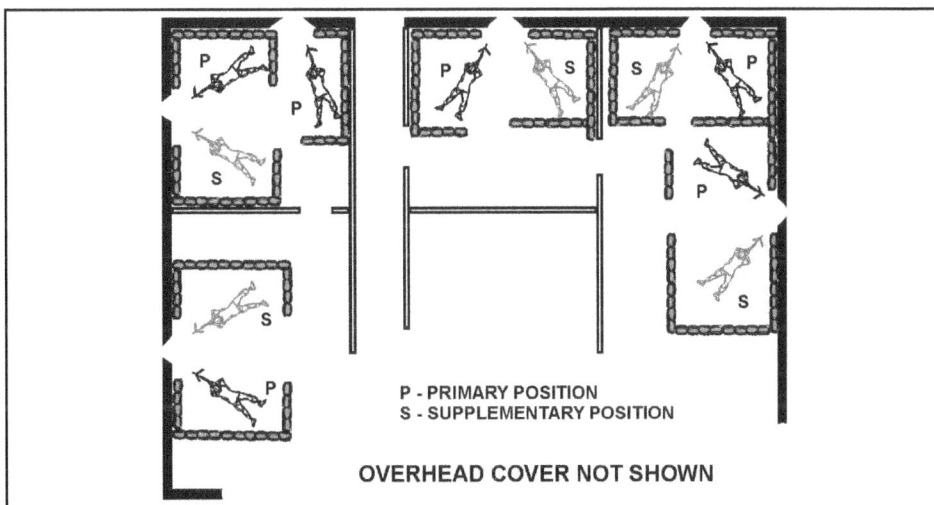

Figure 7-49. Loopholes with primary and supplementary positions

Rooftop Positions

7-205. A rooftop position is usually reserved for snipers as the distance and angle of fire can limit its value as a standard position. A chimney or other protruding structure provides a base from which a position can be prepared. Remove part of the roofing material to allow for firing around the chimney. Stand on beams or a platform with only head and shoulders above the roof and partially protected by the chimney. Placing sandbags on the sides of the position protect the sniper's flanks.

7-206. If the roof has no protruding structure to provide protection, prepare positions from underneath the enemy side of the roof. Reinforce the position with sandbags and remove a small piece of roofing material or gable siding material to allow target engagement. The missing piece of material should be the only outward sign a position exists. Remove other pieces of material to deceive the actual location. The Soldier should be invisible from outside the building, and muzzle flash should be hidden from view.

7-207. Overhead cover for a rooftop position is a challenge. It is usually best to create the position within the attic and then use the roof itself for overhead cover. Typically, this still requires additional structural reinforcement. If on top of the roof, an area can be built up on the reverse slope for overhead cover. Recognition should be made that a rooftop position is fully exposed to both indirect fires and aerial fires.

Machine Gun Positions

7-208. The machine gun can be emplaced almost anywhere. In the attack, windows and doors offer ready-made firing ports, especially for hasty fighting positions. For the defense, and when available in the offense, fortified loopholes that allow the machine gun to be placed on a solid floor are normally preferred positions. Regardless of the openings used, machine guns are best employed inside a building, taking full advantage of interior shadows (figure 7-50).

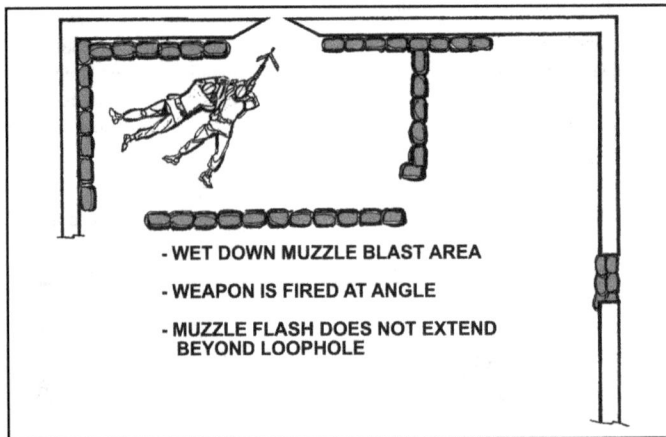

- WET DOWN MUZZLE BLAST AREA

- WEAPON IS FIRED AT ANGLE

- MUZZLE FLASH DOES NOT EXTEND BEYOND LOOPHOLE

Figure 7-50. Use of a loophole with a machine gun

7-209. Grazing fire is best obtained at ground level, while plunging fire is best obtained at higher levels. Increased fields of fire and excellent grazing fire are obtained by locating machine guns in cellars, in the corner of a building, or sandbagged under a building. Where destroyed vehicles, rubble, and other obstructions restrict the fields of grazing fire, elevate the gun to fire over obstacles. Build a rooftop position or platform under the roof in conjunction with a fortified loophole. Loopholes should not be obvious and should be carefully modified.

Antiarmor Positions

7-210. Antiarmor weapons produce backblast and explosive pressure. Gunners must maintain awareness of the angle of fire, the size of the opening, and nearby debris and loose objects. Some antiarmor weapons are less effective at firing angles greater than 20 degrees, while some require an ample opening of at least

10 feet by 15 feet. The antiarmor position must allow for the escape of the backblast and be capable of handing the pressure. (See appendix B for more information.)

7-211. Positions outside of buildings, especially at corners, among rubbled areas, or using destroyed vehicles, readily meet these criteria but may leave the weapon exposed. For a position inside a building, position the weapon to allow the backblast to escape out. This can often be accomplished by creating a large opening in a rear wall or by positioning the weapon to fire out one corner window while the backblast escapes out the adjacent corner window.

7-212. Another technique is to use a rooftop position as an antiarmor position. Firing from the roof allows for the engagement of an armored vehicles most vulnerable point—its top. In all instances, the structure, especially the ceiling, must be sturdy enough to handle the explosive pressure. Once a safe position is identified, fortify and camouflage the same as a barricaded window position.

CAMOUFLAGE

7-213. To survive and win in combat in urban areas, a unit should supplement cover and concealment with camouflage. Most buildings provide numerous natural concealed positions. Armored vehicles can often take advantage of isolated positions under archways or inside small industrial or commercial structures. Thick masonry, stone, or brick walls offer excellent protection from direct fire and can provide concealed routes.

7-214. To properly camouflage men, vehicles, and equipment, Soldiers should study the surrounding area and make positions look like the local terrain. (See STP 21-1-SMCT for details.) Adhere to the following basic rules of camouflage and concealment:

- Avoid areas not in shadows. Buildings in urban areas throw sharp shadows that can be used to conceal vehicles and equipment. However, the position may have to be moved periodically as shadows shift during the day. Positions inside buildings provide better concealment.
- Avoid the area immediately around a window, doorway, or loophole that receives secondary illumination from the sun. Soldiers are better concealed if they fire from the shadowed interior of a room. A lace curtain or piece of cheesecloth provides additional concealment to Soldiers in the interior of rooms if curtains are common to the area.
- Employ deceptive camouflage of buildings. Do not use interior lights.
- Continue to improve positions. Reinforce fighting positions with sandbags or other fragment- and blast-absorbent material. Use sandbags to reinforce the wall below the window and adjacent to the window or door to increase protection for the Soldier. Wire mesh covering the window or door hampers the enemy from throwing in hand grenades.
- Keep positions hidden by clearing away minimal debris for fields of fire.
- Choose firing ports in inconspicuous spots. Avoid single, neat, square, or rectangular firing ports. A lone hole or a regular shape is more easily identified by the enemy.
- Use dummy positions to distract the enemy and make him reveal his position by firing.
- Use wet material in firing positions to keep dust from rising when the weapons are fired.
- Remote radios by placing antennas in upper stories or in adjacent buildings based on remote capabilities. Lay field telephone wire in conduits, in sewers, or through buildings. CPs and logistic emplacements are easier to camouflage and better protected if located underground.

SECTION VII – SUBTERRANEAN OPERATIONS

7-215. In large cities, subterranean features include underground garages, passages, subway lines, utility tunnels, sewers, and storm drains. Most allow troop movement. Even in smaller towns, sewers and storm drains may permit Soldiers to move beneath the fighting to surface behind the enemy. Knowledge of the nature and location of underground facilities is of great value to both the urban attacker and defender. Subterranean routes can grant the attacker use of both surface and subterranean avenues of approach, enabling him to place a smaller force behind the enemy's defenses. Depending upon the strength and depth of the above-ground defense, the attack along the subterranean avenue of approach can become the main attack. Even if the subterranean effort is not immediately successful, it forces the defender to fight on two levels and to extend his resources to more than just street-level fighting.

7-216. The presence of subterranean passages forces the defender to cover the urban area above and below ground with observation and fire. Subterranean passages are more a disadvantage to the defender than the attacker. However, given the confining, dark environment of these passages, they do offer some advantages when thoroughly reconnoitered and controlled by the defender. A small group of determined Soldiers in a prepared defensive position can defeat a numerically superior force. Subterranean passages—

- Provide covered and concealed routes to move reinforcements or to launch counterattacks.
- Can be used as lines of communications, for the movement of supplies and evacuation of casualties, and to cache supplies for forward companies.
- Offer the defender a ready-made conduit for communications wire, protecting it from tracked vehicles and indirect fires.
- Afford the attacker little cover and concealment other than darkness and any man-made barriers.

PLANNING CONSIDERATIONS

7-217. Subterranean areas include natural caves, basements, man-made underground bunkers, tunnels, holes, and sewer systems. Often, enemy personnel use underground sewers and tunnels in the attack of targets and for egress after an attack. (See FM 3-34.170 for details on subterranean detection, reconnaissance, maneuver, and destruction.) To detect or locate subterranean areas, leaders—

- First reduce the geographical area of interest to smaller areas of probable locations.
- Acquire existing blueprints, maps, imagery, video, aerial photographs, and hydrology analysis tools. Overhead imagery may produce results by detecting changes in the appearance of the surface or of the vegetation.
- Actively observe for indicators of probable subterranean access locations.
- Question the local population as to the existence of any subterranean areas.

7-218. Several visual indicators are helpful in detecting actual tunnels. Visual inspections often disclose the general area of a tunnel, but not its precise location. The key to finding a tunnel system is through terrain analysis and a physical ground search of every square meter of an area. Often there are numerous indicators that signal or identify that adversaries within a certain area are using subterranean structures. These indicators include—

- Movement of adversaries in a specific direction.
- Intelligence reports of subterranean structures or activity.
- Failure of cordons to prevent withdrawal or infiltration of known adversary elements.
- Turned or managed soil far away from places of habitation, daily labor, or in mature gardens.
- Enemy contact where the enemy withdraws without decisive engagement by friendly forces.
- Scent of burning wood or food cooking in an uninhabited area.
- Sewer, storm drain, or utility grates or manhole covers.
- Presence of flooring materials in homes, businesses, and other structures not under construction.

7-219. Maximizing the use of these facilities can be a decisive factor during UO. Units planning to conduct subterranean operations should—

- Conduct a thorough reconnaissance of all subterranean systems. Unattended ground sensors may be beneficial in all subterranean operations.
- Determine whether using subterranean avenues of approach or occupying subterranean areas furthers mission accomplishment. Subterranean combat is physically and psychologically demanding and should be carefully thought out prior to committing troops.
- Consider sealing off access routes to underground passages and using smoke to flush out anyone hiding in them as an alternative. If not using tunnels, seal entry points and employ early warning devices and obstacles. Heavy weights or tack-welding (if the capability is available) can block manhole covers.
- Plan for redundant communications (messengers, wire, and radios).

- Plan for additional weapons and ammunition that subterranean operations may require (such as shotguns, pistols, distraction devices, early warning devices).
- Plan for and provide support above ground for those elements that are deployed in subterranean areas. Maintain situational awareness both above and below ground.

SEWERS

7-220. Sewers are separated into sanitary, storm, or combined systems. Sanitary sewers carry waste and are normally too small for troop movement or protection. Storm sewers provide rainfall removal and are often large enough to permit troop and occasional vehicle movement and protection. Except for groundwater, these sewers are dry during periods of no precipitation.

7-221. However, sewers fill rapidly during rainstorms and, though normally drained by electrical pumps, may overflow. During winter, melting snow may preclude their use. Sewer conditions provide an excellent breeding ground for disease, which demands proper troop hygiene and immunization.

SUBWAYS

7-222. Subways tend to run under main roadways and have the potential hazard of having electrified rails and power leads. Passageways often extend outward from underground malls or storage areas, and catacombs are sometimes encountered in older sections of cities. Movement in and clearing of subways may be conducted in the same manners as in hallways.

OBSTACLES

7-223. Obstacles placed at intersections in tunnels are excellent ambush sites and turn the subterranean passages into a deadly maze. Soldiers can quickly construct these obstacles using fencing, barbed or concertina wire, rubble, furniture, and parts of abandoned vehicles interspersed with command-detonated explosives or mines. Locate obstacles at critical intersections in the passage network to trap attackers in a kill zone while allowing defenders freedom of movement.

USE OF WEAPONS

7-224. The limited use of available firepower favors the defender. Underground passageways provide tight fields of fire, amplifying the effect of munitions, such as grenades. The confined space amplifies the sound of weapons firing to a dangerous level. When mines or demolitions are detonated, friendly personnel should be outside tunnels or out of range of the effects.

7-225. The presence of flammable gases can cause a major explosion with the slightest spark. The firing of a weapon could cause an explosion, and smoke grenades may displace oxygen in confined spaces. Employ small-arms weapons as the main weapon system in tunnels and sewers. Use any type of flame or incendiary weapon in a well-vented area.

THREATS

7-226. Consider the threats in subterranean operations that are described below.

ENEMY PRESENCE IN TUNNELS

7-227. The enemy will likely use tunnels and may have the advantage of marked routes and detailed reconnaissance. Because he is able to select ambush positions and withdrawal routes, the defender typically has the element of surprise. A defended position in an underground facility can be very effective in countering enemy subterranean operations. The best underground defensive positions are well protected and canalize the enemy into a killing zone to inflict maximum casualties.

BOOBY TRAPS

7-228. When moving through tunnels, take great care to avoid booby traps. These are normally deployed near junctions and are often operated by tripwires. Standing water in tunnels provides excellent camouflage for antipersonnel mines and booby traps scattered on likely routes.

FLOODING AND CAVE-INS

7-229. With the battle above continuing, flooding and cave-ins are highly possible due to the likelihood of artillery barrages and the use of demolitions. Thus, identifying escape routes is essential.

CHEMICAL HAZARDS

7-230. Chemical defense is a constant concern for Soldiers conducting subterranean operations. In tunnels, Soldiers may encounter chemical warfare agents in dense concentrations. A chemical agent alarm system, carried by the point man, provides instantaneous warning of the presence of chemical warfare agents. M8 and M9 detection papers also test for the presence of chemical agents.

7-231. Large amounts of any type of gas can displace the oxygen in an enclosed space. Some gases cannot be detected by smell. This condition renders protective masks useless and endangers the lives of anyone operating in this type of environment. Unit leaders should be constantly alert to the physical presence of gases and Soldiers showing symptoms of gas exposure.

7-232. The only sure way to protect Soldiers from harmful gases is to ventilate the passageway by forcing fresh air into the site. Removing a manhole cover does not adequately ventilate a subterranean passageway. Respirators that have their own oxygen supply are an acceptable solution when operating in this type of environment. The presence of rodents and other pests in a subterranean environment indicate that there is an adequate amount of oxygen.

CHALLENGES

7-233. Several factors that restrict a Soldier's efforts in accomplishing his mission are particular to subterranean operations. Some of these challenges and their solutions are described below.

TARGET DETECTION

7-234. In the close confines of a tunnel, passive vision equipment requiring ambient light is of little use. To quickly identify enemy personnel or other threats, use an infrared source or white light.

USE OF GRENADES

7-235. Concussion and fragmentation grenades produce a large shock wave and could, if used excessively, collapse the tunnel. Consider using stun grenades in confined spaces. They produce a limited concussion and distraction effect without causing casualties to friendly forces.

MANEUVERABILITY

7-236. The confining spaces of tunnel systems impede the individual's ability to maneuver in subterranean areas. Some techniques used to aid maneuver are described below.

Tag Lines

7-237. A tag line is a flexible handhold that guides Soldiers along a route. Tag lines can aid navigation in confined spaces, where visibility is limited and sense of direction can be lost. Tag lines can be made of rope, string, cable, wire, and so on. Communications wire is an effective item to use as a tag line and can also serve as a primary means of communicating to elements above ground.

Saftey Lines

7-238. Ropes can also function as safety lines to attach team members together to avoid breaks in contact. Leave 5-meter intervals between team members when tying a safety line to them.

PSYCHOLOGICAL CONSIDERATIONS

7-239. Many personnel are unsuited for operations below ground. Subterranean operations are much like night operations. The psychological factors of night operations reduce confidence, cause fear, and increase a sense of isolation. These effects are further magnified in the confines of tunnels. The layout of tunnels could require greater dispersion between positions, further enhancing the feeling of isolation.

RECONNAISSANCE

7-240. A thorough reconnaissance is required to exploit the advantages of underground facilities. Execution of the reconnaissance starts with the entry and ends with a submitted subterranean map. Squad-size elements should perform the reconnaissance. Enough Soldiers are in a squad to gather the required data without getting in each other's way in the confines of the tunnel. Use larger patrols only in extremely large subterranean facilities.

INITIAL ENTRY

7-241. The squad moves to the entrance of the tunnel (usually a manhole) and, with the manhole cover removed, waits 15 minutes before entering to allow any gases to dissipate. The point man descends into the tunnel (safety line attached) to determine if the air is safe to breathe and if movement is restricted. The point man should remain in the tunnel 10 minutes before the rest of the squad follows. If the point man becomes ill or is exposed to danger, he can be retrieved using safety rope.

MOVEMENT

7-242. When the squad is moving through the tunnel, the point man moves about 10 meters in front of the team leader. Other squad members maintain 5-meter intervals. If water in the tunnel is flowing faster than 2.5 meters per second or if the sewer contains slippery obstacles, increase those intervals to allow for squad members to react if one man slips. If using a safety rope, all squad members should remain tied in so they can be retrieved from danger. The rear security man marks the route with the tag line so other Soldiers can find the squad.

MAPPING

7-243. The squad leader should note the azimuth and pace count of each turn he takes in the tunnel. When he encounters a manhole to the surface, the point man should open it and determine the location, which the squad leader then records. Using recognition signals prevents friendly troops from accidentally shooting the point man as he appears at a manhole.

COMPLETION

7-244. Upon return, the squad completes and submits its reconnaissance report. Once the reconnaissance has been conducted, establish security to ensure enemy personnel cannot attack or infiltrate through them.

This page intentionally left blank.

Chapter 8

Light-Heavy Integration

Across the spectrum of combat action in urban areas, powerful combined arms teams produce the best results. Infantry units operating alone suffer from critical shortcomings that can be compensated for only by appropriate task organization with mechanized Infantry, armor, and engineers. These teams must be supported by closely integrated aviation, fire support, communications, and logistical elements. Chapter 8 discusses TTPs that can be employed by light Infantry and heavy armored vehicles during the execution of UO.

SECTION I – ARMORED VEHICLE EMPLOYMENT CONSIDERATIONS

8-1. An effective use of armored combat vehicles in most tactical situations is en masse. Mechanized Infantry/Armored units operating in platoon, company team, and battalion task force strength combine mobility, protection, and firepower to seize the initiative from the enemy and greatly aid friendly success. However, urban combat is often so decentralized, and avenues of approach for vehicles so canalized, that massed armored vehicles cannot be easily employed. However, the heavy firepower, mobility, and armor protection of the tank or BFV is still needed. This urban situation calls for fewer armored vehicles employed over broader areas. The decision to disperse rather than mass armored vehicles should be made only after a careful consideration of the METT-TC situation and anticipated operations in the near future. Decentralized armor support greatly increases a small Infantry unit's combat power. However, dispersed vehicles cannot be easily and quickly concentrated. Their sudden removal from throughout the combat area will necessitate a tactical pause for reorganization and a change of tactical tempo that could disrupt the ongoing combat operation at a critical time.

EMPLOYMENT IN SUPPORT OF INFANTRY

8-2. Armored vehicles can support Infantry during urban combat operations by—

- Providing shock action and firepower.
- Isolating objectives with direct fire to prevent enemy withdrawal, reinforcement, or counterattack.
- Neutralizing or suppressing enemy positions with smoke, high-explosive (HE), and automatic weapons fire as Infantry closes with and destroys the enemy.
- Assisting opposed entry of Infantry into buildings when doorways are blocked by debris, obstacles, or enemy fire.
- Smashing through street barricades or reducing barricades by fire.
- Obscuring enemy observation using smoke grenade launchers.
- Holding cleared portions of the objective by covering avenues of approach.
- Attacking by fire any other targets designated by the Infantry.
- Establishing roadblocks or checkpoints.
- Suppressing identified sniper positions.

LIMITATIONS AND STRENGTHS

8-3. Because of the decentralized nature of urban combat and the need for a high number of troops to conduct operations in dense, compact terrain, Infantrymen will always represent the bulk of forces. At the small-unit tactical level, light Infantry forces have disadvantages that can be compensated for by mechanized Infantry or armor units. Conversely, tanks and mechanized Infantry face problems in the confines of urban areas that place them at a severe disadvantage when operating alone. Only together can these forces accomplish their mission with minimal casualties, while avoiding unnecessary collateral damage. (See chapter 4 for a detail discussion of limitations and strengths).

VEHICLE CHARACTERISTICS

8-4. Fighting in urban areas is centered around prepared positions in houses and buildings. Such positions cover street approaches and are protected by mines, obstacles, and booby traps. Therefore, bridges, overpasses, and buildings must be inspected and cleared of mines before they are used. Reconnaissance parties must ascertain the weight-supporting capacity of roads, bridges, and floors to determine if they can support the weight of BFVs and tanks (table 8-1).

Table 8-1. Vehicle size and weight classification

Vehicle	Weight (tons)	Height (feet)	Width (inches)
M1 Tank	68.7	10.14	143.75
BFV with reactive armor	33	11.3	142.2
BFV without reactive armor	28	11.3	130

ARMORED VEHICLE POSITIONS

8-5. Fighting positions for tanks and infantry fighting vehicles are essential to a complete and effective defensive plan in urban areas. Armored vehicle positions are selected and developed to obtain the best cover, concealment, observation, and fields of fire while retaining the vehicle's ability to move. (See figure 8-1.)

- **Hull Down.** If fields of fire are restricted to streets, hull-down positions should be used to gain cover and fire directly down streets. From those positions, tanks and BFVs are protected and can move to alternate positions rapidly. Buildings collapsing from enemy fires are a minimal hazard to the armored vehicle and crew.

- **Hide.** The hide position covers and conceals the vehicle until time to move into position for target engagement. Since the crew will not see advancing enemy forces, an observer from the vehicle or a nearby infantry unit must be concealed in an adjacent building to alert the crew. The observer acquires the target and signals the armored vehicle to move to the firing position and to fire. After firing, the tank or BFV moves to an alternate position to avoid compromising one location.

- **Building Hide.** The building hide position conceals the vehicle inside a building. If basement hide positions are inaccessible, engineers must evaluate the building's floor strength and prepare for the vehicle. Once the position is detected, it should be evacuated to avoid enemy fires.

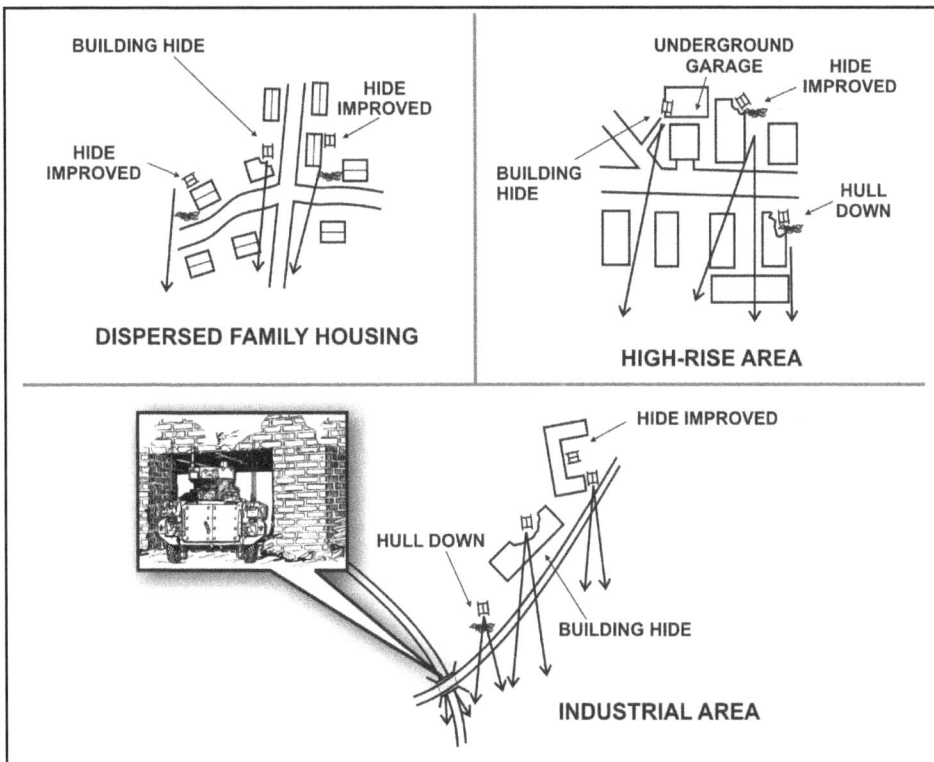

Figure 8-1. Vehicle fighting positions

SECTION II – TASK ORGANIZATION WITH TANKS AT COMPANY TEAM LEVEL

8-6. Tank platoons are normally OPCON to an Infantry company (light, airborne, or air assault) during combined arms operations at the company team level. The four basic techniques of task organizing the tank platoon into an Infantry company for urban combat are—

- **Tank Platoon as a Maneuver Element.** In this technique, the tank platoon leader is responsible for maneuvering the tanks in accordance with the company team commander's intent. With this task organization, likely missions for the tanks would be to support by fire or to overwatch the movement of the Infantry. This task organization is the most difficult to maneuver tanks with the Infantry. However, the tank platoon leader can choose to maneuver the platoon by sections in order to execute the mission. This would provide greater flexibility in supporting the Infantry during the close fight.
- **Tank Sections Under Infantry Platoon Control.** In this technique, tanks would be task organized into two sections and each section would be placed under the OPCON of an Infantry platoon, and maneuvered in accordance with the company team commander's intent. The company team commander relinquishes direct control of the tank maneuver to the Infantry platoon leaders. This technique is very effective in maintaining the same rate of progress between the tanks and the Infantry. However, Infantry platoon leaders are burdened with the additional responsibility of maneuvering tanks. The general lack of experience with tanks and the overall battlefield focus of the Infantry platoon leader can also affect this technique. This technique is best suited when contact with the enemy is expected and close continuous support is required for movement or clearing buildings.

- **Tank Sections Under Company and Platoon Control.** The tank platoon can be task organized into two sections, one under company control, the other under platoon control. The selected maneuver Infantry platoon would have a tank section available to support the close fight. With this technique, the company team commander has a tank section to deploy at the critical place and time of his choosing. This task organization still allows support to the Infantry close fight while keeping additional support options in reserve for the commander to employ. The disadvantages to this technique are that an Infantry platoon leader is maneuvering tanks, instead of the tank platoon leader, and the tanks directly available to the company team commander are cut in half. This technique requires detailed planning, coordination, and rehearsals between the Infantry platoons and tank sections.
- **Infantry Squads Under Tank Platoon Control.** In this technique, the company team commander has the option of placing one or more Infantry squads under the OPCON of the tank platoon leader. He may also retain all tanks under the control of the tank platoon leader or place a tank section under the OPCON of an Infantry platoon leader. This technique will give the company team commander a fourth maneuver platoon, and involves the tank platoon leader in the fight. It works well in a situation where a mobile reserve that needs Infantry protection is required. This technique requires detailed planning, coordination, and rehearsals between the Infantry squads and tank platoon/sections.

CONSIDERATIONS

8-7. None of the techniques described above are inherently better than the other one. The task organization must be tailored to accomplish the mission. Regardless of the technique selected, the guidelines below should be followed.

- Tanks should be used as sections. Single tanks may operate in support of Infantry, however it is preferable for tanks to operate as sections. If using tanks to shield squads and teams from building to building as part of the maneuver plan, the leader of the forward element needs to control the tanks.
- If the company commander is controlling the tanks, he needs to move forward to a position where he can effectively maneuver the tanks in support of the Infantry.
- The task organization should support the span of control. If the company commander is going to control the tanks, then there is no reason to task organize the tanks by section under Infantry platoons.
- Tanks need Infantry support when the two elements are working together. Do not leave tanks alone because they are not prepared to provide local security during the operation. Tanks are extremely vulnerable to dismounted attack when operating on urban terrain. Tanks are most vulnerable and need local security when Infantry are in the process of clearing buildings. Tanks must remain relatively stationary for prolonged periods allowing threat AT teams to maneuver to a position of advantage.

MUTUAL SUPPORT

8-8. Infantry/tank teams work together to bring the maximum combat power to bear on the enemy. The Infantry provides the eyes and ears of the team. The Infantry locates and identifies targets for the tank to engage. It maneuvers along covered and concealed routes to assault enemy elements fixed and suppressed by tank fire. It provides protection for the tank against attack by enemy Infantry. Meanwhile, the tank provides heavy, continuous supporting fires against enemy strongpoints and positions.

MOVEMENT

8-9. The Infantry normally leads movement through urban areas. The tanks follow and provide close overwatch. If the Infantry discovers an enemy position or encounters resistance, the tanks immediately respond with supporting fire to fix the enemy in place or suppress him and allow the Infantry to develop the situation. After sufficient time to develop the situation or conduct short-range reconnaissance, the Infantry squad leader directs the tank to move, if necessary, and identifies specific targets for the tank to engage.

COORDINATION

8-10. Coordination between tank and Infantry leaders must be close and continuous. The tank commander or loader may need to dismount and move, accompanied by the Infantry squad leader, to a position where the route or target can be seen better. Signals for initiating, shifting, or lifting fires must be understood by all. One of the greatest barriers to coordination, command, and control in urban combat is the intense noise. Verbal commands should be backed up by simple, nonverbal signals.

COMMUNICATIONS

8-11. The tank platoon leader and platoon sergeant maintain communications with the company team commander. Individual tanks and Infantrymen communicate with each other using one or more of the following techniques:

- **Messenger.** Use of a messenger is the most secure means of communications available to the tank platoon. When security conditions and time permit, it is the preferred means. It is generally flexible and reliable. A messenger can be used to deliver platoon fire plans, status reports, or lengthy messages. When possible, lengthy messages sent by messenger should be written to prevent mistakes and confusion.
- **Visual Signals.** Visual communications are used to identify friendly forces or to transmit prearranged messages quickly over short distances. Standard arm-and-hand or flag signals work well during periods of good visibility. Crews can use thermal paper, flashlights, chemical lights, or other devices during periods of limited visibility, but they must exercise extreme care to avoid alerting the enemy to friendly intentions. Tank commanders must clearly understand visual signals as they operate across the battlefield; each tank commander must be ready to pass on visual signals from the platoon leader to other vehicles in the platoon and supported Infantry unit. (See STP 17-19K1-SM [the skill level 1 Soldier's manual for MOS 19K] and FM 21-60 for a description of hand-and-arm signals.)
- **Pyrotechnics.** Pyrotechnic ammunition can be used for visual signaling. The meaning of these signals is identified in paragraph 5 of the OPORD and in the signal operation instructions (SOI). The main advantage of pyrotechnics is the speed with which signals can be transmitted. The main disadvantages are the enemy's ability to detect and imitate them and to use them to identify friendly positions.
- **Wire.** This method of communications is especially effective in static positions. The platoon will frequently employ a hot loop in initial defensive positions, OPs, and assembly areas. Unit SOPs, tailored to counter the enemy's electronic warfare capability, prescribe conditions and situations in which the platoon will employ wire. Tank crews can communicate directly with dismounted infantry by routing wire from the vehicle internal communications (VIC)-3 system through the loader's hatch or vision block to a field phone attached to the outside of the tank.
- **FM Radios.** The radio is the platoon's most flexible, most frequently used, and least secure means of communications. It can quickly transmit information with great accuracy. Secure equipment and the ability of the SINCGARS to frequency-hop provide the platoon with communications security against most enemy direction-finding, interception, and jamming capabilities. Sophisticated direction-finding equipment, however, can trace almost any radio signal, allowing the enemy to locate and destroy the transmitter and its operator. Survival of the tank platoon depends on good communications habits, especially when it is using the radio; the platoon leader must strictly enforce radio discipline. The most effective way to use the radio is to follow standard radiotelephone procedures (RTP), including brevity and proper use of approved operational terms; these techniques are covered later in this section.
- **Digital.** Force XXI Battle Command Brigade and Below (FBCB2) enables the platoon leader to transmit digitally encoded information over the SINCGARS radio to other similarly equipped vehicles/units. Linkup refers to the ability of the tank's radio to transmit and receive digital information. When properly linked, the platoon leader receives continuously updated position location information for the platoon's vehicles, as well as for those of the company or troop commander and XO and of adjacent platoons. Using the digital link with other platoon vehicles and the company/troop commander, the platoon leader can also send and receive preformatted reports and overlays with graphic control measures.

Smoke

8-12. The tank's smoke grenade launchers may be used both to protect the tank from enemy fire and to provide concealment for the Infantry forces as they either move across open areas or recover wounded. The use of smoke must be carefully coordinated. Although the tanks' sights can see through most smoke, Infantrymen are at a significant disadvantage when enveloped in dense smoke clouds. The smoke grenade launchers on the tank provide excellent, rapidly developed local smoke clouds, but the grenades produce burning fragments that are hazardous to Infantrymen near the tank and that can ignite dangerous fires in urban areas.

Direct Fire Support

8-13. Tanks provide overwhelming firepower and precision engagements that assist the assaulting forces during isolation of the objective area and seizing a foothold. As the Infantry then moves to clear the position and expand the foothold, the tanks are left in their initial support by fire positions. When possible, tanks should move to subsequent positions where their fires can be used to prevent enemy reinforcement and engage enemy forces withdrawing from the objective. Because of the noncontiguous nature of urban battles, enemy forces may move to the rear or flanks of the tanks and engage them. If a small element of Infantry cannot support the tanks, both vehicles in the section should move to positions of cover and mutual support. Loaders and vehicle commanders should be alert, especially for enemy Infantry approaching from above, the rear, or from the flanks.

Other Considerations

8-14. Other considerations for employing tanks at company team level are to—
- Pay close attention to available terrain that supports tank cross-country movement during planning. While the pace may be slower, security may be significantly enhanced.
- Involve tank platoon leaders and sergeants in the Infantry company-level IPB process. Their expertise will hasten the understanding of what tanks can and cannot do and aid the Infantry company commander in making the best employment decision.
- Use tanks to carry ammunition, water, and other supplies to support the urban fight.
- Plan on keeping tanks mission capable for refueling and rearming. Also, there may be a requirement to recover disabled vehicles. The company XO must coordinate with the battalion S4 to ensure that the proper logistical support is provided for the tanks.
- Specifically allocate time in the planning process for pre-combat inspections (PCI) for the tanks.
- Conduct a combined arms rehearsal at the level that the tanks are task organized. Try to replicate conditions for mission execution during rehearsals; for example, day, limited visibility, civilians on the battlefield, host nation support, and ROE. Include the following:
  - Graphic and fire control measures.
  - Communications.
  - Direct fire plans.
  - Breach drills.
  - Procedures for Infantry riding on tanks. (Tanks can move a maximum of nine personnel.)
  - Techniques for using tanks as Infantry shields.
- Minimize casualties when moving outside or between buildings, do the following:
  - Cover all possible threat locations with either observation or fire.
  - For those areas that cannot be covered with observation or fire, use smoke to set a screen to block enemy observation of friendly movement.
  - Move tanks forward to support Infantry movement. Position the tanks before the Infantry begins moving, whether the tanks are supporting by fire, being used as shields, or both.
  - Preplan positions, if possible, but devise a marking system and communication signals to designate situational dependent positions to help maintain momentum. For example, the VS-17 panel from Building 2 means move to SBF 3.

- When using tanks as a shield for Infantry, move the tanks as close as possible to the start point to allow the Infantry the freedom of movement when exiting the building.
- Tanks need to move at the Infantry's rate of movement.
- When the distance between buildings is short, tanks can position themselves to block the open area from enemy fire.
- Use simple, clearly understood graphic control measures.

TRANSPORTING INFANTRY

8-15. At times, the tank platoon may be required to transport Infantrymen on its tanks (figure 8-2). This is done only when contact is not expected. If the tank platoon is moving as part of a larger force and is tasked to provide security for the move, the lead section or element should not carry infantry.

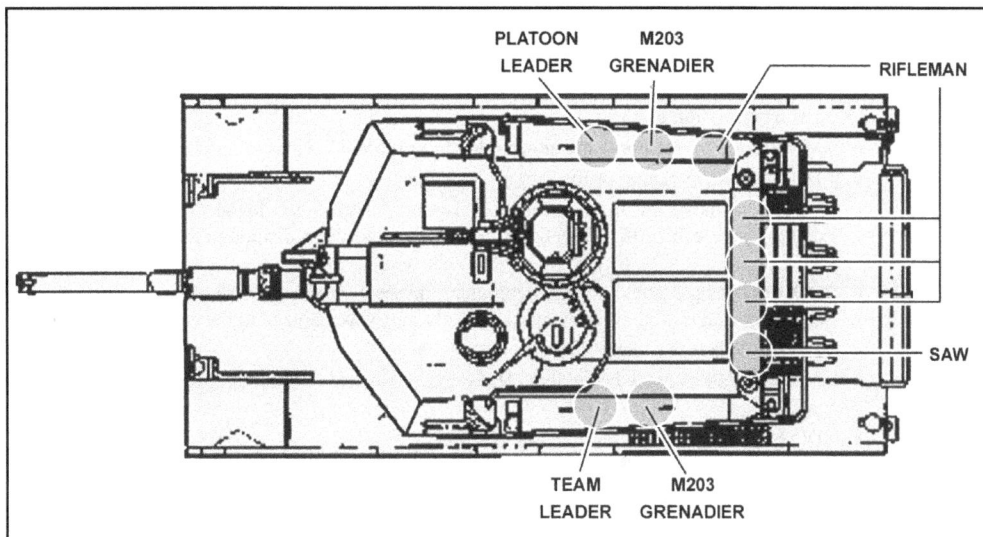

Figure 8-2. Sample positions for Infantry riding on a tank

PROCEDURES, PRECAUTIONS, AND CONSIDERATIONS

8-16. Infantry and Armor leaders must observe the following procedures, precautions, and considerations when Infantrymen ride on tanks—

- Infantrymen should thoroughly practice mounting and dismounting procedures and actions on contact.
- Infantrymen must always alert the tank commander before mounting or dismounting. They must follow the commands of the tank commander.
- Infantry platoons should be broken down by squads, similar to air assault chalks, with the infantry platoon leader on the armor platoon leader's vehicle and the infantry platoon sergeant on the armor platoon sergeant's vehicle.
- Platoon leaders, platoon sergeants, and team leaders should position themselves near the tank commander's hatch, using the external phone (if available) to talk to the tank commander and relay signals to the unit.
- If possible, the lead vehicle should not carry Infantrymen. Riders restrict turret movement and are more likely to be injured or killed on initial contact.

- Whenever possible, Infantrymen should mount and dismount over the left front slope of the vehicle. This ensures that the driver can see the infantrymen and that the infantrymen do not pass in front of the coax machine gun. Infantrymen must ensure that they remain behind the vehicle's smoke grenade launchers. This will automatically keep them clear of all weapon systems.
- Infantrymen must always have three points of contact with the vehicle, and they must watch for low-hanging objects such as tree branches.
- Infantrymen should wear hearing protection.
- Infantrymen should not ride with anything more than their battle gear. Rucksacks should be transported by other means.
- Infantrymen should scan in all directions while riding. They may be able to spot a target the vehicle crew does not see.
- Infantrymen should be prepared to take the following actions on contact:
  - Wait for the vehicle to stop.
  - At the tank commander's command, dismount IMMEDIATELY (one fire team on each side). DO NOT move forward of the turret. DO NOT dismount a vehicle unless ordered or given permission to do so.
  - Move at least 5 meters to the either side of the vehicle.
  - DO NOT move behind or forward of the vehicle.
  - DO NOT move in front of vehicles unless ordered to do so. Main gun discharge overpressure can inflict sever injury or death to forward dismounted Infantrymen (figure 8-3.)
  - DO NOT dangle arms or legs, equipment, or anything else off the side of a vehicle; they could get caught in the tracks, causing death, injury, or damage to the equipment or vehicle.
  - DO NOT place too many riders on the vehicle.
  - DO NOT fall asleep when riding. The warm engine may induce drowsiness; a fall could be fatal.
  - DO NOT smoke when mounted on a vehicle.
  - DO NOT stand near a moving or turning vehicle at any time. Tanks have a deceptively short turning radius.

DANGER

THE OVERPRESSURE FROM THE TANK'S 120-mm CANNON CAN KILL A DISMOUNTED INFANTRYMAN WITHIN A 90-DEGREE ARC EXTENDING FROM THE MUZZLE OF THE GUN TUBE OUT TO 200 METERS.

FROM 200 TO 1000 METERS ALONG THE LINE OF FIRE, ON A FRONTAGE OF ABOUT 400 METERS, DISMOUNTED INFANTRY MUST BE AWARE OF THE DANGER FROM DISCARDING SABOT PETALS, WHICH CAN KILL OR SERIOUSLY INJURE PERSONNEL.

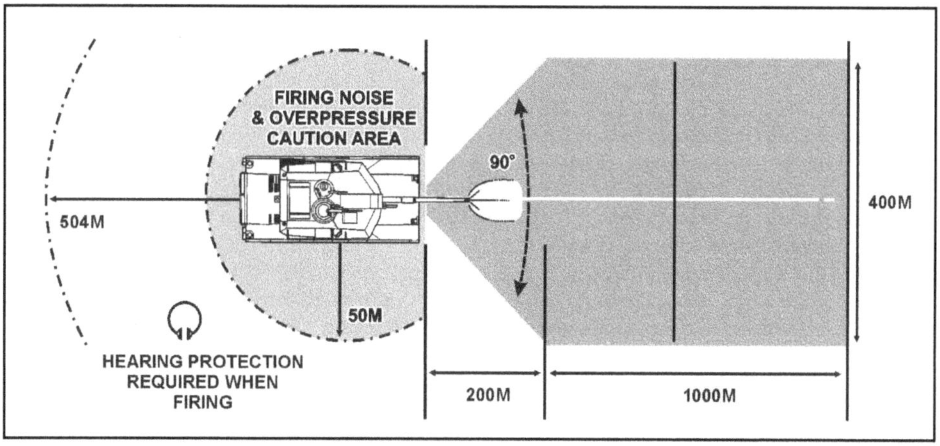

Figure 8-3. Danger areas around a tank firing a 120-mm main gun

ADDITIONAL CONSIDERATIONS AND PREPARATIONS

8-17. Additional considerations and preparations for transporting the Infantrymen include the following:

- Armor—
  - Uses main-gun fire to reduce obstacles or entrenched positions for the Infantry.
  - When OPCON to a Infantry company, platoon or squad, takes directions from the Infantry ground commander (platoon leader/platoon sergeant/squad leader) to support their fire and maneuver.
  - Provides reconnaissance by fire for the Infantry.
  - Should know and understand how the Infantry clears buildings, how they mark cleared buildings, the casualty evacuation plan, signal methods, engagement criteria for tank main gun, front line trace reporting, ground communication from the tank with the dismounted personnel.
  - Uses its night vision capability to augment and supplement the Infantry's night vision capabilities.
- Infantry—
  - Provides real-time information for the tank crewmen to help them overcome tank noise and the lack of ground situational understanding.
  - Provides reconnaissance and fire direction of enemy positions for main gun attack.
- Considerations for dismounted tank security include—
  - Tank crewmen should rehearse the mounting and dismounting of Infantrymen from their vehicle, briefing the Infantrymen on safety procedures for the vehicle and weapons systems.
  - Tank commanders need to rehearse communicating with Infantrymen.
- Vehicle preparation for combat in urban terrain should cover these procedures—
  - Keep at least one ballistic shield to the "dog house" closed (most engagements will be under boresight range and the battlesight technique will suffice).
  - Place sandbags around antenna connections and electrical wiring on the turret top.
  - Place extra coax ammunition inside the turret.
  - Remove all highly flammable products from the outside of the vehicle and from the sponson boxes.

ARMOR VEHICULAR, WEAPONS, AND MUNITIONS CONSIDERATIONS

8-18. Numerous factors related to tanks and their organic weapons and munitions affect the tank platoon's urban operation planning and execution, including—

- The preferred main gun rounds in the urban environment are high-explosive antitank (HEAT), multipurpose antitank with tracer (MPAT-T) (ground mode), and multipurpose antitank-obstacle reducing (MPAT-OR) (XM908). These all perform much better than sabot rounds against bunkers and buildings.
- HEAT ammunition will open a larger hole in reinforced concrete or masonry structures than multipurpose antitank (MPAT) or MPAT-OR (XM908). Both MPAT and MPAT-OR, however, offer greater incapacitation capability inside the structure.
- HEAT ammunition arms approximately 60 feet from the gun muzzle. It loses most of its effectiveness against urban targets at ranges of less than 60 feet.
- MPAT and MPAT-OR rounds arm approximately 100 feet from the muzzle of the gun. Because of the shape and metal components of the projectiles; however, this ammunition remains effective at ranges of less than 100 feet.
- Sabot petals, including those on MPAT and MPAT-OR, endanger accompanying infantry elements. They create a hazard area extending 70 meters on either side of the gun-target line out to a range of 1 kilometer.
- The tank's main gun can depress only to -10 degrees and can elevate only to +20 degrees, which creates considerable dead space for the crew at the close ranges that are typical in the urban environment.
- The external M2 HB machine gun can deliver a heavy volume of suppressive fire and penetrate light construction, buildings, and most barricades. The M2 HB machine gun can elevate to +36 degrees; however, the tank commander must be unbuttoned to fire the M2 on the M1A2 or M1A2 SEP.
- The M240 coax machine gun can effectively deliver suppressive fires against enemy personnel and against enemy positions that are behind light cover.
- The loader's M240 machine gun can effectively deliver suppressive fire against enemy personnel and against enemy positions that are behind light cover; however, the loader must be unbuttoned to operate it. This weapon may be dismounted and used in a ground role if units are equipped with the M240 dismount kit.
- When buttoned up, the tank crew has limited visibility to the sides and rear and no visibility to the top.

Note. FM 3-20.21 explains special uses for tank-mounted machine guns in the urban environment.

SECTION III – INFANTRY/MECHANIZED INFANTRY COMPANY

8-19. The following information refers to mechanized and light Infantry platoons. An attached or OPCON BFV platoon will have Infantry squads that can be employed in the scheme of maneuver. Therefore, platoon integrity with a BFV platoon should be maintained in urban combat and the BFV platoon should be used as a maneuver element.

OFFENSIVE CONSIDERATIONS FOR BFV PLATOON

8-20. The mechanized Infantry platoon provides a very flexible heavy direct fire support asset to light Infantry companies conducting operations on urban terrain. The 25-mm cannon and 7.62-mm coax machine gun, combined with the additional Infantry, Javelin, and tube-launched, optically-tracked, wire-guided (TOW) antitank guided missiles (ATGM), provide the company team commander powerful combat multipliers during urban combat.

TARGET ENGAGEMENT

8-21. Streets and alleys are natural firing lanes and killing zones. Because of this, all vehicular traffic is greatly restricted and canalized, and subject to ambush and short-range attack. Tanks are at a disadvantage because their main guns cannot be elevated enough to engage targets on the upper floors of tall buildings. The BFV, with +60 to -10 degrees elevation of the 25-mm gun and 7.62-mm coax machine gun, has a much greater ability to engage targets in urban terrain.

GENERAL CONSIDERATIONS WHEN USING BFVS

8-22. Light Infantry companies may be task organized with mechanized Infantry platoons when conducting operations in urban terrain. A BFV platoon is capable of providing its own Infantry support. The BFVs should not be separated from their Infantry. Working as a team, Infantrymen (the rifle squads) provide security for the vehicles; the BFVs provide critical fire support for the Infantry company team.

- **Movement.** When moving, if the street is large enough, BFVs should stay close to a building on either side of the street. This allows each BFV to cover the opposite side of the street. BFVs can button up for protection, but the BFV crew must remain alert for signals from Infantry. Coordination between mounted and dismounted elements is critical in urban terrain.
- **ATGMs/ATs.** The BFV lacks adequate armor protection to withstand medium to heavy ATGM fire. It is normally employed after the area has been cleared of ATGM positions or on terrain dominating the city to provide long-range antiarmor support or fire suppression. Light antiarmor weapon (LAW), AT4s, Dragons, or Javelins provide a significant amount of the BFV platoon's short-range antiarmor fires in urban areas; the TOWs provide long-range antiarmor fires. The BFV's 25-mm gun and machine gun are employed while providing direct fire support.

ORGANIZATION AND TASKS

8-23. The BFV platoon comprises mounted and dismounted elements. Based on the company commander's guidance and the factors of METT-TC, the BFV platoon leader will normally determine how his elements will be deployed.

- **Offensive Task Organization.** During offensive operations, the BFV platoon is normally given the mission of providing support for the company team. The company team commander generally will not separate the dismounted element from the mounted element, since the BFVs must have Infantry support during urban combat. If the dismounted element is needed for other tasks, enough local security must be left with the BFVs in order to protect them against enemy counterattack or antiarmor ambushes.
- **Assault Tasks.** An Infantry company team commander may give the BFV platoon the mission of performing assault tasks. The BFV platoon's Infantry would perform these tasks operating in the same manner as light Infantry platoons and squads. If the Infantry is used in this role, enough local security must be left with the BFVs to protect them.
- **Support Tasks.** The most likely tasks that will be given to a BFV platoon supporting a light Infantry company in urban combat will be those assigned to the support element. Direct fire support and other assistance to facilitate the advance of the assault element is provided by the support element. The BFV platoon is well suited to act as the support element for the light Infantry company team during offensive operations. The BFV platoon leader, acting as the support element leader, can provide command and control over his platoon and other support element assets. Specific BFV platoon tasks include, but are not limited to, the following:
  - Suppressing enemy gunners within the objective building(s) and adjacent structures. This is accomplished with the 25-mm gun and 7.62-mm coax machine gun, TOWs, Infantry antiarmor, and small-arms weapons.
  - Breaching walls en route to and in the objective buildings.
  - Destroying enemy positions within a building with the direct fire of the 25-mm gun and the 7.62-mm coax machine gun (when the wall is constructed of light material).
  - Providing replacements for the assault element.
  - Providing a mobile reserve for the company team.

■ Providing resupply of ammunition and explosives.

■ Evacuating casualties, prisoners, and noncombatants.

DIRECT FIRE SUPPORT

8-24. The BFV is best used to provide direct fire support to Infantry. The BFV should move behind the Infantry, when required, to engage targets located by the rifle squads. The dash speed (acceleration) of the BFV enables it to rapidly cross streets, open areas, or alleys (figure 8-4).

● **Weapons.** The BFV mounted element provides fire with its 25-mm gun and 7.62-mm coax machine gun.

● **Safety Considerations.** The use of the 25-mm gun in support of Infantry requires safety considerations. (See appendix B for more information.)

● **High-Explosive 25-mm Rounds Arm 10 Meters from the Gun and Explode on Contact.** Armor-piercing discarding sabot (APDS) rounds discard their plastic sabots to the front of the gun when fired. This requires a 100-meter safety fan (17 degrees either side of the gun-target line for 100 meters) to the front of 25-mm gun. This means that exposed Soldiers cannot go any farther forward than the end of the 25-mm's muzzle or must be a minimum of 100 meters from the muzzle blast.

● **Use of Smoke.** The BFVs' engine exhaust smoke system can be used in urban areas to cover the movement of Infantry. The BFV can also provide a smoke screen by using its smoke grenade launchers. This requires careful analysis of wind conditions to ensure that the smoke does not affect friendly units. This is a difficult task since wind currents tend to be erratic between buildings. The smoke can also screen the movements of the BFVs after the Infantry moves.

Note. On-board smoke only works when the vehicle is using diesel fuel. It will not work with JP-8 fuel.

● **Using the BFV to Isolate a Building.** To isolate a building, the BFVs take an overwatch position. They fire the 25-mm gun and 7.62-mm coax machine gun, and adjust indirect fire to suppress enemy troops in the building and in nearby buildings who can fire at the assault element.

Figure 8-4. Moving with Infantry

DEFENSIVE CONSIDERATIONS FOR THE BFV PLATOON

8-25. The BFV can provide a valuable combat multiplier in the defense. Infantry in the BFV platoon will defend in the same manner as light Infantry platoons. The following are typical defensive tasks that may be given to a BFV platoon:

- Providing fire support for Infantry and mutual support to other BFV teams.
- Destroying enemy armored vehicles and direct fire artillery pieces.
- Destroying or making enemy footholds untenable by fire using the 25-mm gun.
- Providing rapid, protected transport for organic rifle teams or other Infantry elements.
- Reinforcing threatened areas by movement through covered and concealed routes to new firing positions.
- Providing mutual support to other antiarmor fires.
- Providing a mobile reserve and counterattack force.
- Providing resupply of ammunition and other supplies to the Infantry.
- Evacuating casualties, prisoners, and noncombatants.

8-26. The BFVs are integrated into the company team defensive fire plan. The 25-mm gun and 7.62-mm coax machine gun fields of fire cover streets and open areas; TOWs are used to cover Armor avenues of approach. Once placed in position, BFVs should not be moved for logistical or administrative functions. Other vehicles should accomplish these functions, when possible.

- **Positioning of BFVs and Weapons.** Once the company team commander gives the BFV platoon leader his mission, the platoon leader will position his BFVs and Infantry. Dismounted machine guns should be positioned to have grazing fire. For the coax to have grazing fire, the BFV must be in a hull-down position. BFVs are assigned primary, alternate, and supplementary positions. ATGMs should be positioned on upper stories for longer range and to permit firing at the tops of tanks. These positions should permit continuous coverage of the primary sectors and all-round defense.
- **Engagement Ranges.** Due to the close engagement ranges on urban terrain, the 25-mm gun and 7.62-mm coaxial machine gun are used more than ATGMs. The antiarmor capability of the BFV is degraded by short ranges and must be supplemented by Dragons, Javelins, and AT4s. ATGM and AT positions should be placed where they can support the BFV but must not attract enemy attention to the BFV location. Dragons, Javelins, and AT4s are much more effective against the flanks, rear, and tops of enemy armored vehicles and should be positioned to attack those areas. The TOWs are also employed against enemy armored vehicles.
- **Integration of Fires.** All of the BFV's crew-served weapons are integrated with the rest of the company team's weapons and assets. The positions are recorded on a company sector sketch and forwarded to battalion.

This page intentionally left blank.

Appendix A

Urban Environment

The three key components of all urban environments are terrain (natural and man-made), society, and supporting infrastructure. The particulars of these components often vary widely from one urban area to another. Understanding them is critical because they influence all operations. Appendix A discusses various aspects of the urban environment. Familiarity with these aspects is important for both planning and execution during UO.

SECTION I – TYPES OF URBAN AREAS

A-1.   Large urban areas are often composed of more than one municipality, and large municipalities often have subordinate political units. Units should identify and consider the boundaries of these political units during planning on a case-by-case basis. Analyze civil considerations in terms of six factors in ASCOPE. (See FM 2-01.3 for details on ASCOPE.) These characteristics easily align with an urban area's three main components of terrain, society, and infrastructure; and, like them, they are overlapped and interdependent. (See FM 3-06 for details.)

A-2.   Urban areas all over the world share many general characteristics. These characteristics include dense city centers, compartmentalization, sectionalism, infrastructure, mass transportation lines, varied street patterns, and continual modernization. Central to these characteristics is population. There is no international standard of population size for the various types of municipalities. However, within the U.S. and most of the developed countries, the common breakdown for population is as per table A-1.

Table A-1. Descriptions and population sizes of inhabited areas

Area	Description	Population
Homestead	Single family house, with associated buildings, in a rural area.	Under 25
Settlement	Small community or grouping of houses in a rural area.	25 to 100
Village	Small community incorporated as a municipality in a rural area.	100 to 2,500
Town (Rural)	Densely populated urban area incorporated as a municipality and surrounded by rural terrain.	2,500 to 100,000
Town (Urban)	Densely populated urban area incorporated as a municipality and part of a larger urban area.	2,500 to 100,000
City	Large, densely populated urban area incorporated as a municipality that may be part of a larger urban area.	100,000 to 1 million
Metropolis	Very large, densely populated urban area consisting of several cities and towns.	1 million to 10 million
Megalopolis	Huge, densely populated urban area consisting of several large cities and towns.	Over 10 million

VILLAGE

A-3.   Villages are often on choke points, such as in a valley or between high ground and a river, that dominate a single high-speed avenue of approach through the area. If the buildings in such a village are well constructed, they can provide good protection against both direct and indirect fires. Thus, a formidable defense can often be easily developed using the village as a centralized strongpoint. Supporting elements often secure the surrounding terrain (figure A-1).

Figure A-1. Village between a river and a highway

TOWN

A-4. When facing a predominantly armored enemy, small forces can gain an advantage in combat power by defending a town that is a choke point. The small-unit leader positions his available antiarmor weapons on positions dominating critical approaches. To deny the enemy the ability to bypass the town, the defending force should control key terrain and coordinate with adjacent forces. Reserve forces should locate where they can quickly reinforce critical areas. Obstacles and minefields assist in slowing and canalizing the attacker.

CITY

A-5. Cities are large areas characterized by a high building density and varied street patterns. Units should consider them highly restrictive terrain. Cities require a higher density of troops and smaller AO than natural open terrain. Units typically use frontages about one-third the size of those in open areas. Cities typically grow due to a distinct transportation feature, such as a bay, river, or major rail intersection. This feature, both its physical composition and its use, significantly impacts military and nonmilitary operations.

METROPOLIS

A-6. In its simplest form, a metropolis is a very large city with all the characteristics of a typical city. Its complexity is the primary difference. Often a metropolis is composed of multiple cities that have grown together. A metropolis has numerous internal governments and a diverse population.

MEGALOPOLIS

A-7. A megalopolis is a large urban area that typically contains more than one city. The sheer size of a megalopolis guarantees it dominates at least the geographic region it occupies and often the country of which it is a part. A force cannot operate successfully without taking the size of the population and the political and economic impact of the area into account.

SECTION II – URBAN ZONES

A-8. Most cities in the world develop distinct areas or zones within the city that are geographically identifiable. These zones are normally categorized by the predominate activity within their boundaries. The typical urban zones are shown in figure A-2.

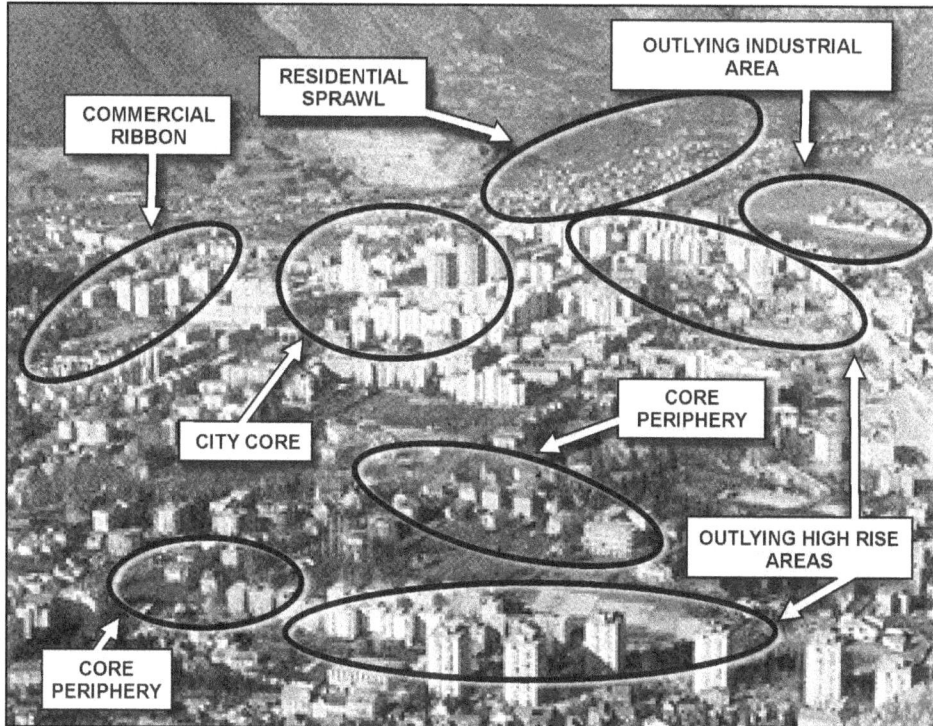

Figure A-2. Urban zones

CITY CORE

A-9. The city core is the heart of the urban area—the downtown or central business district. It is relatively small and compact but contains a larger percentage of the urban area's shops, offices, and public institutions. It normally contains the highest density of multistory buildings and subterranean areas. In most cities, the core has undergone more recent development than the core periphery. As a result, the two regions are often quite different. Today, typical city cores consist of buildings that vary greatly in height.

CORE PERIPHERY

A-10. The core periphery is located at the edges of the city core. The core periphery consists of streets 12 to 20 meters wide with continuous fronts of brick or concrete buildings. The building heights are fairly uniform—2 or 3 stories in small towns and 5 to 10 stories in large cities. Dense random and close orderly block are two common construction patterns that are within the city core and core periphery zones.

HIGH-RISE RESIDENTIAL AREAS

A-11. High-rise residential areas are typical modern construction in larger cities and towns, consisting of multistory apartments, separated open areas, and single-story buildings. Wide streets are normally in rectangular patterns. These areas are often contiguous to industrial or transportation areas or interspersed with close orderly block areas.

COMMERCIAL AREAS

A-12. Commercial areas provide goods and services to the neighborhoods that surround them and to the city as a whole. Specific activities include the buying and selling of goods and services in retail businesses, wholesale businesses, and financial establishments.

INDUSTRIAL AREAS

A-13. Industrial areas are generally on or along major rail and highway routes in urban complexes. Older complexes may be within dense random construction or close orderly block areas. New construction normally consists of low, flat-roofed factory and warehouse buildings. Identification of transportation facilities within these areas is critical because these facilities, especially rail facilities, pose significant obstacles to movement. It is important to identify the type of activity conducted and the toxic industrial material (TIM) that may be present and could affect the mission and Soldiers.

MILITARY AREAS

A-14. Military areas include several types and may be actual fortifications or part of a fortified line. While most of these fortifications are in Western Europe, many are in the Balkans, Middle East, Asia, Africa, and South America. Those in the U.S. are mostly of the coast-defense type. These permanent fortifications can be made of earth, wood, rock, brick, concrete, steel-reinforced concrete, or any combination of said material. Some variants are built underground and employ heavy tank or warship armor, major caliber and other weapons, internal communications, service facilities, and CBRN overpressure systems.

LOW-RISE RESIDENTIAL AREAS

A-15. Low-rise residential areas are normally adjacent to close orderly block areas in Europe. The pattern consists of row houses or single-family dwellings with yards, gardens, trees, and fences. Street patterns are normally rectangular or curving. Residential zones are typically subdivided by income or culturally important factors, such as ethnicity or religion.

STRIP AREAS

A-16. A strip area is a small urban area built predominately along a transportation route, such as a road or river (figure A-3 and figure A-4). The strip area may stand alone or be linked between nearby larger urban areas. If visibility is good and enough effective fields of fire are available, a unit acting as a security force need occupy only a few strong positions spread out along the strip. This can deceive the enemy into thinking the strip is an extensive defensive line. Strip areas often afford covered avenues of withdrawal to the flanks once an attacking force deploys and before the security force becomes decisively engaged.

Figure A-3. Strip area in farmland

Figure A-4. Strip area near river

SHANTYTOWNS

A-17. Shantytowns are areas composed of low-income or unemployed elements of the population living in poorly constructed or older buildings in various states of decay (figure A-5). Most towns and villages in third world countries have shantytowns, which are often in multiple zones throughout the area.

Figure A-5. Shantytown

A-18. Structures within shantytowns are made of readily available materials, such as cardboard, tin, adobe, or concrete block. These less structurally sound buildings have no common floor pattern and often have only one room. Weapon fire in or at a structure may penetrate the walls of one or more adjacent structures and endanger friendly forces as well as noncombatants. There is also an increased risk of easily spread fires.

A-19. Armored vehicles may easily knock down and traverse most shantytown structures without significantly affecting mobility. However, their destruction may cause unacceptable civilian casualties. Mobility becomes more restrictive as narrow paths often do not accommodate vehicles. Commanders should carefully consider the effects of their operations in this area, to include vehicles and weapons, the weaknesses of structures, and the minimal protection and danger of fires. These effects all increase the risk of fratricide and civilian casualties.

SECTION III – STRUCTURES

A-20. Commanders and leaders should be capable of identifying the basic characteristics of buildings within their AOs. They should also understand weapon effects against those buildings. This enables commanders to give clear instructions to their subordinates concerning mission execution. It also assists leaders in choosing the appropriate weapons or explosives to accomplish their respective missions.

A-21. In addition to housing an enemy, the buildings of the city also accommodate the businesses, government, noncombatants, schools, and similar functions critical to the normal conditions of the city. Minimizing collateral damage reduces the hardship within the city and leads to a faster return to normalcy. Planners and personnel should restrain the urge to rubble structures even when they identify enemy within. The Geneva Convention states that "any destruction by the occupying power of real or personal property belonging individually or collectively to private persons, or to the state, or to other public authorities, or to social or cooperative organizations, is prohibited, except where such destruction is rendered absolutely necessary by military operations." While the enemy may be inside the building, so too may be innocent civilians. Therefore, the commander should carefully consider a full range of implications before leveling a building housing the enemy.

ELEMENTS OF BUILDINGS

A-22. For the purposes of this manual, the major elements of a building are the—
- **Foundation.** Foundation supports the load of the building and provides stability.
- **Structure.** Structure supports all imposed loads and transmits them to the foundation.
- **Exterior Walls and Roofs.** Exterior walls and roofs may or may not be part of the supporting structure.
  - *Load-Bearing Walls.* Load-bearing walls support the weight of the building and its contents.
  - *Nonload-Bearing Walls.* Nonload-bearing walls are frame-type structures that have nonload-bearing skin.
  - *Roofs.* Roofs are normally supported by a load-bearing wall or the frame.
- **Interior Walls.** Interior walls may or may not be part of the supporting structure.
- **Environmental Control Systems.** Environmental control systems include heating, ventilation, air-conditioning, and lighting.
- **Vertical Transportation.** Vertical transportation includes elevators, escalators, and stairways.
- **Communication Systems.** Communication systems include internal, external, public address, and closed-circuit television.
- **Water Supply and Waste Disposal.** Water supply and waste disposal include water heaters, toilets, sinks, and exposed pipes.

CHARACTERISTICS OF BUILDINGS

A-23. Five interrelated aspects characterize all buildings—function, size, height, materials, and construction methods. Two additional aspects (exterior openings and floor plans) determine the interior layout of a building.

FUNCTION

A-24. Arguably the most important characteristic is the reason for the building—its function. The four categories of building functions are—
- **Residential.** Residential includes single-family and multi-family housing.
- **Public and Civic.** Public and civic includes church-type and government buildings, schools and gyms, airports, bridges, parks and plazas, and stadiums.
- **Commercial.** Commercial includes hotels, restaurants, and retail stores.
- **Mixed-Use.** Mixed-use includes a combination of commercial and residential buildings.

SIZE

A-25. The four sizes of buildings are small, medium, large, and massive. These four sizes have no firm dimensions and are often relative to the building function and the size of other structures in the surrounding urban area. Residential buildings, particularly single-family homes, are categorized separately from other structures. For this manual, square footage for each of the four building sizes are—

- Small buildings are less than 2,000 square feet in size.
- Medium buildings are 2,000 square feet to 22,000 square feet (one-half of an acre).
- Large buildings are 22,000 square feet (one-half of an acre) to 44,000 square feet (1 acre) in size.
- Massive buildings are greater than 44,000 square feet (1 acre) to 200,000 square feet.

HEIGHT

A-26. A significant urban trend is buildings of ever-greater height and span, which is made possible by the development of stronger building materials and increased engineering knowledge.

A-27. The height of a single floor varies slightly by locale, function, and construction method. However, individual floors, except for the first floor, are normally the same height throughout the building. For the purposes of this manual, 13 feet (approximately 4 meters) is the average height for a floor. The terms commonly used to refer to building height are—

- **Low-Rises.** Low-rises are 5 floors (65 feet) or below, often without an elevator.
- **Mid-Rises.** Mid-Rises are 5 floors (65 feet) to 11 floors (150 feet). Common international building codes require at least one elevator.
- **High-Rises.** High-rises are between 6 and 37 floors high. Most international building codes require at least one elevator, as well as stairs, in all high-rise buildings.
- **Skyscrapers.** Skyscrapers are taller than 500 feet (150 meters) or 37 floors. International building codes require that skyscrapers have at least two elevators and two sets of stairwells that are protected and that span the height of the building.

MATERIALS

A-28. Knowing a building's materials and its basic method of construction is important in UO. Leaders should understand the basic effects that weapons fire, demolitions, blast, and fire have on structures. Leaders should also understand the likelihood of fire starting or spreading and the potential effect the fires will have on thermal imagery, other night vision devices, and the health of Soldiers and the local population.

A-29. The history of building is marked by a trend of increasing durability of building materials. In general terms, the four categories of building construction materials are—

- **Wood.** Wood is limited by its flammable characteristics when other less combustible materials are readily available in the construction of public, civic, and commercial structures.
- **Masonry (Brick, Block, or Stone).** Masonry offers greater load-bearing capacity and fire resistance. Brick is favored for residences, while block is favored for commercial purposes. Stone comprises culturally important buildings.
- **Reinforced Concrete.** Reinforced concrete is a major structural material in most buildings. It is used in all foundations and is commonly used as support columns, load- and nonload-bearing walls, interior walls, and roofs. Reinforced concrete is very strong, resistant to wind and tremors, and provides weatherproofing. Due to its hardness and reinforcing steel bars, it is difficult to breach.
- **Steel or Metal.** Steel or metal is a major structural material in most framed buildings. Many public, civic, and commercial structures use steel frames because of the larger spans and future flexibility required.

CONSTRUCTION METHODS

A-30. Modern construction methods vary greatly based on factors such as available materials, building function, aesthetics, cost, and so on. However, at the most basic levels, the three ways to construct a building are stacking, framing, and hanging. Many buildings are built using a combination of the three methods.

A-31. The most common method of modern building is using the skeleton frame, which essentially consists of vertical members interconnected to horizontal members. Using load-bearing walls for constructing tall buildings has declined steadily and been replaced by using load-bearing columns with either light or heavy cladding covering the exterior openings.

Stacking

A-32. Early stacking was characterized by the use of individual stones or mud bricks. With the introduction of reinforced concrete and the ability to make and transport precast concrete, stacking has evolved to allow the stacking of load-bearing columns, load-bearing walls, floor slabs, roof slabs, and even complete box-like sections.

A-33. Building mid- and high-rise residential buildings commonly uses the stacking method. Since stacked walls are load-bearing walls, they tend to be thick, with 6- to 8-inch walls being common. Stacked walls provide good cover, except at the openings. Most rooms are normally too small for firing close combat missiles. Movement from room to room and floor to floor is often easy.

Framing

A-34. The framing method is based around structural members (often called studs) that provide a stable frame to which interior and exterior wall coverings and roof trusses are attached. All walls and the roof are then covered by various sheathing materials to give weather resistance and lateral strength.

Cladding

A-35. Cladding is the exterior covering for framed buildings. While cladding includes the material that actually covers the structural framework material itself, the focus is on cladding as it covers the exterior space of the structural framework.

Heavy

A-36. Heavy-cladding walls are made of layers of terra-cotta blocks, brick, or stone veneer. Their lower floors can be as thick as masonry walls but not as solid. Heavy-cladding framed buildings are normally in the city core or core periphery. Often, they have a classical architectural style in which each building's design has three sections: the pediment, shaft, and capital. The walls of all floors are normally of the same materials and thickness. Often, the frame members (columns) are visible at the ground floor.

Light

A-37. Most framed buildings built since World War II are light-cladding buildings. They are in core and outlying high-rise areas. Their walls consist of a thin layer of brick, lightweight concrete, or glass. The walls of all floors above the ground floor are the same thickness and made of the same material. On all floors, the windows are set at the same depth throughout. Normally, the frame members (columns) are not visible.

Tilt-Up Walls

A-38. This is a framing method in which complete wall sections, normally large slabs of precast concrete, are tilted up into place. One wall, typically the front, is markedly more open than the other three walls. The roof is often made of either lighter materials or a much thinner slab of concrete. The solid walls provide good cover, although the roof and front wall are often vulnerable. These buildings are built on slabs, which can normally support the weight of vehicles and can therefore provide excellent cover and concealment.

Hanging or Suspension

A-39. In this construction method, floors are suspended from a central core or a group of centralized cores. Individual floors may be reinforced by cables from the central core or overhanging arms to hold each floor. Cable suspension is common for bridge construction and for long-span roofs, particularly sports arenas.

EXTERIOR OPENINGS AND FLOOR PLANS

A-40. Exterior openings and floor plans vary by building function; building size; building material; and, to some degree, building height. However, distinct common trends can be established based on the height and function of a building.

A-41. In general, most buildings limit the number of exterior openings due to privacy requirements, temperature control, and the higher cost of constructing exterior openings. This is especially true for the ground floor of residential buildings. However, for most commercial and service-oriented buildings, the ground floor tends to be open and inviting to attract entry. Other common trends based on the building height and function are described below.

Low-Rise Wood, Light Metal, and Masonry Buildings

A-42. These buildings are rarely built over four floors. At higher floors, using reinforced concrete or steel frame construction usually better achieves cost and safety considerations.

Residential Buildings

A-43. Low-rise wood and light metal frame houses have a great variance of floor plans. Interior walls are often semipermanent and relatively easily to remodel. Direct fire munitions, shell fragments, and shrapnel easily penetrate both exterior and interior walls. Breaching an entry point through walls is fairly simple with an axe or electric saw. The roofs vary greatly from slight, even slopes to steep, multi-slope roofs. Like the walls, most roofs are easily breached, although the footing on sloped roofs can be treacherous.

A-44. Low-rise masonry houses normally have similar floor plans on each floor. As such, once the floor plan of one floor is known, the clearing of additional floors can be based on the known floor plan. Both exterior and interior walls are permanent and are not easily penetrated by direct fire munitions, shell fragments, or shrapnel. Breaching an entry point through a masonry wall requires explosives or an armored vehicle. Roofing material is often masonry, shale, or other rock-like materials, and the roof slant varies from flat to deeply slanted. Breaching deeply slanted roofs or hard surface roofs is often difficult. A sledge hammer can usually breach flat roofs. Use a pry bar to breach shale or slanted roofs.

Public, Civic, Commercial, and Mixed-Use Buildings

A-45. The ground-level floor plans of these buildings are usually different from the upper-level floor plans. The ground floor tends to support the primary purpose of the building, and a large section of the ground floor is often very open, possibly two or three stories high. Rooms (offices) are typically adjacent to this large ground floor area. Exterior walls and any interior load-bearing walls typically extend throughout all floors, reducing in thickness with each level in height. These walls can typically be breached with explosives. Nonload-bearing interior walls are of light construction and easily breached. Roofs are typically flat and can usually be breached with a sledge hammer.

Low-Rise and Mid-Rise Reinforced Concrete Buildings

A-46. Reinforced concrete is relatively inexpensive and easily manufactured. It is used for many public, civic, commercial, and mixed-use buildings and for multi-family low-rise and mid-rise apartments and condominiums. However, single-family residences are rarely made of reinforced concrete.

Residential and Mixed-Use Buildings

A-47. The ground floor of multistory residential or mixed-use buildings is normally markedly different from the upper floors. The floor plans of multistory reinforced concrete buildings are usually based on a centralized hallway, with stairways on opposite ends of the building. All four walls, load-bearing interior walls, and the roof are normally made of reinforced concrete. However, the ground floors of multistory buildings tend to include additional exterior openings and internal space.

A-48. For a residential building or the residential upper floors of a mixed-use building, the floor plans of each residential floor (other than the ground floor) are usually similar. The only common exception to this is the penthouse floor, which tends to have larger size residences. Additionally, the roofs of these buildings often have roof access doors. Normally, the best way to enter this type of building is through a door or a ground floor opening.

Public Gathering Buildings

A-49. Public gathering buildings (such as churches, theaters, auditoriums, and gyms) typically have large, open interiors. Interior walls are often not reinforced concrete and are normally easy to breach or dismantle. The roofs, usually for aesthetic purposes, are often geometric and not easily accessible. Public gathering buildings are most common in the dispersed residential and high-rise residential areas.

Low-Rise and Mid-Rise Steel Frame Buildings

A-50. Steel frame buildings are normally easily recognized because concrete beams and columns surrounding the steel are typically visible from the outside. The floor plans vary greatly depending upon their functions. Additionally, the use of light or heavy cladding varies in terms of aesthetics and function. Light cladding includes glass and light metal coverings. Heavy cladding includes reinforced concrete and thick composite materials. The floors of these buildings are heavier and provide moderate overhead cover.

Office and Residential Buildings

A-51. These buildings normally have three or four small offices or rooms connected together to form an office group or residence. These offices have dimensions based on the distance between the steel columns. These, in turn, are connected to an interior hall that is connected to stairs and often an elevator. Core rooms in framed buildings are much bigger than other buildings. Lighter materials used as partitions often subdivide the core rooms.

Factories

A-52. Factories typically have large windows and open interiors, which favor the use of most weapons. Since the floors are often made to support heavy machinery, they provide good overhead cover.

Commercial Buildings

A-53. Large commercial stores normally have large, open interiors. Steel fire doors, which are heat activated, often exist between sections of the buildings. Once closed, they are difficult to breach or force open, but they effectively divide the store into sections.

Public and Civic Buildings

A-54. Public and civic buildings are rarely, if at all, made to the height of a high-rise or skyscraper. However, public and civic services may be integrated into the lower floors of a high-rise or skyscraper.

High-Rise Reinforced Concrete and Steel Frame Buildings and Skyscrapers

A-55. All high-rise buildings use a skeleton frame, and most have a central core containing two stairwells, elevators, and all other environmental support items. Recently, building designers have considered separating the two central core stairwells. In some cases, lower floors of high-rise building use heavy cladding, while upper floors use light cladding.

TYPICAL DISTRIBUTION OF BUILDINGS

A-56. Certain types of buildings dominate certain parts of a city, which establishes patterns within a city. Analysis of the distribution and nature of these patterns directly affects planning and weapon selection (figure A-6).

Figure A-6. Distribution of building types

A-57. Urban zones and building types are interrelated. Residential areas have predominately low-rise framed or masonry buildings, while commercial and industrial zones have a predominance of masonry and reinforced concrete buildings. Availability of material and local culture determine which, if any, predominates. The central core usually contains the majority of high-rise steel and concrete frame buildings. These multistory buildings have an importance far beyond their contribution to total ground floor area. They occupy core areas (a city's most valuable land) where as centers of economic and political power, they have military significance.

A-58. Open space accounts for about 15 percent of an average city's area. Many open spaces are grass-covered parks, athletic fields, and preserves. Some are broad, paved areas. The largest open spaces are normally associated with suburban residential areas, where large tracts of land often act as recreation areas.

A-59. Streets serving areas that consist of primarily one building type normally have a common street pattern. In downtown areas; for example, high land values often result in narrow angular streets. Street widths are grouped into three major classes:

- Seven to 15 meters, located in older historical sections of pre-industrial cities.
- Fifteen to 25 meters, located in newer planned sections of most cities.
- Twenty-five to 50 meters, located along broad boulevards or set far apart on large parcels of land.

A-60. When a street is narrow, observing or firing into windows of a building across the street can be difficult because an observer is forced to look along the building rather than into windows. When the street is wider, the observer has a better chance to look and fire into the window openings.

SECTION IV – STREET PATTERNS

A-61. The development of street patterns within an urban environment can be attributed to deliberate design, natural features, man-made structures, and the changing needs of the inhabitants. Urban areas can display any of three basic patterns and their combinations—grid, radial, and irregular (table A-2).

A-62. Street patterns influence all warfighting functions. Knowledge of street patterns and widths gives commanders and leaders a good idea of whether or not mounted mobility corridors permit movement and maneuver of wheeled or tracked vehicles, facilitate mission command, and facilitate sustainment operations.

Table A-2. Urban street patterns and effects

Shape	Street Pattern	Effect
	Rectangular or Chessboard	Grid-like streets with parallel streets intersected by perpendicular streets.
	Rayed	Streets fanning out at various angles from a given focal point and through less than 360 degrees.
	Radial	Primary thoroughfares radiating out from a central point, which may extend outward 360 degrees around the central point or within an arc from a point along a natural barrier, such as a coastline.
	Radial-Ring	Loops or rings surrounded by successively larger ones that are usually found in conjunction with larger radial patterns. Radial rings incorporate the elements of both radial and ring or concentric designs.
	Contour Forming	Primary streets running parallel to control lines, with intersecting roads connecting them. Pronounced terrain relief influences construction of roadway along lines of elevation.
	Irregular	Irregular street patterns specifically engineered without geometric patterns for aesthetic or functional reasons.
	Combined Pattern	Any combination of the above.
	Linear Pattern	A primary thoroughfare running down the center with buildings on either side.

SECTION V – HAZARDOUS MATERIALS

A-63. The existence of industrial facilities and activity in urban areas means the presence of TIM, a subset of CBRN hazards. Toxic industrial material is a toxic or radioactive substance in solid, liquid, aerosolized, or gaseous form. It can result in a toxic industrial hazard (that is, the contamination or irradiation of personnel, the environment, an area, or any particular object). Soldiers should be trained and have information available to identify TIM-related markers and placards and to properly and safely respond to the threat.

COMMON PRESENCE

A-64. Toxic industrial material is transported by air, water, road, rail, and pipeline. Large storage facilities, transportation vehicles, and small containers ensure TIM may be almost anywhere. U.S. forces should be able to respond safely, accurately identify the material, assess the threat, and provide for immediate security.

A-65. Toxic industrial material may be encountered by U.S. and friendly forces through purposeful employment or by accidental encounter. Many household hazardous materials easily obtained by the civilian population can be used to cause direct harm to U.S. or friendly forces.

COMMON CONCERNS

A-66. The damage caused by TIM released during UO depends on the—

- Type and size of the discharge.
- Physical phase of the material discharged.
- Terrain of the environment where the release occurs.
- Rate of movement and distance of travel, which can be affected by weather patterns.
- Route of exposure for personnel affected.
- Distance from the point of release.
- Period during which personnel are exposed.
- Length of time between exposure and treatment.

IMMEDIATE HAZARDS

A-67. The most common incidents involve trucks, pipelines, and railroad tankers containing gasoline, chlorine, or other industrial chemicals. Transportation units pose greater hazards than fixed facilities.

A-68. Common risks are irritant gases, especially chlorine, sulfur dioxide, ammonia, and hydrogen chloride. These substances have relatively high toxicity when inhaled and are produced, stored, and transported in large volumes. These vapors tend to remain concentrated downwind from the release point in natural low-lying areas. Their release is most dangerous at night because nighttime weather conditions produce high concentrations that remain near the ground for extended distances. Toxic industrial chemicals are often corrosive and can damage eyes, skin, respiratory tract, and equipment.

A-69. Liquid propane and other fuel storage tanks present a serious threat to forces engaged in UO. Fires on or near these tanks are dangerous. If the fire superheats the tanks, a boiling liquid expanding vapor explosion may result, which can create a significant blast wave and throw huge pieces of the tank well over 100 meters. Small propane tanks can also be used as part of an IED.

LOCATION

A-70. Toxic industrial material may be located throughout any large urban area. Table A-3 shows various urban locations and their commonly associated TIM.

Table A-3. Location and types of toxic industrial material

Location	Type of Toxic Industrial Material
Airports	Aviation gasoline and jet fuel
Farm and garden supply warehouses	Pesticides
Shipping terminals	Bulk petroleum and chemicals
College laboratories	Organic chemicals and radioactive materials
Electronics manufacturers	Arsine and arsenic trichloride
Food processing and storage areas	Ammonia
Glass and mirror plants	Fluorine and hydrofluoric acid
Pipelines and propane storage tanks	Ammonia, methane, and propane
Plastic manufacturers	Isocyanates and cyanide compounds
Landscaping businesses	Ricin (a food and water poison)
Medical facilities	Radioactive isotopes and mercury
Hard rock ore mines	Potassium and sodium cyanide
Pesticide plants	Organophosphate pesticides
Petroleum storage tanks	Gasoline and diesel fuel
Photographic supply distributors	Cyanides and heavy metals
Rail and trucking lines	Anhydrous ammonia, sulfuric phosphoric and hydrochloric acids, and flammable liquids
Chemical manufacturing plants	Chlorine, peroxides, and other industrial gases
Power stations and transformers	Polychlorinated biphenyls

PLANNING CONSIDERATIONS

A-71. A unit's planning should build upon that of the existing groups already involved in TIM planning and response. This includes the Army's chemical and medical branches and numerous U.S. governmental agencies. The first sources of information for basic TIM planning are unit CBRN personnel. The best document for a basic understanding TIM hazards is the U.S. Department of Transportation's Emergency Response Guide (ERG) located at http://www.phmsa.dot.gov/staticfiles/PHMSA/DownloadableFiles/Files/erg2008_eng.pdf.

A-72. This guidebook is the U.S. standard for TIM response. Key planning tasks to identify and plan for possible TIM hazards are—

- Identify all possible industrial plants, storage sites, and shipment depots and pipelines.
- Identify TIM routinely produced, used, or processed in the area.
- Assess the effects of the TIM release as a result of collateral damage or an accident.
- Assess whether deliberate TIM release is a realistic possibility.
- Identify local hazard management procedures and responsible civilian agencies.
- Identify local hazard identification labeling and placard systems.
- Assess the need for specialized protective suits or self-contained breathing apparatus.

ORANGE IDENTIFICATION CODES

A-73. The ERG2008 explains the internationally used orange codes as well as critical information found on most international hazardous material shipping documents (figure A-7 and figure A-8).

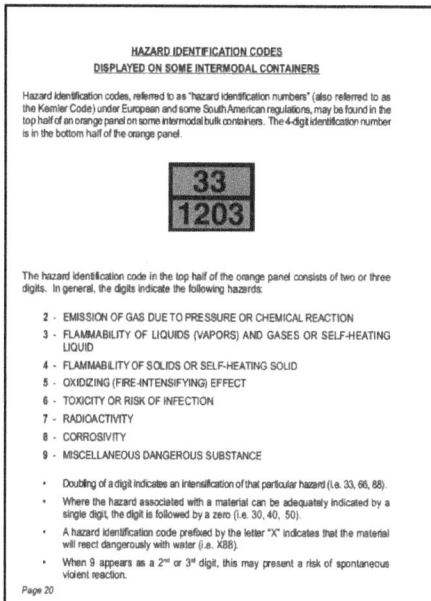

Figure A-7. ERG2008 hazard identification codes

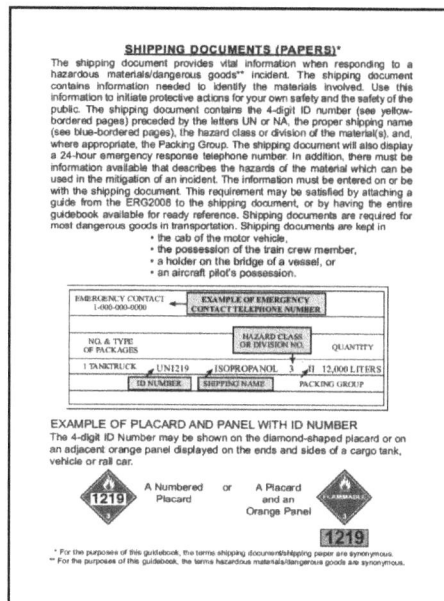

Figure A-8. ERG2008 placard examples

BASIC RESPONSE STEPS

A-74. Soldiers in UO are often first responders to an incident and are, therefore, often the first to come in contact with TIM. When encountering TIM, units should—

- React to contact.
- Establish the perimeter and secure the area.
- Identify the hazard and evaluate all available information.
- Implement initial response measures and assess the situation.
- Obtain help and respond.

EMERGENCY RESPONSE GUIDE RESPONSE STEPS

A-75. The following is an extract from the ERG2008. If possible, all CBRN personnel should have access to this guide. Use ERG Guide 111 for nonexplosive unknown hazardous material (figure A-9). Use ERG Guide 112 for explosive unknown hazardous material (figure A-10).

GUIDE 111 — MIXED LOAD/UNIDENTIFIED CARGO — ERG2008

POTENTIAL HAZARDS

FIRE OR EXPLOSION
- May explode from heat, shock, friction or contamination.
- May react violently or explosively on contact with air, water or foam.
- May be ignited by heat, sparks or flames.
- Vapors may travel to source of ignition and flash back.
- Containers may explode when heated.
- Ruptured cylinders may rocket.

HEALTH
- Inhalation, ingestion or contact with substance may cause severe injury, infection, disease or death.
- High concentration of gas may cause asphyxiation without warning.
- Contact may cause burns to skin and eyes.
- Fire or contact with water may produce irritating, toxic and/or corrosive gases.
- Runoff from fire control may cause pollution.

PUBLIC SAFETY
- CALL Emergency Response Telephone Number on Shipping Paper first. If Shipping Paper not available or no answer, refer to appropriate telephone number listed on the inside back cover.
- As an immediate precautionary measure, isolate spill or leak area for at least 100 meters (330 feet) in all directions.
- Keep unauthorized personnel away.
- Stay upwind.
- Keep out of low areas.

PROTECTIVE CLOTHING
- Wear positive pressure self-contained breathing apparatus (SCBA).
- Structural firefighters' protective clothing provides limited protection in fire situations ONLY; it may not be effective in spill situations.

EVACUATION
Fire
- If tank, rail car or tank truck is involved in a fire, ISOLATE for 800 meters (1/2 mile) in all directions; also, consider initial evacuation for 800 meters (1/2 mile) in all directions.

EMERGENCY RESPONSE

FIRE
CAUTION: Material may react with extinguishing agent.
Small Fire
- Dry chemical, CO₂, water spray or regular foam.
Large Fire
- Water spray, fog or regular foam.
- Move containers from fire area if you can do it without risk.
Fire Involving Tanks
- Cool containers with flooding quantities of water until well after fire is out.
- Do not get water inside containers.
- Withdraw immediately in case of rising sound from venting safety devices or discoloration of tank.
- ALWAYS stay away from tanks engulfed in fire.

SPILL OR LEAK
- Do not touch or walk through spilled material.
- ELIMINATE all ignition sources (no smoking, flares, sparks or flames in immediate area).
- All equipment used when handling the product must be grounded.
- Keep combustibles (wood, paper, oil, etc.) away from spilled material.
- Use water spray to reduce vapors or divert vapor cloud drift. Avoid allowing water runoff to contact spilled material.
- Prevent entry into waterways, sewers, basements or confined areas.
Small Spill • Take up with sand or other non-combustible absorbent material and place into containers for later disposal.
Large Spill • Dike far ahead of liquid spill for later disposal.

FIRST AID
- Move victim to fresh air. • Call 911 or emergency medical service.
- Give artificial respiration if victim is not breathing.
- Do not use mouth-to-mouth method if victim ingested or inhaled the substance; give artificial respiration with the aid of a pocket mask equipped with a one-way valve or other proper respiratory medical device.
- Administer oxygen if breathing is difficult.
- Remove and isolate contaminated clothing and shoes.
- In case of contact with substance, immediately flush skin or eyes with running water for at least 20 minutes.
- Shower and wash with soap and water.
- Keep victim warm and quiet.
- Effects of exposure (inhalation, ingestion or skin contact) to substance may be delayed.
- Ensure that medical personnel are aware of the material(s) involved and take precautions to protect themselves.

Page 168 — Page 169

Figure A-9. Extract from ERG2008 Guide 111

GUIDE 112 — EXPLOSIVES* - DIVISION 1.1, 1.2, 1.3, 1.5 OR 1.6; CLASS A OR B — ERG2008

POTENTIAL HAZARDS

FIRE OR EXPLOSION
- MAY EXPLODE AND THROW FRAGMENTS 1600 meters (1 MILE) OR MORE IF FIRE REACHES CARGO.
- For information on "Compatibility Group" letters, refer to Glossary section.

HEALTH
- Fire may produce irritating, corrosive and/or toxic gases.

PUBLIC SAFETY
- CALL Emergency Response Telephone Number on Shipping Paper first. If Shipping Paper not available or no answer, refer to appropriate telephone number listed on the inside back cover.
- Isolate spill or leak area immediately for at least 500 meters (1/3 mile) in all directions.
- Move people out of line of sight of the scene and away from windows.
- Keep unauthorized personnel away.
- Stay upwind.
- Ventilate closed spaces before entering.

PROTECTIVE CLOTHING
- Wear positive pressure self-contained breathing apparatus (SCBA).
- Structural firefighters' protective clothing will only provide limited protection.

EVACUATION
Large Spill
- Consider initial evacuation for 800 meters (1/2 mile) in all directions.
Fire
- If rail car or trailer is involved in a fire and heavily encased explosives such as bombs or artillery projectiles are suspected, ISOLATE for 1600 meters (1 mile) in all directions; also, initiate evacuation including emergency responders for 1600 meters (1 mile) in all directions.
- When heavily encased explosives are not involved, evacuate the area for 800 meters (1/2 mile) in all directions.

*For information on "Compatibility Group" letters, refer to the Glossary section.

EMERGENCY RESPONSE

FIRE
CARGO Fire
- DO NOT fight fire when fire reaches cargo! Cargo may EXPLODE!
- Stop all traffic and clear the area for at least 1600 meters (1 mile) in all directions and let burn.
- Do not move cargo or vehicle if cargo has been exposed to heat.
TIRE or VEHICLE Fire
- Use plenty of water - FLOOD it! If water is not available, use CO₂, dry chemical or dirt.
- If possible, and WITHOUT RISK, use unmanned hose holders or monitor nozzles from maximum distance to prevent fire from spreading to cargo area.
- Pay special attention to tire fires as re-ignition may occur. Stand by with extinguisher ready.

SPILL OR LEAK
- ELIMINATE all ignition sources (no smoking, flares, sparks or flames in immediate area).
- All equipment used when handling the product must be grounded.
- Do not touch or walk through spilled material.
- DO NOT OPERATE RADIO TRANSMITTERS WITHIN 100 meters (330 feet) OF ELECTRIC DETONATORS.
- DO NOT CLEAN-UP OR DISPOSE OF, EXCEPT UNDER SUPERVISION OF A SPECIALIST.

FIRST AID
- Move victim to fresh air. • Call 911 or emergency medical service.
- Give artificial respiration if victim is not breathing.
- Administer oxygen if breathing is difficult.
- Remove and isolate contaminated clothing and shoes.
- In case of contact with substance, immediately flush skin or eyes with running water for at least 20 minutes.
- Ensure that medical personnel are aware of the material(s) involved and take precautions to protect themselves.

*For information on "Compatibility Group" letters, refer to the Glossary section.

Page 170 — Page 171

Figure A-10. Extract from ERG2008 Guide 112

Appendix B

Weapon Considerations in Urban Operations

Appendix B supplements the technical manuals and field manuals that describe U.S. weapons capabilities and effects against generic targets and their employment. It focuses on organic Infantry weapons, vehicles, and common supporting weapons employed in UO. It also covers basic enemy weapon systems.

SECTION I – URBAN CONSIDERATIONS

B-1. Leaders and Soldiers must carefully choose the correct weapons system and ammunition to employ while conducting UO. Understanding the effects weapons have against various types of structures enhances survivability and limits collateral damage to the civilian population and structures.

COMMON EFFECTS

B-2. Weapons and ammunition exhibit certain common effects in urban terrain. Leaders should take the below effects into account and use or avoid them as the situation demands.

PENETRATION OF STRUCTURES

B-3. Most tactical situations call for penetration of buildings and walls. The amount of penetration a round will achieve against a specific target is unknown until tried. Generally, the smaller the round, the less penetration.

B-4. The following definitions are based on analyses of various studies relating to the size of man-size holes:
- **Loopholes.** Loopholes are firing apertures (a minimum of 8 inches in diameter) made in a structure.
- **Mouseholes.** Mouseholes are openings made to the interior or exterior of a structure (walls, floors, ceilings, and roofs) to aid inter- and intra-building communications and movement. A mousehole is usually a minimum of 24 by 30 inches in size.
- **Breach Holes.** Breach holes are openings made in a structure using mechanical, ballistic, explosive, or thermal means to aid the entry of assault elements. A breach hole is a minimum of 50 by 30 inches in size.

RUBBLE

B-5. An urban area often becomes more of an obstacle to advancing troops and a stronger position for defending troops after being reduced to rubble by weapons fire.

TRAPPED AND INJURED SURVIVORS

B-6. Urban combat can result in large-scale destruction to buildings. Survivors, both military and civilian, may be trapped in the rubble. Extraction efforts may be impossible without heavy construction equipment. Rescue efforts can result in more casualties as the rubble shifts and collapses on would-be rescuers. Once located, casualties should be evacuated quickly and safely. This is often difficult to do without causing additional injury.

RICOCHETS

B-7. Ricochets are a common hazard in UO, especially inside buildings. The walls of an enclosed room present many right angles. When combined with hard surfaces, a bullet may continue to ricochet until its energy is spent. Even after hitting enemy personnel, ball ammunition may pass through the body and ricochet. Body armor and helmets provide some protection from this hazard.

FIRE

B-8. The risk of fire during urban combat is high. Once a large fire starts, it is nearly impossible to extinguish. Fires that rage out of control can cause more damage to the urban area than any other factor. Various factors make containing fires difficult, including—

* Damage to gas lines and water mains.
* Scarcity of firefighting equipment and trained firemen.
* General lack of access caused by rubble blocking the streets.
* Danger posed by combat.

SMOKE AND HAZE

B-9. Limited visibility is common in UO. Fires produce large clouds of often toxic or irritating, choking smoke. Explosions add significant amounts of dust to the atmosphere. Even the effort to rescue personnel trapped within collapsed buildings creates dust.

DAMAGED AND DESTROYED TRANSPORTATION SYSTEMS

B-10. Urban areas are transportation hubs. Urban combat may disrupt the normal flow of traffic, destroying or damaging roads, ports, bridges, and rail lines necessary for the movement and distribution of supplies and goods.

DISPLACED CIVILIANS

B-11. Although many civilian inhabitants of a town flee the fighting, some remain behind in the immediate area of the fighting and are, thus, in danger. Commanders should consider civilians in all planning and make provisions for their protection and evacuation.

COMMON CHARACTERISTICS

B-12. The characteristics and nature of urban combat affect the use of weapons and their results. Common characteristics of urban combat are described below.

ENCLOSED COMBAT

B-13. Whether inside or outside, nearby walls limit the openness of urban engagements. Soldiers should consider their weapon's effects, such as minimum arming ranges, muzzle blast and backblast, the round's effect on the target, and the target's effect on the round. Soldiers should also consider enemy weapons effects on friendly positions.

SHORT ENGAGEMENT TIMES

B-14. Enemy personnel and vehicles typically present only fleeting targets as they can rapidly seek the cover of a nearby wall and then fire from the same or different firing position. Simultaneously, other enemy fire aims to suppress friendly fire and can often hinder deliberate, well-aimed shots.

CLOSE COMBAT

B-15. Close combat is the predominant characteristic of urban engagements. Riflemen should be able to hit targets through bunker apertures, windows, and loopholes. This requires accurate semiautomatic weapons fire with short target acquisition times.

CLOSE ENGAGEMENT RANGES

B-16. About 90 percent of all targets are engaged at a range of 50 meters or less.

BUILDING CONSTRUCTION TYPES

B-17. Over 60 percent of buildings throughout the world are constructed with 12- to 24-inch brick or concrete block.

MODERNIZED BUILDINGS

B-18. Modern engineering and design improvements mean most large buildings constructed since World War II are resilient to the blast effects of bomb and artillery attack. They may burn easily but usually retain structural integrity and remain standing. Burnt high-rise buildings require substantial explosive force to damage further and typically retain their military significance, such as for individual firing or unit positions. A large structure can take 24 to 48 hours to burn out and become cool enough to enter.

ENHANCED DEFENSE

B-19. Many man-made structures provide ready-made strong defensive positions. As a result, units may have to attack this structure before attacking enemy personnel inside. Units should often choose weapons and demolitions for employment based on their effects against masonry and concrete.

HARD, FLAT, SMOOTH SURFACES

B-20. Hard, flat, smooth surfaces are characteristic of urban construction. Rounds usually impact at some angle of obliquity, which normally reduces the effects of a round and increases the threat of ricochets. The tendency of rounds to strike glancing blows against hard surfaces means that up to 25 percent of impact-fuzed explosive rounds may not detonate when fired into rubbled areas.

VERTICAL DEAD SPACE

B-21. The depression and elevation limits for some weapons create dead space. Additionally, tall buildings form deep canyons that inhibit the use of indirect fires. Some weapons systems, especially small-arms weapons, can be fired with the deliberate intent of the rounds ricocheting behind cover to inflict casualties. Target engagement from oblique angles, both horizontal and vertical, demands superior marksmanship skills.

REDUCED VISIBILITY

B-22. Smoke, dust, shadows, and the lack of light penetrating inner rooms all combine to reduce visibility and to increase a sense of isolation. Additionally, rubble and man-made structures by themselves tend to mask fires. As a result, targets (even those at close range) tend to be indistinct.

RISK OF FRIENDLY FIRE

B-23. Urban fighting often becomes confused melees with several small units attacking on converging axes or being attacked from multiple directions. As such, consider the risks from friendly fires and ricochets during planning. Control measures should be continually adjusted to lower risks. Soldiers and leaders should maintain situational awareness, communicate their movement, and clearly mark their progress as per unit SOP to avoid fratricide.

SECTION II – SMALL-ARMS WEAPONS

B-24. Small-arms weapons covered in this section include the 5.56-mm rifle, 7.62-mm machine gun, .50-caliber rounds, 40-mm grenades, and various hand grenades. The shotgun, since it has minimal effect on an urban structure and is excellent for breaching and room clearing, is covered in chapter 7.

RIFLE, CARBINE, AND SQUAD AUTOMATIC WEAPON

B-25. The M16 rifle and M4 carbine are the most common U.S. weapons fired in urban areas. The overall length of both the M16 and the M249 may require individuals to modify handling and firing techniques for interior direct fire engagements. The M4, being shorter and lighter, is often easier to handle inside buildings.

PENETRATION

B-26. Most structural building materials (such as stone, brick, or concrete walls) repel single 5.56-mm rounds. However, continued and concentrated fire can create small breach holes. Armor-piercing rounds are slightly more effective than ball ammunition in creating a wall breach. However, armor-piercing rounds are more likely to ricochet than ball ammunition when the target presents a high degree of obliquity.

B-27. The penetration of 5.56-mm rounds depends on target range and the building material. Maximum penetration occurs at 200 meters. At ranges less than 25 meters, penetration is greatly reduced. The best method for breaching a masonry wall is to repeatedly fire short bursts (three to five rounds) in a U-shaped pattern. The 5.56-mm rounds cannot cut the reinforcing bars in reinforced concrete.

PROTECTION

B-28. Wood frame buildings and single cinder block walls offer little protection from 5.56-mm rounds. Even with reduced penetration at short ranges, an interior wall made of thin wood paneling, sheetrock, or plaster is no protection against 5.56-mm rounds. When clearing such structures, Soldiers must ensure friendly casualties do not result from rounds passing through walls, floors, or ceilings. The following common barriers in urban areas stop a 5.56-mm round fired at less than 50 meters:

- Single row of well-packed sandbags.
- Layer of tightly packed books 18 to 24 inches thick.
- Two-inch concrete wall (nonreinforced).
- Small ammunition filled with sand.
- Cinder block filled with sand.
- Single layer of brick.

MEDIUM AND HEAVY MACHINE GUNS

B-29. The U.S. medium machine gun and the U.S. heavy machine gun provide high-volume, long-range, automatic fires for the suppression or destruction of targets.

EMPLOYMENT

B-30. The primary consideration impacting machine gun employment within urban areas is the limited availability of long-range fields of fire. Although machine guns should be emplaced at the lowest terrain level possible, grazing fire at ground level is often obstructed by rubble. If machine guns are emplaced too high, their plunging fire is limited to a single small open area. Often, the second floor is the best compromise since it is above common debris, allows for relatively low trajectory fire, and the floors above provide indirect fire protection.

PENETRATION

B-31. The penetration ability of the medium and heavy machine guns depends on the range to the target and type of material fired against. The rounds can easily penetrate internal walls, partitions, plaster, floors, ceilings, common office furniture, home appliances, and bedding. Continued and concentrated machine gun fire can breach most urban walls but typically cannot breach thick reinforced concrete walls or dense natural stone block walls.

Medium Machine Guns

B-32. The penetration of the 7.62-mm round is best at 600 meters, but most urban targets are closer. The typical minimum effective penetration range for the 7.62-mm round is 200 meters. At 50 meters, the 7.62-mm ball round cannot reliably penetrate a single layer of well-packed sandbags. At 200 meters, it can penetrate a single sandbag layer but not a double layer. The armor-piercing round does only slightly better against sandbags. It cannot penetrate a double layer but can penetrate up to 10 inches at 600 meters.

B-33. A medium machine gun is difficult to hold steady enough to repeatedly hit the same point on a wall. The dust created by the bullet strikes also makes precise aiming difficult. As such, firing from a tripod is usually more effective than without, especially if sandbags are also steadying the weapon. Short bursts of three to five rounds fired in a U-shaped pattern are best. Breaching cinder block presents a problem for medium machine guns. Rounds easily penetrate the hollow portions of the cinder block but leave a net-like structure of the solid portions. Substantial ammunition is required to destroy this net since many rounds will just pass through the eroded holes. However, a crowbar or axe can remove this web and allow entry through the breach hole.

Heavy Machine Gun

B-34. The .50-caliber round penetrates best at 800 meters. For hard targets, obliquity and range affect the penetration of the .50-caliber round. Both armor-piercing and ball ammunition penetrates 14 inches of sand or 28 inches of packed earth at 200 meters if the round impacts perpendicular to the target. The .50-caliber machine gun can be fired accurately from the tripod using the single-shot mode. This is the most efficient method for producing a loophole. Automatic fire in three- to five-round bursts in a U-shaped pattern is more effective in producing a breach. (See FM 3-22.65 for details.) The .50-caliber round can penetrate common urban barriers, except a 55-gallon drum filled with sand, a car engine block, and sewer covers. Continued and concentrated fire breaches most urban walls, except for the reinforcing bars in concrete or dense natural stone walls.

PROTECTION

B-35. Barriers that offer protection against 5.56-mm rounds are also effective against 7.62-mm rounds with some exceptions. The 7.62-mm round can penetrate a windowpane at a 45-degree obliquity, a hollow cinder block, or both sides of a car body. It can also easily penetrate wood frame buildings.

HAND GRENADES

B-36. Hand grenades are the most used explosive munitions during intense combat in urban areas. As such, individuals should carry additional grenades, and units should have forward stockpiles for resupply. The mission variables, building construction materials, and ROE dictate the type used. Although useful during urban combat, hand grenades (especially fragmentation hand grenades) are difficult to employ safely and involve a high risk of fratricide.

Note. In combat, it may be necessary to reinsert the safety pin into a hand grenade. Take special care to replace the pin properly. If the tactical situation allows, it is safer to throw the grenade rather than to trust the reinserted pin.

TYPES

B-37. The five types of hand grenades are fragmentation, chemical, offensive, nonlethal (stun), and practice. Ground smoke signals are commonly known as smoke hand grenades. Table B-1 describes the employment of these grenades. (See FM 3-23.30 for details.)

Table B-1. Employment of hand grenades and ground smoke signals

Type	Employment
Nonlethal	Use when noncombatants and friendly forces are intermingled with enemy forces and when the structural integrity of the building does not permit the use of fragmentation or concussion grenades. Throw into rooms prior to entering to confuse, disorient, or momentarily distract a potential enemy in forced-entry scenarios.
Chemical	Use for riot control or incendiary purposes to immobilize or destroy vehicles, equipment, munitions, or weapons.
Fragmentation	Throw at assaulting enemy troops between buildings or on streets from windows, doors, or man-made apertures (mouseholes). Grenade fragments cannot penetrate a single layer of sandbags, a cinder block, or a brick building, but they can penetrate wood frame and tin buildings.
Offensive	Use for concussion effects. They are less lethal than fragmentation grenades on an enemy in the open but are effective in enclosed bunkers, buildings, and fortified areas.
Ground smoke signals	The M106 provides a near instantaneous screen of dense smoke and is safe to use inside urban structures, subterranean locations, and caves. Use in lieu of the AN-M8 HC and the M83 TA white smoke hand grenade when inside of confined spaces and when encountering enemy in close quarters.

EMPLOYMENT

B-38. To throw a hand grenade through an adjacent opening or through an above-the-head opening, use the following steps:

(1) Stand near the opening and use the wall of the building as cover.
(2) Quickly lean (adjacent opening) or step out (above-the-head opening) far enough to ensure the opening is free of obstacles. If blocked, do not throw the grenade. Instead, throw a rock or other heavy object to break through the opening. However, breaking through a blockage may telegraph that a hand grenade is soon to follow.
(3) Return to the wall.
(4) Ready the grenade.
(5) If the situation warrants, release the spoon and allow the grenade to cook off for 2 seconds.
(6) Lean (adjacent opening) or step out (above-the-head opening) far enough to lob the grenade through the opening and quickly return to the wall for cover.

GRENADE LAUNCHERS

B-39. The M203 and M320 grenade launcher and the MK19 grenade machine gun fire 40-mm HE and high-explosive dual purpose (HEDP) ammunition. Ammunition for the grenade launchers and the MK19 is not interchangeable, but the grenade and fuze assembly are identical. All provide point and area destructive fires as well as suppression. (See FM 3-22.27 for details.)

EMPLOYMENT

B-40. A grenade launcher is the safest method for putting a grenade through an aperture in urban terrain. When using a grenade launcher to deliver a grenade into a window or doorway, ensure proper standoff for arming the round. (TM 3-22.31 for details.)

B-41. Two considerations affecting the employment of 40-mm grenades within urban areas are the typically short engagement range and the potentially high rate of ammunition expenditure. The 40-mm grenade has a minimum arming range of 14 to 28 meters. If the round strikes an object before it is armed, it will not detonate. Both the HE and HEDP rounds have 5-meter burst radii against exposed troops.

B-42. The 40-mm grenade can suppress the enemy in a building or inflict casualties by firing through apertures. If fired into an interior room, the 40-mm HEDP can penetrate all partition-type walls. However, none of the fragments reliably penetrate interior walls, office furniture, sandbags, helmets, or body armor. Soldiers can use the M203 or M320 from upper stories to deliver accurate fire against the top decks of armored vehicles.

B-43. The MK19 can use its high rate of fire to concentrate rounds against light structures. This concentrated fire can create extensive damage. The 40-mm HEDP round can penetrate the armor on the flank, rear, and top of Soviet-made armored personnel carriers. Multiple hits are needed to achieve a kill.

PENETRATION

B-44. The MK19 individual HEDP round, can penetrate brick (6 to 8 inches), cinder block, and concrete. The only material that has proven resistant to concentrated 40-mm fire is dense, large block stone. No precise data exists as to the number of rounds required to produce loopholes or breach holes with the MK19. However, the round's explosive effects should exceed the performance of the .50-caliber machine gun. The M203 and M320 cannot reasonably deliver the rounds needed to breach a typical exterior wall. Table B-2 shows U.S. and enemy small-arms weapons penetration against common materials found in UO.

Table B-2. U.S. and enemy small-arms weapons penetration against common urban materials

Weapon Type		Min Range	Max Effective Range	Penetration Number of Rounds/Material							
				8" Reinforced Concrete	9" Double Brick	12" cinder block with veneer	12" cinder block with sand	14" Triple Brick	16" Tree Trunk	24" Double Sand Bag	3/8" Mild Steel Door
M16/M4	Point	~	500 m	35	70	60	35	90	1-3	220	1
	Area	~	600 m								
M249	Point	~	800 m	35	70	60	35	90	1-3	220	1
	Area	~	1000 m								
M240B	Point	~	900 m	100	18	30	18	170	1	110	1
	Area	~	1800 m								
M203/M320	Point	14-28 m	150 m	~	2	~	1	3	2	2	1
	Area		350 m								
M2 .50 Cal	Point	~	1500 m	50	~	25	~	15	~	1	1
	Area	~	1830 m								
MK19	Point	18-30 m	150 0m	~	2	~	1	3	2	2	1
	Area		2212 m								
Javelin		65 m	2000 m	1	1	1	1	1	1	1	1
Threat Weapon Types and Penetration Capabilities											
AK 74	Point	~	500 m	Yes	Yes	Yes	Yes	Yes	Yes	No	Yes
	Area	~	800 m								
AKM	Point	~	300 m	Yes	Yes	Yes	Yes	Yes	Yes	No	Yes
	Area	~	800 m								
PKM	Point	~	1000 m	Yes	Yes	Yes	Yes	Yes	Yes	No	Yes
	Area	~	1500 m								
NSV-T	Point	~	800 m	Yes	Yes	Yes	Yes	Yes	Yes	Yes	Yes
	Area	~	2000 m								
GP-30	Point	10-40 m	400 m	Yes	Yes	Yes	Yes	Yes	Yes	Yes	Yes
	Area										
W-87	Point	~	600 m	Yes	Yes	Yes	Yes	Yes	Yes	Yes	Yes
	Area		1500 m								
RPG-7V	Point	18-30 m	200 m	Yes	Yes	Yes	Yes	Yes	Yes	Yes	Yes
	Area		1000 m								
RPG-29	Point	~	800 m	Yes	Yes	Yes	Yes	Yes	Yes	Yes	Yes

SECTION III – SHOULDER-LAUNCHED MUNITIONS

B-45. Shoulder-launched munitions include the improved M72-series LAW, the M136 AT4, the M136 AT4CS, and the M141 Bunker Defeat Munition (BDM). These munitions are used to attack light armored vehicles, field fortifications, and enemy personnel behind cover. They have limited capability against tanks, especially those equipped with reactive armor. These weapons are issued as rounds of ammunition to individual Soldiers in addition to their assigned weapons.

GENERAL

B-46. Due to warhead design and narrow blast effect, shoulder-launched munitions are not as effective against urban structures as heavier weapons, such as a main gun round of a tank. Since they are man-portable, individual rounds, small units may carry multiple rounds to allow for the repetitive firing at select targets.

FIRING AT ARMORED VEHICLES

B-47. Shoulder-launched munitions are most effective when fired at short-range at a vulnerable part of the armored vehicle. Flank, top, and rear shots hit the most vulnerable parts of armored vehicles. As such, the firing of shoulder-launched munitions from the upper floors or roofs of buildings is extremely effective and common in urban terrain. Additionally, these weapons are best employed using volley fire or paired firing, especially when firing at a tank, as multiple hits are normally needed to achieve a kill on a tank. The most effective method of engagement for hitting and killing an armored vehicle is to fire from an elevated position at the top of the armored vehicle. This improves the chance of hitting the armored vehicle and the chance of penetration, which increases the chance of destruction.

B-48. Firing from upper stories protects the shooter from tank main gun and coaxial machine gun fire since tanks cannot sharply elevate their cannons. The M136 AT4CS is the only shoulder-launched munition authorized to fire from an enclosure. Top attacks can be performed from rooftops, allowing for greater angles of fire and protection of the shooter from overpressure effects.

B-49. Many main battle tanks have some form of reactive armor in addition to their thick armor plate. Head-on, ground-level shots against these vehicles have little probability of obtaining a kill. Even without reactive armor, modern main battle tanks are hard to destroy with a LAW. The BMP-2 can elevate its 30-mm cannon to engage targets in upper stories. Additionally, modern threat light armored vehicles, such as the BMP-2, have significantly improved frontal protection against shaped-charge weapons.

B-50. Table B-3 lists considerations for effects of shoulder-launched munitions on heavy armored vehicles. The older the vehicle model, the less protection it has against shoulder-launched munitions. Newer versions may use bolt-on (appliqué) armor to improve their survivability. Some vehicles are equipped with reactive armor, which consists of metal plates and plastic explosives.

Table B-3. Shoulder-launched munition effects on heavy armored vehicles

Munitions	Effects on Heavy Armored Vehicles	Remarks
M72-series	Causes only a small entry hole, though some fragmentation or spalling may occur	Reactive armor may cover the front and sides of the vehicle and can defeat shaped-charge weapons. However, the munitions can restrict the vehicle's mobility and may destroy the vehicle if the round hits a vulnerable spot, such as the engine compartment area.
M136-series	Causes only a small entry hole, though some fragmentation or spalling may occur	
M141 BDM	Can cause a mobility kill by disabling the vehicle's suspension system	The M141 BDM should be a last resort when engaging armored vehicles.

B-51. Table B-4 lists considerations for effects of shoulder-launched munitions on light armored vehicles. All current shoulder-launched munitions are capable of destroying most light armored vehicles if the round hits a vulnerable spot, such as the engine compartment area or fuel tank. Unit leaders should provide squad and platoon supporting fires when engaging light armored troop carriers. Any infantry troops that survive the initial assault may dismount and return fire.

Table B-4. Shoulder-launched munition effects on light armored vehicles

Munitions	Effects on Light Armored Vehicles
M72-series	Can cause a catastrophic kill if the round hits a vulnerable spot, such as the engine compartment area or fuel tank
M136-series	
M141 BDM	

B-52. Table B-5 lists considerations for effects of shoulder-launched munitions on nonarmored vehicles. Nonarmored vehicles, such as trucks and cars, are considered soft targets. Firing along their length (flank) offers the greatest chance of a kill since this type of shot is most likely to hit their engine block or fuel tank. Front and rear angles offer a much smaller target, reducing the chance of a first-round hit.

Table B-5. Shoulder-launched munition effects on nonarmored vehicles

Munitions	Effects on Nonarmored Vehicles	Remarks
M72-series	May penetrate but will pass through the body with limited damage unless the rocket hits a vital part of the engine	When engaging enemy-used privately-owned vehicles, do not fire at the engine compartment area instead of the main body.
M136-series	May penetrate but will pass through the body with limited damage unless the rocket hits a vital part of the engine	
M141 BDM	Causes a catastrophic kill	

FIRING AT STRUCTURES

B-53. The M72-series LAW, the M136 AT4, and the M136A1 AT4CS are shaped-charge weapons that penetrate most field fortifications and buildings. However, penetration does not mean the destruction of the integrity of the position. Typically, a small hole is made in the structure, and only those enemy personnel directly in the path of the spall from a HEAT round become casualties. Other enemy inside a fortification may be deafened, dazed, or shocked, but they eventually return to action. The M141 BDM fires the HE charge that destroys fortifications and substantially damage buildings (table B-6 and table B-7).

Table B-6. M136- and M72-series munitions effects on field fortifications or bunkers

Aimpoint	Effects	Recommended Firing Technique
Firing Port or Aperture	Rounds fired into firing ports or apertures may be wasted. Rounds detonate inside the rear of the position cause little structural damage to the position, equipment, or personnel within unless they are hit directly.	Coordinate fire: fire an M72- or M136-series shoulder-launched munition at a point 6 to 12 inches from the front edge of the firing ports in the berm.
Berm	Firing at the berm causes the round to detonate outside the fighting position or inside the berm, creating only a small hole in the berm, dust, or minor structural damage to the position and no damage to personnel or equipment unless they are hit directly.	
Window	The round may travel completely through the structure before detonating. If not, it creates dust and causes minor structural damage to the rear wall and little damage to personnel or equipment unless they are hit directly.	Coordinate fire: fire 6 to 12 inches from the sides or bottom of a window. M136- and M72-series rounds explode on contact with brick or concrete, creating an opening with a size determined by the type of round used.
Wall	The round detonates on contact, creating dust and causing a small hole and minor structural damage but little damage to personnel or equipment unless they are hit directly.	
Corner	Corners are reinforced and, therefore, harder to penetrate than other parts of a wall. The munitions detonate sooner on a corner than on a less dense surface. Detonation should occur in the targeted room, creating dust and causing overpressure, which can temporarily incapacitate personnel inside the structure near the point of detonation. M136-series munitions cause more overpressure than M72-series munitions.	

Note. Fire small-arms weapons at enemy-held positions to prevent personnel within from returning fire.

Table B-7. M141 bunker munitions effects on field fortifications or bunkers

Aimpoint	Effects		Recommended Firing Technique
Bunkers	Rounds fired into firing ports or apertures can destroy standard earth and timber bunkers and hasty urban fighting positions. Rounds detonate inside the rear of the position, causing major structural damage. Damage to enemy equipment may be minor unless it is hit directly. The round causes injury or death to occupants.		Coordinate fire: fire a shoulder-launched munition at and through firing ports.
Buildings	Windows or Doorways	Rounds fired through windows or doorways can destroy the contents of the building. Destruction may not be contained within a single room. Rounds and debris from the round and material may pass through into other sections of the building, causing collateral damage. Damage to enemy equipment may be minor unless it is hit directly. The round causes injury or death to occupants.	Coordinate fire: fire an M141 BDM at the center of the visible part of a window or door.
	Walls	Rounds fired at walls will penetrate double-reinforced concrete walls up to 8 inches thick and triple-brick structures. The initial blast opens a hole in the wall but may or may not completely penetrate the building.	Coordinate fire: fire one or more M141 BDM at the center of the desired location for the opening. Fire a second round through the opening to destroy targets within the structure. **Note.** It takes more than one round to create a man-size hole. Use pair or volley fire, placing the rounds about 12 to 18 inches apart.
Underground Openings	Rounds fired through underground openings can collapse the opening or destroy the contents within it. Destruction may not be contained within the opening. Rounds and debris may pass through into other sections of the opening, causing further damage. Damage to enemy equipment may be minor unless it is hit directly. The round causes injury or death to occupants at the front entrance. Others farther into the opening may be incapacitated or die from the concussion, heat, and debris caused by the explosion.		Coordinate fire: fire one or more M141 BDM.

Firing Ports or Windows

B-54. Rounds fired directly into firing ports or windows typically detonate on the rear wall of the structure, causing limited damage to equipment and personnel inside. For best effect, aim shaped-charge weapons about 6 inches below or to the side of a firing aperture to maximize blast effects on the interior.

Sandbagged Emplacements

B-55. Because sandbags absorb much of the energy from a shaped charge, aim at the center of the firing aperture. Even if the round misses the aperture, the bunker wall area near it is usually easier to penetrate.

Berms or Walls

B-56. Firing directly at a berm or wall typically produces only a small hole, causing little or no damage to the position, equipment, or personnel behind the wall unless the round penetrates and directly hits equipment or personnel. For best effect, fire at a point 6 to 12 inches from the edge of the top or side edge of the berm or wall to maximize blast effects on the interior. Specific wall material effects follow:

- **Stone.** Stone is the most difficult to penetrate of all common building materials. The AT4 usually does not penetrate a heavy European-style stone wall. Surface cratering is usually the only effect.
- **Brick.** Brick is also difficult to breach with light recoilless weapons. Multiple firings can breach some brick walls, especially if they are less than three bricks thick. Weapons such as the AT4 may require three to five rounds to penetrate brick walls. The BDM produces a hole in brick or mud walls that is often large enough to be a breach hole.

- **Wood.** Wood offers little resistance to light recoilless weapons, which penetrate and splinter even heavy timbered walls. The AT4 and BDM have a devastating effect against wood frame walls. A single round produces a breach hole and significant spall.

PROTECTION

B-57. Soldiers must consider the effects of backblast when employing shoulder-launched munitions, protecting themselves from the blast, overpressure, and heat. During UO, the backblast area is more hazardous due to the channeling effect of enclosed spaces, narrow streets, and alleys. Anyone not able to vacate the caution zone should be behind cover. All personnel should be out of the weapons danger zone. When firing the M72 LAW, AT4, and TOW missile from masonry and frame buildings and sandbag bunkers—

- The safest place for Soldiers in the room is against the wall from which the weapon is fired.
- The key difference between firing from an enclosure and firing in the open is the duration of the pressure fluctuation.
- Little hazard exists to the gunner or crew from any type of flying debris. However, firers should take advantage of all available sources of ventilation by opening doors and windows to help clear the room of smoke and dust and reduce the effective duration of the overpressure.
- No substantial degradation occurs to the operator's tracking performance as a result of obscuration or blast overpressure.
- The greatest hazard that can be expected is hearing loss. As such, all room occupants should wear hearing protection.
- Frame buildings, especially small ones, can suffer structural damage to the rear walls, windows, and doors. Large rooms suffer slight, if any, damage.

M72A7 LIGHT ANTIARMOR WEAPON

B-58. The M72A7 LAW offers significantly enhanced capability beyond that of the M72A3.

RANGE AND PENETRATION

B-59. The M72A7 LAW has a minimum range of 25 meters, a maximum range of 1,400 meters, a maximum effective range of 220 meters, and a maximum engagement range of 350 meters. The 66-mm rocket can penetrate 150 millimeters of armor.

FIRING FROM AN ENCLOSURE

B-60. In accordance with TB 9-1340-230-13, firing the M72A7 LAW from an enclosure is prohibited.

PROTECTION

B-61. Like all recoilless weapons, the backblast area of the LAW must be clear of personnel. Figure B-1 depicts the M72A7 backblast area. (See TM 3-23.25 for details.)

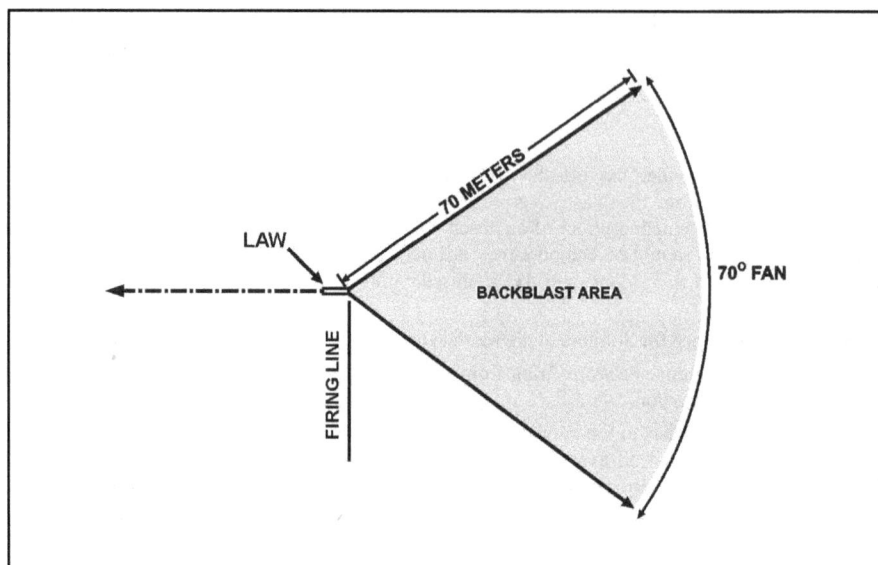

Figure B-1. M72A7 backblast area

M136 AT4

B-62. The M136 AT4 is a lightweight, self-contained, shoulder-launched munition designed for use against the improved armor of light armored vehicles. It provides lethal fire against light armored vehicles and has some effect on most enemy field fortifications.

RANGE AND PENETRATION

B-63. The AT4 has a minimum range of 34 meters, a maximum range of 2,100 meters, a maximum effective range of 300 meters, and a maximum engagement range of 500 meters. The AT4's warhead has excellent penetration ability and lethal after-armor effects. The shaped-charge explosive penetrates more than 14 inches (350 millimeters) of armor. Penetration of a soft target is enhanced by the high kinetic energy retained by the rocket as it impacts the target. The rocket configuration also provides directional stability as the rocket enters soft targets, which greatly enhances lethality, especially when engaging targets at oblique angles. This directional stability after impact keeps the rocket from deflecting away from the target wall.

FIRING FROM AN ENCLOSURE

B-64. Do not fire the AT4 from an enclosure or in front of any barrier that could interfere with the backblast.

PROTECTION

B-65. The total backblast area extends 100 meters to the rear of the AT4 in a 90-degree fan (figure B-2). (See TM 3-23.25 for details.)

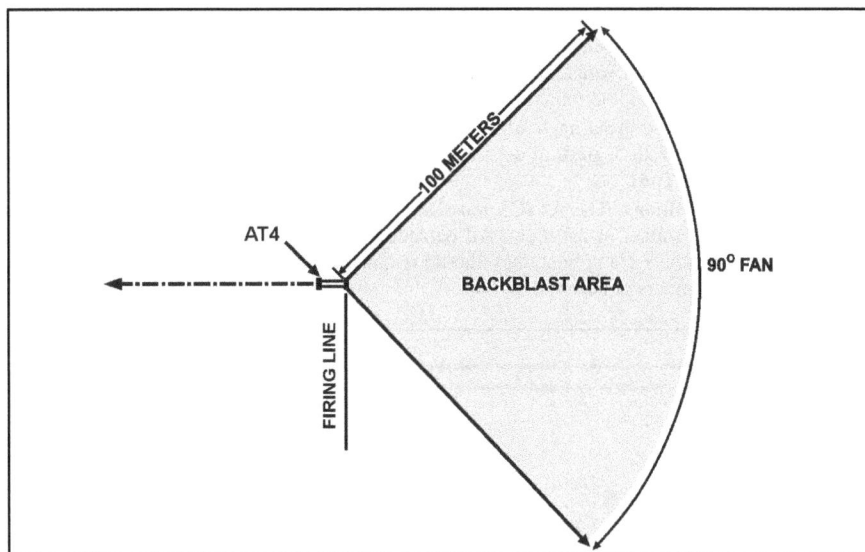

Figure B-2. M136 AT4 backblast area

M136A1 AT4CS 84-mm LAUNCHER

B-66. The M136A1 AT4CS is similar to the AT4 but uses a different propulsion system that permits the AT4CS to be fired from an enclosure. As such, it is important to be able to identify the visual differences between the AT4CS and the AT4. A clearly displayed marking stating CONFINED SPACE identifies the launcher as an AT4CS.

RANGE AND PENETRATION

B-67. The AT4CS has a minimum range of 9 to 15 meters, a maximum range of 2,100 meters, a maximum effective range of 300 meters, and a maximum engagement range of 400 meters. Caution should be taken when engaging targets at less than 30 meters due to fragmentation. The AT4CS can penetrate 15.7 inches (400 millimeters) of armor, which is slightly more than the AT4.

FIRING FROM AN ENCLOSURE

B-68. The AT4CS has been rated safe for use from an enclosure when the enclosure meets the following minimum requirements:
- **Construction.** The building should be sturdily constructed to reduce the structural damage that would occur in a weakly constructed enclosure, such as one made of wood frame construction.
- **Size of Enclosure.** A room should have a minimum inside area of 12 by 15 feet (about 3.5 by 4.5 meters) with a minimum ceiling height of 7 feet (2.1 meters).
- **Ventilation.** To allow for ventilation of the backblast, at least 20 square feet of open area, such as a standard 3- by 7-foot doorway, must be available and open on a side or rear wall. Any additional doors or windows should be opened to increase ventilation and reduce overpressure, noise, and blast effects. On the front wall, windows and doors need to be reinforced rather than removed since removing would draw attention to the position. A blanket hung 1.5 to 2 meters behind the weapon and 15 to 30 centimeters from the rear wall considerably reduces sound pressure.
- **Objects and Debris.** Any objects or debris to the rear of the weapon should be removed to prevent them from flying around the room and possibly injuring personnel as a result of the backblast. Any equipment kept in the room when firing must be covered as it will be exposed to countermass spray (corrosive saline solution). Keep soft objects, such as furniture and pillows, to help absorb overpressure.

- **Clearance.** Firing the AT4CS requires a minimum opening of 36 by 36 inches (1 by 1 meter) minimum. The fins open approximately 10 inches (25.4 centimeters) wide shortly after exiting muzzle. Use caution when aiming weapon (muzzle) to prevent fins from impacting window or doorsill. Fire weapon no more than 4 inches (10 centimeters) from door or window frame.
- **Firing Angle.** The firing angle of the weapon must not exceed 45 degrees left or right from the vertical plane or 20 degrees of depression. Do not fire weapon at any angle of elevation (figure B-3 and figure B-4).
- **Personnel Positions.** The AT4CS must be fired in standing position, with no more than two additional personnel in the room. All personnel within the enclosure should wear earplugs. If any other Soldiers are present, they should remain forward of the rear of the launcher and avoid standing in corners or near walls.

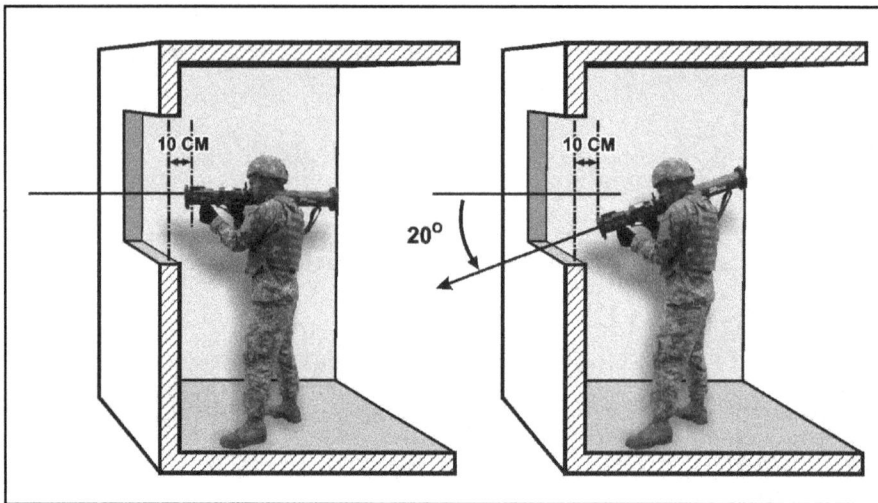

Figure B-3. Vertical firing angle

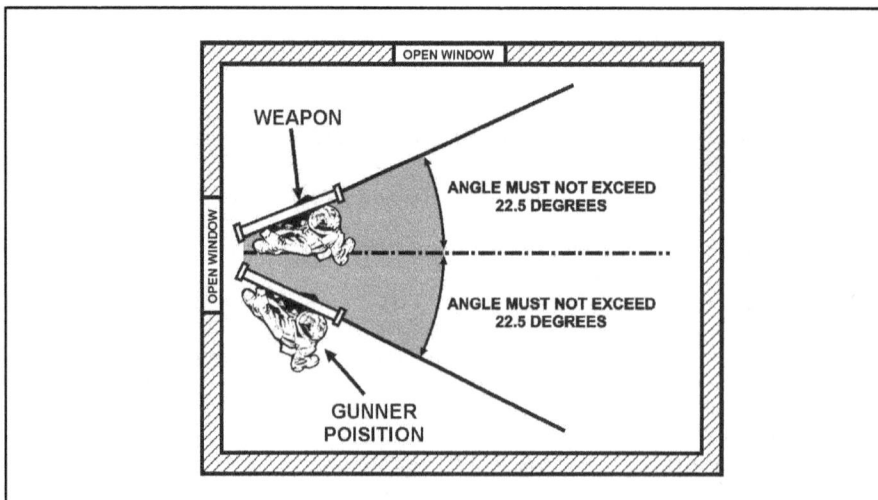

Figure B-4. Horizontal firing angle

PROTECTION

B-69. The backblast area is to the rear of the launcher in a 50-degree fan (figure B-5). (See TM 3-23.25 for details.)

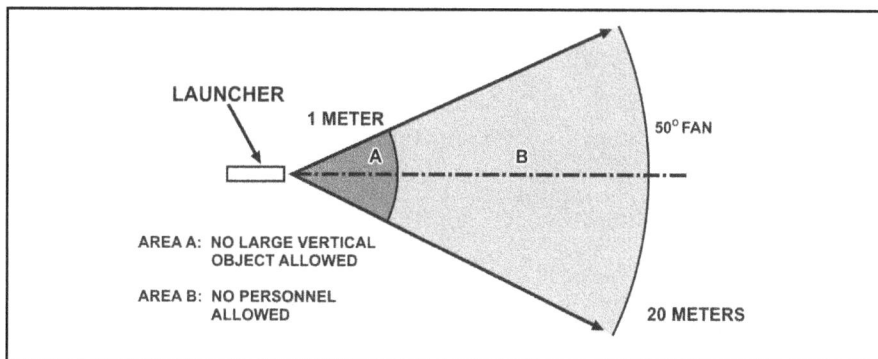

Figure B-5. M136A1 AT4CS backblast

M141 BUNKER DEFEAT MUNITION

B-70. The BDM is a lightweight, man-portable assault weapon that fires an 83-mm HEDP rocket that is effective against walls, bunkers, and light armored vehicles. The BDM can destroy most bunkers with a single hit. While multiple shots create breach holes even in reinforced concrete, they do not cut reinforcing steel bars.

B-71. The warhead automatically adjusts for the target type on impact. If the warhead hits a soft target, such as a sandbagged bunker, the fuze delays warhead detonation until the rocket has buried deep into the target, devastating the target. Rocket impact on a building wall or lightly armored vehicle causes the fuze to detonate immediately. The warhead's HE charge is compressed against the target, resulting in enormous target holes and large fragments inside the vehicle or behind the wall.

RANGE AND PENETRATION

B-72. The effective range is between 15 and 250 meters, maximum range is 2,000 meters, and maximum engagement range is 500 meters. The penetration and breaching of walls is a common task for the BDM in UO. The BDM is the only Army shoulder-launched munition combat-proven to destroy earth and timber bunkers, breach up to 8 inches of reinforced concrete, breach up to 12-inch triple brick walls, and defeat light armored vehicles by penetrating up to 20 millimeters of armor.

FIRING FROM AN ENCLOSURE

B-73. Do not fire the BDM from an enclosure or in front of any barrier that could interfere with the weapon's backblast. (See TM 3-23.25 for details.)

PROTECTION

B-74. Do not attempt to fire the weapon unless danger zones are clear of personnel and obstructions. Keep the backblast area clear of personnel (figure B-6). The BDM backblast area consists of two areas:

- **Danger Area.** No personnel are allowed in this area. Severe injury may be sustained from blast and flying debris.
- **Ear Protection Caution Area.** All personnel should wear hearing protection devices in this area. Sound pressure levels may exceed 140 decibels.

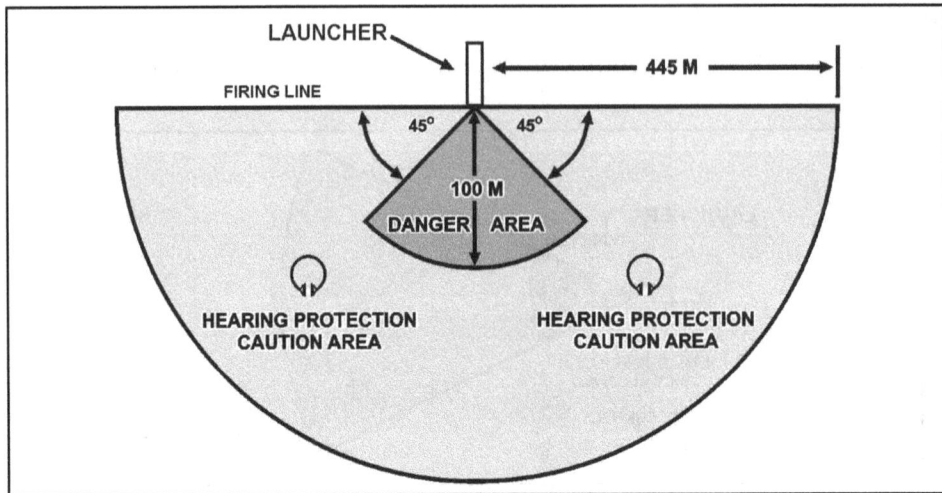

Figure B-6. Bunker defeat munition backblast surface danger zones

SECTION IV – CLOSE COMBAT MISSILES

B-75. Close combat missiles include the Javelin and the TOW missile. They are used mainly to defeat main battle tanks and other armored vehicles. They have a moderate capability against bunkers, buildings, and other fortified targets commonly found during combat in urban areas. Close combat missiles provide precision long-range direct fire capability to platoons and companies. The fire-and-forget capability of the Javelin and the 10-digit grid coordinates afforded by the far target locator provide precision fires against a wide array of fleeting and static targets.

JAVELIN

B-76. The Javelin is a fire-and-forget weapon system that can destroy tanks and fortified positions. (See FM 3-22.37 for details.)

RANGE AND PENETRATION

B-77. The minimum engagement range is 65 meters, and the maximum range is 2,000 meters. Engagement areas in urban terrain should be developed to ensure the Javelin achieves this minimum arming distance. In the top-attack mode, the missile strikes the thinner armor on the top of an armored vehicle rather than the thicker frontal and side armor plates. Top attack also prevents an enemy target from protecting itself by moving behind frontal cover. When used in urban areas or where obstacles might interfere with the top-attack flight path of the missile, the Javelin can also be fired in the direct-attack mode.

B-78. Penetration of urban targets does not mean a concurrent destruction of the structural integrity of a position. When engaging a position in a building, gunners should normally use the direct-attack mode to hit the target. When engaging a position or bunker in the open, use either attack mode.

DEAD SPACE

B-79. Few areas in most urban environments permit fires much beyond the minimum arming distance. Ground-level long-range fires down streets or rail lines and across parks or plazas are possible. The Javelin may be effective from the upper stories or roofs of buildings to fire into other buildings. The Javelin gunner should take into consideration the targeting dead space that is sometimes caused by the background of the target and its heat signature. When firing from the upper stories of a building towards the ground, the missile seeker sometimes cannot discriminate between the target and surrounding rubble, buildings, or paving if that background material has the same temperature as the target.

BACKBLAST

B-80. The Javelin's soft-launch capability enables the gunner to fire from within an enclosed area with a reduced danger from backblast overpressure or flying debris. Personnel within the enclosure should still wear appropriate protective gear.

B-81. When firing a Javelin from inside a room—
- Select a building of sturdy construction.
- Ensure ceiling height is at least 7 feet and floor size is at least 15 by 12 feet.
- Ensure window opening is at least 5 square feet.
- Ensure at least 20 square feet of ventilation, preferably to the rear of the weapon. An open 7- by 3-foot door provides minimum ventilation.
- Remove all glass from windows and all small, loose objects from the room.
- Clean the room of debris and wet the floors to prevent dust and dirt (kicked up by the backblast) from obscuring the vision of other Soldiers in the room.
- Allow sufficient room for the missile container to extend beyond the enclosure.
- Ensure all personnel in the room are forward of the rear of the weapon.
- Ensure a clearance of 6 inches between the launch tube and the firing aperture.

TOW MISSILE

B-82. The TOW missile, especially when using the Bunker Buster missile, is extremely effective against fortified positions. Within urban areas, it is best employed along major thoroughfares and from the upper stories of buildings to attain long-range fields of fire. (See FM 3-22.34 for details.)

PENETRATION

B-83. The TOW missile can penetrate and destroy heavily armored tanks. All TOW missiles can defeat triple sandbagged walls, double layers of earth-filled 55-gallon drums, and 18-inch log walls. The shaped-charge warhead produces relatively little spall. Enemy personnel not standing directly behind or near the point of impact of a TOW missile may escape injury. Available TOW missiles include the—
- **Basic TOW.** The basic TOW missile can penetrate 8 feet of packed earth, 4 feet of reinforced concrete, or 16 inches of steel plate.
- **TOW Bunker Buster.** The TOW bunker buster missile can create an entry hole into a room. It can also neutralize enemy personnel and equipment in a room when fired through an opening and detonated on the back wall. The subsequent thermobaric effects inside a room are devastating. The fragmentation of the titanium warhead case renders the room(s) useless as a fighting position and destroys any enemy personnel within the blast radius. A single TOW Bunker Buster missile creates a 22-inch hole in 8-inch double reinforced concrete. It completely destroys an 8- by 8-foot cinder block wall. Firing a second TOW Bunker Buster missile below the first creates a breach hole in the wall.
- **TOW 2B.** The TOW 2B missile flies over the target and fires onto the thinner top vehicle armor. Because of this feature, the TOW 2B missile cannot be used to attack nonmetallic structural targets. Gunners must avoid firing directly over friendly vehicles, disabled vehicles, or large metal objects.

DEAD SPACE

B-84. Three aspects of dead space that affect the firing of TOW missiles are—
- **Arming Distance.** The TOW missile has a minimum arming distance of 65 meters, which can limit its use in urban areas. As a result, EAs in urban terrain must be developed. Ground-level, long-range fires down streets or rail lines and across parks or plazas are possible. The TOW missiles may be used from upper stories or roofs of buildings to fire into other buildings.
- **Maximum Depression and Elevation.** The maximum depression and elevation limits of the ITAS mount could result in dead space and preclude the engagements of close targets. A TOW ITAS crew located any higher than the sixth floor of a building cannot engage a target at the

minimum arming range due to maximum depression limits. At 100 meters, the TOW ITAS crew can be as high as the ninth floor and still engage the target (figure B-7).

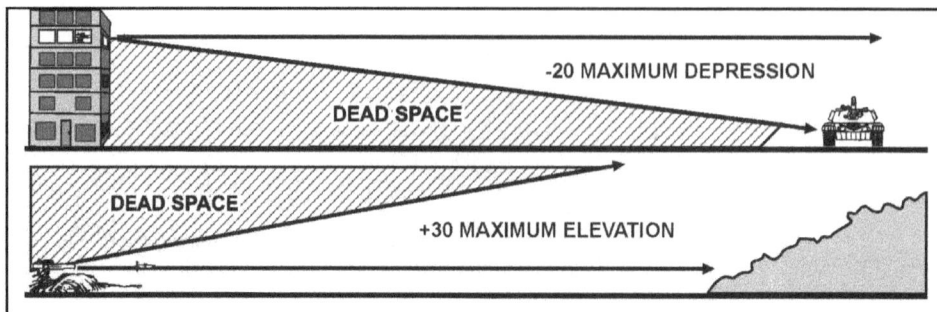

Figure B-7. TOW ITAS maximum elevation and depression limitation

- **Backblast.** This is more of a concern during combat in urban areas than in open country. The backblast can pick up and throw any loose rubble in the caution zone. The channeling effect of walls and narrow streets is even more pronounced due to the greater backblast. If the TOW missile backblast strikes a wall at an angle, it can pick up debris or be deflected and cause injury to unprotected personnel. When firing a TOW missile from inside buildings, all personnel should wear appropriate protection (figure B-8).

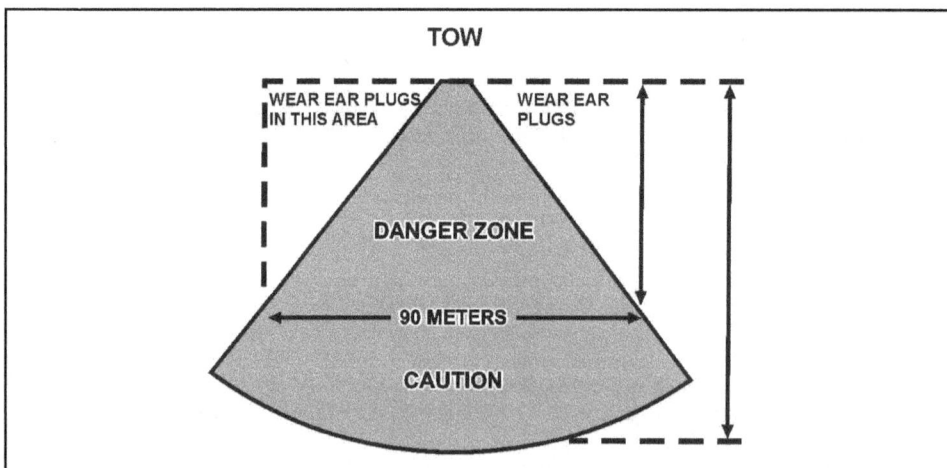

Figure B-8. TOW missile backblast in an open street

B-85. When firing a TOW missile from inside a room—

- Select a building of sturdy construction.
- Ensure ceiling height is at least 7 feet. Ensure floor size is at least 15 by 15 feet.
- Ensure at least 20 square feet of ventilation (room openings), preferably to the rear of the weapon. An open 7- by 3-foot door provides minimum ventilation.
- Remove all glass from windows and all small loose objects from the room.
- Clean the room of debris and wet the floors to prevent dust and dirt (kicked up by the backblast) from obscuring the vision of other Soldiers in the room.
- Ensure all personnel in the room are forward of the rear of the weapon.
- Ensure a clearance of 9 inches between the launch tube and the firing aperture.

OBSTACLES

B-86. An obstacle is any object that can interfere with TOW missile flight. Maintain at least 3.5 feet (1 meter) of vertical clearance over obstacles. Other obstacles for TOW missiles include—

- **Water.** Firing across bodies of water wider than 1,100 meters can reduce the range of the TOW missile. Signals being sent through the command-link wires are shorted out when a large amount of wire is submerged in water. If the range is less than 1,100 meters, the missile's range is not affected. Maximum and limited firing ranges over water vary according to missile type. A TOW missile position should be as high above and as far back from the water as the tactical situation allows.
- **Electrical Power Lines.** Firing over power, street car, and electric train lines may cause the command-link wires to make contact with live high-voltage power lines. If this occurs, personnel can be injured, control of the missile can be lost, and the launcher electronics may be damaged.
- **Windy Conditions.** Gusty, flanking, or quartering winds can cause the launch tube to vibrate and spoil the tracking performance. Strong winds can be present around tall buildings. Erecting a windscreen next to the launcher helps to reduce this problem. Strong winds can move the missile around during flight, but the weapon system itself can compensate for wind effects as long as the crosshairs are kept on the center mass of the target.
- **Smoke and Area Fires.** Smoke can obscure the line of sight and hide the target when using the daysight. When obscuration is encountered, the gunner should switch to the night vision sight mode. Fire can burn through the command-link wire, causing loss of control of the missile. The gunner should avoid firing through fire and over fires if there is a possibility that the wires will contact the fire before missile impact.

SECTION V – VEHICULAR WEAPON SYSTEMS

B-87. This section discusses five armored vehicles capable of providing supporting direct fire during UO: M1 Abrams tank, Stryker MGS, BFV, Stryker ICV, and MRAP vehicle. The breaching effects of each of these armored vehicles, especially the 120-mm tank cannon, are major assets to Infantry fighting in urban areas.

M1 ABRAMS TANK

B-88. The M1-series tank has excellent cross-country mobility, sophisticated communications, enhanced target acquisition, lethal firepower, and effective armor protection. In combination, these factors produce the shock effect that allows units with M1 tanks to close with and destroy the enemy in most weather and light conditions.

ARMAMENT

B-89. The M1 tank is armed with three types of weapons:

- **Main Gun.** The tank's main gun can only depress to -10 degrees and elevate to +20 degrees, which creates considerable dead space at the close ranges. The lower depression limit creates a 35-foot (10.8-meter) dead space around the tank. On a 16-meter-wide street, this dead space extends to the buildings on each side (figure B-9). Similarly, there is a zone overhead in which the tank cannot fire (figure B-10). This offers ideal locations for enemy short-range antiarmor weapons. It also exposes the tank's most vulnerable areas: the flanks, rear, and top. Infantry should provide close protection. The M1-series tanks also have a blind spot caused by the 0-degree of depression available over the rear deck. To engage targets in this area, the tank must pivot to orient the main gun over either side of the vehicle.
- **Coaxial Machine Gun.** The coaxial machine gun is aligned with the main gun by way of a machine gun mount near the breech ring. It is sighted and fired from either the gunner's station or the commander's station in the same manner as the main gun.

- **Flexible Machine Guns.** The commander's M2 and the loader's M240 machine gun can elevate to +36 degrees. However, on the M1A2 System Enhancement Package, both weapons must be fired from the open hatch position. On the M1A1, the loader's machine gun must be fired from the open hatch position.

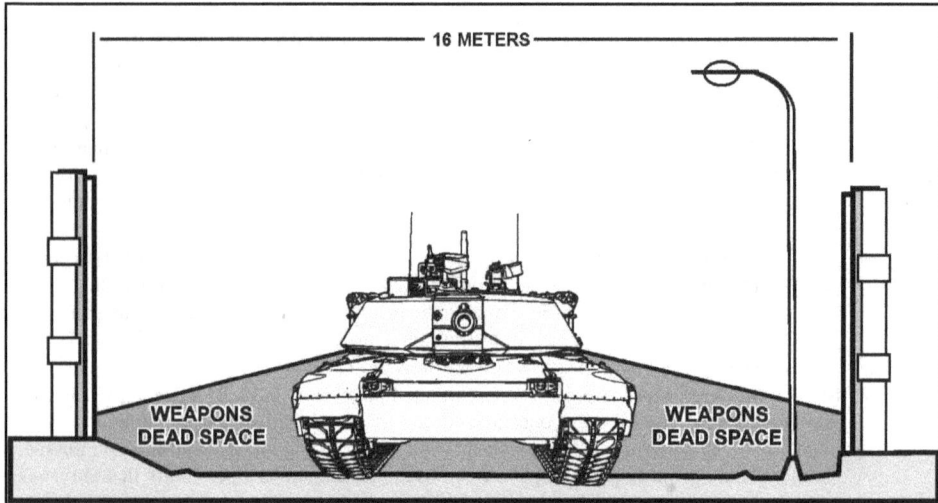

Figure B-9. Dead space at street level

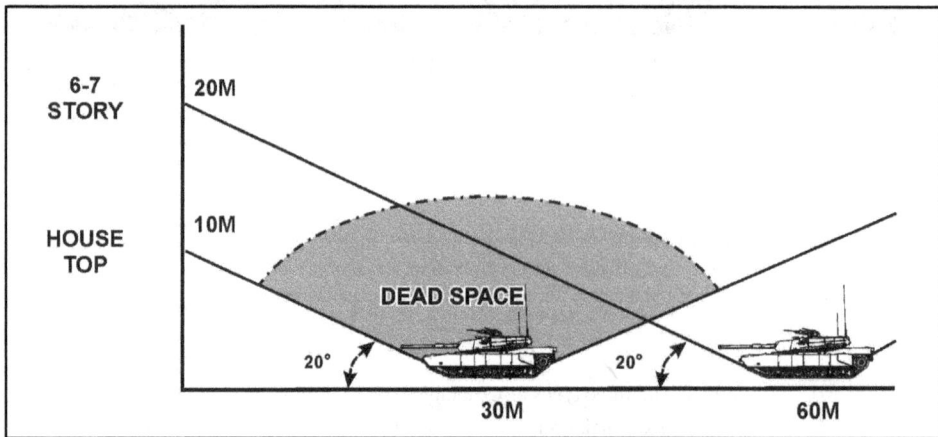

Figure B-10. Dead space above street level

EFFECTS

B-90. Effects are broken down into categories of weapon effects and one category of mechanical effects.

Weapons Effects

B-91. Weapons effects are described below.

Armor-Piercing Fin-Stabilized Discarding Sabot with Tracer

B-92. The armor-piercing fin-stabilized discarding sabot with tracer (APFSDS-T) round works best against armored vehicles. It operates by utilizing kinetic energy. Therefore, the round does not need to arm. Because of this, the round can be fired at almost any range. The APFSDS-T round can penetrate deeply into a structure but does not create as large a hole or displace as much spall behind the target.

High-Explosive Antitank with Tracer

B-93. The HEAT round arms within 30 meters. On a 16-meter-wide street, HEAT ammunition does not arm quickly enough to engage a structure directly perpendicular to the direction of travel. However, a HEAT round fired at a structure less than 30 meters away still provides some kinetic effects, to include casualties inside the building. The effectiveness of unarmed HEAT rounds is unpredictable and highly variable. When armed, the HEAT round creates a larger hole in reinforced concrete or masonry structures than the other rounds.

B-94. The HEAT round also has an anti-helicopter capability. It is most effective against masonry walls. One HEAT round normally creates a breach hole in all but the thickest masonry construction. A single round demolishes walls constructed with brick veneer or wood frame. However, the HEAT round cannot cut all the reinforcing rods, which are often left in place, hindering entry.

Multipurpose Antitank with Tracer

B-95. The MPAT-T round is effective against urban structures and arms approximately 30 meters from the muzzle of the gun. It effectively penetrates structures even when unarmed. The effectiveness of the MPAT-T round against heavy armor is limited to attacks from the side and rear and could result in a mobility kill. The MPAT-T projectile is effective against light armored vehicles. A consideration when using the MPAT-T round in an urban environment is the proximity fuze. The proximity fuze sometimes functions prior to the intended target, causing a premature detonation and possible unintended damages.

B-96. The MPAT-T is effective against buildings with wooden walls over 1-inch thick. Impact against a thinner wall structure (plywood sheathing without striking supporting members) may produce only a small hole as the projectile passes through the wall without detonating if the fuze is set to ground mode. Impact against a supporting structure (roof rafter or wall stud) causes detonation of the warhead, a subsequent hole, and lethal fragmentation effects to personnel located inside. Impact against concrete walls yield holes of about 24 inches in diameter, but reinforcing bars embedded within the concrete are not likely to be cleared from the hole unless struck directly.

B-97. The MPAT projectile is extremely effective against earthen, timber, and sandbag bunkers. The projectile tends to bury itself into the bunker structure before warhead detonation. When this occurs, the detonation produces lethal effects to personnel within the structure as well as a highly destructive effect to the bunker structure itself. When switched to the "A" or "air" mode, the MPAT-T round is effective against helicopters. Its proximity fuze can produce kills without actually impacting the aircraft. If the projectile is on a direct-impact flight path, the proximity fuze may function, but it detonates when the projectile strikes a solid part of the helicopter.

High-Explosive Obstacle Reducing with Tracer

B-98. The high-explosive obstacle reducing with tracer (HE-OR-T) round is effective against urban structures and arms approximately 30 meters from the muzzle of the gun. It effectively penetrates structures even when unarmed. The HE-OR-T round has a rubbling capability.

B-99. The HE-OR-T projectile is effective against concrete obstacles. The projectile penetrates several inches before the warhead detonates. This penetration fractures the concrete obstacle from within, breaking it into smaller blocks, which can be cleared with a bulldozer blade.

Canister Round

B-100.   The canister round is primarily used in an antipersonnel role against troops in the open. It can also be used in an antimaterial role to defeat nonarmored vehicles and surfaced laid obstacles, such as concertina wire.

Mechanical Breaching

B-101. The tank is effective at breaching reinforced doors, fences, or walls to create entry points by ramming. To breach structures, it is recommended that the front hull be used to make head-on contact with the structure. However, unless a blade or other externally mounted attachment is used, the headlights and fenders will be damaged. Care should be taken to avoid covering the driver's vision ports with rubble. Also, avoid using the rear of the tank as the grille and external phone are easily damaged by rubble.

PROTECTION

B-102. Tank cannons create an overpressure and noise hazard to exposed Soldiers. All dismounted Soldiers should wear appropriate protection and avoid the tank's frontal 60-degree arc during firing. The overpressure from the tank's 120-mm cannon can kill a dismounted Soldier within a 90-degree arc extending from the muzzle of the gun tube out to 200 meters.

B-103. Discarding sabot petals, including those on MPAT and HE-OR-T rounds, endanger accompanying Infantry elements. They create a hazard area from 200 to 1,000 meters along a tank's line of fire on a frontage of about 400 meters. Dismounted Infantry must be aware of the danger from discarding sabot petals, which can kill or seriously injure exposed personnel (figure 8-3, chapter 8).

STRYKER MOBILE GUN SYSTEM

B-104. The MGS provides direct supporting fires to Infantry squads during the assault. Its function is to destroy or suppress hardened enemy bunkers, machine gun positions, and sniper positions and to create breach points in urban, restricted, and open rolling terrain. The MGS is not a tank and should not be employed in the same manner as a tank. The MGS optic system is extremely valuable in detecting the slightest change to the environment, to include recent holes, debris, wire, and IEDs.

ARMAMENT

B-105. Table B-8 shows the effective ranges of the MGS weapons systems. The MGS is armed with three weapons:

- **Main Gun**. The MGS has a weapons dead space similar to the tank (figure B-11). The MGS 105-mm main gun uses four primary rounds—APFSDS-T, high-explosive antitank with tracer (HEAT-T), high-explosive plastic with tracer (HEP-T), and canister.
- **Coaxial Machine Gun**. This machine gun is aligned with the main gun.
- **Flexible Machine Gun**. This machine gun has the best elevation. However, the firer must expose himself to fire it.

Table B-8. Effective ranges of the mobile gun system weapons systems

Weapon System	Effective Range
105-mm main gun	2,000 meters
7.62-mm coaxial machine gun	900 meters
.50-caliber flexible machine gun	1,800 meters

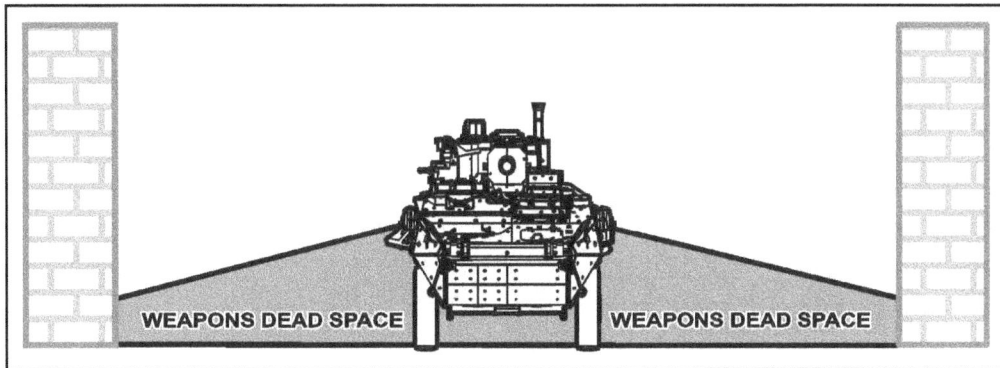

Figure B-11. Mobile gun system dead space at street level

EFFECTS

B-106. For UO, the primary desired effects are creating an entry point into a structure, destroying a strongpoint, and destroying personnel or light material.

Creating an Entry Point

B-107. The HEP-T round is the primary round against field fortifications, bunkers, buildings, crew-served weapon emplacements, and troops where blast concussion and fragmentation are desired with secondary armor defeating capabilities. It damages buildings due to its blast overpressure and concussion and creates casualties due to its fragmentation. It has a secondary use of creating Infantry breach points. It is effective at opening a hole (22 to 27 inches in diameter) in 8-inch double reinforced concrete. The HEP-T round arms between 11 and 17 meters. Four rounds of HEP-T are needed to create an Infantry entry point measuring 30 by 50 inches in an 8-inch thick wall.

Destroying a Strongpoint

B-108. Firing two MGS rounds, one HEAT and one HEP-T, is best to destroy a basic bunker. A more advanced bunker may require additional rounds. The first round fired is the HEAT. The HEAT round displaces more of the typical covering material used to reinforce and conceal most bunkers. The jet stream produced by the round provides more incapacitation to the inhabitants than the HEP-T round. The second round fired is a HEP-T round into the hole created by the HEAT round to destroy the bunker.

Destroying Personnel or Light Material

B-109. The M1040 canister round is the primary round for defeating troops in the open. It has a secondary, anti-materiel role to defeat light walls, unarmored vehicles, and surfaced laid obstacles. The canister round has no minimum arming range. It spreads approximately 2 meters in height and width for every 10 meters in range.

PROTECTION

B-110. Discarding sabot petals endanger accompanying Infantry elements. They create a hazard area from 200 to 1,000 meters along the MGS line of fire on a frontage of about 140 meters. Dismounted Infantry must be aware of the danger from discarding sabot petals, which can kill or seriously injure exposed personnel. Additionally, MGS cannons create an overpressure and noise hazard to exposed Soldiers. All dismounted Soldiers should wear appropriate protection and avoid the MGS's frontal 60-degree arc during firing (figure B-12).

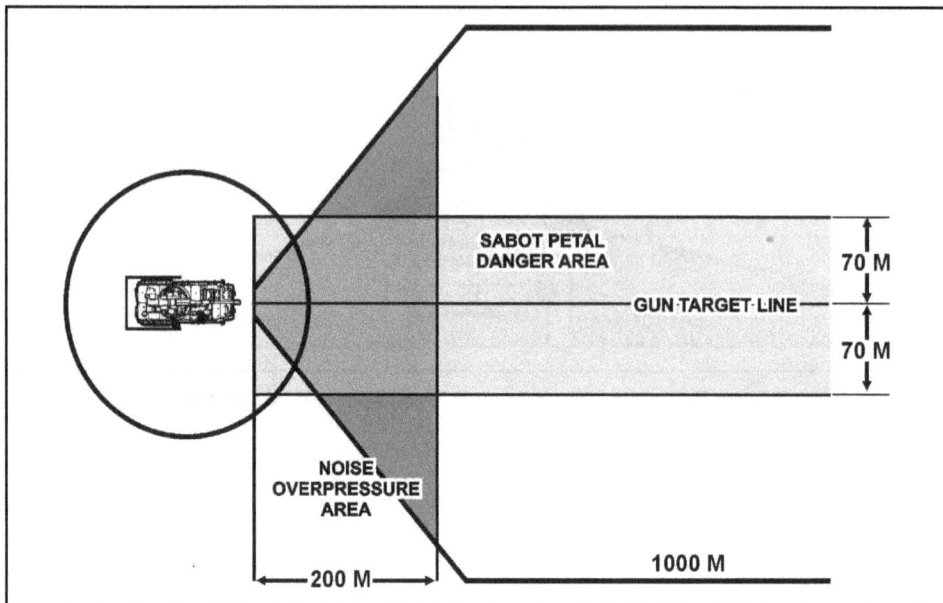

Figure B-12. Danger areas around a mobile gun system firing a 105-mm main gun

BRADLEY FIGHTING VEHICLE

B-111. The primary role of the BFV during combat in urban areas is to provide suppressive fire and to breach exterior walls and fortifications. It can also protect Soldiers when they move during UO.

ARMAMENT

B-112. The armament of the BFV consists of a 25-mm main gun, the 7.62-mm coaxial machine gun, and TOW missile launcher.

- **Main Gun.** The 25-mm automatic chain gun is an effective weapon for urban combat. The BFV can elevate its 25-mm gun to +60 degrees but can only depress to -10 degrees, which like the M1 creates considerable dead space at street level. On a 12-meter-wide street, this dead space will extend one to two meters form the buildings on each side (figure B-13). Similarly, there is a zone overhead in which the BFV cannot fire (figure B-14). The 25-mm gun fires—
  - Three combat rounds—APFSDS-T, armor-piercing discarding sabot with tracer (APDS-T), and high-explosive incendiary with tracer (HEI-T).
  - Two training rounds—target practice with tracer (TP-T) and target practice discarding sabot with tracer (TPDS-T).
- **Machine Gun.** The 7.62-mm coaxial machine gun is used to engage dismounted infantry, crew-served weapons, antitank guided missile teams, RPG launcher teams, thin-skinned vehicles, and lightly constructed positions. (See the earlier section on medium and heavy machine guns for information on the M240 machine gun.)
- **TOW Missile.** See section IV for the capabilities of the TOW missile.

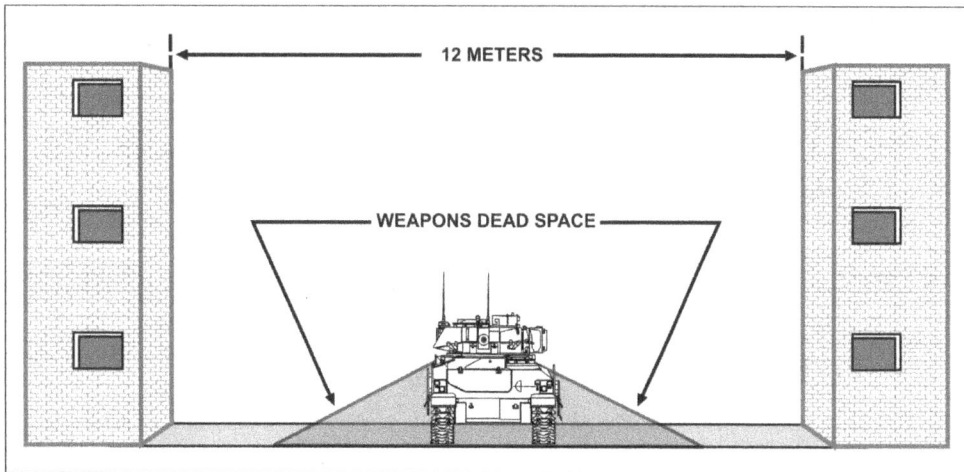

Figure B-13. BFV street level dead space

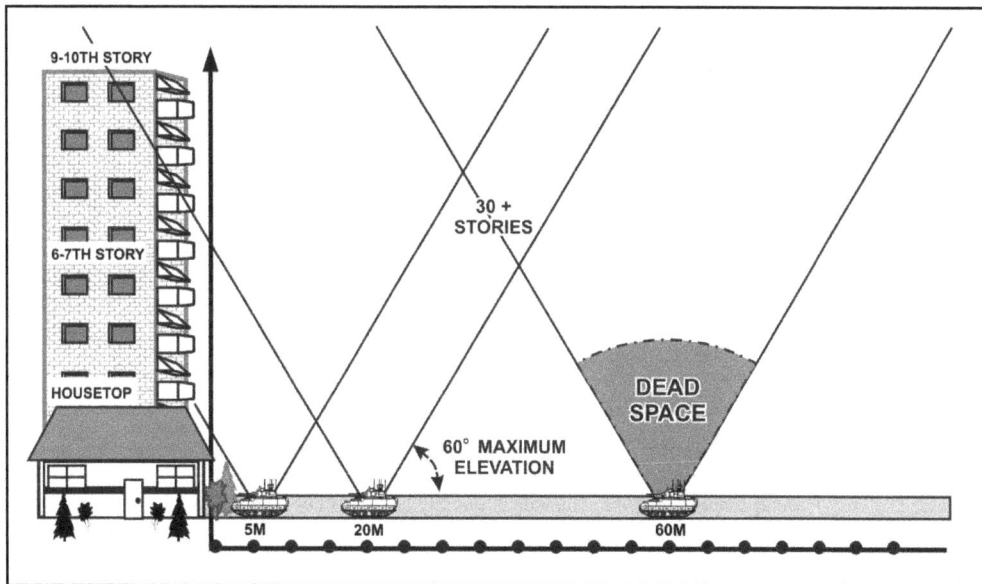

Figure B-14. BFV above street dead space

EFFECTS

B-113. Although the penetration achieved by the three combat rounds differ slightly, all are eventually effective. However, the target practice with tracer training round is significantly more effective against urban structures, although it has little utility against enemy armored vehicles. Soldiers should consider using more effective weapons before expending large amounts of 25-mm ammunition to breach walls.

Armor-Piercing Discarding Sabot with Tracer Round

B-114. The APDS-T and APFSDS-T rounds are similar. The major difference is the APFSDS-T is fin stabilized and contains depleted uranium. They both penetrate urban targets by retaining their kinetic energy and blasting a small hole deep into the target. The APDS-T round gives the best effects behind the wall, and the armor-piercing core often breaks into two or three fragments, which can create multiple casualties. The APDS-T needs as few as four rounds to begin achieving lethal results behind a wall. Table B-9 explains the number of APDS-T rounds needed to create different size holes in common urban walls.

Table B-9. Breaching effects of APDS-T rounds on urban walls

Target	Loophole	Breach Hole
3-inch brick wall at 0-degree obliquity	22 rounds	75 rounds
3-inch brick wall at 45-degree obliquity	22 rounds	35 rounds
8-inch reinforced concrete at 0-degree obliquity	22 rounds	75 rounds*
8-inch reinforced concrete at 45-degree obliquity	22 rounds	40 rounds*
* Reinforcing rods still in place.		
Note. Obliquity tends to increase the amount of wall material removed.		

B-115. When firing single rounds, the APDS-T round provides the greatest capability for behind-the-wall incapacitation. The APDS-T round can penetrate over 16 inches of reinforced concrete with enough energy left to cause enemy casualties. It penetrates through both sides of a wood frame or brick veneer building. The APDS-T round easily penetrates field fortifications. Table B-10 explains the number of APDS-T rounds needed to create different size holes in common bunkers.

Table B-10. Breaching effects of APDS-T rounds on bunkers

Bunker Type	Penetration	Loophole	Small Breach Hole
36-inch sand or timber at 0-degree obliquity	1 round	25 rounds	40 rounds
36-inch sand or 6-inch concrete at 0-degree obliquity	6 rounds	6 rounds	20 rounds

Armor-Piercing Fin-Stabilized Discarding Sabot with Tracer Round

B-116. The APFSDS-T round contains depleted uranium. The depleted uranium is only used in combat and should be reserved for defeating enemy armor and not for penetrating urban targets. The APFSDS-T round can be used to penetrate urban structures, but should only be used as a last option due to the dangers associated with depleted uranium in urban areas. Its effects are nearly identical to the APDS-T and are covered above under the APDS-T.

High-Explosive Incendiary with Tracer Round

B-117. The HEI-T round does not provide single-round perforation or incapacitating fragments on any external masonry structural wall. It can create first-round fragments behind wood frame and brick veneer walls. The HEI-T round cannot penetrate a bunker as quickly as the APDS-T round, but it can create more damage inside the bunker once the external earth has been stripped away. Against a heavy bunker, about 40 rounds of HEI-T are needed to strip away the external earth shielding and breach the inner lining of concrete or timber. The HEI-T round is also useful for suppression against known or suspected firing ports, such as doors, windows, and loopholes.

B-118. The HEI-T round penetrates urban targets by blasting away chunks of material. The HEI-T round does not penetrate an urban target as well as the APDS-T, but it creates the effect of stripping away a greater amount of material for each round. The HEI-T does more damage to an urban target when fired in multiple short bursts because the accumulative impact of multiple rounds is greater than the sum of individual rounds. Table B-11 explains the number of HEI-T rounds needed to create different size holes in brick or concrete.

Table B-11. Number of HEI-T rounds needed to create different size holes in brick or concrete

Target	Loophole	Breach Hole
3-inch brick wall at 0-degree obliquity	10 rounds	20 rounds
3-inch brick wall at 45-degree obliquity	20 rounds	25 rounds
8-inch reinforced concrete at 0-degree obliquity	15 rounds	25 rounds
8-inch reinforced concrete at 45-degree obliquity	15 rounds	30 rounds

B-119. The 25-mm gun has different effects when fired against different urban targets. The impact of the 25-mm gun on typical urban targets is often magnified if the firing is in short bursts. At close ranges, the gunner should shift his point of aim in a spiral pattern to ensure that the second and third bursts enlarge the hole. Even without burst fire, sustained 25-mm gunfire can defeat almost all urban targets.

Reinforced Concrete Walls

B-120. Reinforced concrete walls, which are 12 to 20 inches thick, are relatively easy to penetrate, fracture, and clear away the concrete. However, the steel reinforcing rods, normally 3/4 inch thick and 6 to 8 inches apart, often remain in place. This creates a "jail window" effect that prevents entry but allows grenades or rifle fire to be placed behind the wall. There is no quick way of cutting these steel rods. Although, they can be cut with demolition charges, cutting torches, or special power saws.

Brick Walls

B-121. The 25-mm gun defeats brick walls regardless of their thickness.

Bunker Walls

B-122. The 25-mm gun is devastating when fired against sandbag bunker walls. Obliquity has the least affect on the penetration of bunker walls. Bunkers with earth walls up to 36 inches thick are easily penetrated. At short ranges typical of combat in urban areas, defeating most bunkers is easy, especially if the 25-mm gun can fire at an aperture.

PROTECTION

B-123. The APDS-T round creates a hazardous situation for exposed personnel because of the discarding pieces of sabot that are thrown off the round. These discarding pieces could injure or kill personnel not under cover forward of the 25-mm gun's muzzle and within the danger zone. Crew members must consider the safety of the Soldiers on the ground prior to firing any ammunition with discarding sabot projectiles (figure B-15). The danger zone extends at an angle of about 10 degrees below the muzzle level, out to at least 200 meters, and about 30 degrees left and right of the muzzle.

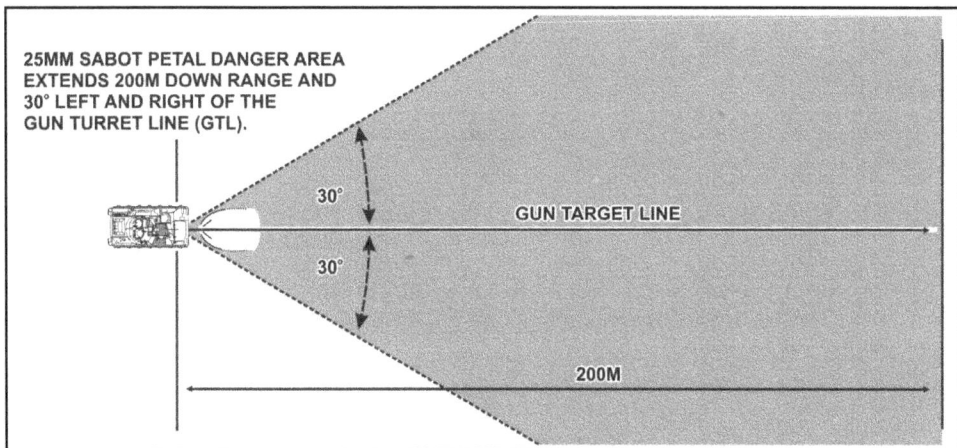

Figure B-15. Sabot petal danger area

B-124. The TOW weapon system has a backblast area that extends 75 meters to the rear of the vehicle in a 90-degree cone (figure B-16). This area comprises both a 50-meter danger zone and an additional 25-meter caution zone. The Bradley must be positioned so that no personnel, unarmored vehicles, or obstructions (such as walls, embankments, or large trees) remain in the backblast area for its missile.

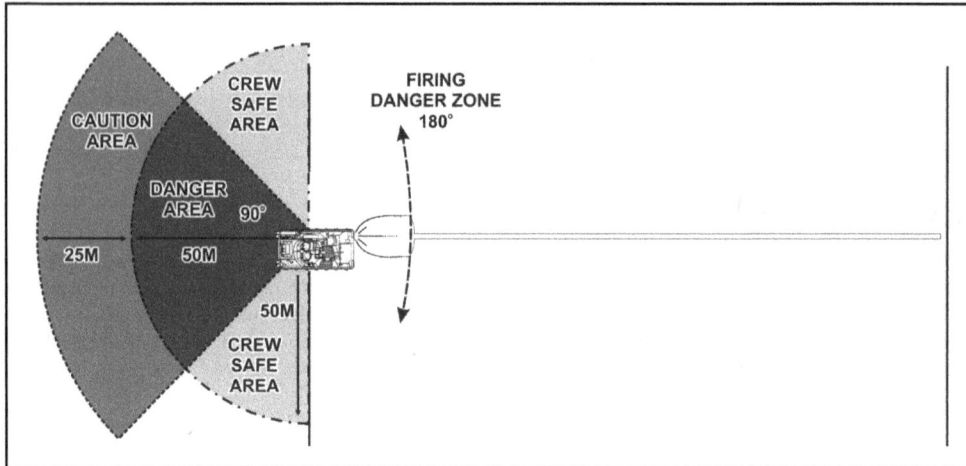

Figure B-16. Danger zone

STRYKER INFANTRY CARRIER VEHICLE

B-125. The ICV can support the Infantry with suppressive fire and provide protection by negating the effects of enemy small-arms weapons, either by driving Soldiers up to a building or by acting as a shield while the Infantry moves behind it along a street.

ARMAMENT

B-126. The main armament of the ICV is the remote weapon system, which accommodates either an MK19 40-mm grenade machine gun or a .50-caliber HB M2 machine gun. Both weapons can be controlled under the vehicle's protective armor.

EFFECTS

B-127. See the earlier section on heavy machine guns and grenades.

PROTECTION

B-128. While the ICV is not vulnerable to small-arms weapons, it is vulnerable to most other weapons systems, particularly antitank weapons.

MINE RESISTANT AMBUSH PROTECTED VEHICLE

B-129. The MRAP vehicle's mission role is similar to the Stryker in many respects. MRAP provides small units with protected mobility and mounted firepower. Squads and platoons use MRAP vehicles to conduct both mounted and dismounted missions. (See Center for Army Lessons Learned [CALL], Handbook No. 11-11 and TC 7-31 for details.)

ARMAMENT

B-130. Armament may include an M2 50-caliber heavy machine gun, MK-19 automatic grenade launcher, or M240 medium machine gun.

EFFECTS

B-131. See the earlier section on heavy machine guns and grenades.

PROTECTION

B-132. MRAP is designed for the distinct purpose of increasing the protection of Soldiers against small-arms fire and the detonation of mines or IEDs employed singularly or in combination. With increased protection, an MRAP vehicle can reduce its standoff to potential threats or move through potential danger areas when METT-TC dictate the increased risk.

B-133. Units successfully employ MRAP vehicles by understanding the vehicle's capabilities and limitations while integrating protection with training to standard, detailed planning, smart tactics, and well-rehearsed drills. MRAP vehicles operate under the full spectrum of weather and terrain conditions, to include limited off-road operation across firm soil and obstacles such as debris.

B-134. Exiting the vehicle in response to an ambush and loading or unloading equipment and casualties are difficult due to the steps and back hatch on some MRAP variants. Units must train and rehearse individuals and teams to streamline the process for mounting and dismounting operations under various conditions, especially in an emergency.

B-135. The field of view from the armored windows is limited for Soldiers, which results in blind spots and overall poor visibility.

WARNING

Operating on single-lane and/or steeply crowned rural roads, roads with no shoulders, roads with soft shoulders and/or washouts around culverts, and especially any road bordering water (such as canal, irrigation ditch, or pond) requires extreme caution. The majority of MRAP vehicle rollovers are due to road, shoulder, or bridge approaches giving way under the MRAP vehicle's weight and high center of gravity.

B-136. Trafficability studies/products must be available to the leaders and Soldiers operating MRAP vehicles. They can factor AO-specific trafficability and terrain limitations into their composite risk management and combat planning processes.

SECTION VI – INDIRECT FIRE WEAPONS

B-137. This section discusses mortars, artillery, and naval gunfire effectiveness in urban areas. HE fragmentation is the most commonly used round. White phosphorus is effective in starting fires in buildings and forcing the enemy out of cellars and light-frame buildings. It is also the most effective mortar round against dug-in tanks. Even near misses blind and suppress the tank crew, forcing them to close their hatches. GPS-enhanced munitions, such as the 155-mm Excalibur HE and guided MLRS unitary HE warhead rounds may be employed against well-located targets. Their near-vertical attack trajectories make them suitable for employment in urban terrain.

GENERAL

B-138. While mortars and artillery are clearly different as indirect fire weapons, they do share common considerations. The considerations are described below.

DEAD SPACE

B-139. Enemy targets on the far side of buildings cannot be effectively engaged if they are in the dead space created by the height of the building. As a general principle, the size of this dead space is half the height of the building for mortars (high-angle fire) and five times the height of the building for artillery (low-angle fire). By firing at maximum elevation, the size of this dead space can be reduced to about half, but it cannot be eliminated.

CREST

B-140. A crest is a terrain feature of such altitude (tall buildings) that it restricts fires into an area. It may limit the minimum elevation of a weapon, create dead space, or both. (See FM 6-40 for details.) These features can interfere with a round's trajectory, especially low-angle fire, causing premature impact, detonation, or round deflection.

OBSERVATION

B-141. Observation in urban terrain is severely restricted. Enemy targets are often only visible when they are within one block of the observer or on the same street as the observer. Positions in tall buildings can provide long-range observation but normally only from the tops of buildings. To engage the enemy, the forward observer should be positioned well forward. Many fire missions are either on streets that lead up to friendly positions or on targets that are within one block of the observer or friendly positions. Select and construct positions with the understanding that probable errors associated with indirect fire occasionally cause rounds to strike the top or rear of any nearby tall buildings.

Shapes of Targets

B-142. The three basic shapes of targets in urban terrain are—

- **Point.** Point targets are less than 200 meters wide. They are the most common type of target due to the restricted sight lines, the use of street intersections as adjustment points, and the typical kill zones being no wider than a single street or building. Point targets can be engaged by a single gun, a section, or platoon. Using a high rate of fire from a single tube puts a higher percentage of rounds in a small target area as opposed to using the same number of rounds from multiple tubes. Maximum effect, however, can be achieved through accurate initial and massed fires that surprise and shock the enemy.
- **Linear.** Linear targets are more than 200 meters but less than 600 meters long. In UO, they typically occur along streets. Due to the layout of the streets, they are normally either perpendicular or parallel to the gun-target line. However, occasionally they approach at some other angle. For linear targets, the forward observer includes the attitude of the target with the call for fire. The fire direction center may have to issue separate gun data to each tube to orient the sheaf correctly to bring effective fire on the target.
- **Area.** Area targets are not as common in urban terrain as point or linear targets. However, area targets are common for parks, plazas, or other large open areas. They may also occur over a group of similar buildings where the enemy is suspected of massing or assembling their forces.

RUBBLING

B-143. Indirect fires may create unwanted rubble. Rubble can provide substantial cover for dismounted Soldiers and act as a severe obstacle to vehicular movement. The close proximity of friendly Soldiers requires careful coordination.

AMMUNITION

B-144. FM 3-09.32 contains extensive information on delivery systems and munitions available for them. When viewing this data from UO perspective, remember that the risk estimates are based on open field environment and must be adapted for the urban environment. The desired target area effects drive the FS effort. Planners first identify munitions that provide the desired effects and then select the delivery systems to deliver those munitions that minimize the undesired effects. Give special consideration to fuze and shell combinations when buildings and the ROE limit the effects of munitions.

FUZE TYPES

B-145. A fuze is a device to explode a projectile. Mortar and artillery fuzes have similar actions.

- **Proximity or Variable Time.** Proximity or variable time fuzes are radio-activated fuzes that detonate at a predetermined height of burst. Combined with an HE shell, they can clear enemy positions, observers, and antennas off building roofs. However, the varying heights of nearby buildings may cause the premature detonation of proximity fuzes.
- **Point Detonating.** Point detonating fuzes function on impact. They are effective against exposed personnel, unarmored vehicles, and light material. They are less effective against personnel under cover or in buildings.
- **Delay.** Delay fuzes function a set time after impact and are effective in penetrating walls or roofs of buildings before detonating.
- **Multi-Option.** Multi-option fuzes are manually set prior to firing and function in any one of the above categories.
- **Concrete Piercing.** Concrete piercing fuzes are used on artillery rounds to penetrate concrete and earth structures.

SHELL TYPES

B-146. Mortar and artillery shells fall into the same general categories described below.

High-Explosives

B-147. HEs are the most used type of indirect fire round during urban combat. They give good results against all lightly built structures. For more study structures, the 105-mm artillery and 120-mm mortar are best, while well-built reinforced concrete structures may require 155-mm artillery for maximum effectiveness.

B-148. Accurately adjusted, concentrated artillery fire (HE fuzed with quick and delay) at breach sites is effective in obstacle reduction. These fires significantly weaken wire obstacles with mines and booby traps. They do not significantly affect metal tetrahedrons or concrete dragon's teeth.

Family of Scatterable Mines

B-149. Use a family of scatterable mines to impede enemy movements. The effectiveness of a family of scatterable mines is reduced when delivered on a hard surface.

Illumination

B-150. The presence of buildings greatly influences the effects of illumination rounds. Deep canyons formed by buildings severely limit the effect and duration of illumination on the target even if properly placed. Use of illumination tends to favor the defender. Illumination rounds can ignite fires that may burn or smoke enemy out of buildings. Because of heat, the building may be unusable to the enemy for days. Consider the following effects before using illumination:

- Friendly casualties from stray rounds, large fires, and the impact of illumination round canisters.
- Effect on planned operations resulting from burning buildings or heavy smoke.
- Collateral damage and civilian casualties
- Limitations placed on the use of illumination by the ROE.
- Placement.
  - Behind the objective during the offense may put the enemy in shadows rather than in the light.
  - Behind friendly troops in the defense may put them in the shadows while placing the enemy troops in the light.

- Short duration of effective illumination because of the shadows produced by the buildings and the drift of the illumination round.

Infrared Illumination

B-151. Infrared illumination rounds significantly enhance the available level of light used by night observation devices. This allows friendly forces the capability to better negotiate terrain, improve targets acquisition, and to more effectively engage targets at night. Looking through night observation devices using infrared illumination rounds provides a clearer and sharper image of objects than observing with the naked eye using white light illumination rounds. Infrared illumination rounds also do not create enhanced areas of shadows as white light illumination rounds do. Rather, they only create areas where less infrared illumination is present.

Smoke

B-152. Smoke missions are vital in UO to provide obscuration for assaulting or withdrawing forces. Planners should account for the duration the smoke lasts when planning for white phosphorus smoke. It is important to remember that mortars use white or red phosphorus rounds for smoke missions. These rounds burn until all the oxygen in the immediate area or the phosphorus is exhausted. The man-made topographical relief of urban terrain reduces wind speed and increases atmosphere mixing. As such, smoke tends to persist longer and give greater coverage than in open terrain.

SPECIAL TARGETS

B-153. Certain targets, such as armored vehicles, the tops of buildings, and the front of buildings require special considerations to ensure effectiveness.

Armored Vehicles

B-154. While artillery fire can disable armored vehicles, it is difficult to hit an armored vehicle in urban terrain. Mortars also have difficulty hitting an armored vehicle and, except for the 120-mm mortar, cannot normally disable armored vehicles. Artillery and mortar fire can, however, be a combat multiplier when used with direct fire weapons. Indirect fire is effective in—

- Forcing the enemy to close their hatches during movement.
- Slowing the enemy's advance.
- Making it hard for the enemy to determine his exact location.
- Decreasing the probability the enemy sees obstacles or mines.
- Masking friendly antiarmor weapons fire against enemy armor.

Tops of Buildings

B-155. Enemy soldiers can be forced off building roofs by using HE rounds with proximity fuzes or, if rounds are prematurely detonating, time fuzes. When firing at the top or upper stories of buildings, the forward observer must provide the vertical interval. Enemy located in an attic or on the floor immediately below in mass construction buildings can be engaged with delay fuzes. Mass construction buildings have weak roofs and attic floors. Because these are point targets, use only one gun.

Fronts of Buildings

B-156. Enemy hasty positions or observers in the front side of buildings, or in a large open area in front of a building, can be engaged using proximity fuzes. Effectiveness depends on the amount of window surface. Shell fragments normally will not penetrate walls. Most casualties are caused by the secondary hazard of flying glass. For maximum effectiveness, the trajectory of the rounds should be the lowest point possible that clears the buildings along the gun-target line and enables the rounds to impact far enough down the building to hit the target. If the goal is to blow building fragments into the street to cause casualties, employ delay fuzes. The 60-mm mortar in the handheld mode can be effective against this type of target.

ANGLE OF FIRE

B-157. The angle of fall of indirect fire rounds tends to cause the rounds to impact on the roofs or upper stories of buildings. As such, the urban terrain greatly restricts low-angle artillery and naval fires because of overhead masking, which creates dead space behind buildings. High-angle fires are the normal method of engagement during combat in urban terrain. They can be fired by both mortar and field artillery weapons and are less affected by urban terrain due to their higher trajectory. For low-angle fire, dead space that cannot be struck is about five times the height of the building behind which the target sits. For high-angle fire, dead space is only about one-half the height of the building (figure B-17).

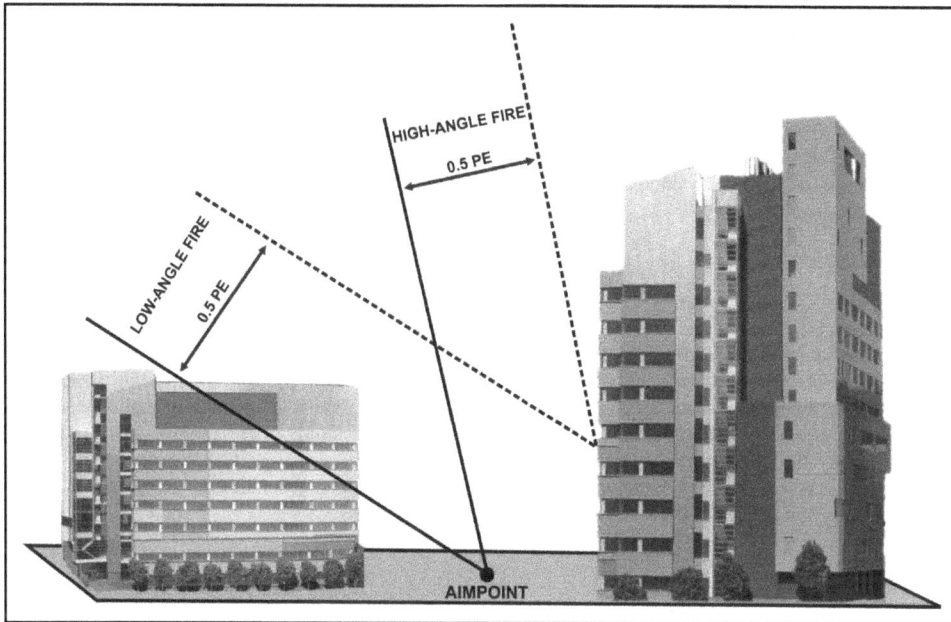

Figure B-17. High-angle and low-angle trajectories

MORTARS

B-158. Mortars are well suited for urban combat because of their high rate of fire, steep angle of fall, and short minimum range. Commanders should plan mortar support as part of the total FS system. (See FM 7-90 for details on the tactical employment of mortars.)

B-159. Mortar rounds that do not directly impact a structure, such as proximity fuzed rounds, cause minimal structural damage and few interior casualties. Proximity fuzes may detonate prematurely if the round passes too close to a building. As such, to be effective, rounds or their effects must penetrate the structure. Due to the high angle of mortar fire, the only practical structural target on a building is the roof. However, the structure can be affected by mortar hits on nearby ground. If the goal is to create building fragments or interdict personnel using select apertures, aerial burst can be of value.

B-160. The roofs of mid- and high-rise buildings are typically concrete, while the roofs of low-rise buildings are extremely varied. Concrete roofs are difficult to penetrate with mortar rounds. Mortar rounds with delay fuzes can penetrate the top floor. However, additional penetration is rare since each additional floor is also concrete. Roofs not made of concrete are easier to penetrate. Depending on the type of building construction material, mortar rounds can penetrate multiple floors, especially wood floors. Interior damage is significant in the room of impact but limited outside that room due to interior walls. Use HE delay fuzes for deeper penetration and to maximize interior effects. Use HE point detonating rounds to maximize the

Appendix B

effect against the structure. HE point detonating rounds are effective against flimsy construction, especially that found in shantytowns.

60-MM MORTAR

B-161. The 60-mm mortar has a limited effect on structural targets and cannot penetrate most rooftops even with a delay setting. The 60-mm round at terminal velocity and 0-degree obliquity is expected to penetrate nearly 4 inches of reinforced concrete. Fragments from 60-mm HE rounds landing as close as 10 feet away cannot penetrate a single sandbag layer or a single-layer brick wall. Normally, the blast will not collapse a properly constructed bunker but can cause structural damage. Normally, the 60-mm mortar will not crater a hard-surfaced road.

81-MM MORTAR

B-162. The 81-mm mortar has limited effect on structural targets and cannot significantly crater a hard-surfaced road. With a delay setting, the 81-mm round can penetrate the roofs of light buildings. The 81-mm round at terminal velocity and 0-degree obliquity is expected to penetrate up to 6 inches of reinforced concrete.

120-MM MORTAR

B-163. The 120-mm mortar is effective against structural targets. With a delay fuze setting, it can penetrate deep into a building and cause extensive damage. The 120-mm round at terminal velocity and 0-degree obliquity is expected to penetrate up to 12 inches of reinforced concrete. A minimum of 18 inches of packed earth or sand is needed to stop the fragments from a 120-mm HE round impacting 10 feet away. The effect of a direct hit from a 120-mm round is equivalent to almost 10 pounds of explosive material, which can crush fortifications built with commonly available materials. The 120-mm mortar round can create a large but shallow crater in a road surface, but it is not deep or steep-sided enough to block vehicular movement. However, craters can be deep enough to damage or destroy storm drain systems, water and gas pipes, and electrical or phone cables.

ARTILLERY

B-164. Artillery support is significant to the combined arms concept if the ROE allow its use. Use artillery rounds with delay fuzes to penetrate buildings and cause interior casualties or with variable time fuzes to clear rooftop observation and weapons positions with relatively little collateral damage. Use terminally guided rounds, such as the 155-mm Excalibur or guided MLRS munitions, to effectively destroy enemy occupied buildings while minimizing collateral damage. Artillery in the direct fire role is extremely effective in reducing strongpoints, breaching sturdy buildings, and isolating an objective. In other than high-intensity conditions, artillery typically employ terminally guided munitions to reduce collateral damage.

105-MM ARTILLERY ROUND

B-165. While the target effects of the 105-mm round are much less destructive than larger caliber weapons, it is still a valuable urban weapon. It will cause significant damage to buildings constructed with lightweight material and even penetrate single layer stone and brick walls or lightweight reinforced concrete.

155-MM ARTILLERY ROUND

B-166. Heavy artillery rounds are necessary to penetrate thick reinforced concrete, stone, or brick structures. Even with heavy artillery, large expenditures of ammunition are required to knock down buildings of any size. HE 155-mm rounds can penetrate up to 38 inches of brick and nonreinforced concrete and up to 28 inches of reinforced concrete with considerable damage beyond the wall. HE rounds with concrete-piercing fuzes provide an excellent means of penetrating strong reinforced concrete structures. One round can penetrate up to 46 inches. Five rounds are needed to create a 1.5-meter breach in a 1-meter-thick wall. About 10 rounds are needed to create such a breach in a wall 1.5 meters thick.

MULTIPLE LAUNCH ROCKET SYSTEM GUIDED UNITARY ROCKET

B-167. The M31A1 guided MLRS unitary rocket contains a 200 pound class preformed fragmentation warhead and has a range of 15 to 70+ kilometers. The combination of range, accuracy, and fuze settings allows this rocket to be effective in an urban environment with low collateral damage.

ARTILLERY DIRECT FIRE

B-168. Self-propelled artillery pieces can provide long-range direct fire against tough or important urban targets during urban combat. This may also occur when supporting tanks are unable to elevate sufficiently to engage a target on the upper floors of a building or where larger caliber HE fires are needed. It is best to use self-propelled field artillery in this role but only after an analysis of the need for heavy HE direct fire. The tradeoff is the extreme decentralization of artillery firepower. Self-propelled artillery pieces are not as heavily armored as tanks, and towed artillery has no crew protection. Both self-propelled and towed artillery have the same need for ground security and target designation as tanks. Towed artillery is more difficult to employ in the direct fire mode if the maneuverability of the towing vehicle is affected by limited clear spaces. Light artillery (105-mm) may be moved by the crew for short distances.

B-169. Normally, only employ field artillery in the direct fire role when tanks, BFVs, and other direct fire systems are not available or are not able to achieve the desired effects on the target.

B-170. Large-caliber artillery rounds provided by direct fire are effective for destroying targets in buildings. Self-propelled 155-mm howitzers can use direct fire to destroy or neutralize bunkers, heavy fortifications, or enemy positions in reinforced concrete buildings.

Positions

B-171. The Infantry needs to reconnoiter and occupy positions where the howitzer can provide direct FS. These positions should be free from enemy direct fire but still allow direct fire by the howitzer on the target. Although these systems seem formidable, they provide less crew protection than a BFV and contain large amounts of onboard ammunition and propellant. They are susceptible to catastrophic destruction by heavy automatic weapons, light cannon, and antitank fire.

Protection

B-172. Infantry should provide local security and prevent enemy ground assault, sniper fire, and antitank fire.

NAVAL GUNFIRE

B-173. Because of its flat trajectory, naval gunfire is affected by terrain masking. It is usually difficult to adjust onto the target because the gun-target line is constantly changing. The most common naval cannons used to support ground troops are the 5-inch .54-caliber gun and the newer 5-inch .62-caliber gun. Both have a high rate of fire and are roughly equivalent to the 155-mm howitzer in target effect.

SECTION VII – AIR-DELIVERED MUNITIONS

B-174. This section discusses munitions that are deliverable by rotary-wing and fixed-wing aircraft.

ROTARY-WING AIRCRAFT

B-175. Army aviation forces provide a significant advantage during UO. They should be fully integrated into the military decision-making process to ensure effective combined arms employment. This requires that aviation and ground maneuver forces synchronize operations by operating from a common perspective.

B-176. Ground units may receive support from a variety of attack reconnaissance helicopters, including the AH-64 and OH-58D. Attack reconnaissance helicopters can provide area fire to suppress targets and precision fire to destroy specific targets or breach structures. Attack reconnaissance helicopters can also assist with surveillance and communications using their advanced suite of sensors and radios.

B-177. Other supporting (lift) helicopters, such as the UH-60 and CH-47, may also have weapon systems that aid in the suppression of enemy forces when conducting UO. However, their primary role is to transport personnel, equipment, and supplies to those critical urban areas that may be inaccessible to ground transportation. Lift helicopters can provide a distinct advantage by placing personnel and weapon systems at critical locations at critical times to surprise and overwhelm the enemy.

B-178. Some of the weapons systems used are—

- **Hellfire Missiles.** Hellfire missiles have a larger warhead and greater range than TOW missiles. Several warhead options are available for the Hellfire missile. The primary warhead uses a shaped charge with a contact fuze to defeat heavy armor. A second option uses a shaped charge, a contact fuze, and a fragmentation sleeve to produce an antipersonnel, antivehicle effect against troops and vehicles in the open. A third warhead variant uses a metal augmented blast fragmentation warhead with a delay fuze to perforate typical urban structures to provide antipersonnel effects inside the structure. Laser target designation for the Hellfire missile sometimes may not be possible due to laser reflections off glass and shiny metal surfaces. Therefore, visual acquisition by the aircrew is a primary method of target identification. The use of a Hellfire missile against targets in the upper stories of high buildings is highly effective and produces minimal collateral damage.
- **The 2.75 Rockets.** The 2.75 rockets are effective against enemy forces and light vehicles in the open or under light cover. They only provide a suppressive effect against enemy in well-built masonry or concrete structures. Other warhead options include red and white phosphorus smoke and overhead covert and overt illumination.
- **The .50-caliber Machine Guns.** The .50-caliber machine guns are effective against enemy forces and light vehicles in the open or under light cover, with similar effects as a ground mounted .50-caliber machine gun.
- **The 20-mm Cannons (U.S. Marine Corps Helicopters).** The 20-mm cannons are effective against enemy forces and light vehicles in the open or under light cover. They are ineffective against well-built masonry or concrete structures. The 20-mm cannon ammunition produces many ricochets, especially when antipersonnel ammunition is fired into urban areas.
- **The 30-mm Cannons.** The 30-mm cannons are accurate weapons and can penetrate standard masonry and concrete structures. They are effective against personnel and light armored vehicles.

FIXED-WING AIRCRAFT

B-179. Close air support to ground forces fighting in urban areas is a difficult mission for fixed-wing aircraft. Targets are hard to locate and identify, enemy and friendly forces may be intermingled, and enemy short-range air defense weapons are hard to suppress. Because only one building can separate enemy and friendly forces, accurate delivery of ordnance is required. Marking panels, lights, electronic beacons, smoke, or some other positive identification of friendly forces is needed. A unit may be supported by Air Force, Marine Corps, Navy, or multinational fixed-wing fighters and attack aircraft while fighting in urban areas. Fixed-wing aircraft can carry a wide variety of weapons, to include—

- **General-Purpose Bombs.** General-purpose bombs from 500 to 2,000 pounds are effective in creating casualties among enemy troops located in large buildings. High-dive angle bomb runs increase accuracy and penetration but also increase aircraft exposure to antiaircraft weapons. Low-dive angle bomb runs using high drag (retarded) bombs can place bombs into upper stories, but penetration is not good. Sometimes bombs pass through light-cladding buildings and explode on the outside.
- **Laser-Guided Bombs.** Laser-guided bombs can be effective against HPTs. The U.S. Air Force has developed special, heavy, laser-guided bombs to penetrate hardened weapons emplacements. Problems associated with dense smoke and dust clouds hanging over the urban

area and laser scatter can restrict their use. If the launching aircraft can achieve a successful laser designation and lock-on, these weapons have devastating effects, penetrating deep into reinforced concrete before exploding with great force. If launched without a lock-on or if the laser spot is lost, these weapons are unpredictable.

- **The 20-mm Cannons.** The 20-mm cannons are moderately effective for strafing exposed enemy personnel in urban areas but lack accuracy and penetration. The 20-mm cannon rounds penetrate slightly better than the .50-caliber round but can ricochet badly, and tracers can start fires.
- **The 30-mm Cannons.** The 30-mm cannons fired from the A-10 aircraft are accurate weapons. They are moderately effective against targets in urban areas and can penetrate most masonry and concrete structures.

AC-130

B-180.   The AC-130 aircraft has weapons that can be effective during UO. It can deliver accurate fire from a 20-mm Vulcan cannon, 40-mm rapid-fire cannon, and 105-mm howitzer. The 105-mm howitzer round is effective against the roof and upper floors of buildings. The AC-130 is accurate enough to concentrate its 40-mm cannon and 105-mm howitzer fire onto a single spot to create a rooftop breach, allowing fire to be directed deep into the building.

This page intentionally left blank.

Glossary

AG	assistant gunner
AO	area of operations
APDS	armor-piercing discarding sabot
APDS-T	armor-piercing discarding sabot with tracer
APFSDS-T	armor-piercing fin-stabilized discarding sabot with tracer
ARNG	Army National Guard
ARNGUS	Army National Guard or the United States
ASCOPE	areas, structures, capabilities, organizations, people, and events
ATGM	antitank guided missile
ATTP	Army Tactics, Techniques, and Procedures
BCT	brigade combat team
BDM	Bunker Defeat Munition
BFV	Bradley fighting vehicle
BP	battle position
BSB	brigade support battalion
BSTB	brigade special troops battalion
CAL	caliber
CBRN	chemical, biological, radiological, and nuclear
CCIR	commander's critical information requirements
COA	course of action
COAX	coaxial
CP	command post
EA	engagement area
eng	engineer
EPW	enemy prisoner of war
ERG	Emergency Response Guide
FBCB2	Force XXI Battle Command Brigade and Below
FEBA	forward edge of battle area
fld	field
FM	field manual
FO	forward observer
FS	fire support
FSC	forward support company
GPS	Global Positioning System
GREM	grenade rifle entry munition
Gren	grenadier
GTL	gun turret line
HBCT	heavy brigade combat team
HE	high-explosive

HEAT	high-explosive antitank
HEAT-T	high-explosive antitank with tracer
HEDP	high-explosive dual purpose
HEI-T	high-explosive incendiary with tracer
HE-OR-T	high-explosive obstacle reducing with tracer
HEP-T	high-explosive plastic with tracer
HHB	headquarters and headquarters battery
HHC	headquarters and headquarters company
HHT	headquarters and headquarters troop
HN	host nation
HPT	high-payoff target
HUMINT	human intelligence
HVT	high-value target
IBCT	Infantry brigade combat team
ICV	Infantry carrier vehicle
IED	improvised explosive device
IFV	Infantry fighting vehicle
IPB	intelligence preparation of the battlefield
ITAS	Improved Target Acquisition System
JP	Joint publication
LAW	light antiarmor weapon
ldr	leader
LZ	landing zone
MANPADS	Man-Portable Air Defense System
MBA	main battle area
MCoE	Maneuver Center of Excellence
med	medical
MEDEVAC	medical evacuation
METT-TC	mission, enemy, terrain and weather, troops and support available, time available, and civil considerations
MG	machine gunner
MGS	mobile gun system
MI	military intelligence
MICO	military intelligence company
MLRS	Multiple Launch Rocket Systems
mm	millimeter
MP	military police
MPAT	multipurpose antitank
MPAT-OR	multipurpose antitank-obstacle reducing
MPAT-T	multipurpose antitank with tracer
MRAP	mine resistant ambush protected
NSC	network support company
OAKOC	observation and fields of fire, avenues of approach, key terrain, obstacles, and

	cover and concealment
OBJ	objective
OP	observation post
PCI	pre-combat inspection
Plt	platoon
PMESII-PT	political, military, economic, social, information, infrastructure, physical environment, and time
PZ	pickup zone
ROE	rules of engagement
RPG	rocket-propelled grenades
RS	reconnaissance squadron
RTO	radiotelephone operator
RTP	radiotelephone procedures
SAW	squad automatic weapon
SBCT	Stryker brigade combat team
sgt	sergeant
SINCGARS	Single-Channel Ground and Airborne Radio System
SOF	Special Operations Forces
SOI	signal operation instructions
SOP	standing operating procedures
SOSRA	suppress, obscure, secure, reduce, and assault
sqd	squad
STP	soldier training publication
TC	training circular
TIM	toxic industrial material
tm	team
TOW	tube-launched, optically-tracked, wire-guided
TP-T	target practice with tracer
TPDS-T	target practice discarding sabot with tracer
TRADOC	U.S. Army Training and Doctrine Command
TTP	tactics, techniques, and procedures
UAS	unmanned aircraft system
UO	urban operations
USAR	United States Army Reserve
VIC	vehicle internal communications
XO	executive officer

This page intentionally left blank.

References

DOCUMENTS NEEDED

These documents must be available to intended users of this publication.

Center for Army Lessons Learned (CALL), Handbook Number 11-11, *MRAP M-ATV Observations, Insights, and Lessons*, February 2011.

FM 2-0, *Intelligence*, 23 March 2010.

FM 2-01.3, *Intelligence Preparation of the Battlefield/Battlespace*, 15 October 2009.

FM 2-91.4, *Intelligence Support to Urban Operations*, 20 March 2008.

FM 3-0, *Operations*, 27 February 2008.

FM 3-06, *Urban Operations*, 26 October 2006.

FM 3-06.1, *Aviation Urban Operations-Multiservice Procedures for Aviation Urban Operations*, 9 July 2005.

FM 3-06.20, *Cordon and Search Multi-Service Tactics, Techniques, and Procedures for Cordon and Search Operations*, 25 April 2006.

FM 3-07, *Stability Operations*, 6 October 2008.

FM 3-07.1, *Security Force Assistance*, 1 May 2009.

FM 3-09.31, *Tactics, Techniques, and Procedures for Fire Support for the Combined Arms Commander*, 1 October 2002.

FM 3-09.32, *J-FIRE Multiservice Tactics, Techniques, and Procedures for the Joint Application of Firepower*, 20 December 2007.

FM 3-11.4, *Multiservice Tactics, Techniques, and Procedures for Nuclear, Biological, and Chemical (NBC) Protection*, 2 June 2003.

FM 3-20.21/MCWP 3-12.2, *Heavy Brigade Combat Team (HBCT) Gunnery*, 3 September 2009.

FM 3-20.96, *Reconnaissance and Cavalry Squadron*, 12 March 2010.

FM 3-21.10, *The Infantry Rifle Company*, 27 July 2006.

FM 3-21.20, *The Infantry Battalion*, 13 December 2006.

FM 3-21.75, *The Warrior Ethos and Soldier Combat Skills*, 28 January 2008.

FM 3-22.9, *Rifle Marksmanship M16-/M4-Series Weapons*, 12 August 2008.

FM 3-22.10, *Sniper Training and Operations*, 19 October 2009.

FM 3-22.27, *MK 19, 40-mm Grenade Machine Gun, Mod 3*, 28 November 2003.

FM 3-22.34, *TOW Weapon System*, 28 November 2003.

FM 3-22.37, *Javelin–Close Combat Missile System, Medium*, 20 March 2008.

FM 3-22.65, *Browning Machine Gun, Caliber .50 HB, M2*, 3 March 2005.

FM 3-23.30, *Grenades and Pyrotechnic Signals*, 15 October 2009.

FM 3-24.2, *Tactics in Counterinsurgency*, 21 April 2009.

FM 3-28, *Civil Support Operations*, 20 August 2010.

FM 3-34.2, *Combined-Arms Breaching Operations*, 31 August 2000.

FM 3-34.22, *Engineer Operations–Brigade Combat Team and Below*, 11 February 2009.

FM 3-34.170, *Engineer Reconnaissance*, 25 March 2008.

FM 3-34.214, *Explosive and Demolitions*, 11 July 2007.

FM 3-37, *Protection*, 30 September 2009.

FM 3-50.1, *Army Personnel Recovery*, 10 August 2005.

FM 3-90, *Tactics*, 4 July 2001.

FM 3-90.5, *The Combined Arms Battalion*, 7 April 2008.

FM 3-90.6, *Brigade Combat Team*, 14 September 2010.

FM 5-0, *The Operations Process*, 26 March 2010.

FM 5-19, *Composite Risk Management*, 21 August 2006.

FM 6-40, *Tactics, Techniques, and Procedures for the Field Artillery Cannon Battery*, 23 April 1996.

FM 7-90, *Tactical Employment of Mortars*, 9 October 1992.

FM 21-18, *Foot Marches*, 1 June 1990.

FM 21-60, *Visual Signals,* 30 September 1987.

JP 1, *Doctrine for the Armed Forces of the United States*, 14 May 2007.

JP 3-0, *Joint Operations*, 17 September 2006.

JP 3-06, *Joint Urban Operations*, 8 November 2009.

STP 17-19K1-SM, S*oldier's Manual, MOS 19K, M1A1 & M1A2 SEP Armor Crewman, Skill Level 1, 13 January 2011.*

STP 21-1-SMCT, *Soldier's Manual of Common Tasks, Warrior Skills, Level 1*, 18 June 2009.

TB 9-1340-230-13, *Operator's and Field Information for Rocket, High Explosive, 66 Millimeter: Light Anti-Armor Weapon (LAW), Heat, M72A7,* 31 December 2007.

TC 21-24, *Rappelling*, 9 January 2008.

TM 3-22.31, *40-mm Grenade Launchers,* 17 November 2010.

TM 3-23.25, *Shoulder-Launched Munitions*, 15 September 2010.

RELATED PUBLICATIONS

None.

REFERENCED FORMS

DA forms are available on the Army Publishing Directorate Web site: www.apd.army.mil.

DA Form 2028, *Recommended Changes to Publications and Blank Forms.*

PRESCRIBED FORMS

None.

INTERNET WEBSITES

Websites are listed were current as of May 2011. Some of the documents and individual and collective tasks referred to in this publication may be accessed at one of the following Army websites:

Army Knowledge Online, https://akocomm.us.army.mil/usapa/doctrine/index.html

Center for Army Lessons Learned (CALL), http://usacac.army.mil/cac2/call/index.asp

Digital Training Management System, https://dtms.army.mil/DTMS

Reimer Doctrine and Training Digital Library, http://www.train.army.mil

StrykerNet, https://strykernet.army.mil

US Army Publishing Directorate, www.apd.army.mil

U.S. Department of Transportation, *Emergency Response Guidebook,.* http://www.phmsa.dot.gov/staticfiles/PHMSA/DownloadableFiles/Files/erg2008_eng.pdf

Index

multipurpose antitank (MPAT), 8-10, B-21, B-22

multipurpose antitank with tracer (MPAT-T), 8-10, B-21

multipurpose antitank-obstacle reducing (MPAT-OR), 8-10

N

noncombatants, xv, xxi, xxvii, 1-25, 2-2, 4-11, 4-13, 6-3, 7-25, 7-30, 7-32, 7-34, 7-35, 7-36, 7-37, 7-39, 7-40, 7-50, A-5, A-6

O

observation and fields of fire, avenues of approach, key terrain, obstacles, and cover and concealment (OAKOC), 3-5, 6-5

observation posts (OP), 1-20, 1-24, 2-5, 4-15, 5-9, 5-18, 5-21, 6-2, 6-3, 6-10, 6-12, 8-5

operational control (OPCON), 8-3, 8-4, 8-10

P

paramilitary, xv, xvii, 1-19, 4-11

political, military, economic, social, information, infrastructure, physical environment, and time (PMESII-PT), xxviii, 1-7

R

radiotelephone procedures (RTP), 8-5

rocket-propelled grenades (RPG), xvii, B-24

rules of engagement (ROE), xxi, xxvii, xxviii, 1-12, 2-3, 2-6, 2-7, 4-10, 4-14, 4-16, 5-12, 5-13, 5-14, 5-17, 5-19, 5-20, 5-26, 6-5, 6-6, 6-9, 6-11, 6-14, 7-22, 7-35, 8-6, B-5, B-31, B-34

S

signal operation instructions (SOI), 8-5

Single-Channel Ground and Airborne Radio System (SINCGARS), 4-14, 8-5

Special Operations Forces (SOF), 1-1, 1-2, 1-21, 4-13, 7-36

squad automatic weapon (SAW), 7-7

standing operating procedures (SOP), 2-9, 5-14, 5-17, 6-7, 7-1, 7-24, 7-32, 7-33, 7-39, B-3

Stryker brigade combat team (SBCT), xxv, 1-1, 1-3, 1-4, 1-5, 2-6, 2-11, 3-11, 4-5

suppress, obscure, secure, reduce, and assault (SOSRA), 2-10, 5-10, 7-15

T

tactics, techniques, and procedures (TTP), xi, 2-9, 2-14

target practice discarding sabot with tracer (TPDS-T), B-24

target practice with tracer (TP-T), B-24

terrorists, xvii

toxic industrial material (TIM), A-4, A-12, A-13, A-14, A-15

tube-launched, optically-tracked, wire guided (TOW), 8-10, 8-11, 8-13, B-11, B-16, B-17, B-18, B-19, B-24, B-36

U

unmanned aircraft system (UAS), xxviii, 1-12, 1-14, 1-19, 1-20, 2-4, 2-6, 3-3, 4-10, 4-11, 4-14, 5-9, 5-12, 5-16, 5-25

urban
area, xii
environment, xii
infrastructure, xiii, xv
population, xii
society, xiv
terrain, xii, xiii
threat, xvii
threat traditional, xvii

urban environment
air-delivered munitions, B-35
ammunition, B-31
angle of fire, B-33
artillery, B-34
basic response steps, A-15
Bradley Infantry fighting vehicle, B-24
characteristics of buildings, A-6
city, A-2
city core, A-3
close combat missiles, B-16
commercial areas, A-4
common characteristics, B-2
common concerns, A-13

common effects, B-1
common presence, A-13
construction of building, A-8
core periphery, A-3
elements of buildings, A-6
emergency response guide response steps, A-15
exterior openings and floor plans, A-9
fixed-wing aircraft, B-36
function of building, A-6
general shoulder-launched munitions, B-7
grenade launchers, B-6
hand grenades, B-5
hazardous materials, A-13
height of building, A-7
high-rise residential areas, A-3
immediate hazards, A-13
indirect fire weapons, B-29
industrial areas, A-4
Javelin, B-16
location, A-13
low-rise residential areas, A-4
M1 Abrams tank, B-19
M136 AT4, B-12
M136A1 AT4CS 84-mm launcher, B-13
M141 bunker defeat munition, B-15
M72A7 light antiarmor weapon, B-11
materials for building, A-7
medium and heavy machine guns, B-4
megalopolis, A-2
metropolis, A-2
military areas, A-4
mortars, B-33
naval gunfire, B-35
orange identification codes, A-14
planning considerations, A-14
rifle, carbine, and squad automatic weapon, B-4
rotary-wing aircraft, B-35
shantytowns, A-5
shoulder-launched munitions, B-7
size of building, A-7
small-arms weapons, B-4
street patterns, A-12
strip areas, A-4
structures, A-6
Stryker Infantry carrier vehicle (ICV), B-28
Stryker mobile gun system (MGS), B-22
TOW missile, B-17

ATTP 3-06.11
(FM 3-06.11)
10 June 2011

By order of the Secretary of the Army:

MARTIN E. DEMPSEY
General, United States Army
Chief of Staff

Official:

JOYCE E. MORROW
Administrative Assistant to the
Secretary of the Army
1113301

DISTRIBUTION:

Active Army, Army National Guard, and U.S. Army Reserve: To be distributed in accordance with the initial distribution number (IDN) 111232, requirements for ATTP 3-06.11.